CONFLICT & CONTINUITY
in Brazilian
Society

CONFLICT

& CONTINUITY
in Brazilian
Society

edited by HENRY H. KEITH &

S. F. EDWARDS

UNIVERSITY OF SOUTH CAROLINA PRESS

Columbia, South Carolina

To
ARTUR HEHL NEIVA *(1909–1967)*
and
GEORGE C. A. BOEHRER *(1921–1967)*

FIRST EDITION
Copyright © 1969 by THE UNIVERSITY OF SOUTH CAROLINA PRESS
Published in Columbia, S.C., by The University of South Carolina Press, 1969
Standard Book Number: 87249-170-6
Library of Congress Catalog Card Number: 73–86193
Manufactured in the United States of America by
Thos. J. Moran's Sons, Inc.
Designed by Robert L. Nance

PREFACE

IT is with great pleasure that I accept the invitation to write a few words as a preface to the interesting and important volume entitled *Conflict and Continuity in Brazilian Society*.

As a career diplomat, I feel that history is unquestionably an important subject for furthering international relations. I am sure that these studies will be useful, not only to complement the already known facts about our own history and its interpretation, but also to contribute to a better understanding of Brazilian reality by our American friends and neighbors.

I must say that I was deeply impressed by the quality of the studies presented to the Seminar on Latin American History held at the University of South Carolina in October, 1967, as well as by the number of participants present. Some years ago it would have been impossible to gather such a numerous and notable group of American professors of Brazilian history. Much has been done in the field of historical research in my country but much still remains to be uncovered, and we welcome the efforts of historians from all countries who wish to join us in this task. The publication of these studies is a very worthwhile objective, and I am convinced that this volume will be extremely useful for professors and students of history alike everywhere interested in my country.

I am very grateful to President Thomas F. Jones of the University of South Carolina for the support he gave to this seminar and his hospitality at Columbia. May I add my admiration for the university, which has been looking to the future without rejecting its past so full of traditions; for this reason, it is progressing so much. I commend the work and interest of Professors Robert D. Ochs, Henry H. Keith, S. F. Edwards, and all those who have contributed with their knowledge and presence to the success of the seminar and now, it is hoped, of this volume.

Vasco Leitão da Cunha
Ambassador of Brazil

CONTENTS

---

*   Affiliations of contributors are those in effect at the time of the meeting of the Brazilian History Seminar at the University of South Carolina, October 1967.

INTRODUCTION

THE essays in this volume were first presented at the Seminar on Latin American History held at the University of South Carolina (Columbia), October 19–21, 1967. This meeting was, to the best of our knowledge, the first scholarly gathering devoted exclusively to Brazilian history ever to take place in the United States. In the words of Professor Alan K. Manchester, a participant and one of the American pioneers in the study of Brazilian history: "Until the last ten years, working in Brazilian history was a lonely occupation. It seems little short of a miracle that one could assemble a dozen and a half, or more, knowledgeable people in the field."

The success of the seminar reflects the growing maturity of historical scholarship, especially in this country, concerned with the Luso-Brazilian world. For this compelling reason, we felt a duty and a responsibility to bring the fruits of research of these leading scholars to the attention of students everywhere who are interested in the field of Luso-Brazilian history. It is hoped that this volume will be of special value to the advanced student who wishes to strike out in new directions in historical research and writing.

In different ways, these studies address themselves to the central theme of conflict and continuity in Brazilian society during its more than four and one-half centuries of existence. The reader, however, is entitled to ask: Why adopt this theme as the key to an understanding of the historical evolution of Brazil? Conceivably, it might be argued that the theme itself does not represent a valid dichotomy and that the more traditional choice of "continuity and change" would be more meaningful. The use of this unconventional theme—conflict and continuity in Brazilian society—thus calls for a word of explanation. It is the very "unopposite" nature of much of Brazil's historical development which prompted us to select the conflict-continuity dichotomy rather than that of continuity-change. Conflict is, of course, present in the historical development of all societies, but what is of interest in the Brazilian experience is that the forces of continuity limited the role which conflict played in altering social, political, and economic arrangements. Conflict was a constant companion of the basic pattern of continuity, but it usually did not cause sweeping social and political transformations. Thus, it seemed that the "unopposite" conflict-continuity dichotomy held much more promise of yielding meaningful interpretations of Brazilian history than the more conventional opposites of continuity and change. Another reason for choosing this dichotomy as the mode of analysis was to test the traditional view of the Brazilians—and the Portuguese before them—as nonviolent and accommodationist in the solution of social, political, economic, and cultural problems.

The organization of the essays in a meaningful way presented a problem: they did not lend themselves easily to arrangement in neat historical time segments. This was true simply because, as perhaps we should have realized from the outset, there was such a marked degree of overlap because the theme arched over artificial chronological boundaries. It became increasingly apparent that the very nature of most of Brazilian history from the discovery to the present reflected this overlapping characteristic. Having rejected a straight chronological organization, then, we decided upon an institutional approach as the best means of arranging the essays, realizing that this approach was also not without its drawbacks.

The present division has resulted in an uneven distribution of the essays in the chosen categories. This was due to the fact that there was no attempt to suggest specific topics or approaches to the contributors; each scholar was allowed to address himself to the overall theme to the degree and in the manner which his special interests and imagination led him. Consequently, some of the essays undoubtedly hew more closely to the theme than others, but this should only demonstrate the highly individual ways in which the historical imagination works. This collection of essays thus offers the additional advantage to the student of being an interesting experiment in historiography.

In terms of the contribution to historical scholarship, each of these essays appears to belong to one of three types: *(a)* provocative and original re-examination of the traditional—revision, if you will; *(b)* exploration of *terra incognita* in historical research; or *(c)* overarching synthesis of historical evidence. (Even so, one must enter the caveat that there are sometimes overlaps here, too.) In the first group, one might place the essays by Professors Diffie, Cardozo, Manchester, Keith, and Young (with respective commentaries by Professors Schneider, Burns, Graham, Love, and Macaulay). The second group could perhaps include the studies by Professors Alden, Bernstein, and Boehrer (with commentaries by Father Kiemen and Professors Carl and Warren, respectively). In the last group there would be the bold attempt at synthesis by Professor Lôbo. The highly personal nature of all attempts at historical synthesis has led us to exclude a formal commentary on her paper.

Perhaps the greatest utility of these essays is the number of searching questions to which they have given rise; they are broadly indicative of a growing refinement in analysis in the field of Brazilian history. On Portuguese economic policy Professor Diffie asks whether the Portuguese Crown was, as has been supposed, less exclusivist than the Spanish vis à vis foreign merchants in Portugal and her possessions, especially Brazil; Professor Alden turns his attention to the economic role of the Jesuits in Brazil, asking to what extent economic motivations were operative in the decision by the Portuguese Crown to expel the order from Brazil. Two interesting questions are raised relating to the Church and its capacity to reform from within: Professor Cardozo explores the question of the actual role of the Enlightenment in the Church in Portugal and in Brazil; and Professor Boehrer takes up the twin questions of regalism and reformism within the Brazilian Church in the latter half of the nineteenth century. Questions relating to the polity are raised, centering on two momentous events in Brazilian history: Professor Manchester asks whether the transfer of the Portuguese Court to Rio de Janeiro was a precipitate action or a carefully planned maneuver and Professor Young probes the question of whether the Vargas Revolution really represented a sharp break with the Brazilian past. Reviewing the entire span of Brazilian history, Professor Keith asks to what extent the non-violent character of Brazilian evolution is an historical myth; and Professor Lôbo addresses herself to the larger question of why Brazilian social and economic development has moved so slowly throughout its history. These important questions, appropriately discussed and criticized by the commentators, bring up in their turn additional questions for examination by the student. By asking such penetrating questions of the historical evidence the authors have performed a service for scholars seeking a deeper understanding of one of the world's most fascinating countries.

The essays in this volume appear in substantially the form in which they were submitted by their authors; this has been done at their specific request. The editors have therefore confined their task, in the main, to such technical details as standardizing spellings and forms of citation in order to attain as much consistency as possible throughout the collection of essays. In no case was the content of the essays altered in any significant way; the essays must stand, then, on their own merits.

Without the constant support and encouragement of many persons the seminar, and this volume, would not have been possible. We express our special thanks to His Excellency Vasco Leitão da Cunha, Ambassador of Brazil, who generously took time from his many diplomatic duties to launch the seminar. Special thanks should go also to President Thomas F. Jones and other officials of the University of South Carolina, who were always generous in their support—both moral and material. A strong vote of thanks is reserved to Professor Robert D. Ochs and his staff of the Department of History at the university for their unfailing kindness, confidence, and plain hard work from the inception of the project to its culmination. To the staff of the University of South Carolina Press, and to our colleagues, students, and friends, we should like to express our appreciation for their cordial interest and assistance.

HENRY H. KEITH
S. F. EDWARDS

Berkeley, California, and
Columbia, South Carolina
Spring, 1969

CONFLICT & CONTINUITY
in Brazilian
Society

THE LEGAL "PRIVILEGES" OF THE FOREIGNERS IN PORTUGAL AND SIXTEENTH-CENTURY BRAZIL

Bailey W. Diffie
City College of the City University of New York

ONE established "fact" concerning early Brazilian history is that the Portuguese monarchy followed a policy of exclusivism and monopoly. This conflicts at first glance with another, which we know to be true, that many foreign merchants and other foreigners were present in the first years of the Colony, including the year of discovery.

The supposed "fact" of exclusivism and monopoly was only in part true, as will become evident as we go on. The foreigners were in Brazil quite legally in accordance with rights they had long enjoyed in Portugal and with specific grants of privilege from the king. There were, of course, numerous foreign ships along the coast of Brazil which were not legal from the Portuguese point of view and against which Portugal was warring, eventually successfully. These are not the foreigners under consideration in this paper.

During the early years of the Colony the policy followed by Portugal with reference to Brazil and her Far Eastern possessions was about the same as that followed by other nations of the time with reference to fiscal controls. The stricter defense of exclusive rights which we associate with Portugal and Spain was to come later, when the rivalry of foreign nations made it necessary in the eyes of the two leading colonial powers to tighten their defenses or lose out entirely in the lands they had been the first to discover.

Foreign ships, foreign merchants, and foreign agents of European merchants were all found in Portuguese overseas possessions legally, and foreigners commanded ships in the colonial trade. The colonials themselves were allowed trade with friendly foreign nations so long as a stop was made in Portugal. Thus, neither monopoly nor exclusive

1

trade was the rule, though it is true that the Portuguese Crown conducted business in its own name or through its agents. All this came
about in the normal course of Portuguese development.

Commerce with Brazil was open to all private merchants of the Portuguese kingdom, without regard to nationality. Foreign merchants,
subjects of friendly countries, could trade with and live in Brazil (as well
as Africa and the Far East) on the same terms as the Portuguese themselves. Most goods could be bought and sold by private merchants
though there were certain royal monopolies in this system, among them
the well-known monopolies of brazilwood and slaves. If we do not wish
to consider this "free trade" in our modern sense, we shall nevertheless
see that it is not too far from a modern economy in which nations
through tariffs, port regulations, control of water routes, and other
means restrict commerce in favor of their own nationals.

This fact is so contrary to the usual view that we find it hard to accept.
Through examination of some of the history of Portugal we shall see
why, in the early colonial years, it was true of Brazil and other overseas
possessions of Portugal.

Among the foreigners who from the earliest years traded with and
sometimes either resided in or whose agents were present in Brazil, we
find such names as Fugger, Welser, Seitz, Rem, Hirschfogel, Hochstetter,
Ratt, Paris, Ximenes, Marchioni, Morelli, Affaitati, and others who will
be mentioned. Vespucci, whatever the facts about the much-disputed
voyages, was in Brazil on a Portuguese expedition.

There were foreigners in the armada of Martim Afonso de Sousa,
which the Portuguese did not think strange. Pero Lôpes de Sousa remarks in his *Diário* that on his expedition to Rio de la Plata "Eu trazia
comigo alemães e italianos . . . e franceses." Of the 320 men "a sôldo do
rei" who came with Tomé de Sousa in 1549, not counting the simple
mariners, we find many with foreign names, such as Argüello, Lamego,
Lantim, de Luca, Castelhano, Bruges, Soap, Recarte Francês, Canteira,
Aguirre, Galego, Verdelho, Soajo, Salamanca, Guilhen, and others. Luis
Sarmienti in a letter of 1554 reports that Luis de Melo brought "more
than fifty Castillians and more than forty Frenchmen." Among the foreigners who left distinguished families in Brazil were the Espinoza,
Eoban, Cavalcanti, Linz, Toscano, Zorilha, Adorno, Dore, Bandeves,
and Málio.

From a wide variety of documents of the time comes the impression
that a large number of foreigners were in all the captaincies, many of
them merchants on their own account or agents for foreigners resident

in Europe. In 1587 a Duarte Arquer, "mercader flamengo que aqui re-
sidia" in Salvador, Bahia, owned an *urca* "com marinheiros flamengos"
captured by English pirates. Seven Flemings were in Pernambuco at the
time of the first visitation of the Inquisition in 1595, one of them an
André Pedro, merchant, agent of merchants resident in Germany. Pyrard
found a number of foreigners of various nationalities living in Brazil in
1612.[1]

It must be stressed that many of these foreign residents and much of
their business of importing and exporting was legal. They had a long
tradition in Portugal before Brazil was known. When the discovery
came, they came with it by right of privileges granted them and their
predecessors for generations and even centuries before. Their presence
is an illustration of the natural transfer of Portuguese (or Spanish or
English) institutions to their new possessions, a transfer which historians
from time to time rediscover.[2]

The privileges granted to foreigners in Portugal go back to the beginning of the nation. When the fleet of the Second Crusade which sailed
from the English Channel in 1147 stopped over in Portugal long enough
to aid in the capture of Lisbon, many of its members remained in Portugal where King Afonso Henriques granted them land, trade rights, and
personal privileges.[3]

A similar thing happened in Spain. When King Ferdinand III of
Castille captured Seville in 1248, he rewarded the Genoese who had
helped him. In 1251 they received their own "barrio, é Alfándiga é forno
é baño . . . eglesia é poder de presentar el capellán al Arzobispo de Sevilla." [4] Much other legislation from time to time shows both the rights
given to and the restrictions laid on foreigners in Spain, and among them
are named Genoese, Piacenzans, Catalans, French, English, and others.
For example, there was a street of the Portuguese in Seville. The strong
influence of the Genoese in Spain has often been noted by historians.
This influence continued down to and after the discovery of America
and was felt in America.[5] The Spanish side of this is not our primary
interest at this time, but we must note it in order to better understand
what was a common practice among nations of that time, the granting
of privileges of both a commercial and personal kind to foreigners as a
means of stimulating trade. Such privileges were mutual, Portugal or
Spain giving and receiving from the Genoese, or English, French or other
nationalities.

Although the presence of foreigners in Portugal, as said before, can be
traced to very early times, we need not dwell on the period before 1317.

In that year King Dinis of Portugal called Manuel Pessagna from Genoa, named him *almirante-môr* of Portugal in perpetuity for himself and his heirs, and contracted with him to bring twenty captains to command the King's ships. This marks an advance for the Portuguese, who were already experienced sailors in the rough Atlantic and who knew well the trade routes northward to France, England, and the North Sea, where they had traded since the twelfth century at least. As one of many examples of Portugal's trade position at this time we may cite agreements already made with England, France, and others for trade and protection of merchants. An outstanding instance of the importance of the Portuguese traders abroad is found in 1293 when King Dinis recognized a mutual aid agreement which his merchants trading to the north, mainly in Bruges, made among themselves to insure their ships, property, and persons. Bringing the Pessagno family and their captains was but another step in Portugal's progress. At this time many other foreigners lived in, traded in, or stopped over en route from northern Europe to the Mediterranean, or *vice versa*. Genoese and Venetians were among the most important of these, but others were likewise there, as numerous records show.[6]

The act of the time which was to influence most what we are concerned with was the charter given to the Bardi family of Florence in 1338. They were granted the "liberties" (as the expression then was) to live in, trade, travel within the country, discharge cargo, have their own consul, and be exempt in their ships and persons from the king's corsairs unless carrying forbidden merchandise to the Moslems. The charter they received was similar to that already granted by the French and English to the Portuguese and was typical of the times, when the merchants formed a sort of international community, with branches of the families in two or sometimes several countries or cities.[7]

The 1338 grant to the Bardi family became a model for other Italians, as well as the French, English, and eventually the Germans and Flemings, all citing it when petitioning the Portuguese Crown. Throughout this century and the next, to the moment of da Gama's trip to India and Cabral's discovery of Brazil, foreign merchants were to play a large part in the development of Portugal's economy. Such foreigners became firmly rooted in Portugal, some becoming citizens with descendants still known in Portugal to this day, the Pessanha (or Peçanha) family being an example.[8]

Portuguese sailors were among those who explored the Atlantic in the fourteenth century. Although this is not the place to debate the difficult question of when and by whom the coast of Africa, the Canary Islands, the Madeira Islands, and the Azores were first discovered and settled, we can note that there was at least one voyage authorized by the Portuguese king to the Canaries, the most likely date being 1341 on the basis of the rather scarce evidence we now have. There had been a settlement in the Canaries by Lancelloto Malocello (or Marocello) of Genoa as early as 1312 which lasted for many years. We know of Catalan, Mallorcan, and Andalusian voyages during the fourteenth century before the first permanent settlement came by Jean de Bethencourt and Gadifer de la Salle in 1402 under Castilian auspices.[9]

Portugal was the only nation that made such effort during the fifteenth century to explore the African coast and the Atlantic, except the Spanish occupation of part of the Canaries, just cited, and the English voyages made out of Bristol after 1480 looking for islands which proved to be mythical.[10] We are not concerned here with exploration as such but only with Portugal's attitude toward the foreigners in her midst. The country was "swarming" with them, as Fernão Lopes remarks in his chronicle of King Fernando. Some of these already in Portugal by the time of Henry the Navigator, and some who came later, participated in the discovery and development of new lands. Far from repelling the foreigners, Portugal welcomed them; Prince Henry was particularly cordial.

After the Madeira Islands were occupied (about 1420; the exact date has never been precisely established), among the donataries later was Bartolomeu Perestrello, described as a Genoese noble, who was appointed captain of Pôrto Santo Island.[11] Columbus was to marry into the Perestrello family[12]

Three foreign names are associated with the discovery of the Cape Verde Islands—the two Genoese Antônio Usodimare and Antônio de Noli, and the Venetian Alvise Cadamosto. There is still a sharp division among historians, with which we are not here concerned, about who was the first discoverer.[13]

The point most important to notice is that in 1454 when Cadamosto inquired of some merchants and sailors about Henry's policies, "asking if the said Senhor would allow anyone who wished to make this voyage, they replied yes, if either of two conditions was met," a quarter of the goods for Henry if the merchant supplied the ship and the goods, or half if the ship was supplied by Henry and the goods only by the mer-

chant.[14] When Cadamosto interviewed Henry, he found him most cordial and thereafter made two voyages to the coast of Africa and the Cape
Verde Islands, living in Portugal for several years.

When the Azores Islands were discovered and colonized, so many
Flemings were settled there by mid-fifteenth century that they were
known as the Flemish Isles and many assumed incorrectly a Flemish
discovery.[15] Among the settlers was Jos de Hurtere, donatary of the
islands of Faial and Pico. His daughter married Martin Behaim, the
German author of the famous world globe of 1492. Behaim first came to
Portugal in 1484. He claimed to have accompanied Diogo Cão on the
second voyage along the African coast, 1485–1486. Some have doubted
this, but he seems to have known something of Africa as far as some
point south of the Congo River.

Another foreign settler in the Azores was Luca di Cazzana, described
by Damião Peres as a "rich merchant established in the Azores." He
financed several unsuccessful voyages into the Atlantic from the Azores
in search of an island that had been seen to the west of Madeira in the
mid-fifteenth century. The Fleming Jacome of Bruges was the colonizer
of the island of Terceira and its captain until his death about 1472.

The Portuguese founded the *feitoria* and fort of São Jorge da Mina
on the Guinea coast in 1482 as a center of their trade for the gold and
other products of that region. Among the foreigners who were here was
Christopher Columbus.[16]

The Fleming, Ferdinand van Olmen (or Ferdinand of Ulm), captain
of the island of Terceira, was one of the unsuccessful searchers for land
to the west, in 1486–1487.[17]

During the same period of the fifteenth century when the exploration
of the African coast and the settlement of the Atlantic islands had occupied some of the energy of Portugal, more of it had gone into cultivating the trade routes known for centuries. The close contacts with
northern Europe which we have seen developing from the first days of
the Portuguese nation, and which included political contacts as well,
reached a point in the fifteenth century where it would no longer be
correct to consider Portugal an immature economic nation.[18] The great
majority of the people might be agricultural, as they were, but the active
forces of the nation were now commercial, and in terms of the time
we might also say industrial, and in active cooperation with the many
foreign merchants who lived in or who were represented by agents
living in Portugal. Trade from northern Europe to the Mediterranean,
both the Christian and the Moslem areas of the Mediterranean, and

with the Atlantic coast of Africa, in large part passed through Portugal or came directly from the areas Portugal had developed. Portugal did not find it to her advantage to exclude foreigners from her trade, though at times there were protests from Portuguese business interests about the preference given to foreigners or about the foreigners learning the secrets of the Africa trade, as in the *Côrtes* of 1481.

The development of the African trade opened up through Portuguese explorations intensified the interest of foreign merchants and bankers, particularly the Italians. As has been said earlier, already in the fourteenth and fifteenth centuries Portugal was the home of thousands of foreigners.

The letters of Bartolomeu Manni and Bernardo di Mariano concerning the market opportunities in Portugal in 1399–1400, found in the archives of Francisco di Mareo Datini, show that his trade embraced Portugal, Spain, the Mediterranean, and northern Europe.[19] Martim Lem, or Leme, a merchant from Bruges established in Lisbon, obtained a ten-year monopoly on the export of cork, on June 7, 1456. The next year, on August 8, 1457, Lem obtained for his fellow Flemings a charter of privilege from Afonso V, which conceded to shipmasters, mariners, pilots, and merchants the right to bear arms, and the redress of grievances in overcharges by the collectors of the customs (*escrivães de alfândega*). In 1468 and 1478 Afonso reaffirmed and granted other favors, and the same was done by João II in 1483.[20] The Lomelini, a family of Italian merchants also established in Portugal in the fifteenth century, were at times associated with Leme. They were among the most important foreign merchants of the country.[21]

The attraction of Portugal for foreign merchants and bankers, considerable during the Middle Ages, grew greatly with Portugal's developing African and island commerce and took a great leap forward with the return of Vasco da Gama in 1499.[22] The news that the Portuguese had made direct contact with the great markets of the East came as a major blow to the Rialto, Venice's center for the sale of the spices which hitherto came in through a slow and costly route from the East into the Mediterranean. Barcelona, Marseilles, and other spice-trading cities were also hurt. Spice now became more plentiful, prices fell (at first disastrously), and it seemed for a time that Lisbon might take over entirely the whole of the eastern trade.

Venice and the other cities were not, however, to surrender so easily. We can look forward half a century at this point and find them largely recovered from the first ill effects of Vasco da Gama's discovery and still active in the spice trade.[23] They were too rich, too powerful, and too well connected with the Turks in the eastern Mediterranean, and the Moslems of the Red Sea, and the Indian trade to be pushed out. The new route was too long and the ships of the day still inadequate for efficient commercial exploitation. The cost of spice in the long run proved to be not much less than on the old routes, once the Venetian-Turkish-Indian-Arabic merchants understood their problem and worked to overcome the Portuguese rivals.[24]

One of the moves of the Venetians and other Italians was to transfer more of their activity to Portugal, as they had already begun to do in Spain after the news of Columbus' return had reached Italy in 1493. The Italians were in fact indispensable in the Iberian economy of the day. After the expulsion of the Jews they were even more needed as international merchants and bankers.[25] It will be recalled that it was Genoese merchants in Spain who financed Columbus' part of the costs of his voyages and helped the sovereigns raise their part. Nor were the Portuguese monarchs able to do without them. Furthermore, the Germans who had already begun to penetrate Portugal and Spain were to become more necessary during the sixteenth century when Spanish and Portuguese commitments almost overnight required sums in financing that dwarfed previous state needs. The income was much larger, true, but never enough to meet the sums wanted by Manoel the Fortunate and João III of Portugal and of Charles V of the Holy Roman Empire and Spain. All Western Europe and the Mediterranean became one commercial world, with Portugal and Spain standing in the middle of the sea route from the north into the Mediterranean, Portugal being the entrepôt for eastern goods and Brazil as Spain was for the rest of America. Portugal's main outlet was in Antwerp, where the Feitoria de Flandres had been moved from Bruges in 1496.[26]

So it was that Portugal (and Spain) needed the foreign merchants as much as they needed the new markets so long sought and so suddenly opened up.

For her eastern trade Portugal needed goods of exchange. This was more difficult than it had been for the African trade. In Africa the unsophisticated economy was satisfied with items of often insignificant value which could be exchanged for gold, silver, peppers (malagueta), and other goods, and for slaves. The situation in India and other parts of the East was different. There the Portuguese found they must trade gold, silver, copper, tin, and other expensive items, of which they had an insufficient supply, for the pepper, ginger, nutmeg, allspice, cinnamon, clove, silks, and other things for which they had a market in Europe. The long-developing mutual dependence of Portuguese and foreign merchants, which had given rise to the Portuguese *feitorias* in Flanders and elsewhere and to the presence of foreign merchants in Portugal, was now greater than ever. And as the Portuguese monarchy, perhaps more heavily and directly engaged in its nation's business than any other royal house in Europe, needed the merchants to carry on the so-called monopoly it held in Africa, the East, and Brazil, it was in no position to deny to them now the privileges hitherto granted and often renewed for several centuries past. The Portuguese kings called themselves "Lords of the Conquest, Navigation and Commerce of Ethiopia, Arabia and India," and the privileges hitherto granted to foreigners in their realms were thus without question at first extended to the new parts of the realm, albeit with same royal right to grant or withhold concession to foreigners as well as to Portuguese.

The foreign participation in the new overseas trade, eastern and Brazilian, began at once. Foreigners perhaps participated in the financing of Vasco da Gama's first expedition of discovery, which would have been logical. We know that in Cabral's voyage to India in 1500, during which Brazil was discovered (by chance or by design, we shall not attempt to discuss here), foreign merchants sent their ships, their men, and their merchandise.[27]

Among the principal Italian merchant-bankers were the Marchioni and Sernigi of Florence. Bartolomeu Marchioni and Girólamo Sernigi had been in Portugal since the mid-fifteenth century. Both Afonso V and João II, before the discoveries, and Manoel I afterward, were involved in financial transactions with them. In 1486 João II got letters of credit from them for Pero de Covilhã, his envoy to the East. In 1500 Manoel I received large sums from Marchioni in connection with the African trade, including the slave trade.

In the fleet of Cabral, Bartolomeu Marchioni and Girólamo Sernigi were associated with Dom Alvaro, brother of the Duke of Bragança, in sending one of the ships. When João de Nova, who was himself a Galician, sailed for India in four ships in 1501, one of his ships belonged to Marchioni and was commanded by his fellow Florentine, Fernando Vineti. On the second Vasco da Gama voyage to India in 1502, in which Estevam da Gama commanded one section of the fleet, Mateo di Benigno was sent as factor for the Affaitati family of Cremona. His account of this voyage, which he sent home to his employer, is a prime source of our knowledge. One of the ships was commanded by Giovanni Buonagrazia, who was to die in India. Another Italian, Giovanni da Empoli, sailed with Afonso de Albuquerque in 1503 as factor for Marchioni. Still another was Buonavita de Albon.[28]

This same year, 1503, was to see the organization of the Casa da India, which was to become the center of Portugal's newly established trade.[29]

The German merchants and bankers, who had gained a foothold in Portugal later than the Italians, were not to be far behind in the participation in the Indian and Brazilian trade. The spices of the East would attract their interest on the one hand and the brazilwood for the textiles of Flanders and the other parts of northern Europe on the other. German privileges in Portugal date particularly from the time of Afonso V (1438–1481) and more specifically from the grants of 1503.[30]

The first important shift of the Germans from the Rialto to Portugal came in 1503 when the Welsers of Augburg sent Simon Seitz to Lisbon as their agent. They and other German firms were to become indispensable to Portuguese trade because they controlled the minerals of central Europe without which there could be no adequate amount of trade goods to exchange for the spices of the East. Seitz made a contract with Manoel I which enabled him to found a branch of the firm of Anton Welser, Konrad Vohlin and Company. The same year Lucas Rem also came to Lisbon as their representative to fit out three ships and load them. The Welser agents were aided by the German printer Valentim Fernandes, who had been in Lisbon since about 1495, knew Portuguese, took a great interest in all matters of discovery, and to whom we owe a great deal of what little information has come down to us from these early years.[31] The German humanist Konrad Pentinger, son-in-law of Anton Welser, personal friend of Damião de Goes and Valentim Fernandes, was also useful to the Welsers.

The year 1503 was that of the return of the second Vasco da Gama voyage from India. It was also the year when Nicolau von Rechtergen obtained additional privileges for the Flemings. Thus, the Germans and Flemings were on the ground in time to meet the incoming Vasco da Gama ships. It should be noted that Emperor Maximilian of the Holy Roman Empire was the nephew of King Manoel of Portugal. The privileges granted to the "citizens of the empire of the very August Maximilian our beloved nephew" are excellent though not unique examples of why the newly discovered lands were open to the trade of foreigners. Among such privileges were the right to buy and sell any kind of merchandise "throughout our realms and overlordship in person or through their agents." The privileges were spelled out in numerous clauses and were to run from February, 1503, for fifteen years. Not the Welsers alone, but all German firms whose capital was 10,000 cruzados or more were granted the same privileges. In October, 1504, Lukas Rem, another Welser representative, got the right to send factors in the armadas to India.

In the great fleet of Francisco de Almeida of 1505 both the Italians and Germans had a large share.[32] The Marchioni, Sernigi, and Affaitati of Italy and the Welsers, the Fuggers, and the Hochstetters were represented. The Welsers had the heaviest German investment, 20,000 florins, the others 4,000 each, while the Italians invested some 29,400 florins. The profits ran to 150 percent or more. When Tristão da Cunha sailed in 1506 the larger part of the fleet was privately owned, according to Castanheda. This fleet was heavily hit by shipwreck and thereafter the foreign merchants in general bought from the Portuguese in Lisbon or Antwerp, allowing the Portuguese to take the greater risk.

A Fugger representative arrived in Lisbon in October, 1503, gaining from Manoel the same privileges granted to the Welsers, which were those the Italians had long enjoyed. The Fuggers, richer than the Welsers, were to grow even richer in the sixteenth century thanks to the new worldwide trade and to decline only when caught in the net of financing kings who bankrupted themselves and their bankers in endless wars. The powerful position of the Germans in mining made them particularly useful to the Portuguese monarchs. They likewise held a strong position in Spanish mines and in the financing of the Spanish monarchs. Another German firm which was active in the Iberian trade was the Hochstetters, also of Augsburg. Its center in Antwerp, the most important in north European trade, and the location of Portugal's most important feitoria, was in the street of Kipdorp, next to the Portuguese feitoria. The Hochstetters held a strong position in the silver mines of the Tyrol, as well as an interest in mercury, where they were badly hurt when mercury was found in Hungary and Spain. Still other Germans in the Portuguese trade were the Herwarts of Augsburg and the Paungartners of Nuremberg, both interested in mining.

The Spanish firm of the Haro family of Burgos was active in Portugal from the end of the fifteenth century, with offices in Antwerp and Lisbon. They shipped copper, silver, and cloth from Antwerp to Lisbon and were also involved in Portugal's African trade.

The Schetz family, one of the richest Flemish merchant-bankers, founded by Erasmus Schetz, had branches in Leipzig and Lisbon, exporting metals from Antwerp to Lisbon. They held a strong position in the zinc mines of Limbourg. As is well known, they were among the important foreigners in the early trade and development of Brazil.

If the India trade which was a royal monopoly needed foreign capital, so much more would the Crown need and welcome foreign capitalists to take the risks in Brazil where the expenses were great and the rewards far less in the beginning than from the richer East. Bartolomeu Marchioni participated in the expedition of 1501–1502 to Brazil, sent after getting the news of Cabral's discovery. In 1502, the king let a contract for three years to Fernão Loronha (or Noronha, usually) who headed a group of New Christians to develop the land "which Vespucci discovered" (in the words of Pietro Rondinelli, our source of information, writing from Seville, on October 3, 1502). Noronha is described as an opulent merchant and as a *fidalgo* with a coat of arms. He contracted to send six vessels a year, explore an additional 300 leagues of hitherto undiscovered coast, construct and maintain a fort, and to enjoy extensive trade rights with the obligation to make specified payments to the Crown.[33]

The first expedition to carry out this contract sailed in June, 1503, with six vessels, only two of which were destined to return to Portugal.[34] The loss of the four vessels is almost the only news we have of this expedition. We do not know for certain that other voyages were made under this contract. It was renewed, however, on expiration in 1506. The Italian merchant Lunardo da Cá Masser, writing in 1507, says that Noronha took a ten-year concession at a rental of 4,000 ducats annually for the brazilwood monopoly. Importation of such wood from India was prohibited. Thus, we know little of this. We do know with unusual accuracy of the "Bretôa," a vessel which sailed in February, 1511, and of which we have a record of the *armadores* who were Noronha's associates, of the *regimento*, the *roteiro*, and the cargo. Among the participants in financing were Bartolomeu Marchioni, Benedito Morelli, and Francisco Martins. The *Newen Zeytung auss Presillg Landt*, published in 1515 by a German who was a commercial agent in Madeira, mentions Cristóbal de Haro, Spaniard, among the armadores of ships to Brazil in 1513.

As Brazil became settled, around São Vicente and Santos there sprang up sugar mills owned by Portuguese and foreigners, among the latter being the Schetz, who were Flemings, and the Doria, Italians (Genoese). Pero Magalhães de Gândavo, author of the *Tratado da terra do Brasil* and *História da província de Santa Cruz a que vulgarmente chamamos Brasil*, was, though a native of Braga, descended from the Flemings, as his name indicates.[35]

Yet another Italian family to gain fame and riches in Brazil were the Adornos: Paolo, Guiseppe, and Francesco. Established in Portugal about 1500, and somewhat later in Brazil, they became cane planters and manufacturers of sugar.[36]

We may close this brief introduction to the reasons for the legal presence of foreigners in early Brazil by mentioning Lucas Giraldi, a Florentine merchant-banker who established himself in Lisbon in the early sixteenth century.[37] He was a friend of Giovanni da Empoli, who made his first voyage to India in 1503 on the vessel sent by Bartolomeu Marchioni. Giraldi was also connected with the Affaitati of Cremona (interested in the sugar of Madeira), who formed part of the group of spice contractors which included the Affaitati, Francisco Mendes (New Christian), Afonso de Torres, Gabriel de Negro, "and other Italians, Spaniards, and Portuguese." In 1533 he obtained from João III a *carta patente* for the same "liberdades and privilegios" held by the German merchants.

In 1540, 1544, 1546, and 1551, he was the outfitter (armador) of vessels. In 1540 he may have gone to India himself as captain of the "Urca." We find him protesting the failure of the Portuguese to cut off the trade from the East through Ormuz, saying that goods from there were underselling Portuguese and coming into the Mediterranean and all Christendom. His activities covered the Portuguese world.

Our particular interest in him does not concern his European and eastern interests, which nevertheless are essential to understanding his importance, but his Brazilian activities. On March 26, 1547, he obtained from Jorge de Figueiredo Correia, captain-donatary of Ilheus, a *sesmaria* of two leagues waterfront and three leagues inland. This was an hereditary grant, with rights to build a villa and fortifications, and with jurisdiction and *senhorio*. The captain-donatary retained his superior rights as did the king over the donatary, but for practical effects the grant made the holder near sovereign. The enumeration of his rights and privileges was quite extensive. Though *sesmarias* were usually for a period of five years if not proved up, he was given fifteen years. He contracted to send 100 persons in the armadas of 1547 and 1548 including "free men and slaves," to provide arms, to set up sugar mills, sawmills, cotton mills, grain mills, and to install salt pans, etc. Though we do not know all the results of this *sesmaria*, his interest continued. In 1561 he bought the captaincy from Jerónimo de Alarcão de Figueiredo for 4,825 *cruzados*. It was inherited by his son Francisco Giraldi in 1565, to whom it was confirmed by the king in 1566.

14   BAILEY W. DIFFIE

Much further evidence could be adduced to show the presence of
foreigners in early Brazil. With additional research, a major work on
this subject could, no doubt, be produced. To cite further examples
here would not add strength to the principal thesis of this study: that
foreigners were in early Brazil by reasons of the legal standing they had
acquired in the realms of Portugal from a time dating back several
centuries.

NOTES

1 This interpretation of Portuguese policy is persuasively presented by Mario
   Neme, "Notas para uma teoría do comércio colonial português," *Anais do Museu
   Paulista*, XVII (1963), 7–40. A large number of foreigners in Brazil are named
   in *Documentos históricos da Biblioteca Nacional* (Rio de Janeiro), Vols. XIII
   and XIV. The original of Francisco Pyrard de Laval, *Viagem* (2 vols.; Pôrto,
   1944), in French, covers his voyage around the world, 1601–1611. The legal aspect of Portuguese colonial policy is covered in Antônio da Silva Rego, *Portuguese Colonization in the Sixteenth Century: A Study of the Royal Ordinances*
   (Johannesburg, South Africa, 1959).
2 Eduardo Ibarra y Rodríguez, "Los precedentes de la Casa de Contratación de
   Sevilla," *Revista de Indias*, I (1940), 5ff. and *passim* through further volumes
   shows that the principles on which the Casa was built had been long developing
   in Spain. An article of a few years later by Charles Verlinden, "Le problème de
   la continuité en histoire coloniale: de la colonisation médiévale a la colonisation
   moderne," *Revista de Indias*, XI (1951), 219–36, calls attention to the transfer
   of people, institutions, and culture from the mother countries to the colonies.
3 Concerning the privileges of foreigners in Portugal the principal works are:
   Victor Ribeiro, *Privilégios de estrangeiros em Portugal (Inglêses, Francêses,
   Alemães, Flamengos e Italianos)* (Coimbra, 1917); Henrique da Gama Barros,
   História da administração pública em Portugal nos séculos XII–XV, ed. Tor-
   quato de Sousa Soares (11 vols.; 2nd ed.; Lisbon, 1945–1960), *passim*. This work
   is fundamental not only to the subject here treated, but to all medieval Portugal.
   In João Martins da Silva Marques, *Descobrimentos portuguêses*, Vol. I and
   Suplemento (Lisbon, 1944), the principal privileges are published under the
   year of the grant, arranged in chronological order. The Italians in Portugal are
   best treated in Prospero Peragallo, *Cenni intorno alla colonia italiana in Portogallo nei secoli XIV, XV, XVI* (2nd ed.; Genoa, 1907), and in Luigi Federzoni,
   ed., *Relazione storiche fra l'Italia e il Portogallo, memorie e documenti* (Rome,
   1940); and in still other works, such as Carlos de Passos, "Relações históricas
   luso-italianas," *Anais Academia Portuguêsa de História*, 2nd ser. VII (1956),
   143–240; Yves Renouard, "Les rélations du Portugal avec Bordeaux et la Roch-
   elle au Moyen-Âge," *Revista Portuguêsa de História*, VI (1955), 239–55. A brief
   treatment can be found in Bailey W. Diffie, *Prelude to Empire: Portugal Overseas before Henry the Navigator* (Lincoln, Neb., 1960). Merchants of later
   years often compiled copies of the privileges for their own use. Such copies are
   found in libraries and private hands, as for example Ms. 628 in the University
   of Coimbra Library, and Additional Ms. 23:727 in the British Museum. A recent

work on the sixteenth century is Maria Valentina Cotta do Amaral, *Privilégios de mercadores estrangeiros no reinado de D. João III* (Lisbon, 1965).

4 See Ibarra, "Los precedentes de la Casa."

5 See a series of articles by Enrique Otte, "Gonzalo Fernandez de Oviedo y los Genoveses: el primer registro de Tierra Firma," *Revista de Indias*, XXII (1962), 515ff.; "Empresarios españoles y genoveses en los comienzos del comercio trasatlantico: la Avería de 1507," *Revista de Indias*, XXIII (1963), 519ff.; and in XXIV (1964), 475ff. Also see Ruth Pike, "The Genoese in Sevilla and the Opening of the New World," *Journal of Economic History*, XXII (1962), 348–78.

6 In addition to citations in n. 3, above, see: José Benedito de Almeida Pessanha, *Os Almirantes Pessanhas e sua decendência* (Pôrto, 1923); L. Saavedra Machado, "Os inglêses em Portugal," *Biblos: Revista da Faculdade de Letras da Universidade de Coimbra*, in a series beginning with Vol. VIII (1932) and running through to Vol. XIII (1937); A. Beardwood, *Alien Merchants in England, 1350–1377* (Cambridge, Eng., 1931); Emile Vandenbussche, *Flandre et Portugal* (Bruges, 1874), with additional material in the review *La Flandre*, which Vandenbussche edited: Conde de Tovar, *Portugal e Veneza na Idade Media ate 1495* (Coimbra, 1933); V. M. Shillington and A. B. Wallis Chapman, *The Commercial Relations of England and Portugal* (London, 1907).

7 R. Doehard, *L'expansion économique belge au Moyen-Âge* (Brussels, 1946); R. de Roover, "L'évolution de la lettre de change, XIV–XVII siècle," in the *Collection Affaires et Gens d'Affaires* (Paris, 1953); Michel Mollat, *Le commerce maritime normand a la fin du Moyen-Âge* (Paris, 1952); Yves Renouard, *Les hommes d'affaires italiens du Moyen-Âge* (Paris, 1949); A. Sapori, "Le marchand italien au Moyen Age," in the *Collection Affaires et Gens d'Affaires* (Paris, 1952); Virgínia Rau, "Feitores e feitorias—instrumentos do comércio internacional português no século XVI," *Brotéria*, LXXXI (July–Dec., 1965) 458–78, and an offprint with supporting documents.

8 See n. 6, above.

9 An excellent example of the international character of Atlantic exploration is seen in the discovery and settlement of the Canary Islands, where Portuguese, Italians, Catalans-Mallorcans, and Spaniards all were involved, the successful colonization being by French leaders under Spanish auspices. See: B. Bonnet Reveron, "Las expediciones a las Canarias en el siglo XIV," *Revista de Indias*, V (1944), 577ff., and running through several issues, with excellent research and notes on other medieval exploration as well as the Atlantic; E. S. Rafols, "Portugal en las islas Canarias," in *Congresso do Mundo Português, Publicações*, III (Lisbon, 1940); Florentino Pérez Embid, *Los descubrimientos en el Atlántico y la rivalidad castellano-portuguesa hasta el Tratado de Tordesillas* (Seville, 1948); António Rumeu de Armas, *España en el Africa Atlántica* (Madrid, 1956); compare the works by Spaniards just mentioned to get a difference of views with Damião Peres, *História dos descobrimentos portuguéses* (2nd ed.; Coimbra, 1960), and Guido Po, "Le scoperte maritime dei portoghesi" in *Congresso do Mundo Português, Publicações*, III (Lisbon, 1940), and other articles by Po in the same volume; and for further comparison see Charles de la Roncière, *La découverte de l'Afrique au Moyen-Âge* (3 vols.; Cairo, 1923–1927).

10 For explorations, in addition to the works cited above, particularly Peres, *História dos descobrimentos portuguêses*, which is the most satisfactory one-volume history of Portuguese discoveries, see: José Ramos Coelho, ed., *Alguns documentos do Archivo Nacional da Tôrre do Tombo* (Lisbon, 1892); Duarte Leite, *História dos descobrimentos; Colectânea de esparsos*, edited and with extensive notes and comments by V. Magalhães Godinho (2 vols.; Lisbon, 1958–

1960) of very special value because of the quality of scholarship of both the author and the editor; Alberto Iria, *Descobrimentos portuguêses: o Algarve e os descobrimentos* (2 vols.; Lisbon, 1956), a companion volume to Silva Mârques, *Descobrimentos;* Julio Gonçalves, "Da expansão geográfica de portûgesa; notas critíticas," *Boletim da Sociedade Geografia de Lisbôa,* LXXVII (1959), 3–13, one of the calmest voices in the area in which much agitated writing is common; Charles M. De Witte, "Les bulles pontificales et l'expansion portugaise au XVe-siècle," separata from *Revue d'Histoire écclesiastique de Louvain* (1958) ; Jaime Cortesão, "Teoría geral dos descobrimentos portuguêses," in Congresso do Mundo Português, *Publicações,* III (Lisbon, 1940) , and numerous other writings of this historian, who is the foremost exponent of discoveries he believes were made by the Portuguese and intentionally kept secret by the Portuguese kings; William J. Blake, *Europeans in West Africa, 1450–1560* (London, 1942) . For the diplomatic aspect see F. M. da Costa Lôbo, *A acção diplomática dos portuguêses nos sèculos XV e XVI destinada a realização de descobertas e conquistas* (Lisbon, 1937) . The basic chronicle of the explorations of Henry the Navigator is Gomes Eanes de Zurara, *Crônica da Guiné,* ed. José de Bragança (Pôrto, 1937) .

11 The date of the first discovery and colonization of the Madeira Islands is one of the many moot points of discovery history. On this see: M. Higino Vieira, "Descobrimento do arquipélago da Madeira: estado actual do problema," *Revista da Faculdade de Lêtras* (Lisbon) , VI (1938–1939) , 209–36; Peres, *História dos descobrimentos portuguêses,* pp. 27–32, 57–71; Antônio Gonçalves Rodrigues, *D. Francisco Manuel de Melo e o descobrimento da Madeira (a Lenda de Machim)* (Lisbon, 1935) .

12 Leite, *História dos descobrimentos,* I, 270–77.

13 On the discovery of the Cape Verde Islands the differences of views are great. Three men are given credit for the discovery between 1455 and 1560, or approximately: Alvise da Ca da Mosto (Cadamosto) , Antonio de Noli, and Diogo Gomes. Some have ascribed the discovery to Vicente Dias in 1445. See Peres, *História dos descobrimentos portuguêses,* pp. 189–205; Julio Monteiro Júnior, "A descoberta das ilhas de Cabo Verde e ainda um problema," *Boletim da Agência Geral de Colônias,* No. 261 (1947) , 30–44; Julio Gonçalves, "Alvise da Ca da Mosto e o V centenário caboverdiano: com uma carta do Exmo. Almirante Gago Coutinho," in *Boletim da Sociedade de Geografia de Lisbôa,* LXXV (1957) , 399–404; Orlando Ribeiro, "Primordias da ocupação das ilhas de Cabo Verde," *Revista da Faculdade de Lêtras* (Lisbon) , II series, no. 1, vol. XXI (1955) , 92–122; Leo Magnino, "Antonio de Noli e a colaboração entre portuguêses e genoveses nos descubrimentos," *Studia,* X (1962) , 99–117; Charles Verlinden, "Antônio de Noli e a colonização das ilhas de Cabo Verde," *Revista da Faculdade de Lêtras* (Lisbon) , III series, no. 7 (1963) , 28–45; see also "Navegações de Luis de Cadamosto," in Silva Mârques, *Descobrimentos, Suplemento,* pp. 164ff.

14 Vitorino Magalhães Godinho, *Documentos sôbre a expansão portuguêsa* (3 vols.; Lisbon, 1945–1946) , III, 112; see also Godinho, *História econômica e social da expansão portuguêsa* (Lisbon, 1947) .

15 Peres, *História dos descobrimentos portuguêses,* pp. 73–92; Leite, *Descobrimentos,* I, 277–81; Godinho, *Documentos,* I, 207–23; Manuel Monteiro Velho Arruda, ed., *Colecção de documentos relativos ao descobrimento e povoamento dos Açores* (Ponta Delgada, 1932) ; Sousa Gomes, "O descobrimento e os descobridores das ilhas dos Açores," *Boletim da Sociedad de Geografia de Lisbôa,* LXVI (1948) , 527–55; Jules Mees, *Histoire de la découverte des Iles Açores et de l'origine de leur dénomination d'iles flamandes* (Ghent, 1901) .

16 Peres, *História dos descobrimentos portuguêses,* 253–86, 287–314; Domingo Man-

fredi Cano, "Colón en el Africa ocidental," *Africa* (Madrid), 219 (1960), 106–108.

17 Peres, *História dos descobrimentos portuguêses,* 329–36; Peres, "Considerações relativas ao projecto de navegação ocidental por Ferdinand van Olmen em 1486," *Boletim da Sociedade de Geografia de Lisbôa,* LXX (1952), 343–46; Charles Verlinden, "Un précurseur de Colomb: le Flamand Ferdinand van Olmen (1487)," *Revista Portuguêsa de História,* X (1962), 453–65, reasons that as there were many similarities between the contract of Van Olmen (Ulm) with João II in 1486 and Columbus with Ferdinand and Isabella in 1492, Van Olmen should be considered a predecessor of Columbus, though he discovered nothing.

18 Astrogildo R. de Melo, "O comércio européu nos séculos XV e XVI e o florescimento de Espanha e Portugal," *Boletim da Cadeira de História da Civilização* (Faculdade de Filosofia da Universidade de São Paulo), No. 2 (1940); Jacques Heers, "L'expansion maritime portugaise a la fin du Moyen-Âge: la Méditerranée," *Revista da Faculdade de Lêtras* (Lisbon), XXII (1956), 84–112.

19 Virgínia Rau, "Cartas de Lisbôa no Arquivo Datini de Prato," *Estudos Italianos em Portugal,* Nos. 21–22 (1962–1963), 3–13.

20 Manuel Nunes Dias, *O capitalismo monárquico português (1415–1549); contribuição para o estudo das origens do capitalismo moderno* (2 vols.; Coimbra, 1963–1964), II, 322ff.; Sousa Viterbo, "O monopólio da cortiça no século XV," *Archivo Histórico Portuguêz,* II (1904), 41ff.

21 Virgínia Rau, "Uma família de mercadores italianos em Portugal no século XV: os Lomellini," *Revista da Faculdade de Lêtras* (Lisbon), XXII (1956), 56–83.

22 The *História da expansão portuguêsa no mundo,* ed. Antônio Baião, Hernani Cidade, and Manuel Murias (3 vols.; Lisbon, 1937–1940), is the best single work from which to get a view of both exploration and colonization. There are several editions of the "Diary" of the voyage of da Gama (not by da Gama himself). See *Diário da viagem de Vasco da Gama,* ed. Antônio Baião and A. de Magalhães Basto (Pôrto, 1945). See also: T. O. Marcondes de Sousa, "A primeira viagem de Vasco da Gama a India," *Revista de História* (São Paulo), XIX (1959), 289–301, for an "Ensaio Crítico" on the controversies surrounding the route followed and other aspects of da Gama's voyage; Charles A. Julien, *Les voyages de découverte et les premiers etablissements (XV e XVI siècles)* (Paris, 1948); and Julio Gonçalves, *Os portuguêses e o Mar das Indias* (Lisbon, 1947).

23 The first panic at the news of da Gama's return soon gave way to a determination on the part of Venice, Barcelona, and other "spice" cities to get in on the Portuguese-India trade on the one hand and to protect their Mediterranean-Near Eastern route on the other. They were largely successful in both. See F. Braudel, *La Méditerranée et la monde méditerranéen a l'époque de Philip II* (Paris, 1949); V. Magalhães Godinho, "Le repli venetien et égyptien et la route du Cap" in *Hommage a Lucien Febvre* (Paris, 1953), II, 284ff.; Francisco Guerra, "La política imperial sobre las drogas las Indias," *Revista de Indias,* XXVI (1966), 31ff., particularly pp. 48–49.

24 One of the bad problems of the Portuguese on the long run to India (and to Brazil) was shipwreck. See Damião Peres, *Viagens e naufrágios célebres dos séculos XVI, XVII e XVIII* (Pôrto, 1938); M. Pires da Silva, *Vicissitudes e ameaça comercial da rota portuguesa do Cabo* (Lisbon, 1947); P. Sardella, "Nouvelles et speculations a Venise au debout du XVIe siècle," *Cahiers des Annales,* No. I (Paris, n.d.). The attacks of the English and Dutch greatly contributed to the Portuguese problems. See "England and Holland Conquer the Trade of the World," *News and Rumor in Renaissance Europe (The Fugger Newsletters),* ed. George T. Matthews (New York, 1959), item 255.

25 The works on Italians in Portugal are cited in n. 3, above. See also: Achille
    Pellizzari, "Portogallo e Italia nel secolo XVI, studi e ricerche" (Naples, 1914),
    cited in *Revista de História* (São Paulo), III (1914), 266. For the Jews see:
    J. Lúcio de Azevedo, *História dos christãos nôvos portuguêses* (Lisbon, 1922);
    J. Mendes dos Remédios, *Os judéus em Portugal* (Coimbra, 1895); J. Amador
    de los Rios, *História social, política y religiosa de los judíos de España y Portugal*
    (2 vols.; Buenos Aires, 1943), and many other editions.
26 J. Maurício Lopes, *Les portugais a Anvers au XVIe siècle* (Antwerp, 1895);
    José da Silva Figueiredo, "Os peninsulares nas 'guildas' de Flandres (Bruges e
    Antuerpia)," *Ocidente*, XVIII (1942), 236–37; J. Denuce, *L'Afrique au XVIe
    siècle et le commerce anversais* (Antwerp, 1937); L.V.D. Essen, *Contribution a
    l'histoire du port d'Anvers et du commerce d'exportation des Pays-Bas vers
    l'Espagne et le Portugal a l'époque de Charles-Quint* (Antwerp, 1921); José
    Gentil P. da Silva, "Contratos da trazida de drogas no século XVI," *Revista da
    Faculdade de Lêtras* (Lisbon), XV (1949), 5–28.
27 W. B. Greenlee, *The Voyage of Pedro Alvares Cabral to Brazil and India* (Lon-
    don, 1938); Gago Coutinho, "A descoberta do Brasil em 1500 e o seu estudo no
    volume publicado em 1938 pela Hakluyt Society," *Boletim da Sociedade de
    Geografia de Lisbôa*, LVIII (1940), 263–83, in which Coutinho sustains the
    thesis of a pre-Cabral Portuguese discovery of Brazil and of the Cabral voyage
    as a deliberate stopover in a land already known; for a viewpoint directly op-
    posite that of Coutinho and others upholding the intentionality of Cabral's
    discovery, see T. O. Marcondes de Sousa, *Algumas achêgas a história dos de-
    scobrimentos marítimos* (São Paulo, 1958), and *Americo Vespucci a suas via-
    gens*, No. 10 in *História da Civilização Brasileira* (São Paulo, 1949), as well as
    several articles running through the *Revista de História* (São Paulo) from 1950
    on; Manuel Nunes Dias has a good study in his "Partilha do mar oceano e de-
    scobrimento do Brasil," *Studia*, XII (1963), 273–463; for the most important
    documents see *Os sete únicos documentos de 1500 conservados em Lisbôa refer-
    entes a viagem de Pedro Alves Cabral* (Lisbon, 1940).
28 Leite, *Descobrimentos*, II, 61–62, 68–69, 181–99; Dias, *Capitalismo monárquico*,
    II, 208–10; T. O. Marcondes de Sousa, *O descobrimento da América e a suposta
    prioridade dos Portuguêses*, pref. J. Capistrano de Abreu (2nd ed.; São Paulo,
    1944), pp. 156–59.
29 *Regimento das Cazas das Indias e Mina*, ed. Damião Peres (Coimbra, 1947).
30 Luis Saavedra Machado, "Os Alemães em Portugal desde os tempos primitivos
    até fins do século XIV," *Biblos: Revista da faculdade de Letras da Universidade
    de Coimbra*, II, 73–88; J. Denuce, "Privilèges commerciaux accordés par les rois
    de Portugal aux Flamands et aux Allemands (XVe e XVIe siècle)," *Archivo
    Histórico Portuguêz*, VII (1909), 310–19, 377–92; J. Baptista Barreiros, *La parti-
    cipation des Allemands lors de la découverte des Indes* (Braga, 1931); A. H. de
    Oliveira Mârques, "Relações entre Portugal e a Alemanha no século XVI," *Re-
    vista da Faculdade de Lêtras* (Lisbon), III (1960), 36–55; Hermann Kellenbenz,
    "Os mercadores alemães de Lisbôa por volta de 1530," *Revista portuguêsa de
    História*, IX (1960), 125–40; R. Carandé, *Carlos V y sus banqueros* (Madrid,
    1949); Dias, *Capitalismo monárquico*, II, 172.
31 *O manuscrito de Valentim Fernandes*, ed. Antônio Baião (Lisbon, 1940).
32 *Fundação do Estado da India em 1505*, ed. Alexandre Lobato (Lisbon, 1955);
    Dias, *Capitalismo monárquico*, II, 171–85, 209–13; Marcondes de Souza, *De-
    scobrimento da América*, pp. 156–59.
33 Leite, *Descobrimentos*, I, 644–46; II, 69–73, 160ff., 179ff. Whether Noronha him-
    self was a New Christian or a descendant of a family of nobles from the time of
    the capture of Ceuta in 1415 is a matter of dispute among historians.

34 The question of who commanded the 1501–1502 expedition, of which Vespucci formed a part, is one of the subjects of rancorous dispute. Leite, *Descobrimentos,* I, 644–45; II, 160–64, 281–82, 286ff., says that Fernão de Noronha commanded.

35 Capistrano de Abreu, *História colonial* (2nd ed.; Rio de Janeiro, 1932) , pp. 77–79, 100; and *Ensaios e estudos (crítica e história),* pp. 299ff.

36 Prospero Peragallo, "Viaggio di Geronimo da Santo Stefano e d'Geronimo Adorno in India nel 1494–1499," *Bollettino della Società Geografica Italiana,* 4th ser. II (1901) , XXXVIII, 24–40.

37 Virginia Rau, "Um grande mercador-banqueiro italiano em Portugal: Lucas Giraldi," *Estudos Italianos em Portugal,* Nos. 24–25 (Lisbon, 1965) , 3–35.

COMMENTARY

Susan C. Schneider
University of Texas, Austin

A NEW image of the Portuguese colonial empire is emerging from the works of recent authors. Instead of viewing the empire as an exclusively Portuguese enterprise, some historians have begun to recognize that the Court of Lisbon not only tolerated but even encouraged an amazing amount of foreign participation in the early imperial venture. Professor Diffie is one of the main proponents of this revisionist trend, and in this study he presents evidence which will cause many further modifications of the old picture of the sixteenth century Portuguese Empire.

Foreigners in Portugal, as Professor Diffie stresses, had long enjoyed not only commercial but extensive civil and religious privileges as well. The English, Dutch, Irish, and Germans could worship as they pleased within the confines of their own homes. As early as 1405, the English had a "judge conservator" appointed especially to handle their commercial cases. The Flemings had such an official by the 1470's.[1] Foreigners in Portugal likewise had the right to have their own consuls and separate cemeteries. Foreign merchants had wide-ranging commercial privileges. German merchants, for example, were exempt from paying import duties on several thousand dollars' worth of cloth imported annually for their own personal use. Nor did German merchants have to pay the import duty on copper, silver, or mercury, a valuable privilege. In some cases, foreigners did not have to pay the duties on spices bought from the fleet and marketed abroad. Furthermore, foreigners had the right of having their goods dispatched first in the Custom's House.[2] But these privileges resembled those enjoyed by alien merchant communities everywhere in Europe.

Only the Portuguese kings, however, allowed foreigners to enjoy these

20

same privileges in the overseas possessions as well. For nearly a century, Portugal allowed all Catholic foreigners, whether or not they resided in the Mother Country, to buy and sell freely in all parts of her empire. Furthermore, foreign merchants could build and use their own ships, as long as they employed a Portuguese crew and Portuguese officers. Besides requiring strict adherence to the Catholic religion, the Portuguese kings placed few restrictions on the foreigners living and trading in their colonies. In Brazil, foreigners could not trade with the Indians.[3] Moreover, in some cases, foreigners did have to pay an additional tax, but this was not a great burden since they were exempt from many of the taxes paid by native Portuguese. Otherwise, the foreigners trading in the Portuguese empire enjoyed equal, if not greater, privileges than did nationals.

Foreigners quickly took advantage of the privileges conceded them. Professor Diffie quotes Fernão Lopes, the chronicler, who maintained that the Portuguese possessions in the East "swarmed" with them. In 1506, three boats financed by German and Italian capitalists returned from the East with a profit of 175 percent.[4] In 1510, Albuquerque mentioned Germans resident in Gôa, and German religious founded convents in both Gôa and Macau early in the sixteenth century.[5] The same thing occurred in Portugal's Atlantic empire. Italians controlled the sugar production in Madeira and the Azores. The Flemings helped to finance the first Brazilian sugar mill established at São Vicente in 1533, and within a hundred years, Dutch merchants estimated that they had secured one-half to one-third of the carrying trade between Brazil and Europe.[6] In fact, an almost symbiotic relationship developed between Brazilian sugar and Dutch capital. Indeed, Brazilian sugar production owed its success not only to the capital, but also to the technical know-how and the skillful marketing procedures of the Low Countries.[7]

After Columbus' discoveries, Spain also attracted great numbers of foreigners, and contemporary accounts describe the influx of Portuguese, Italian, and German merchants into Seville. Foreigners entered the Spanish New World possessions, and control of much of the Spanish colonial trade passed into their hands. Nonetheless, except for a brief liberal period under Charles V, the Spanish official ideology, unlike the Portuguese, remained hostile toward foreigners. In 1501 and again in 1538, the Spaniards barred foreigners from the Indies. Spanish kings, like Ferdinand and Isabella, encouraged the immigration of foreign artisans. However, they reserved the colonial spoils for themselves and their subjects. Professor Diffie fails to make this important distinction between the attitudes of Spain and Portugal.

A policy of exclusivism would have been difficult to enforce in an empire as decentralized as the sixteenth century Portuguese. While the Spanish concentrated commerce in one port at home and three ports in America, the Portuguese allowed ships to travel between Vianna, Aveiro, Pôrto, Lisbon, Lagos, Funchal, and the various ports of the colonies. There were other reasons for the lax Portuguese attitude toward foreigners. The rapid rate at which sugar deteriorated hindered the establishment of a strict fleet system, necessary for a rigid commercial monopoly. To market the agricultural products derived from their colonies, the Portuguese relied on foreign merchants.

The xenophobic exclusivism usually attributed to both Iberian empires did not actually begin with the Portuguese until the last decade of the sixteenth century, after the unification of the Spanish and Portuguese crowns. In 1591, the Portuguese possessions were attacked. On February 9 of the same year, the home government restricted the Brazil trade to Portuguese merchants and to Portuguese markets. Three years later, the government for the first time formally prohibited the Dutch from trading with Brazil. In 1605 the Crown forbade all transactions with foreigners in the overseas possessions.[8] Although these restrictions were rarely enforced, they demonstrate the change in Portugal's official attitude toward foreigners.

The life of Ferdinand Cron, the best known of the German merchants in Gôa, illustrates this transformation from an open to a closed policy. Sent by the Fuggers and the Welsers to the Orient, Cron established a factory in Cochim in 1587. He married the daughter of a Portuguese *fidalgo*, became a resident of Gôa, and participated actively in its municipal government. A respected citizen, Cron lent money to the viceroys and furnished them with important information about the activities of the Dutch in India. As a reward for these services, the King made Cron a *fidalgo* and a member of the Order of Christ, two honors which carried sizable financial benefits. In 1619, Crown officials accused Cron of collaborating with the Dutch and imprisoned him, confiscating all of his property. Unable to prove the charges of treason, the Portuguese authorities freed him soon thereafter, but in 1622, King Felipe IV ordered an investigation of Cron to be held in Lisbon. The charges were again dropped, but only after Cron had spent five years in jail.[9]

Political events in the seventeenth century did cause a minor reversal in the new policy. Forced to rely on British aid, the Portuguese Crown by the Treaty of 1654 strengthened the privileges of English merchants in Portugal and Brazil. For the first time, the English consul, instead of being appointed by the Portuguese king, was chosen by his own government. England and the United Provinces also forced the Portuguese government to permit four merchants of each nationality to reside in Bahia and Rio de Janeiro. In only fifty years, the openness of the early Portuguese policy had disappeared completely. A privilege once freely given was now granted grudgingly and only under great pressure. Charles R. Boxer has written that by the second half of the seventeenth century, "any attempt to increase legitimate foreign trade with Brazil at once aroused antagonism at Lisbon and Bahia." [10]

By the end of the eighteenth century, the Portuguese imperial policy had completely lost its earlier permissiveness. During the rule of the Marquis of Pombal, the Portuguese government even began to encroach upon the long-established privileges of foreigners in the Mother Country. After the famous Lisbon earthquake of 1755, the Portuguese authorities imposed a new duty to pay for the reconstruction of the city. They extended this tax to British merchants as well as to nationals, even though the treaties between Portugal and England forbade such a measure. In addition, they drew up new customs valuation lists, which no longer favored the British.[11] Monopoly and exclusivism had, indeed, become the correct terms of description for the Portuguese empire.

Exclusivism, however, did not, as Professor Diffie has shown, characterize the early period of Portuguese imperialism. His research conclusively demonstrates that in the sixteenth century Portugal openly and officially encouraged foreign commercial participation at home as well as in the empire. Official hostility to foreigners developed in the seventeenth and eighteenth centuries. Above all, Professor Diffie's findings emphasize the need for a revision of the current tendency to view the Portuguese colonial empire as a static system existing for three centuries without change.

NOTES

1 Victor Ribeiro, *Privilégios de estrangeiros em Portugal (Inglêses, Francêses, Alemães, Flamengos e Italianos)* (Coimbra, 1917) , *passim.*
2 "Privilégios concedidos a alemães em Portugal—certidão de Duarte Fernandes (1589) ," *Anais das Bibliotecas e Arquivos de Portugal,* I (1962) , 119–59 and 131–33.

3   F. A. Varnhagen, *História geral do Brasil* (São Paulo, 1927–1930), I, 147.

4   Herman Kellenbenz, "Fuggers em Portugal" in Joel Serrão, ed., *Dicionário de história de Portugal* (Lisbon, 1963–1967), II, 308.

5   Herman Kellenbenz, "Alemães em Portugal," in *ibid.*, I, 90–91; J. B. Amancio Gracias, *Alemães na India nos séculos XV a XVIII* (Lisbon, 1941), pp. 10–41.

6   C. R. Boxer, *The Dutch in Brazil* (Oxford, 1957), p. 20, quoted in Celso Furtado, *The Economic Growth of Brazil,* trans. Richard W. de Aguiar and Eric C. Drysdale (Berkeley, 1965), p. 17.

7   Furtado, *Economic Growth*, pp. 16–18.

8   "Alvará em que se prohibe irem Naos, ou Navios Estrangeiros a India, Brasil, Guiné e Ilhas, ou outras Províncias de Portugal" *Boletim do Conselho Ultramarino, Legislação Antiga* (Lisbon, 1867) I, 188–90.

9   Kellenbenz, "Ferdinand Cron," in Serrão, *Dicionário,* I, 752.

10 *The Golden Age of Brazil* (Berkeley, 1962), p. 157.

11 A. R. Walford, *The British Factor in Lisbon* (Lisbon, 1940), pp. 51–52.

ECONOMIC ASPECTS OF THE EXPULSION
OF THE JESUITS FROM BRAZIL:
A PRELIMINARY REPORT*

Dauril Alden
University of Washington, Seattle

THE first New World colony to receive members of the newly founded Society of Jesus (1540) was Brazil, where the initial contingent of Black Robes landed in 1549; the first New World colony from which the society was expelled, some two hundred and ten years later, was also Brazil. During the intervening centuries the Black Robes made their presence felt in that colony in a remarkable variety of capacities—as outstanding missionaries and militant defenders of Indian rights, as advisors to senior administrative officers, as the educators of most of that tiny fraction of literate colonial youth, as the builders of the colony's largest libraries, as pathfinders through its backlands, and as linguists, historians, anthropologists, botanists, pharmacists, physicians, architects, and craftsmen of one sort or another. Such activities have been examined by a number of writers,[1] the most noteworthy among whom is Serafim Leite, S. J., the author of the massive and authoritative *História da companhia de Jesús no Brasil*.[2] Scattered throughout Father Leite's ten hefty volumes are also references to the Jesuits as horticulturalists, stockbreeders, plantation supervisors, and managers of urban real estate. From time to time he also furnishes indications of the value and extent of some of the order's properties in Brazil. But although Father Leite suggested the need for a comprehensive study of the society's economic role in the colony,[3] he has never pub-

* Part of the research for this paper was completed during the summer of 1967 in the Hispanic Foundation (Library of Congress), the Oliveira Lima Library, and the Newberry Library, and I wish to express my appreciation to the custodians of those facilities, respectively Dr. Howard F. Cline, Professor Manoel Cardozo, and Dr. Lawrence W. Towner, for their numerous courtesies. I also wish to acknowledge the assistance of two of my colleagues, Professors Howard Kaminsky and Paul Mosher.

lished such a work,[4] and those who have written on the economic history of the colony have ignored the subject.[5]

It may be that filling this important gap in our knowledge exceeds the talents and energies of a single investigator. In any event, I have a more limited objective in mind: an assessment of the extent to which the Crown's decision to expel the Jesuits from its domains was economically motivated and the economic consequences of that action.[6] When I began my inquiry several years ago, I started with the following questions: (a) how did the Society of Jesus become a major owner of urban and rural properties, including Negro slaves, in Brazil? (b) to what extent did its economic activities arouse complaints from competitive economic interests in the colony and what influence did such criticisms exert upon royal policy? (c) how extensive and how valuable were the Black Robes' possessions in Brazil at the time of their sequestration? and (d) what disposition did the Crown make of them after their confiscation? It is evident that the search for answers to these and related questions will have to be further extended in Portuguese and Brazilian archives and very likely be carried on in depositories in Rome as well. Meantime, in the following sections I offer interim findings with respect to the first three of these questions.

I. THE SOURCES OF JESUIT WEALTH IN BRAZIL

At the time of their expulsion there were 474 Black Robes in the Province of Brazil and another 155 in the Vice Province of Maranhão.[7] The fathers, their neophytes, and their Indian wards were widely scattered among the society's educational, spiritual, agricultural, pastoral, recreational, and medical facilities which extended from the upper Amazon as far south as Paraná and Santa Catarina. Those facilities included nineteen colleges, five seminaries, several hospitals, upwards of fifty missions (*aldeias*), and uncounted houses of instruction, novitiates, and retreats.[8]

The construction and maintenance of such installations and the care for their personnel naturally required substantial means of support. That support came from a variety of sources. Initially, the fathers relied upon alms contributed by the founding settlers of Bahia, but such offerings and the food and clothing allowances that the Crown provided were hardly sufficient to sustain the Jesuits' ambitious missionary and educational enterprises.[9] Those operations were placed on a firmer foundation in 1550, when the society received its first land grant (*sesmaria*) in

Brazil.[10] That grant was partly intended to aid the establishment of the order's first *colégio* in Salvador. In later decades of the sixteenth century additional colleges were founded in Rio de Janeiro and in Pernambuco. They, too, were assigned *sesmarias*[11] and were endowed with revenues derived from the tithes (*dízimos*). The amount of such endowments at first depended upon the number of fathers assigned to each college district, but although the number of priests in those districts continued to increase during the seventeenth and eighteenth centuries, the endowments remained fixed after 1575.[12] When the society expanded its activities to the Amazon area in the seventeenth century and a separate vice province was formed there, the Crown also endowed the northern missions, though on a smaller scale than it had done in the Province of Brazil.[13]

These grants of lands and endowments represented the extent of the Crown's *direct* economic assistance to the Jesuits.[14] In time, by the late seventeenth century at least, the magnitude of that aid was far exceeded by the level of private beneficence and by the amount of capital which the Jesuits were able to generate from their growing number of properties. Within the first years of their arrival in Brazil the Jesuits became recipients of undeveloped lands and livestock given to them by such noteworthy figures as Brás Cubas and Diogo Álvares (better known as Caramurú), but bequests of large parcels of improved rural and urban real estate, including sugar plantations, cattle ranches, town mansions, and business offices, appear to date from the second decade of the seventeenth century.[15] The size of such bequests and the stipulations attached to them varied considerably. Bequeathers commonly instructed that part of the funds they assigned to the Society be reserved for masses for their souls and those of their families. Exceptional was Domingo Afonso Certão, the famous co-founder of the cattle ranges of Piauí, who in his fascinating will instructed that five daily masses be said for his soul in the church of the colégio of Salvador and that an additional weekly mass be sung in the church of the novitiate of the same city "until the end of the world." [16] Many benefactors directed the padre-trustees to sell their properties, settle the benefactors' debts, establish the legacies they reserved for their heirs, and apply the remainder to pious works, such as annual gifts to the poor, special masses, or improvements in particular sanctuaries where they had worshiped. A few gave the Society cash to be invested in interest-bearing loans or in rental properties. Some instructed that the bulk of their estates be used to endow new colleges or other kinds of educational facilities. Others simply left their properties to the rectors of the colleges, who were given the option to keep them for the order or to dispose of them as they thought best. Since these wills were customarily prepared with the assistance of the Jesuits themselves, there were inevitable charges that the fathers applied death-bed coercion to secure particularly valuable portions of their benefactors' estates, but it would not be easy today to find convincing proof of such allegations.[17]

In addition to gifts from royal and private benefactors, the Jesuits also obtained properties through direct purchases.[18] Whenever possible, they added to their most promising estates in order to secure access to better water transportation or irrigation facilities, more area to plant sugar or to graze livestock, and for other purposes. It was as a result of many separate purchases, gifts, and lawsuits extending over more than a century that they managed to enlarge the famous *fazenda* of Santa Cruz in the Captaincy of Rio de Janeiro until it measured more than 100 square leagues and became the domicile of more than a thousand persons, most of whom were Negro slaves.[19] The fathers also bought unimproved lots and single and multi-storied dwellings in the colonial towns in anticipation of their future expansion needs and to provide rental income for existing facilities.[20] Whenever particular properties ceased to fit into their plans, the Jesuits sold them to other orders or to private individuals.[21]

The Jesuits utilized their properties in various ways. On their farms they raised a wide variety of indigenous and European crops. Among the more important of the former were manioc *(farinha)*, rice, cotton, and tobacco; among the latter were various kinds of legumes, citrus fruits, and wheat. Such produce was intended principally to feed the fathers and their charges, but surpluses were sold to persons outside the order. The prime market for the Jesuits' most lucrative crop, cane sugar, was, of course, the kingdom. Although the Black Robes began cultivating sugar soon after their arrival in Brazil, they did not acquire their first grinding mill until 1604, when the *engenho* of Camamú was built in Bahia on a site selected by Father Fernão Cardim. That engenho was destroyed by the Dutch in 1640, but the fathers continued to acquire other large mills by gift (as in the case of the famous Sergipe do Condé) or by purchase (e.g., the engenho of Pitanga, also in Bahia) until each of their major colégios was able to draw part of its income from one or more sugar plantations. By my count the Jesuits had a total of seventeen sugar plantations, each equipped with one or more engenhos, at the time of their expulsion.[22] Such installations included not only crushing mills and other apparatus related to the processing of sugar but also brandy stills, blacksmiths, coopers, potters, and weaving shops, and in some instances construction yards capable of producing water craft ranging in size from Amazonian canoes to ocean-going smacks. In addition to food farms and sugar plantations, each college also possessed a number of stock ranches which produced mainly milk and beef cattle but also horses, pigs, sheep, goats, and barnyard fowl. At the time of their sequestration there were, for example, 16,580 livestock on the *fazenda do colégio* in northern Rio de Janeiro, an estimated 32,000 head scattered among thirty ranches in Piauí, and more than 100,000 head of cattle on seven ranches on the island of Marajó.[23]

The properties which the Jesuits operated themselves were managed by one or two padres who supervised the labor of Negro slaves, as in the case of sugar plantations, or Indians, as on the Amazonian cattle ranches. The Society of Jesus was probably the greatest institutional slaveholder in Brazil; certainly it possessed the largest number of slaves confined to a single plantation in all of colonial America.[24]

The Jesuits also leased and rented grazing and agricultural lands, though the income they received from such properties was far less than they gained from their urban holdings.[25] Their greatest portfolio of urban real estate was in the city of Salvador (Bahia), where at the time of the expulsion (1759–1760) they possessed 186 dwellings worth 152,165,000 *réis* and yielding an annual income of 10,918,160 *réis*.[26] A report prepared two decades earlier reveals that in the city of Rio de Janeiro, where the order had its second largest number of urban properties (seventy), it received 5,824,280 *réis* in yearly rentals. By contrast, in the same year the two colleges in São Paulo possessed only six urban properties which gave them an annual income of 980,000 *réis*.[27] Another survey of the 1740's shows that the two colleges in Pernambuco owned forty urban rental properties which yielded a yearly income of 751,000 *réis*.[28] According to the calculations of Father Leite, the Society's urban properties in Salvador and Recife became their most lucrative source of income at the time of their sequestration.[29]

When the Jesuits were expelled, they were undoubtedly the wealthiest religious order in Brazil.[30] Besides royal and private donations and earnings from the direct operation and rental of urban and rural properties, that wealth derived from investments in interest-bearing loans (about which I have no information[31]), and from the sales of so-called Amazonian spices, including cacao, cloves, cinnamon, pepper, sarsaparilla, dyestuffs, and even turtle butter. Until the completion of further archival research, it is impossible to give more than a rough guess as to the total worth of the Jesuits in 1759. The evidence at hand, consisting of inventories taken of some of the Jesuits' larger sugar plantations, surveys of their most important urban properties at the time of their confiscation, and reports concerning the sales of some of those properties, suggests a total figure in excess of 1,000 *contos*.[32]

II. CONFLICTS BETWEEN THE JESUITS AND THEIR RIVALS BEFORE 1722

Considering the Jesuits' extensive property holdings in Brazil, the economic privileges they enjoyed by right and by self-assertion (of which more will be said later), the special favor they long possessed with Portugal's sovereigns and with high colonial officers like members of the Sá family, and the efforts they constantly made to safeguard the Amerindians against predatory seculars, it is not surprising that the Black Robes came under attacks from rival special interest groups. Those attacks began very soon after the fathers first arrived in the colony. Long before questions concerning their economic activities arose, the Jesuits were pitted against seculars over the control of the Indians. The seculars wanted them concentrated in villages easily accessible to their plantations in order to exploit their labor. The missionaries wished to protect the Indians against exploitation and to facilitate their indoctrination in the precepts of Christianity by isolating them as much as possible from the colonists and insisted that they should serve as intermediaries between the Indians and the settlers in matters of labor and trade. In general policies and in special legislation, beginning in 1570, the Crown supported the Jesuits' attempts to defend the Indians until the 1750's. Nevertheless, by the end of the sixteenth century the natives had been virtually eliminated from many parts of the eastern littoral as a result of their destruction through enslavement and exposure to European and African diseases and their flight to the interior, where they and their cousins were pursued by the missionaries and their rivals.[33]

That pursuit intensified during the seventeenth century as the Portuguese expanded their conquests both in the south and in the north. In the south, slave-hunting Paulista *bandeirantes* struck southwest from São Paulo and between 1628 and 1641 overran and destroyed two mission fields newly founded by Jesuits based in Spanish Paraguay and were prevented from doing further damage only when the Black Robes succeeded in arming their wards.[34] In 1640 when the Jesuits in São Paulo read to their flocks a papal brief which condemned all enslavement of the Amerindians, the populace rebelled and expelled them from the Captaincy. And their brethren in Rio de Janeiro barely escaped the same fate.[35]

As the Portuguese contemporaneously expanded around the hump toward the Amazon, the competition between the colonists and the Black Robes for the bodies and souls of the Indians created new tensions between the Jesuits and their rivals. The result on two occasions (1661–1662 and 1684) was the ouster of the Black Robes from the State of Maranhão. If on the first occasion the Crown contented itself with the restoration of the Jesuits and the issuance of a general pardon for those responsible for their exile, it was less lenient the second time, when three leaders of the tumult were hanged and several others were given less severe sentences.[36]

The second restoration of the Jesuits in the State of Maranhão was followed by the issuance of a set of regulations (the *regimento* of 1686) which was to govern relations between the Black Robes and the other orders active in the Amazon area (principally the Franciscans, Carmelites, and Mercedarians), the Indians, and the settlers for the next seventy years. Key provisions of this document are worth noting, since they became vital issues during the Jesuits' most troubled decade, the 1750's. The regimento awarded the missionaries spiritual, political, and temporal jurisdiction within the mission villages *(aldeias)* they administered and from which all colonists were barred. The Jesuit colleges in São Luis and Belém were each assigned an aldeia of Indian workers exclusively for their support. In addition, every Jesuit residence situated at a distance of thirty or more leagues from either college was authorized to make use of twenty-five Indians (later interpreted to mean twenty-five families) for mission tasks. All public officials, including royal governors and municipal councils, concerned with regulating relations between Indians and colonists, such as the procurement of ransomed captives *(resgates)* from the remote interior, the distribution of Indian workers, and the determination of their periods of service and wages, were enjoined to act in consultation with the missionaries.[37]

These regulations were more favorable to the Jesuits than to any other order and reflect the very close relations which existed between the society and the government of Pedro II (1683–1706). So, too, does a renewal in 1684 of a decree *(alvará)* originally issued during the reign of King Sebastian (1557–1578) exempting the Jesuits from payment of all customs duties on goods they shipped to and from Brazil.[38] During the same decade the Crown more than doubled the stipend of the Black Robes assigned to Maranhão, strongly censured a governor who questioned whether the Jesuits had a right to certain *aldeias*, and informed him that the King expected his governors to render all possible assistance and protection to the padres to facilitate their labors.[39]

Nevertheless, it was during the reign of Pedro II and that of his immediate predecessor, João IV (1640–1656), that the Crown began to take serious cognizance of colonial complaints of the excessive wealth of the Jesuits and other religious orders. Those complaints date back at least to 1603, when the *câmara* of Gôa warned that if the Estado da India were lost,

it will be the fault of the Fathers of the Company [of Jesus], who, having permission from Your Majesty as we will note and prove, have . . . as big a revenue in this State as amounts to half of the revenues of your Treasury. They are absolute lords of the greater part of this Island, and they buy up everything, so that inevitably within ten years there will not be a house or a palm-grove which they will not own. The citizens are being dispossessed of them all, *which is the reason why this State is so poor.* . . .[40]

I have added emphasis to the last part of this complaint, because the contention that the alleged prosperity of the orders, particularly the Jesuits, was responsible for the misery and poverty of the king's subjects became a very familiar, though never satisfactorily documented, refrain in the memorials and dispatches of opponents of the Jesuits in later days.

Some four decades after the aldermen of Gôa expressed this warning, the câmara of Rio de Janeiro rebuffed the efforts of its governor, Salvador de Sá, to persuade the council to vote additional revenues for local defenses, pointing out that the city had already contributed a great deal to that end and that the Black Robes "are very rich and the lords of the best properties in [this] land and [possess] half *(2 partes)* of the lands and cattle in it." [41] Their complaint was echoed sixteen years later by the municipal council of Salvador, which lamented: "The Religious Orders, which in this captaincy possess much property and many sugar mills, estates, farms, houses, cattle and slaves, refuse to contribute anything at all to the expenses of the war [Portugal's struggle for liberation from Spain, 1640–1668], so that the rest of the people are heavily burdened and the poor suffer continual oppression." To these complaints Francisco Barreto, the prestigious governor-general of the State of Brazil, added another when he wrote the Crown criticizing the religious orders, especially the Jesuits, for their refusal to pay tithes upon their numerous, prosperous properties.[42]

The conflict between Crown officers and tithe contractors on the one hand and the religious orders, especially the Jesuits, on the other concerning payment of the tithe is a familiar one to students of colonial Spanish America and it should come as no surprise that it was a seemingly never-ending one in Brazil too.[43] By the bull *Super specula* (1551), collection of the tithes in Brazil was awarded to the sovereigns of Portugal in their capacity as Grand Masters of the Order of Christ, which was theoretically responsible for the colonial Church.[44] The following year royal officials for the first time attempted to levy the tithe upon Jesuit properties in Brazil but were rebuffed by Padre Manoel da Nóbrega, the society's first Vice Provincial in Brazil, who asserted that his order had been exempted from such payments.[45] Perhaps the padre was referring to the bull *Licet debitum* of Paul III (October 18, 1549), the first of many papal statements upon which the Jesuits were to rely to justify their refusal to pay the dízimos. What their defenders have never made clear is whether such legislation ever had the Crown's sanction to be applicable to the Church in Brazil.[46]

What is clear is that the Jesuits and the other missionary orders in Brazil persistently refused to comply with the Crown's injunctions to pay tithes on their properties. In 1614 Philip III (1598–1621) noted with displeasure the inability of his predecessors to impress the orders with the necessity of contributing to the tithe funds and implied that his government was determined to rectify this situation.[47] Nevertheless, as already observed, Governor General Barreto declared in 1661 that the orders were continuing to refuse to pay tithes. What response the Crown made to his complaint is unknown. Certainly the governments of Pedro II and João V (1706–1750) undertook repeated efforts to compel the orders to pay dízimos and threatened to deprive them of their properties, excepting the initial grants for new colleges, if they failed to comply. In 1711 the Crown directed that in order to avoid further "damage" all future land grants to colonists would contain as a condition of their acceptance the pledge that they would not be later conveyed to the orders except with the stipulation that their possessors agree always to pay the dízimos.[48]

The first Bragançan kings also endeavored to deal with a related grievance of their colonists, namely, that the religious orders, especially the Jesuits, had too much land. In 1642 when Father Luis Figueira went to

Lisbon seeking permission to establish Jesuit missions in the Amazon, João IV consented but "made it clear that the Jesuits would not be allowed to acquire property without the permission of the Crown." [49] Such a stipulation was entirely consistent with royal legislation dating back to the *Código Afonsino* (1446), which strictly forbade religious orders to acquire property without possessing royal license to do so.[50] The inclusion in that injunction in subsequent codes, the *Manuelinas* of 1521 and the *Filipinas* of 1603, besides the enactment of additional legislation on the same point, indicates that such warnings were more honored in their breech than in their observance.[51] In 1690 and again in 1711 the Crown directed that neither convents nor monasteries in Brazil "can nor ought to acquire lands and retain them, except for those which were [bestowed] upon them for their establishment, because of the pernicious consequences which result from similar acquisitions and the disorders [that they cause] among the vassals of those states [i.e., the captaincies]. . . ." [52] Seven years later, when the Overseas Council directed the governor of Rio de Janeiro to inform it concerning the extent to which the three nonmendicant orders in the Captaincy (the Benedictines, Carmelites, and Jesuits) held properties there, the Governor replied that their superiors had proven evasive to his request for information, while the câmara of Rio de Janeiro complained of the "inconveniences" which such properties caused the Crown and its vassals, having been accumulated contrary to the laws of the realm. The Council then sternly admonished the heads of the orders to comply with its directive. The result was possibly the first comprehensive survey of properties owned by the orders in that captaincy.[53] Whether similar surveys were undertaken in other captaincies at this time has yet to be discovered. Certainly, this one does not seem to have led to any change in royal policy. Four years later, however, the Jesuits were confronted for the first time by one of their most persistent and intractable enemies, the famous Paulo da Silva Nunes, populist spokesman of the Amazon.

III. THE CAMPAIGN OF PAULO DA SILVA NUNES
AGAINST THE JESUITS, 1722–1746

The Black Robes experienced some of their greatest achievements and some of their most bitter sorrows in the Amazon. In 1693, when the Crown moved to terminate long-standing rivalries among the four religious orders seeking to carry the faith to the primitive Amerindians of the Amazon by dividing that vast area among them, the Jesuits secured

the largest and most favorable territory.[54] If the Black Robes were grati-
fied by that award and by the terms of the regimento of 1686, they were
displeased by the Crown's decision to reverse an earlier stand and again
make licit the capture of Indian slaves under certain conditions. The
new law of 1688 authorized offensive campaigns against hostile, pagan
Indians, provided that the nature of their hostility was first verified in
writing by Franciscan and Jesuit missionaries who were to accompany
the ransoming expeditions *(resgates)*. For understandable reasons, the
Black Robes wanted no part of such a sordid business and they appear
to have tried to frustrate the new law by declining to participate in the
resgates.[55] That did not prevent unscrupulous slavers from finding ways
of securing captive labor, often with the connivance of royal governors.[56]

It was following the recall of one such governor, the famous annalist
Bernardo Pereira de Berredo,[57] that Paulo da Silva Nunes made his first
public efforts to bring about the ouster of the Jesuits from the Amazon.[58] Considering his importance, we know little about Silva Nunes's
background or the specific reasons for the intensity of his hatred of the
Jesuits. Evidently a Peninsular by birth, he appeared in Pará as a soldier
during the War of the Spanish Succession (1702–1713). In Belém he
attached himself to the entourage of Captain-General Cristovão da
Costa Freire (1707–1716), either as his secretary (as he claimed) or as
his barber (as the Jesuits later asserted). Utilizing his palace connections, Silva Nunes became governor of two lower Amazon towns (Vigia
and Icatú), superintendent of fortifications, and a captain of a colonial
militia company. This last distinction gained him entry into the local
aristocracy, if it can be called that, and Silva Nunes married a descendant of one of its most celebrated seventeenth-century warrior-explorer
forebears, Pedro Teixeira.[59]

When a senior magistrate *(desembargador)* who accompanied Berredo's successor, João da Maia da Gama (1722–1728), to Belém launched
an inquiry into the treatment of Indian captives, he found a number of
colonists guilty of participating in unauthorized slaving expeditions.
Such changes produced widespread unrest throughout Pará. Defama-
tory broadsides *(pasquins)* appeared denouncing the Black Robes, who
were believed to be the instigators of the investigation, and called for
their expulsion from the captaincy.[60] In a meeting of the municipal
council of Belém, Paulo da Silva Nunes read a lengthy brief in which he
defended the colonists and denounced the Jesuits for having frustrated
the Crown's directives concerning the supply of Indian workers for the
settlers, for having made themselves the absolute masters of the abo-

rigines, and for engaging in commerce in Amazonian spices to the prejudice of the royal treasury.[61] Unimpressed by these charges and persuaded by the Jesuit inspector (*visitador*) that Silva Nunes was the leader
of the colonists' movement against the Black Robes, Maia da Gama
had him arrested and temporarily confined to a fortress. That seems to
have quelled the unrest, but it marked only the beginning of Silva
Nunes' unrelenting campaign to discredit the Jesuits and to secure their
permanent banishment from the Amazon.

Shortly after his release, Silva Nunes fled to Lisbon bearing a lengthy
memorial signed by Paraense malcontents, expressing their grievances
against the Captain-General and the missionaries. In this first of many
memorials that he was to prepare during the next two decades while
serving as the official agent (*procurador*) of the colonists living in the
State of Maranhão, Silva Nunes alleged that the padres were the source
of all discord within that State. They were accused of exerting limitless,
despotic influence over Crown officers, white colonists, and the Indians.
They were charged with inciting Negro servants to abandon their owners and with supplying the Indians with firearms with which they had
murdered white settlers. He asserted that within some of their missions
the fathers maintained gaols where even white trespassers had been confined in irons. Furthermore, he said, their missions and colleges were
more akin to vast customs houses, where scandalous illicit trade was
carried on, than places of prayer. Even worse, the Jesuits were accused
of engaging in treasonable relations with Portugal's neighbors in the
Amazon region, the Dutch, the French, and the Spanish. The memorial-
ist concluded with the inevitable statement that the State of Maranhão
had the potential of becoming exceedingly prosperous but was on the
verge of economic ruin and would be destroyed if His Majesty did not
provide immediate, effective remedies.

What remedies did the procurator have in mind? First, that the religious should be barred from exercising temporal, political, or economic jurisdiction within the aldeias. Second, that they ought to be prohibited from continuing to instruct the Amerindians in the *língua geral*
and be required to teach them Portuguese instead.[62] Third, that the
missionaries should be compelled to admit inspectors to their facilities
to examine their behavior. And fourth, that the Crown arrange to send
fifty families each year from its Atlantic islands to the Amazon area in
order to populate the backlands and assist in the region's economic development.[63]

Shortly after Silva Nunes reached Lisbon, he acquired an important ally, former Captain-General Berredo, who had left Belém under a cloud and was doubtless anxious to blacken the reputation of his successor. Like Silva Nunes, he, too, was no friend of the Jesuits. It was Berredo who persuaded the câmara of Belém to contribute to Silva Nunes's expenses and it was he who gave the lobbyist funds out of his own pocket when the procurator was destitute.[64] It was probably he who opened doors that would otherwise have remained closed to the procurator,[65] particularly those of influential persons in the kingdom who shared his own hostility toward the Black Robes.

During the mid- and late 1720's Silva Nunes continued to draft lengthy memorials buttressed with citations to classical authorities, learned jurists such as Solórzano Pereira, and previous royal legislation, endeavoring to emphasize the bestiality of the Indians while putting the colonists' motives in the best possible light. He argued that the savages, whom he suggested may have been the descendants of the Jews, were "not true men but arboreal brutes incapable of participating in the Catholic faith." They were such "squalid savages, [so] ferocious, and so base" that they scarcely resembled humans. And he asked: "If the Ethiopians can be made captives, why can not the Indians of Maranhão?" Actually, he assured the Court, the whites really did not intend to enslave the Indians at all; they only wished to employ them in their fields and mills, paying them wages, feeding, clothing, and teaching them Christian doctrines and good customs. He argued that married white officers *(cabos)* be named to replace the missionaries as administrators of the *aldeias* so that, among other things, they could minister to the physical afflictions of the Indians.[66]

For several years Silva Nunes's memorials appear to have been officially ignored, even though many of his allegations were supported by statements sent to the Overseas Council by câmaras in Maranhão and Rio de Janeiro[67] and by Alexandre de Sousa Freire, captain-general of Maranhão (1728–1732), a close friend of Berredo and an employer of Silva Nunes who represented his interests in Court.[68] But by the end of the decade this growing body of criticism of the Jesuits was beginning to produce results. One was the Overseas Council's announcement (in 1728) of a new law concerning the procurement of Indians from the interior. Official (but not private) ransoming expeditions were again authorized in order to provide the planters with workers, but the Indians were to remain free rather than become slaves.[69] A *carta régia* of 1729 also reiterated the Crown's insistence that property originally granted to private individuals could not be transferred to religious orders unless such conveyances explicitly reserved its right to collect the dízimos. Still another royal order of these years called upon the Jesuits to submit an accounting of properties they had acquired in Pará as a result of bequests and other arrangements.[70]

In the face of the apparent toughening of the Crown's policy toward the Black Robes, two prominent figures rose to their defense. One was Father Jacinto de Carvalho, formerly a missionary in the Amazon and more recently confessor to both Maia da Gama and Sousa Freire, who in 1729 took up his pen as the newly named procurator of the Jesuit missions in Maranhão and wrote a lengthy rebuttal to the charges of Silva Nunes.[71] The other was former Captain-General Maia da Gama, who in 1730 complied with the Overseas Council's request for comment on Silva Nunes's memorials and pronounced them to be factually baseless and as born out of the lobbyist's long-standing personal hatred of the Black Robes.[72]

In 1734 the Crown turned over most of this mass of conflicting testimony to a senior magistrate, desembargador Francisco Duarte dos Santos, and sent him to Maranhão to ascertain to what extent the charges against the Jesuits were correct and to recommend whatever changes he felt were necessary in its policies toward the Indians and the missionaries.[73] The Jesuits emerged from that investigation with a clean bill. After receiving oral and written testimony for a year and undertaking tours to appropriate places in order to verify the assertions and counter-assertions, the desembargador submitted a perceptive report in which he stated his conclusions forcefully and unequivocally. First, he failed to find evidence corroborating the settlers' perennial claim that they were compelled to live in great misery without sufficient workers because of the activities of the missionaries. He pointed out that the colonists owned many sumptuous homes of recent construction in Belém, that they could afford to dress in clothing made from good quality fabrics imported from France and Italy, and that many of their estates contained from fifty to more than two hundred slaves, most of them Indians, many of them obviously not acquired through legal channels since they were unregistered. Second, he found little support for the colonists' contention that offensive campaigns against the Indians were necessary in order to protect their properties against raids by wild savages. Third, he was convinced that if the oft-repeated proposal of Silva Nunes that temporal, political, and economic jurisdiction over the missions should be transferred from the missionaries to married white officers were ever put into practice, within a few years "the aldeias would remain only a memory." Consequently, "I am of the opinion that the missionaries [should continue to] administer the *aldeias* in temporal as well as in spiritual matters, as in the past." Fourth, he absolved the Jesuits from the charge that they conducted large-scale illicit trade in colonial and European products. It was true, he admitted, that their *fazendas* were prosperous, but the goods they produced were used primarily for the support of their missions, and the surpluses sold to the colonists were made available at their own requests and at reasonable, rather than exhorbitant, prices. It was also true that large quantities of spices came down river in Jesuit barges, but there was no reason why the colonists could not emulate the missionaries in tapping the forests of their resources except that they preferred to load their canoes with illegal cargoes of Indian slaves. On the other hand—and this was the magistrate's second important recommendation—he did not favor the missionaries' continued involvement in commercial activities, presumably because he realized that this was a major source of the settlers' complaints against them, and therefore he strongly urged that the Crown provide the missionaries with adequate financial support so that they could dispense with their trading operations.[74]

The response of the Overseas Council to the desembargador's report was mixed. Implicitly, at least, it went along with his recommendation that the missionaries' authority over their aldeias not be altered. But upon the advice of treasury officers, it voted against the magistrate's proposal that the Crown increase its financial support of the missions.[75]

Even as the desembargador was dismissing many of Paulo da Silva Nunes's charges as mere "fantasies," that implacable Jesuitophobe was drafting new memorials. In 1734, the very year that the royal investigator was sent to Belém, Silva Nunes composed still another diatribe against the Jesuits in which he expanded upon old and added new charges. Among the latter was his assertion that there existed a Jesuit conspiracy against the rights of the Crown and its colonists which extended into the very chambers of the Overseas Council, where the Society continually intrigued against colonial officers who opposed its activities. He also warned that the Jesuits were continuing to defy the injunctions of the Crown to teach their neophytes the Portuguese language and to pay tithes upon their properties, much to the prejudice of legitimate commerce. For reasons not clear, when he submitted this memorial to the Overseas Council in 1735, Silva Nunes moderated its tone and abbreviated its length. But at the same time he added an appendix listing the properties and alleged incomes of the religious orders

active in the Amazon. Three years later the tireless petitioner wrote his
final brief against the Black Robes, merely repeating his old allegations.
Then, burdened by debts and abandoned by friends, he entered a debt-
or's prison from which he emerged eight years later (in 1746) to be taken
to his grave.[76]

It would be easy to dismiss Paulo da Silva Nunes as a mere crank and
a failure, but such an assessment would be a serious underestimation of
his importance. He was clearly an intelligent, if misdirected, man, but
to what extent the scholarly apparatus which accompanied his memorials was the product of his own researches or was contributed by unknown persons for whom he served as spokesman is a question which
can not now be decided. It is true that Silva Nunes failed to live long
enough to see his major goal achieved, but his influence, both immediate
and in the long run, was far from inconsequential. Although a direct
causal connection cannot be traced at this time, it is not unlikely that
his last memorials had a bearing upon the Crown's decision to revive the
dízimo issue with the religious orders in the late 1720's and again in the
1730's.[77] Nor is it unlikely that they influenced the Crown to direct colonial authorities during the early 1740's to investigate how much property the orders possessed in Brazil in violation of the ordinances of the
realm.[78] It is true that these measures did not lead to any significant
changes in royal policy during the 1740's, but they and the memorials
that Silva Nunes wrote helped to prepare the way for the decisive blows
that befell the Society of Jesus during the fateful 1750's. It was then that
high royal authorities would paraphrase Silva Nunes with approbation,
and it was in the middle of that decisive decade that the Portuguese
government assembled and published his last series of memorials under
the title *Terribilidades jesuíticas no governo d'el-rei d. João V* (Lisbon,
1755) .[79] Thus, in the long run, to paraphrase Professor Boxer, the poi-
sonous seeds that Paulo da Silva Nunes had planted during the 1720's
and 1730's produced bitter fruit for the Black Robes.[80]

IV. THE CLIMAX OF PORTUGUESE JESUITOPHOBIA:
THE FATEFUL FIFTIES

The catastrophic series of developments during the 1750's which ultimately brought forth the Portuguese government's order expelling
the Society of Jesus from all its dominions must be studied in three—
very likely four—theaters: the missions' lands of what became the Bra-

zilian state of Rio Grande do Sul, the State of Maranhão, the kingdom, and probably Rome as well. I have space here to consider in detail only the second of these *loci contentiones.*

The Jesuits' tribulations in this decisive decade began with the signing of the Treaty of Limits (1750) between Spain and Portugal. That agreement, which superseded the ancient, unworkable Treaty of Tordesillas (1494), was intended to bring to an end the centuries-old territorial disputes between the two Iberian powers in South America. One of its key provisions called for the exchange of the Portuguese smuggling entrepôt of Colônia do Sacramento for the so-called Seven Missions' lands east of the Uruguay River in western Rio Grande do Sul. Such missions and the flourishing cattle ranches assigned to them had been nourished since the beginnings of the century by the so-called Spanish Jesuits for the care of their Guaraní neophytes. For understandable reasons these Black Robes were reluctant to abandon such a promising field and they pulled every string they could to persuade Spanish authorities not to carry out the terms of the exchange provisions. But to no avail. Early in 1753, when a joint Iberian survey party reached the cattle station of Santa Tecla, its progress was blocked by a group of armed Guaraní warriors and the party was forced to turn back. When subsequent negotiations failed to persuade the Indians to cease their resistance, it was broken by force after a frustrating two-year campaign (1754–1756) in which normally uncongenial Spanish and Portuguese soldiers fought together against motley levies of Guaraní warriors whose defense, they became convinced, was organized and directed by the Jesuits.[81]

Although Black Robes in the Province of Brazil and in the Vice Province of Maranhão were not directly involved in the war, their order's opposition to the treaty of 1750 and its rumored role in the Guaraní war were sufficient to cast suspicion on the motives of all Jesuits living in Portuguese lands and served to give credence to the allegations which one of their most fearsome opponents, Francisco Xavier de Mendonça Furtado, made against them. One of two younger brothers of Sebastião José de Carvalho e Melo, better known as the Marquis of Pombal, Mendonça Furtado was sent to Belém in 1751 with two assignments, one to serve as the chief Portuguese commissioner of the northern joint boundary survey team, and the other to fill the office of governor and captain-general of the State of Maranhão. A one-time naval officer, Mendonça Furtado was imperious, hard-driving, crude, violent tempered, ambitious though completely loyal to his elder brother, pious in an Old

Testament sense, gullible but suspicious of the motives of anyone, particularly one whom he regarded as an inferior, who held views contrary to his own; he was therefore entirely uncompromising.[82]

Mendonça Furtado reached his station in September, 1751, a year or so after his elder brother assumed his first cabinet post and began his twenty-seven-year dominance of Portugal. Whether Mendonça Furtado's primary mission in coming to Brazil was to assist his brother in the destruction of the Society of Jesus has long been a moot point. Those who deny that there was any such fraternal conspiracy point out that the Captain-General's instructions spoke favorably of the Jesuits' charitable treatment of the Indians.[83] But they must also take into consideration two of the so-called secret articles of those instructions which, even though they did not specifically mention the Jesuits, were obviously written with them primarily in mind. Article 13 warned that if the regulars, a term which Portuguese writers of this time often used as synonymous with Jesuits, offered opposition to the Crown's Indian policies, they should be informed that the King expected them to be the first to obey his orders, particularly "because the fazendas which they possess are entirely or for the most part [held] contrary to . . . the law[s] of the kingdom . . . ," and that the King could enforce such legislation if the orders continued to be negligent or obstreperous. Article 14 was equally menacing:

As the excessive power which the ecclesiastics have in that State, principally in the temporal dominion of their aldeias, has come to my royal attention, you will secure the necessary information, taking counsel with the bishop of Pará who will instruct you with the truth[84]. . . to inform me if it will be more convenient [that] the ecclesiastics remain only with the spiritual dominion, giving them allowances from my royal treasury, for which purpose you should suggest who ought to cultivate the same [missions'] lands, all of which you will . . . inform me, verifying also the truth of the fact with respect to the . . . excessive power and great capital of the regulars; and in all this you should proceed with great caution, circumspection, and prudence.[85]

Whatever predisposition the new Captain-General may have had toward the Jesuits in the past,[86] those instructions, which revived many of the issues concerning the activities of the Black Robes that had been debated during the preceding reign, surely conditioned the attitude that the new administrator would take toward the Black Robes. What his attitude actually was became apparent when Mendonça Furtado set down some of his earliest impressions concerning conditions in his state, less than two months after his arrival there. The lands were very rich, he wrote his brother, and one of their most important resources was the Indians who were for the most part intelligent and docile, but they were terribly abused by the missionaries who possessed complete sovereignty over them, not only those living within the mission compounds, but "all those infinite numbers of unhappy people who are born in these backlands." The *aldeias,* he continued, were virtually separate republics. Within them the name of the king was unknown and the same was true of the Portuguese language; within them the Indians were scandalously allowed to associate in their minds their own pantheon of gods with the Christian God and saints; within them the missionaries despotically wielded the whip, from which there was no appeal save to their own superiors, who even arranged their marriages and sold them into slavery. Because of the missionaries' control over the lives of the Indians and their refusal to pay taxes for which the colonists were liable, he continued, the religious were monopolizing the lucrative spice trade of the interior, and dominated the fish and meat markets in the towns. Furthermore, their convents were veritable factories, producing all sorts of goods for outsiders as well as for their own establishments, and the profits they earned were deposited in strongboxes instead of circulating in the State. The Captain-General's conclusion was inevitable: the economic activities of the missionaries, particularly the Jesuits, were seriously damaging the state and were ruining the colonists who were being reduced to the "last stages of poverty and misery." [87]

Paulo da Silva Nunes, whose memorials Mendonça Furtado cited with approval on more than one occasion,[88] could not have put the case better. But there was a vast difference between the amount of influence that that obscure, long-exiled, recognizably prejudiced lobbyist could bring to bear and that of one of His Majesty's highest-ranking colonial officers, whose impressions were fresh and assumed to be objective and whose dispatches were directed to the colonial secretaries and to the *de facto* prime minister of Portugal, his own brother.

Throughout the early 1750's, Mendonça Furtado, a pre-Actonian exponent of the dictum that "power tends to corrupt and absolute power corrupts absolutely," continued to excoriate the Jesuits who, he insisted, had destroyed the former prosperity of the state[89] and were preventing its recovery. They regarded themselves, he charged, as "sovereign and independent" of all royal authority. Within their chapters *(definitórios)* they decided which laws were in their best interests and would be obeyed and those which were inimical to them and would be ignored, but they were ever ready to insist that legislation which restricted the opportunities of the colonists be rigorously enforced. Their behavior was not truly religious, for religion had become a mere pretext to them, "as it is in the majority of the nations of the North." Not only was this the case with the Jesuits, he said, but also with those who followed their lead, the Franciscans *(Capuchos)*, Mercedarians, and Carmelites who in America had lost that sense of spiritual dedication that had distinguished them in the kingdom and became mercenary-minded, jealous of their privileges, and disobedient to the king's officers. He urged that the most "prideful and troublesome" of the missionaries be removed from the Amazon and that their superiors in Lisbon should be admonished concerning the scandalous commercial activities of their field workers.[90]

In February, 1754, Mendonça Furtado made far-reaching recommendations concerning the future status of the Jesuits in the Amazon region. Responding to an inquiry from the Overseas Council as to the yield and value of the Jesuits' properties, he undertook a personal inspection of those in the vicinity of the capital under the pretext of "mere curiosity and diversion." On the basis of that tour he submitted a general report describing the kinds of activities to which each fazenda was devoted and suggested without offering any specific evidence that all were flourishing.[91] Then he turned to the question posed by Article 14 of his instructions, i.e., whether the missionaries' properties should remain in their possession or be taken over by the Crown in return for allowances provided by the king. Unhesitatingly Mendonça Furtado declared that the Crown ought to assume control of the properties and he proceeded to indicate why. First, such a move would strike a serious blow at the pretentions of the "most powerful enemy of the State," namely the Society of Jesus. Second, in the hands of the king's vassals those estates would yield far more than the cost of the allowances, since their new owners would pay the dízimos and customs duties. Third, the "great number" of Indian slaves whom the Jesuits used to cultivate their fields would be set at liberty and their Negro slaves could be auctioned at great profit to His Majesty. Fourth, the Jesuits would therefore become "transformed from the managers of estates into missionaries and conquerors of souls," the *raison d'être* for their presence in the colony. The Captain-General then made two further recommendations: first, that the number of missionaries attached to each college or monastery be limited according to the amount of subsidy the King could afford; second, that once the Jesuits had been deprived of their fazendas, it would be "totally useless and fruitless" for them to continue to retain their temporal authority over the missions. And without their ability to depend upon Indian laborers, they would cease to be "lords of all the precious spices of the back country." In conclusion, he wrote, either His Majesty wished to re-establish the prosperity of the state, or he must allow it to remain in its present ruinous condition. If the King intended to achieve the former objective, he was convinced that his proposals offered the only means of doing that.[92]

Soon after completing this important dispatch, Mendonça Furtado set off on his arduous, exasperating, frustrating trip up the Amazon to the Rio Negro, where he was supposed to be met by the Spanish boundary commissioner to preside over the first steps in the delimitation of the new dividing line between the two empires in the north. While vainly awaiting the arrival of the Spaniards, the Captain-General visited a number of Jesuit missions and engaged in countless polemics with the Black Robes over the amount of rations and numbers of Indians they provided him.[93] The shortages of both, together with the unexplained delays in the appearance of the Spaniards, the uncorroborated testimony which former employees of the Black Robes furnished the Captain-General against the padres, his periodic bouts of ill health, and the reports that he received from Lisbon concerning the southern boundary party's difficulties with the Guaraní, served to convince Mendonça Furtado that the Society of Jesus was engaged in a vast conspiracy throughout the continent to prevent the Iberian powers from implementing the Treaty of Madrid.[94] He would gladly exchange places with Gomes Freire de Andrada, the Portuguese high commissioner in the south, he wrote, for at least the latter's adversaries were visible and he possessed adequate means to defeat them, whereas his own enemies were hidden and were waging the "most cruel war imaginable" against him.[95]

It was while he was on one of his visits to the "enemy's" camp that the Captain-General became even further convinced of the baseness and treacherous motives of the Jesuits who labored in the Amazon. In October, 1755, he went to the aldeia of Trocano on the Madeira River to preside over its re-establishment as a Portuguese town *(vila)*, renamed Borba a Nôva.[96] Upon entering a large thatched-covered dwelling which served as the residence of the padre in charge of the aldeia and as the mission chapel, the first thing to catch his eye was the altar with the Holy Scriptures upon it. And scarcely a meter *(vara)* away was a large balance, the sort which the Jesuits used to weigh the spices which they purchased from Indians living outside the mission. The shocking juxtaposition of these two objects reminded the Captain-General of the scene when Christ expelled the money-changers from the temple.[97] What better evidence was needed to demonstrate how mercenary the Black Robes had become?

It was while he was staying at the same mission that Mendonça Furtado witnessed an alarming demonstration of Jesuit firepower. Decades before, Captain-General Maia da Gama had authorized the Black Robes to mount two small-caliber cannon at the mission in order to frighten off groups of wild Indians who were raiding the *aldeia*. The German-born fathers who were living at the mission when Mendonça Furtado was there, both of whom were later described by Carvalho as "disguised engineers," were very proud of their artillery and discharged it on several festive occasions during his stay. Taken together with reports of Jesuit artillery in Paraguay, this was proof to the Captain-General—and to his brother—that the Black Robes constituted an armed menace.[98] For their audacity Fathers Anselmo Eckart and Antônio Meisterburg were among twenty-one Jesuits who for similar "crimes" were expelled from the State of Maranhão in 1757 and 1758 and were confined for the next two decades in prisons throughout the kingdom.[99]

In December, 1756, Francisco Xavier de Mendonça Furtado returned to Belém, having abandoned hope of encountering the Spanish boundary commissioner and having urgent matters which required his attention in the capital.[100] The most important among them concerned the implementation of two new laws which, coupled with the recent establishment of the royal monopoly company for the economic development of Maranhão and Pará (1755), posed serious threats to the economic future of the Jesuits in the Amazon region. The first was the so-called law of Indian liberties, which directed enforcement of the long-ignored bull *Immensa pastorum* (1741), in which Benedict XIV absolutely condemned enslavement of the Indians by seculars or ecclesiastics, "even the Company of Jesus," under any pretexts.[101] The second abolished the temporal jurisdiction of the missionaries over the Indians in the State of Maranhão and ordered their aldeias converted into civil communities,[102] thus adopting an old proposal of Paulo da Silva Nunes and one more recently put forth by Mendonça Furtado, as Carvalho readily acknowledged.[103] Both of these important laws naturally affected all the orders active in the Amazon region, but they were directed primarily against the Black Robes, and in anticipation of their opposition to them Carvalho cautioned his brother to keep their texts secret until he found a propitious moment to announce them.[104]

Early in February, 1757, shortly after his return to the capital, Mendonça Furtado called a special meeting of the missions board *(junta das missões)* at which he divulged the text of the law of June 7, 1755, which secularized the missions.[105] Although the Jesuits reacted to the Crown's decision with apparent equanimity, they soon found themselves embroiled in a series of controversies which further exacerbated relations between them and agents of the Crown and which led ultimately to the seizure of their properties in the State of Maranhão and in other parts of the colony. One of those controversies arose at another meeting of the missions board later the same month, when Dom Frei Miguel de Bulhões, bishop of Pará, suddenly demanded that all missionaries who remained living in their former aldeias must now submit to his control. The issue of episcopal visitation with respect to members of the regular branch of the clergy was an old one in Brazil, as it was in Spanish America,[106] and the fact that Bulhões decided to press the matter at this time suggests that he was aware that similar authority had been granted to the bishops of Gôa since 1731 and sensed that in its present mood the Crown was prepared to back his demand in Maranhão. The heads of three of the orders must have realized that, too, for they reluctantly yielded to the Bishop's insistence, but the Vice Provincial of the Jesuits replied, as his predecessors had always done in similar cases, that it would be contrary to the Society's *Institutes* to accept episcopal supervision. Instead, he proposed that the Black Robes who continued to minister to the spiritual needs of the Indians in the former aldeias be regarded as auxiliaries *(coadjutores)* of the Bishop but remain free from his control.[107] But such a compromise was unacceptable to Bulhões and the issue continued to smolder until the final expulsion.

Other controversies between the Black Robes and their adversaries concerned economic matters. In April, 1757, the Vice Provincial addressed a memorial to the Captain-General in which he asked that the Black Robes be permitted to continue to draw spices from the interior in order to satisfy the debts of the *aldeias* to their colleges or, alternatively, that the Crown make other provision to settle those obligations. He also asked that the Jesuits be allowed to continue to utilize Indian slaves to which they had been legally entitled prior to the new law abolishing Indian slavery. The Captain-General bruskly rejected these requests on the ground that the Jesuits had no legitimate debts in the state but merely wished to continue to monopolize its commerce, to exploit the Indians, and to be a burden to the royal treasury.[108]

In the face of this rebuff, the Black Robes, upon instructions from the

Vice Provincial, began removing religious objects, cattle, canoes, and other articles from the aldeias. Some were sold; others were stored in their colleges and houses. When he learned of the Vice Provincial's order, the Captain-General was furious, for he insisted that all appurtenances of the missions properly belonged to the new communities and that their removal was further evidence of the Jesuits' arrogance, despotic behavior, and determination to defy the will of the Crown.[109] When the Jesuits insisted that the goods they were taking were *bens industriais* which they had contributed to the aldeias and were legally their own property, Mendonça Furtado became so incensed that he drafted a prolix paper running to one hundred numbered paragraphs in which he presented a general critique of the economic activities of the Black Robes in the State of Maranhão.[110] First, he declared that their commercial activities were contrary to canon law and were therefore illegal; properties assigned to the missions as a result of such activities could therefore not belong to the Society and since they were acquired as a result of the exploitation of the Indians, they rightfully belonged to them. Second, he contended that such commerce had never been necessary to further the spiritual mission of the Society. Next, he examined the Jesuits' claim that the former missions were heavily in debt to their colleges and asserted that such obligations were artificially contrived. The Society could not possibly be in debt, he affirmed, since it was notorious to everyone that the college of Belém possessed "great magazines" in which the fathers gathered the products of the vast trade they illicitly conducted in the interior with wild tribes and even with Spanish settlements. And it was also well known, he continued, that the Jesuits' fazendas contained large shops where artisans labored steadily, day and night, Sundays, and even saints' days, producing goods which they sold to the community at more than double the prices of similar items in Lisbon. By comparison with the vast profits the Black Robes garnered from such enterprises, the Captain-General concluded that their expenses were very modest. It was an impressive paper, whether prepared upon instructions from Lisbon or on the Captain-General's own initiative and with anyone's assistance we do not know. Significantly, although Mendonça Furtado buttressed his brief with citations to canon law, collections of papal edicts, and even the *Política indiana* of Solórzano y Pereira, he failed to provide the specific sort of statistical evidence necessary to make his assertions convincing. No matter; the authorities in Lisbon were persuaded by the logic of his arguments and in

July, 1757, they ordered the Black Robes expelled from the Amazon backlands.[111]

There remained to be determined the fate of the Jesuits' ranches on the island of Marajó and on the adjacent mainland. In June, 1757, the Captain-General reported on a proposal by the Crown made a year previous that the religious orders be divested of their surplus properties while being permitted to retain some of their fazendas for their sustenance with the stipulation that they agree to make prompt payment of the tithes on such properties. Consistent with the views he had expressed three years before, Mendonça Furtado strongly advised against adoption of the plan, among other reasons because he was convinced that the orders would soon seek to expand their holdings and would plead for new exemptions from the Crown's restrictions, so that "in a few years we would be faced again with the very malady that we wish to avoid," namely the dominance of the economy of the state by the religious. He argued again that it would be much better to take away all of the orders' properties, reduce the number of their priests in Maranhão, and pay them stipends out of the treasury. They would then cease to be public merchants and become spiritual leaders instead. As he had in 1754, Mendonça Furtado forecast that in the hands of seculars the confiscated properties would contribute significantly to an increase in the prosperity of the state and consequently in the revenues of the Crown.[112]

Before the Crown had time to consider these reflections, Dom Francisco turned his attention to the perennially vexing *dízimo* question. As early as 1751 he had pointed out that since the Carmelites had agreed to pay the donatary of the island of Marajó the *redízima* (i.e., a feudal fee amounting to 1 per cent of the tithe due on a particular piece of land), they could not logically dodge payment of the *dízimos*. He observed that three of the orders, the Mercedarians, Jesuits, and Carmelites, possessed large herds of livestock on the island and that if they were required to pay the tithe on such animals, the revenues would be substantial.[113] In 1756, while Mendonça Furtado was still in the Amazon, the Crown instructed his interim replacement, Bishop Bulhões, to investigate large-scale thefts of wild cattle (*gado do vento*) on the island, reminding him that according to a royal edict of 1728 all such cattle belonged to the Crown. Accordingly, the Bishop issued a *bando* to that effect and appointed a receiver (*rendeyro do vento*) to round up such cattle. That move particularly affected the religious orders, the principal ranchers on the island, and in 1757 all save the Jesuits offered a counter-proposal. Admitting that the *gado do vento* belonged to the king, they asked to be allowed to continue to exploit them, promising in return to pay an extraordinary dízimo amounting to 14 percent plus a third of the hides of wild bulls they slaughtered. At first the Jesuits refused to be associated with this proposal, but eventually the fathers yielded and in October of that year, Mendonça Furtado reported with obvious satisfaction the signing of the agreement.[114]

In August of the following year the colonial secretary approved this agreement. But at the same time he directed that the "covetous" Jesuits be required to submit proofs showing not only their ownership of the ranches they occupied on Marajó but also royal licenses which exempted them from the ancient ordinances forbidding the Church to own landed property. Should they be unable to produce such licenses, said the secretary, their properties should be seized.[115] Acting on this directive, the Captain-General established a special board, consisting of himself, his successor, the bishop, and three magistrates, and demanded that the Jesuits produce documents confirming that they held their ranches legitimately and with royal consent. When the board examined the materials the Black Robes presented, it failed to find the required exemptions and in February, 1759, the ranches were confiscated along with more than 130,000 head of livestock.[116]

Two weeks later, on March 3, Francisco Xavier de Mendonça Furtado turned over to a successor the responsibilities of his office and prepared to sail home, where he would be rewarded for his service in Brazil by being appointed colonial secretary, a post he held until his death in 1769. Whether during his final days in Pará Dom Francisco reviewed his record of achievement over the previous seven and a half eventful years is not known; if so, he must have derived satisfaction from such musings. Whatever other accomplishments may have impressed him, he certainly realized that he had played a major role in convincing the highest royal authorities, particularly his brother, soon to be the Conde de Oeiras, that the Jesuits had outlived their usefulness to the Crown and had become a serious threat to it. It was largely on the basis of his prejudicial reports that the Crown removed the long-time protective mantle of the missionaries from the Amazonian Indians and exposed them to unrestricted exploitation by their secular rivals, despite a law which on paper set the Indians at liberty. Mendonça Furtado had succeeded where the tireless Paulo da Silva Nunes had failed: he had convinced the Crown that the commercial activities of the Jesuits seriously jeopardized the possibilities of the economic development of northern

Brazil and deprived the king of vast revenues. And it was in response to his lengthy but persuasive critiques of the economic role of the Jesuits that the Crown invoked long dormant laws to justify the seizure of Jesuit properties in the Amazon and also in other parts of Brazil in the years immediately preceding the expulsion of the Society.[117] But although Mendonça Furtado had the satisfaction of seeing the Jesuits driven from their missions and ranches and individually expelled from Maranhão, he was not present in the colony when the final royal order arrived banishing the Black Robes from the Portuguese Empire, though he must have anticipated it. It was signed exactly six months after he surrendered his post.

The *carta régia* of September 3, 1759, which definitively exiled the Jesuits from all Portuguese dominions, marked the climax of steadily deteriorating relations between the Society of Jesus and the Crown of Portugal, or rather its prime mover, Sebastião José de Carvalho e Melo, during the 1750's and particularly after 1755.[118] Whether or not Jesuit historians and others who share their view are correct in their assertion that Carvalho owed his appointment to the cabinet to Jesuit influence,[119] there can be no doubt that that strong-willed, hard-working, perennially suspicious, intolerant Portuguese minister became determined to root out all vestiges of Jesuit influence in Portuguese lands. In the course of what clearly became a deliberate campaign against the Black Robes, if, indeed, it did not begin as such, Carvalho made extensive use of the "evidence" he received from his brother, Mendonça Furtado, from Gomes Freire de Andrada, captain-general of Rio de Janeiro and chief Portuguese boundary commissioner in the South, and from other colonial officers to prove the existence of a Jesuit conspiracy against the Crown and the necessity of bringing about a radical reform of the Society or its extirpation.

As João Lúcio de Azevedo has written, the long-simmering feud between the Jesuits and Carvalho first came into the open with the sermon of Padre Manoel Ballester who, scarcely a month after the establishment of the Maranhão trading company (1755), warned that those who invested in the company "would not be a member of the Company of Christ." Although the *padre* subsequently tried to explain away the meaning of his warning, it was not lost upon Carvalho, who ordered his exile from Court and soon after had the procurator-general of the Vice Province of Maranhão, Padre Bento da Fonsêca, imprisoned.[120] The following year Carvalho, by then in possession of a large file of dispatches from his brother full of adverse testimony against the Jesuits in Maranhão, informed the papal *nuncio* that something would have to be done about the behavior of the Black Robes in the Amazon who were utilizing their power to abuse the Indians and to defy the officers of the king.[121]

Further warnings came in 1757, following the Pôrto wine producers' rebellion, an uprising which the government accused the Jesuits of fomenting. In consequence, the Black Robes were banned from appearing at Court or from preaching in the cathedral. Carvalho explained to the nuncio that such measures were necessary because of the Jesuits' rebellion in the State of Maranhão and renewed his contention that the fathers were defying the laws of the realm and the edicts of the popes by denying the Indians their freedom, appropriating their property, and engaging in forbidden commercial activities. He assured the nuncio that he had proof of such crimes and warned that if the Jesuits were not immediately disciplined, within a decade they would become so powerful that all the armies of Europe would be unable to oust them from the vast territory they held in the heartland of South America, where they kept hundreds of thousands of slaves in fortified locations prepared by European engineers disguised as Jesuits. The same charges were repeated by the Portuguese envoy in Rome, who urged the Pope to take effective remedies to reform the morally corrupt Society.[122]

That demand was renewed the following year, when the envoy submitted as part of his government's evidence the famous "Brief Account of the Republic founded by the Jesuits in the Overseas Dominions of Spain and Portugal," a manifesto originally printed in the form of a pamphlet and either written by or under the supervision of Carvalho. In it the government reviewed the efforts of its agents to take possession of the missions' lands, described what it called the Jesuit-directed Guaraní uprising and the Black Robes' rebellion against its high commissioner in the Amazon, and asserted that the fathers were continuing to ignore its laws and those of the Church by keeping the Indians in slavery, dominating their agriculture and trade, and were indulging in "seditious machinations" against the Crown.[123] The envoy informed Benedict XIV that his government would insist upon either a severe reform of the Society or its abolition.[124] Reluctantly, on April 1, 1758, the Pope designated Cardinal Francisco Saldanha, a kinsman of Carvalho and very much beholden to him for past favors for himself and for members of his family,[125] as reformer and visitor of the Jesuits in Portugal and instructed him to investigate the government's charges of the Society's wrongdoing, particularly its commercial ventures which were said to be contrary to Church policy and responsible for the loss of vast royal revenue.[126]

The Jesuits were convicted before they had been tried. Although the Cardinal did not begin his inquiry until May 31, he issued an edict a week later asserting that he had definite information that banking and commercial operations were being carried on in every Jesuit college, residence, novitiate, and other facility, contrary to the canons and papal bulls. Threatening them with excommunication, the Cardinal ordered the Black Robes to cease such activities immediately and to turn over to him all of their bookkeeping records. It is interesting to note that although this edict was not published until June 7, it was actually dated May 15.[127] Two days after its publication the Patriarch of Lisbon announced that he was suspending all Jesuits within his jurisdiction from preaching or hearing confessions "from just causes, for the honor of God, and for the benefit of Christian people." [128] Further trials were in the offing.

On September 3, 1758, José I, King of Portugal, was mysteriously but unsuccessfully assaulted while en route to his palace after a nocturnal tryst with his paramour. Curiously, not until December 13 were the first suspects arrested, all of them members of the high nobility and persons who were on intimate terms with the Jesuits. The same night all Jesuits living in the capital were confined under what amounted to house arrest, a measure necessary, said Carvalho, to protect them from the mob which was convinced that they were involved in the abortive regicide plot. A month later ten prominent Black Robes, including the Provincial of Portugal and the saintly ascetic missionary and preacher Gabriel Malagrida, were accused of being the instigators of the plot. On January 19, 1759, the King signed an order confiscating all Jesuit properties in the kingdom on the pretext that the fathers had been behind the Guaraní War and the attack against his life.[129] Soldiers then entered Jesuit residences throughout the kingdom and conducted a frantic but fruitless search for the hoards of treasure which the fathers had long been rumored to possess. No such bonanzas were found, but the search was destined to be repeated in many parts of the Iberian world in ensuing months and years. The final expulsion decree, which called for the confiscation of the Jesuits' remaining possessions throughout the empire, was signed by the King on the first anniversary of his fortuitous escape from his alleged assassins.[130] Although that decree was in a sense anti-climatic, in view of the Crown's previous measures against the Black Robes, it was nevertheless an essential step from the point of view of

the Jesuits' adversaries, for it marked the final success of their long, unrelenting campaign against the Society of Jesus.

V. CONCLUSION

It would be a mistake to ascribe the expulsion of the Jesuits from
Portugal and her empire to any single factor. Obviously, the Crown's
decision was the product of many influences. As was the case with the
subsequent expulsions of the Society of Jesus from French and Spanish
lands (respectively in 1764 and 1767), regalism played a very important
role.[131] The government of the future Marquis of Pombal, whether or
not responding to Jansenist or heretical British influences, as some writers have contended, simply would not tolerate the existence of any element in society that was critical of its policies and not fully subservient
to the will of the king, as interpreted by his ministers. Although the
Jesuits were the prime target of that government's anticlericalism, it
should not be forgotten that it was also hostile to other missionary
orders in Brazil and that several of them were expelled from the colony
in later years.[132] The Portuguese government's conviction that there
existed a Jesuit "conspiracy" against the Crowns of Portugal and Spain
was also a manifestation of its regalist orientation, for, as Magnus
Mörner has recently written, "From the point of view of regalism, the
worst sin of all was any sign of well organized and coordinated ecclesiastical action in opposition to the policy of the Crown." [133] The consistent and persistent refusal of Black Robes in both empires to pay the
tithes, their unwillingness to submit to episcopal discipline, their opposition to the Treaty of Madrid, and the resistence of Jesuit-influenced
Indians to the terms of that agreement, all appeared from a regalist
perspective to be evidence of such a conspiracy.

It may be, too, that the Portuguese government, which was sufficiently
sensitive about what passed at this time for "public opinion" to attempt
to mold the attitudes of other European governments toward the Jesuits
by publishing a series of white papers against the Black Robes, sensed
that the 1750's was a propitious time to oust the Jesuits from its dominions because of their waning popularity. Despite their many admirable
qualities, the fathers had a remarkable capacity for making bitter enemies, both outside and inside the Church, among other reasons, because
they were extremely jealous of their prerogatives, legalistic to the point
of pettifoggery, self-righteous, contemptuous of their opponents, and as

uncompromising as their rivals. Such rivals included not only colonists and royal officials but also members of other missionary orders and the episcopacy. It is evident that there were some within both groups of Churchmen who cooperated closely with the Crown in bringing about an end to the Jesuits' stay in Brazil, and that the episcopacy and other orders were among the beneficiaries of the Black Robes' expulsion. It is difficult to determine what "public opinion" concerning the Jesuits really was in eighteenth-century Brazil, partly because of the absence of suitable media of expression and also because what we know of the views of the colonists comes to us largely from the quills of far from unbiased royal officials. Nevertheless, it seems significant that when news of the Black Robes' banishment spread throughout the colony, there was not a single tumult in protest against the Crown's action, such as there was in New Spain.

Churchmen were not, of course, the only or even the chief beneficiaries of the misfortunes which befell the Jesuits, for both the Crown and private interests, including planters, ranchers, renters, and merchants, were substantial gainers. This brings me to the main thesis of this paper: my conviction that the expulsion of the Jesuits from Brazil was dictated largely by economic considerations. Those considerations included optimistic predictions by critics of the Jesuits that the Crown would secure vast wealth through the confiscation of the Black Robes' properties. But I suspect that what impressed such critics even more was their conviction that it was essential to eliminate the economic role of a dominant, tax-exempt or at least nontaxpaying institution, whose activities, they were persuaded, inhibited the economic development of Brazil and deprived the Crown of enormous revenues. These were the points that Mendonça Furtado stressed repeatedly in his lengthy dispatches, though in truth virtually every argument that he advanced against the Jesuits can be found in the writings of Paulo da Silva Nunes, that still shadowy figure about whom we need to know a great deal more. But unlike the ministers of João V, those of José I were acutely aware of the Crown's urgent need for additional income and they were therefore especially receptive to the charges that Mendonça Furtado reiterated, even though they were put forth in the absence of what we would consider the elementary evidence necessary to sustain them.

But it is not sufficient to identify and weigh the many factors which brought to a climax the long struggle between the Jesuits and their adversaries. It is the historian's task to make judgments, something too few of us are wont to do, as to the validity of the charges and counter-assertions made by critics of the Jesuits and by the Black Robes them-selves. We are not yet in a position to make such an assessment. For example, until we have analyzed records showing how the Black Robes actually managed their manifold economic enterprises and have ac-counted for their income and traced their expenditures, we cannot speak with any authority concerning the profitability of their numerous under-takings, much less calculate whether such activities were unduely bur-densome for the colonial economy or the king to sustain. And until we have an opportunity to examine the reports that the fathers regularly made to their superiors concerning their stewardship of the Society's properties, we can not determine whether the inventories that royal agents made of such properties after their seizure were accurate, in-flated, or undervalued appraisals of their value. And until we have available more of the Jesuits' own writings during the 1750's, we can not decide upon the real merits of the accusations their enemies leveled against them during those critical years.

The expulsion of the Jesuits from Brazil solved one set of troublesome problems, but it raised still others—among them, whether the Crown ought to manage the sequestered properties itself or dispose of them to private individuals. The arguments advanced pro and con and the solu-tion eventually adopted is an interesting and complex story, but one that will have to be reserved for another occasion.

NOTES

1 Serafim Leite, *Artes e ofícios dos Jesuítas no Brasil (1549–1760)* (Rio de Janeiro, 1953) ; John Bury, "Jesuit Architecture in Brazil," *The Month, n.s.* IV (1950) , 385–408; Lúcio Costa, "A arquitetura dos Jesuitas no Brasil," *Revista do Serviço do Patrimônio Histórico e Artístico Nacional* (Rio de Janeiro) , V (1941) , 1–100; Alfred Métraux, "The Contribution of the Jesuits to the Exploration and Anthropology of South America," *Mid-America,* XXVI (July, 1944) , 183–92; E. Bradford Burns, "Introduction to the Brazilian Jesuit Letters," *ibid.,* XLIV (July, 1962) , 172–86; and Manoel Xavier de Vasconcelos Pedrosa, "O exercício da medicina nos séculos xvi–xvii e a primeira metade do século xviii no Brasil colonial," IV Congresso de História Nacional, *Anais* (Rio de Janeiro) , VIII (1951) , 268–74.
2 10 vols.; Rio de Janeiro-Lisbon, 1938–1950; hereinafter cited as *HCJB.*
3 See *ibid.,* IV, 209, n.2, and I, 75.
4 For a bibliography of Father Leite's writings, see Miquel Batllori, comp., *Biblio-grafia de Serafim Leite, S.J.* (Rome, 1962) .
5 Roberto C. Simonsen, *História econômica do Brasil (1500–1820)* (3rd ed.; São Paulo, 1957) ; Caio Prado Júnior, *História econômica do Brasil* (8th ed.; [São

Paulo], 1963) ; and Celso Furtado, *The Economic Growth of Brazil: A Survey from Colonial to Modern Times,* trans. Ricardo W. de Aguiar and Eric C. Drysdale (Berkeley, 1963) .

6   The only work in English concerning the Jesuits' expulsion from the Portuguese empire is Alfred Weld, S.J., *The Suppression of the Society of Jesus in the Portuguese Dominions* (London, 1877) , a study based upon inadequate sources and one that is factually inaccurate. It is at once a bristling condemnation of the Marquis of Pombal for his responsibility for the suppression and a militant defense of the innocence of the Society and its members. Nowhere does the author discuss the economic foundations of the order in Brazil, and he completely ignores economic aspects of its expulsion. I have used a copy in the library of Alma College, Alma, Cal.

7   *HCJB,* VII, 240. Throughout this paper I have used "Maranhão" to signify the *Estado do Maranhão,* rather than merely the captaincy-general of that name.

8   Serafim Leite, *Suma histórica da companhia de Jesús no Brasil . . . 1549–1760* (Lisbon, 1965) , Appendix IV.

9   D. Alden, "The Early History of Bahia, 1501–1553" (unpublished Master's thesis, University of California, Berkeley, 1952) , p. 197, and contemporary sources cited there.

10 For the *sesmaria* of "Água dos meninos" granted by Tomé de Sousa to Manoel da Nóbrega on Oct. 21, 1550, see Serafim Leite, ed., *Monumenta brasiliae,* I *(1538-1553)* (Rome, 1956) , 194–96.

11 Serafim Leite, "Terras que deu Estácio de Sá ao colégio do Rio de Janeiro. A famosa sesmaria dos Jesuítas. Documento inédito quinhentista," *Brotéria,* XX (1935) , 90–108; reprinted in *Monumenta brasiliae,* IV (1960) , 219–39. I have not seen the text of the original grant to the college at Recife.

12 Leite, *Suma histórica,* p. 177.

13 See "Livro grosso do Maranhão," *Anais da Biblioteca Nacional do Rio de Janeiro* (hereinafter cited as *ABNRJ*) , LXVI (1948) , 56–57, 77–78, and 91–92.

14 I emphasize *direct* assistance because the Crown also provided the society with other types of economic aid, such as exempting its goods from assessments of customs duties and, in the Amazon, the assignment of groups of Indians to work on the order's properties. In addition, the fathers claimed that they were entitled to what amounted to another form of subsidy from the Crown, namely exemption from payment of the tithes on their properties. *Q.v.* discussion below.

15 "Relação dos bens sequestrados aos regulares proscriptas, e expulsos da companhia . . . de Jesvs onerados com encargos pios, com declaraçaó dos nomes dos instituidores, dos titulos por que disposeraó das obras pias, que ordenaraó, dos bens e rendas, que para este effeito deixeraó, e do que estes annualmente produzem em rendimentos certos, e incertos, . . ." Bahia, Oct. 1, 1761, Arquivo Histórico Ultramarino, Lisbon (hereinafter cited AHU) , Documentos da Bahia, No. 5586; "Relações dos bens apprehendidos e confiscados aos Jesuitas da capitania de S. Paulo . . ." (1761) , Arquivo do Estado de São Paulo; *Publicação official de documentos interessantes para a história e costumes de São Paulo* (hereinafter cited as *DI*) , XLIV, 337–78.

16 "Testamento de Domingos Afonso Certão, descobridor do Piauhy," Bahia, May 12, 1711, *Revista do Instituto Histórico e Geográfico Brasileiro* (hereinafter cited as *RIHGB*) , XX (1857) , 140–50.

17 For one very suspicious instance which, however, concerns a bequest made in Angola rather than Brazil, see carta régia of Feb. 15, 1625, in Antônio Brásio, ed., *Monumenta missionaria africana,* 1st ser., *África ocidental (1611–1621),* VII (Lisbon, 1955) , 394–95. I am indebted to Professor Engel Sluiter, University of California, Berkeley, for this reference.

18   E.g., Biblioteca Nacional, Rio de Janeiro, *Documentos históricos,* LXII (1943),
     140ff.; LXII (1944), *passim;* and LXIV (1944), 3–112. I have not included in
     this section properties which the Jesuits may have acquired as a result of mort-
     gage of foreclosures, since I have no information that would indicate how im-
     portant a source of acquisition that practice may have been.

19   "Treslado do autto de inventário da real fazenda de Santa Crus e bens que nella
     se acharam. . . ," May 6, 1768, A. J. Melo Morais Filho, ed., *Archivo do Districto
     Federal: revista de documentos para a história da cidade do Rio de Janeiro*
     (hereinafter cited as *RADF*), I (1894), 73–77, 124, 182–92, 217, 333–39, 418–25.

20   A few such examples are given at the end of the Bahian report of 1761 cited in
     n. 15 above.

21   For one example of a sale of land by the Jesuits to the Carmelites for cash, see
     "Regizto de hum documento de venda que fizeráo oz padrez da companhia, ao
     convento do Carmo dezta cidade . . . anno de 1595," *RADF,* III (1896), 251.

22   This count is based upon a variety of contemporary and later sources, the latter
     including *HCJB, passim.* The number of Jesuit plantations devoted mainly to
     sugar growing varied from time to time as new fazendas were acquired and as
     some of the older ones showed signs of diminishing fertility and were converted
     to other uses. Thus, the fazenda of Muribeca (Espírito Santo) became a cattle
     ranch and most of the Engenho Velho plantation (Rio de Janeiro) was parceled
     out into rental plots.

23   Leite, *Suma histórica,* Chap. XI. See also n. 115 below.

24   The incomplete Santa Cruz inventory (see n. 19) suggests that the total number
     of slaves on that plantation in 1759 may have reached 1,600 or 1,700. According
     to Alberto Lamego, there were 1,435 slaves on the "fazenda do colégio" in
     northern Rio de Janeiro at the time of its seizure; *A terra Goytacá á luz de
     documentos inéditos,* III (Brussels-Paris, 1925), 163. By contrast, the largest
     number of slaves reportedly owned by a single slaveholder in the English main-
     land colonies at the time of the Revolution was 490. Louis Morton, *Robert
     Carter of Nomini Hall . . .* (Williamsburg, 1945), p. 101, n.43. The information
     that I have been able to gather about slaveholding in eighteenth-century Spanish
     America indicates that slave concentrations on single plantations were not nearly
     as large as they were on these two Jesuit fazendas. When the full inventories of
     the Society's properties in Bahia become available, it is likely that they will
     reveal slave populations at least as large as those on Santa Cruz.

25   In the 1750's the Jesuits had 273 renters on portions of their Engenho Velho
     fazenda in Rio de Janeiro. *RADF,* I (1894), 73n. For an example of the terms of
     grazing privileges they licensed on the same fazenda, see *ibid.,* 427. Examples of
     their rental agreements are given *ibid.,* 426–27, 455–60, 550–62, and II (1895),
     9–17, 62. In Bahia at the time of the expulsion, 58 small plots which the fathers
     rented yielded an estimated annual income of 300,000 réis. See n. 26.

26   Calculated on the basis of an inventory entitled "Termo das declaraçoens e
     valiaçoens que fizerao os avaliadores do conselho e mestres das obras da cidade
     [do Salvador]," March 26, 1760, AHU, Docs. da Bahia, No. 4952. The inventory
     includes not only urban properties with dwellings attached to them, but also a
     wharf belonging to the order (worth an estimated 3,600,000 réis), "Çitioz que
     occupaváo os Padres" which could be rented, others which had been rented in
     the past, and miscellaneous property. The total appraised value for all of these
     properties was put at 190,886,000 réis, their annual rental at 11,415,200 réis.
     These estimates may have been inflated, for Father Leite cites a contemporary
     source which indicates that the college of Salvador received 8,880,000 réis from
     its urban properties in 1757. *HCJB,* V, 579, n.1.

27   "Relaçao de todas as casas, foros e chãos que ha nesta cidade pertencentes aos

padres da companhia nas ruas que abaixo se declara," July 8, 1740, *RADF*, II (1895) , 366–71.

28 "Relação de todos os conventos e hospícios que há dentro do destricto d'este governo de Pernambuco com o numero de religiozos e rendas, que tem cada um," n.d., *ca.* 1740's, *ABNRJ*, XXVII (1906) , 416.

29 *HCJB*, V, 479, 579 n.l.

30 Cf. the reports of the heads of the Benedictine, Carmelite, and Franciscan orders to the Crown concerning their holdings and income in Brazil in 1764–1765, and, for the captaincy of Rio de Janeiro, the value of the possessions of the same orders as reported by the Conde de Rezende (Viceroy of Brazil) in 1797, *RIHGB*, LXV:1 (1902) , 118–65; *ibid.,* XLVI:1 (1883) , 187–88.

31 The provincial of the Benedictines reported to the Crown, for example, that the monastery of São Paulo had on loan 3,468,865 réis, but that 1,160,000 réis was considered uncollectable because of bankrupcies and the deaths of creditors who left no recoverable estates. Frei Francisco de São José to Francisco Xavier de Mendonça Furtado, May 12, 1765, *RIHGB*, LXVI:1 (1904–1905) , 137–65, Appendix G.

32 A rough estimate that I hope to refine as I have the opportunity to analyze more of the property inventories that I have collected.

33 On the beginnings of the conflict between the Jesuits and the colonists over the treatment of the Indians, the standard works remain Alexander Marchant, *From Barter to Slavery: The Economic Relations of Portuguese and Indians in the Settlement of Brazil, 1500–1580* (reprint; Gloucester, Mass., 1966) , and Mathias C. Kiemen, *The Indian Policy of Portugal in the Amazon Region, 1614–1693* (Washington, D. C., 1954) ; see also, Charles R. Boxer, *Salvador de Sá and the Struggle for Brazil and Angola 1602–1686* (London, 1952) , pp. 124–25.

34 For an introduction to the literature concerning the bandeirantes, see Richard M. Morse, comp., *The Bandeirantes: The Historical Role of the Brazilian Pathfinders* (New York, 1965) .

35 For details, see Boxer, *Salvador de Sá*, pp. 129–37, and *HCJB*, VI, 252–65, 416–21.

36 Kieman, *Indian Policy of Portugal*, pp. 115–16, 146ff. For the royal pardon of 1663, see provisão of Sept. 12, 1663, "Livro grosso do Maranhão," I, 31–32.

37 Kiemen, *Indian Policy of Portugal*, pp. 158–62; *HCJB*, IV, 369–74.

38 Carta régia of Nov. 4, 1684 (renewing *alvará* misdated May 4, 1543 [*sic* for 1573]), José Justino de Andrade e Silva, comp., *Collecção chronológica da legislação portuguêsa . . .*, X (Lisbon, 1859) , 22–23.

39 Cartas régias, Jan. 4, 1687, and March 23, 1688 (two dispatches) , *Anais da Biblioteca e Arquivo Público do Pará* (hereinafter cited as *AAP*) , I (Belém, 1902) , 90–93, 95–96.

40 Quoted in Charles R. Boxer, *Portuguese Society in the Tropics: The Municipal Councils of Góa, Macao, Bahia, and Luanda, 1510–1800* (Madison, Wis., 1965) , p. 17.

41 Reply of the câmara to a petition by Sá, Nov. 16, 1641, Eduardo de Castro e Almeida, comp., *Inventário dos documentos relativos ao Brasil existentes no Arquivo da Marinha e Ultramar de Lisbóa*, VII (Rio de Janeiro, 1934) , 16–17.

42 Boxer, *Municipal Councils*, p. 89, from which the quotation is also taken. I do not know the extent of Jesuit fiscal contributions to the seventeenth-century wars of Portugal, but it may be noted that the Society was the fourth-largest contributor to the ransom fund exacted from the city of Rio de Janeiro by the French privateer Duguay-Trouin in 1711. "Relação das pessoas, e das quantias com que contribuirão para o resgate desta cidade, rendida pelos francezes em 11 de Setembro de 1711," in Antonio Duarte Nunes, "Almanac histórico da cidade de S. Sebastião do Rio de Janeiro" (1799) , *RIHGB*, XXI (1858) , 31.

43   For the conflict over the orders' refusal to pay tithes in the Spanish colonies, see
     Lillian Estelle Fisher, *Viceregal Administration in the Spanish American Colonies*
     (Berkeley, 1926), pp. 199–200; Guadalupe Navarro, *Los diezmos en Mexico
     durante el tiempo de la colonia* (Rome, 1936), Chap. V; and Woodrow Borah,
     "Tithe Collection in the Bishopric of Oaxaca, 1601–1867," *Hispanic American
     Historical Review*, XXI (1941), 386ff.
44   The basic study remains Oscar de Oliveira, *Os dízimos eclesiásticos do Brasil
     nos períodos da colónia e do império* (Juiz de Fóra, 1940).
45   Nóbrega to Simão Rodrigues, Aug. [?], 1552, Afranio Peixoto, ed., *Cartas do
     Brasil 1549–1560* (Rio de Janeiro, 1931), p. 139.
46   See Oliveira, *Dízimos eclesiásticos*, p. 70.
47   *Ibid.*, p. 90.
48   Provisão of Nov. 2, 1692 (referring to an earlier provisão of Jan. 17, 1685, which
     I have not seen), "Livro grosso do Maranhão," I, 130–31; king to *provedor da
     fazenda* (Pará), Jan. 11, 1701, *ibid.*, 203–204; *idem* to Christovão da Costa Freire
     (captain-general of Maranhão), April 4, 1709, and *idem* to *idem*, June 27, 1711,
     ibid., II, 37–38, and 88. As evidence of the Society's concern over the Crown's
     efforts to force it to pay the tithe, see the instruction of Michael Angelus Tam-
     burinus (general) to Padre Ignacio Ferreira (superior of the Vice Province of
     Maranhão), Oct. 22, 1712, in João Lúcio de Azevedo, *Os Jesuítas no Grão Pará:
     Suas missões e a colonização . . .* (1st ed.; Lisbon, 1901), pp. 332–33.
49   Kiemen, *Indian Policy of Portugal*, p. 52.
50   *Ordenações do Senhor Rey d. Affonso V* (Coimbra, 1792), Liv. II, tits. XIII and
     XIV.
51   *Código philippino ou ordenações e leis do reino de Portugal recompiladas por
     mandado d'el–rey d. Philippe I*, ed. Cândido Mendes de Almeida (14th ed.; Rio
     de Janeiro, 1870), Liv. II, tit. XVIII, which includes references to appropriate
     sections of the Manuelinas.
52   Quoted in an undated petition (*ca.* 1740) of Manuel Ferreira Feital and Antônio
     de Alvarenga, Castro e Almeida, *Inventário*, VII, 384–85.
53   Overseas Council to Antônio Brito de Menezes (governor of Rio de Janeiro),
     Sept. 22, 1718, *RADF*, III (1896), 186–88; "Lista das propriedades que possuem
     os padres da companhia do Rio de Janeiro e parte dos da comarca thè o anno
     de mil e sette centos e dezoito," *ibid.*, II (1895), 370–72; "Registo das listas das
     terras dos padres da companhia, de S. Bento e do Carmo, sitas no districto de
     Cabo Frio, que remetterão os officiaes da câmara ao corregedor (i.e., ouvidor) da
     comarca," Dec. 26, 1719, *ABNRJ*, LXXI (1951), 44–46.
54   Kiemen, *Indian Policy of Portugal*, pp. 176–78.
55   *Ibid.*, pp. 164–66.
56   Azevedo, *Os Jesuítas*, pp. 160–63.
57   Captain-general of Maranhão 1718–1722, author of the tedious but important
     Anais históricos do Maranhão (Lisbon, 1749), and in later years a distinguished
     soldier in North Africa.
58   Traditionally Silva Nunes's hostility is said to date from 1722, when he was first
     imprisoned for his censorious remarks against the Jesuits, but João da Maia da
     Gama, successor of Berredo and a noted Jesuitophile, contended that his hostility
     was in evidence before that date. See n. 72 below.
59   Azevedo, *Os Jesuítas*, pp. 167–68.
60   Similar broadsides were circulated in Belém in 1688. Kiemen, *Indian Policy of
     Portugal*, p. 169.
61   João da Maia da Gama to the Crown, Aug. 28, 1722 (two dispatches), in Alexan-
     dre João Melo Moraes, *Corographia . . . do império do Brasil*, IV (Rio de Janeiro,
     1860), 291n.–294n.

62 The *língua geral* was something of a common dialect by which the Jesuits (and others familiar with it) could communicate with Indians of various tongues. In 1689 the câmara of Belém complained to the King that the fathers were ignoring an order to teach the língua geral to Portuguese youth, something essential as they succeeded their fathers as supervisors of Indian plantation labor. Kiemen, *Indian Policy of Portugal,* p. 170. By the time of Silva Nunes, however, the Jesuits were being criticized for the opposite reason. A carta régia of Sept. 12, 1727, did, in fact, instruct the Jesuits to see that their wards were better instructed in Portuguese. *AAP,* II, 190–91. But for some of the practical problems involved, see Maia's defense of the Jesuits (cited n. 72).

63 Azevedo, *Os Jesuítas,* pp. 168, 178.

64 Berredo to câmara of Belém, April 6, 1726, Melo Moraes, *Corographia,* IV, 291n.

65 In 1726, for example, Silva Nunes reported that he had already had two promising private conferences with an unnamed secretary of state. Silva Nunes to câmara of São Luis do Maranhão, March 31, 1726, *ibid.,* 288.

66 Azevedo, *Os Jesuítas,* pp. 170, 176.

67 "Representação dos senhores de engenho e lavradores de canna de Marepicû, freguezia de N. S.ª da Conceição e districto do Rio de Janeiro, contra as usurpações de terrenos que lhes tinham feito os padres da Companhia de Jesus e os religiosos de N. S.ª do Carmo" (1730), Castro e Almeida, *Inventário,* VII, 62; câmara of Rio de Janeiro to the king, Aug. 12, 1731, *RADF,* II (1895), 281–84 (complaining about the illicit commerce of the Benedictines and their preference for Peninsular- rather than colonial-born recruits).

68 Azevedo, *Os Jesuítas,* p. 174. See cartas régias of July 28 and Aug. 1, 1729, and Jan. 11, 1731, *AAP,* IV (1905), 55, 57–58, and 66–67, referring to Sousa Freire's contention that the Jesuits were using mission Indians to plant tobacco and sugar and to work in their engenhos, contrary to his standing instructions.

69 Carta régia of April 13, 1728, "Livro grosso do Maranhão," II, 223–24; see Azevedo, *Os Jesuítas,* pp. 175–77 for an analysis and comparison of this law and that of 1718, which was more favorable to the colonists' interests.

70 Carta régia of Jan. 24, 1729, *DI,* XVIII (1896), 267–68; *HCJB,* IV, 202.

71 "Papel que o padre Jacinto de Carvalho . . . apresentou a el-rei para se juntar aos dous requerimentos do procurador das câmaras do Maranhão e Pará," Dec. 16, 1729, Melo Moraes, *Corographia,* IV, 305n.–330n. For a biographical sketch and an annotated listing of the procurator's writings, see *HCJB,* VIII, 149–53.

72 "Parecer de João da Maia da Gama . . . sôbre os requerimentos que a el-rei apresentou Paulo da Silva Nunes, contra os missionários," Feb. 22, 1730, Melo Moraes, *Corographia,* IV, 258n.–274n.

73 Alvará of April 13, 1734, *ibid.,* 253n.–254n.

74 "Informação e parecer do desembargador Francisco Duarte dos Santos . . . ," July 15, 1735, *ibid.,* 123n.–150n. (This is the second of two long documents which run at the bottom of these pages and is in smaller type than the first.)

75 Azevedo, *Os Jesuítas,* p. 183, where unfortunately no source is given. Presumably the treasury officers knew that the Crown had not paid living allowances (*côngruas*) to the Maranhão missionaries for many years (see the second Maia da Gama letter of Aug. 28, 1722 [cited n. 61], p. 293) and was in no condition to pay even larger sums.

76 Azevedo, *Os Jesuítas,* pp. 184–87.

77 Oliveira, *Os dízimos eclesiásticos no Brasil,* p. 73, citing an order of Feb. 21, 1739, from the general of the order to the vice provincial of Maranhão advising him that it was still hoped that the question could be resolved favorably to the Society but that if it could not, a new royal decree requiring the orders to pay

the *dízimos* would be obeyed by Jesuits pending further appeals. In the meantime, it was necessary to observe great prudence to avoid "males mais graves."

78 Cartas régias of July 9, 1740, and Jan. 21, 1743, Biblioteca Nacional, Rio de Janeiro, *Documentos históricos,* I (1928), 398–99, 440–41; see also, the Overseas Council's resolutions of May 31, 1740, and May 25, 1741, quoted at the beginning of the report cited in n. 27.

79 I have not seen this volume, but it is cited in Azevedo, *Os Jesuítas,* p. 187.

80 Charles R. Boxer, *The Golden Age of Brazil.* . . . (Berkeley, 1962), p. 289.

81 I have examined the Guaraní war in somewhat more detail in my *Royal Government in Colonial Brazil* (Berkeley, 1968), Chap. IV, sec. 2.

82 These impressions are based largely on my reading of the Captain-General's correspondence (see n. 87). For a summary of the views of contemporaries and later historians, see J[oão] Lúcio de Azevedo, *Estudos de história paraense* (Pará, 1893), pp. 13–17.

83 This is the view of Azevedo *(ibid.,* pp. 20–26, and *Os Jesuítas,* p. 238) and of those who follow him, e.g., Marcus Cheke, *Dictator of Portugal: A Life of the Marquis of Pombal 1699–1782* (London, 1938), p. 56; cf. *HCJB,* VII, 338–39.

84 I.e., Dom Frei Miguel de Bulhõese Sousa, a Benedictine who proved to be no friend of the Black Robes.

85 The instructions, dated May 31, 1751, were first published by Azevedo, *Os Jesuítas,* pp. 348–56.

86 An intriguing and an important subject which, so far as I know, no author has successfully examined.

87 [Mendonça Furtado] to [Sebastião José de Carvalho e Melo], Nov. 21, 1751, *A Amazônia na era pombalina: Correspondência inédita do governador e capitão-general do estado do Grão Pará e Maranhão Francisco Xavier de Mendonça Furtado, 1751–1759,* ed. Marcos Carneiro de Mendonça (3 vols.; Instituto Histórico e Geográfico Brasileiro, Rio de Janeiro, n.d. *[ca.* 1964]), I, 63–78 (hereinafter cited as *C/FXMF).* The bulk of the documents included in this invaluable but perplexing collection consist of dispatches written by Mendonça Furtado to the Crown between 1751 and 1757 (despite the title); most of them are printed from registers in the British Museum but (again despite the title) some are from the well-known *AAP* series. The editor, whose notes are sometimes helpful but are not as numerous or enlightening as they should be, seems to feel that this correspondence explains why the Jesuits' final expulsion was fully warranted, but he fails to appreciate the fact that his collection lacks the other side of the story—the letters written by the Jesuits themselves. Furthermore, many of the dispatches published here are covering letters for important enclosures not found in the registers in Belém or in London. Users of this collection are warned that the *índice* of Vol. III does not list the last eighty-one pages of the volume, a group of miscellaneous documents.

88 Mendonça Furtado to Carvalho e Melo, Oct. 25, 1752, *C/FXMF,* I, 254; *idem* to Tomé Joaquim da Costa Corte Real, *ca.* May 23, 1757, *ibid.,* III, 955.

89 In his dispatch of Dec. 29, 1751, cited below, the Captain-General contended that ". . . êste Estado se fundou, floresceu e nêle se estabelceram infinitos engenhos e plantações, enquanto as Religiões não tiveram êste alto e absoluto poder" but failed to indicate precisely when that millenium existed.

90 Mendonça Furtado to Carvalho e Melo, Dec. 29, 1751, Jan. 2 and Oct. 25, 1752, and Jan. 26, 1754, *C/FXMF,* I, 143–48, 155–57, 252–55, and II, 465–70.

91 "Memória das fazendas que até agora tenho podido averiguar que têm os padres da companhia nesta capitania do Pará, e das notícias que até agora achei delas," Feb. 8, 1754, *ibid.,* II, 485–89.

92 Mendonça Furtado to Carvalho e Melo, Feb. 18, 1754, *ibid.,* 498–505.

93 In 1753 the Crown directed the heads of the Jesuit, Carmelite, Mercedarian, and Franciscan orders to furnish the Portuguese commissioner with whatever provisions and Indian workers he needed from their missions, promising adequate compensation for such services. General order of May 18, 1753, British Museum, Add Mss. 20987 (Bancroft Library Microfilm Collection, University of California, Berkeley) .

94 Mendonça Furtado to Carvalho e Melo, July 7 and 9, and Nov. 20, 1755, *C/FXMF*, II, 714–21, 738–39; III, 870–71; *idem* to Luis da Cunha [Manoel], Oct. 12, 1756, *ibid.*, III, 948; Diogo de Mendonça Corte Real (colonial secretary) to Mendonça Furtado, May 1, 1755, Jaime Cortesão, ed. and comp., *Alexandre de Gusmão e o Tratado de Madrid (1750)*, V (Rio de Janeiro, 1963) , 431 (expressing the hope that Mendonça Furtado would not encounter the great difficulties then besetting the southern boundary party because of the Jesuit-led Guaraní resistance) .

95 Mendonça Furtado to Carvalho e Melo, July 7, 1755, *C/FXMF*, II, 714.

96 This was the first Jesuit mission in the Amazon to be secularized. The ostensible reason for doing so was to establish a rest stop for travelers en route between the Amazon and Mato Grosso, but the real purpose was to erect a check point to stop the alleged flow of contraband from the gold-producing interior to the coast. Carvalho e Melo to Mendonça Furtado, March 14, 1755, *ibid.*, 661.

97 Matt 21: 12–13; Mark 11: 15–17; Luke 19: 45–46; or John 2: 14–16. The source (n. 98) does not make clear which passage the Captain-General had in mind.

98 Azevedo, *Estudos*, pp. 127–29.

99 Among the twenty-one were the *cronista* and the vice provincial of Maranhão and the rectors of the colleges in Maranhão and Pará. *HCJB*, VII, 352.

100 Mendonça Furtado to Carvalho e Melo, Oct. 14, 1756, *C/FXMF*, III, 992–93. For the inability of the Spanish commissioner to make contact with his Portuguese counterpart because of navigational problems and the alleged lack of cooperation of the Jesuits, see Demetrio Ramos Pérez, *El tratado de límites de 1750 y la expedicion de Iturriaga al Orinoco* (Madrid, 1946) , pp. 197ff. and 214ff.

101 Law of June 6, 1755, *Colecção dos breves pontificos e leys régias, que forão expedidos e publicadas desde o anno de 1741, sôbre a liberdade das pessoas, bens, e commércio dos Indios do Brasil; . . .* (Lisbon, 1760) , No. II. The text of the bull comprises No. I of this collection, one of a number of white papers which the Portuguese government circulated, some in translation, during the decade 1757–1767 to gain support for its campaign against the Jesuits.

102 Law of June 7, 1755, *ibid.*, No. III.

103 Carvalho e Melo to Mendonça Furtado, March 14, 1755, *C/FXMF*, II, 660.

104 Mendonça Furtado to Carvalho e Melo, Nov. 12, 1755, *ibid.*, 821.

105 [*Idem* to the Crown], April 8, 1757, *AAP*, IV (1905) , 182–84. The junta das missões of the State of Maranhão, one of several such boards which existed in various parts of the Portuguese empire, was established in 1680. Its members included the Captain-General, various other royal officials, the Bishop (at this time of Pará) , and the heads of the several missionary orders active in the region.

106 See Robert C. Padden, "The Ordenanza del Patronazgo, 1574: An Interpretative Essay," *The Americas*, XII (April, 1956) , 333–54.

107 [Mendonça Furtado to the Crown], April 8, 1757, cited n. 105; petition of Francisco de Toledo (vice provincial) , *ca.* Feb. 10, 1757, *AAP*, IV (1905) , 207–209.

108 Mendonça Furtado to Carvalho e Melo, April 25, 1757, *C/FXMF*, III, 1034–38.

109 *Idem* to *Idem*, May 2, 1757, *ibid.*, 1039–40; also published in *AAP*, IV (1905) , 209–12. This was actually the second round of the Captain-General's dispute with the Jesuits over ownership of the appurtenances of their former missions. The first began with a dispute over the alleged looting of the former aldeia of

Trocaño, the new community of Borba a Nôva. See *idem* to Padre Anselmo Eckart, Borba a Nôva, Dec. 31, 1755, *C/FXMF*, III, 890, and *idem* to Carvalho e Melo, Oct. 13, 1756, *ibid.*, 949–54. In the latter dispatch the Captain-General enclosed a signed statement by a Carmelite missionary admitting that all of the appurtenances of the missions were owned by the missions, rather than his order.

110 *Idem* to Tomé Joaquim da Costa Corte Real, *ca.* May 23, 1757, *ibid.*, 955–76. The paper, which in this edition is undated but bears the title "Papel . . . na qual se mostra que a negócio que os padres fazem nem é lícito, nem necessário, nem, em conseqüencia déle, há bens industriais, e que os que adqüirem nas aldeias são para o comum delas," was sent to Lisbon in two installments. See p. 970n. The second part of the memorial, which carries the date, author, and addressee given here, is also published in *AAP*, IV (1905) , 212–20.

111 Decree of July 10, 1757, cited without source by Ernesto Cruz, "Seqüestro dos bens dos regulares da companhia de Jesus no Pará, Maranhão e Piauí," Instituto Histórico e Geográfico Brasileiro, *Anais do Congresso Comemorativo do Bicentenário da Transferência da Sêde do Governo do Brasil (1963)*, III (Rio de Janeiro, 1967) , 14.

112 [Mendonça Furtado] to Carvalho e Melo, June 16, 1757, *C/FXMF*, III, 1098–1104.

113 *Idem* to Diogo de Mendonça Corte Real, Dec. 23, 1751, *ibid.*, I, 131–32.

114 *Idem* to Tomé Joaquim da Costa Corte Real, June 7, Oct. 8 and 18, 1757, *AAP*, V, 215–20, 298–301; VI (1907) , 44–46.

115 Tomé Joaquim da Costa Corte Real to Mendonça Furtado, Aug. 2, 1758, *C/FXMF*, III, 1187; also published in Ernesto Cruz, "O Pará dos séculos xvii e xviii," IV Congresso de História Nacional, *Anais*, III (Rio de Janeiro, 1950) , 26n., where the date is erroneously given as 1753.

116 Mendonça Furtado to T. J. da Costa Corte Real, Feb. 22, 1759, *AAP*, VIII (1913), 25–27. An inventory taken a few months later revealed that the Jesuits had possessed 134,465 cattle and *bestas* on four large and three smaller ranches on Marajó. [Manoel Bernardo de Melo de Castro] to *idem*, July 30, 1759, *ibid.*, 56–59; also published *ibid.*, II (1902) , 152–53, n. 2.

117 In the spring of 1758 the Crown dispatched a special board consisting of three magistrates from the prestigious Casa de Suplicação to Bahia with instructions to seize all Jesuit properties in that captaincy-general if the Black Robes proved unable to produce licenses authorizing them to possess such property. King to Manoel Estevão de Almeida de Vasconcelos Barberino, May 8, 1758, Castro e Almeida, *Inventário*, I, 332–33. Similar orders were sent to the captains-general of Rio de Janeiro and Pernambuco on July 21 and Aug. 23, 1759. Conde de Bobadela to desembargador Manoel da Fonsêca Brandão, Nov. 2, 1759, *RADF*, I, (1894) , 288–89; carta régia to Luíz Diogo Lôbo da Silva, Aug. 23, 1759, *Revista do Instituto Archeológico, Histórico, e Geográfico Pernambucono*, No. 43 (1893), 34–38. On another occasion I expect to analyze the activities of the Bahia board on the basis of extensive manuscript sources that I have collected.

118 The literature concerning the uneven struggle between the future Marquis of Pombal and the Jesuits is vast, and I have thus far examined only a small part of it. In preparing this section I have found particularly helpful João Lúcio de Azevedo, *O Marquês de Pombal e a sua época* (2nd ed.; Lisbon, 1922) , Chaps. 4–6; Ludwig, Freiherr von Pastor, *The History of the Popes from the Close of the Middle Ages,* trans. E. F. Peeler, XXXVI (St. Louis, Mo., 1950) , 8–23, 294–343; and Christoph Gottlieb von Murr, *História dos Jesuítas no ministério do marquêz de Pombal,* trans. and ed. J. B. Hafkemeyer, S.J., published as Vol. III of *Revista do Instituto Histórico e Geográfico do Rio Grande do Sul* (Pôrto Alegre, 1903) . Written by a German Protestant on the basis of materials made available to him by former Jesuits and originally published in Nuremburg in

two volumes in 1787–1788, this is the earliest scholarly account of the expulsion of the Jesuits from the Portuguese empire.

119 Cf. Weld, *The Suppression of the Society of Jesus*, pp. 8ff., and Lamego, *A terra Goytacá*, III, 84ff.

120 Azevedo, *Estudos*, pp. 62–63.

121 Pastor, *History of the Popes*, XXXVI, 10.

122 *Ibid.*, pp. 10–12, 16.

123 Originally published in 1757, the "Relação abreviada" was reissued several times in pamphlet form and was included among the "proofs" which accompanied the Portuguese government's major white paper against the Jesuits, the *Deducção chronológica*, published in three volumes in 1768. See *Provas da parte primeira da deducção chronológica e analytica, e petição de recurso do doutor Joseph de Seabra da Sylva*, I (Lisbon, 1768), 336–72.

124 Pastor, *History of the Popes*, XXXVI, 18.

125 *Ibid.*, 295.

126 *Ibid.*, 22–23.

127 *Mandamento* of Francisco Cardinal Saldanha, May 15, 1758, *Col. dos breves pontifícios*, No. 8; also published in Melo Moraes, *Corographia*, IV, 542–48.

128 As quoted in Pastor, *History of the Popes*, XXXVI, 296; see also his comment on p. 298 concerning the legality of the patriarch's action.

129 See Murr, *História dos Jesuítas*, Chap. XIII, for a unique discussion of the seizure and sale of Jesuit holdings in Portugal.

130 For the text, which repeats in substance and language the major accusations leveled against the Jesuits by the Portuguese government throughout the later 1750's, see Antônio Delgado da Silva, *Collecção da legislação portuguêsa de 1750 a [1820]*, I (Lisbon, 1830), 713–16.

131 For a recent restatement of the importance of regalism in the expulsion of the Society from Spanish dominions, see Magnus Mörner, "The Expulsion of the Jesuits from Spain and Spanish America in 1767 in Light of Eighteenth-Century Regalism," *The Americas*, XXIII (Oct., 1966), 156–64. Although Professor Mörner recognizes the importance of other factors in motivating the expulsion (p. 163), he ignores the role of economic influences.

132 Thus, in response to the recommendation of Mendonça Furtado, the Capuchos and the religious of Conceição da Beira e Minho were banished from Pará in 1758. Cruz, "O Pará dos séculos xvii e xviii," p. 32. In 1794 the Mercedarians were likewise removed from the Amazon and their properties seized. Domingos Antônio Raiol (Barão de Guajará), "Catechese de índios no Pará," *AAP*, II, 153–54.

133 "The Expulsion of the Jesuits," p. 158.

COMMENTARY

Fr. Mathias C. Kiemen, O.F.M.
Academy of American Franciscan History
Washington, D.C.

HISTORICAL problems that are highly polemic pose special difficulties for the conscientious historian. Professor Alden has plunged into one of the most controversial questions in the history of Brazil: the expulsion of the Jesuits. Not satisfied with that, he has taken precisely the most tender part of the question: the economic. Is it true that the fathers of the Society of Jesus were building an empire within an empire? Were they becoming so economically powerful that they posed a danger to the state? What was the extent of their riches? Were they as rich as some writers claim? Or were the claims exaggerated?

I think it is undeniably true that from 1700 to 1759 it is almost impossible to find in contemporary Portuguese sources a nonpolemic, coldly objective statement about Jesuit missions and property in Brazil. The question was extremely complex. There were so many factors to consider: *fazendas*, slaves, missions, canoes and their part in commerce, Indian rowers, Indian servants, Indian and Negro slaves, the amounts of *drogas* brought out from the interior, the sale of goods, food, and cattle at exorbitant prices to the colonists, the reason for such enormous herds of cattle and horses on the island of Marajó, the treatment of the Indians, the methods of *descimentos* and *resgates* and the Jesuits' part in them, the wealth of the Jesuit missions in the North and South of Brazil. Still other questions come to mind: the amount of the profits of the Jesuit fathers, the relations with other religious in the state, the rivalry in the Amazon region between the Jesuits and the Carmelites, and, to a lesser degree, with Franciscans, the monopolistic tendencies of the Society of Jesus in almost all their missionary endeavors.

Professor Alden has courageously attempted to answer some of these

66

complicated questions and has done so in a masterful way. It was difficult, however, for him to keep the treatment to purely economic reasons
for the expulsion. The questions mentioned in the above paragraph are
so closely intertwined with the purely economic one of the riches of the
Jesuits that the author finds himself being carried a little far afield occasionally. This is not surprising.

Having worked for over twenty years in this general field of history,
I cannot but admire the amount of material that Professor Alden has
gathered on this intriguing subject. But there is no danger he will exhaust the documentation. Serafim Leite, S. J., author of the ten-volume
history of the Jesuits in Brazil, calls the documentation on Maranhão
alone a "papelada infinita." I thought I had gathered the greater part
of material in official archives, but he has found more. However, I still
believe that there still remains for both of us a good deal of material in
the *Arquivo Nacional da Tôrre do Tombo*, the *Arquivo Histórico Ultramarino*, the *Biblioteca de Évora*, and the *Biblioteca Nacional*, all of
Portugal. One source which neither of us has searched is the central
Jesuit archive in Rome, and this is the most important of all to ascertain
the economic resources of the Jesuits in Brazil.

This writer finds himself almost in complete agreement with Professor Alden's findings and conclusions. Having said this, I would like
to comment briefly concerning some small points.

It will, I believe, be absolutely necessary for him to go through the
Cartório dos Jesuítas in the Arquivo Nacional da Tôrre do Tombo, to
deal adequately with the question of Jesuit properties in Portugal and
Brazil. This *cartório* consists of 120 thick *maços* or bundles, almost entirely made up, to the best of my recollection, of rental receipts and
similar economic documents. I do not believe that a careful study has
been made of them because I myself numbered the last twenty or so
bundles in 1951.

The author says: "By my count, the Jesuits had a total of seventeen
plantations, each equipped with one or more *engenhos* at the time of
their expulsion." He bases this statement upon a "variety of contemporary and later sources, the latter including [Leite's *História*]." Leite
is a good source for such a statement, but I wish he had been more explicit about his other sources.

Professor Alden also mentions that the Jesuit plantations were often
"managed by one or two padres." I believe there were also some who had
only one or two lay brothers as managers. Could this be one of the reasons that even the Jesuit superiors themselves spoke of a relaxation in

the eighteenth century of the ancient severe discipline at the time of Father Vieira?

An important and somewhat amazing statement is made by Professor Alden when he mentions that the "Society of Jesus was probably the greatest institutional slaveholder in Brazil; certainly it possessed the largest number of slaves confined to a single plantation in all of colonial America." He does not document the latter half of the sentence specifically, giving it merely as his opinion "according to the information I have been able to gather." Whether completely true or not, however, it brings out the bigness of the Jesuit operation in what was certainly one of the poorer states of the New World. Certainly this bigness called attention to them and caused enmity on the part of the less fortunate colonists. We see this in our own day with regard to United States and European holdings in underdeveloped nations.

A capital point was made by Professor Alden in regard to the urban properties of the Jesuits. The value of these holdings was enormous. When we stop to consider that 950 *milréis* were considered sufficient to support thirty Jesuits in Maranhão for a year, what must we think of urban properties worth 152,165 *milréis* yielding an annual income of 10,918 *milréis*? And this from only one city? Such sums would, I believe, be in the millions today.

The writer mentions that "in general policies and in special legislation, beginning in 1570, the Crown supported the Jesuits' attempt to defend the Indians until the 1750's." It was hardly that clear-cut. It seems to me that the Crown vacillated weakly between protecting and exploiting the natives, or allowing their exploitation, but could usually be brought around to the side of the angels through Jesuit pressure at Court. Sometimes, however, this took years of effort by the Society. And, of course, each time they increased the number and ferocity of their enemies, because the result of the Jesuits' efforts usually touched the officials and colonists in the pocketbook.

The author mentions a survey of the property of religious undertaken in the area of Rio de Janeiro in 1718 and 1719. He concludes: "whether similar surveys were undertaken in other captaincies at this time has yet to be discovered." Similar surveys were made, at least in the north. On August 28, 1706, the *provedor da fazenda* of Belém, Pará, gave an account of "os bens e o pagamento de impostos" of the religious in that state. This was repeated on February 8, 1718.[1] In 1728, as is well known, Governor Sousa Freyre sent an extensive account of their properties to the Court.

The story of Paulo da Silva Nunes, the "populist spokesman" of the Amazon, as Alden calls him, cries out for a definitive biography. What was the iron purpose of will that drove this man to fight the Jesuits during more than twenty long years, without ever slackening his efforts, in the face of official disinterest and even active opposition? And finally, can it be possible, as Azevedo states, without giving his source,[2] that the Jesuits succored Nunes with money when he was in debtor's prison during the last eight years of his life, in return for all his orginial papers? If so, where are these papers now? I believe that Professor Alden's treatment of Nunes is one of the high spots of his paper, but I would like to see much more information on this enigmatic character.

For the record, I believe that Dom Miguel de Bulhões e Sousa was a Dominican, not a Benedictine.[3] Also, there were no "Capuchins" in Maranhão at this time. The term causing the trouble is "Capuchos," which was the term applied vulgarly to the reformed friars of the Order of Friars Minor (Franciscans) in Portugal. Three Portuguese provinces of Franciscans were represented in Maranhão and Pará: Santo Antônio, Piedade, and Conceição: they were all "Capuchos."

One of the contentions of the Jesuits throughout most of the colonial history of Brazil was that their colleges and novitiates could not adequately be supported in this unfriendly and poor country without fazendas and Indians to work them. The royal *dotação* and *côngrua*, even if always paid promptly (which it was not), could not begin to buy all the things necessary. Produce and food and meat were necessary and the only sure way of obtaining them, they felt, was to have their own plantations. As the time came nearer to 1759, this argument was impugned by their enemies. Finally the Indians were "set free" of the paternalistic rule of the padres in 1757 (Law of 1755). But wasn't it ironical that already in 1761, two years after the Jesuits' expulsion, Governor Póvoas of Maranhão wrote to Furtado strongly urging that the old college of the Jesuits, which was now being used for the civil education of boys, keep the same fazendas as before with all their slaves.[4] So, apparently, the Jesuits were correct in their contention after all.

The questions raised by the liquid assets of the Jesuits have still not been satisfactorily answered, in my opinion. I believe that this was of even greater importance than landed property, because of the relative lack of money in circulation and the almost total lack of risk capital in Brazil. These liquid assets, together with the sophisticated credit system in operation between the Jesuit mission procurator in Lisbon and his local counterparts, gave the Society a tremendous advantage over

the merchants of the area, and, in my opinion, was just as strong a reason for hatred of the Jesuits as the Indian and *fazenda* question. In
matters such as the above, the undeniably strong worldwide organization of the Jesuits must have been the despair of the individual civilian
merchant, no matter what his riches and his connections at Court.

Perhaps the objective truth about the relative economic position of
the Jesuits can never be established. However, in the interim, it would
seem that the report of *desembargador* Francisco Duarte dos Santos on
the Jesuit missions in 1734 probably comes closest to the truth. He did
not find proof of great misery among the settlers; he opted for continued Indian control by the missionaries rather than by married white
Indian agents; he absolved the Jesuits of charging exorbitant prices for
the goods they sold to the colonists. His final conclusion, however, was
telling: he did not favor the missionaries' continued involvement in commercial activities and strongly urged the Crown to provide the missionaries with adequate financial support so that they could cease their commerce. The Crown, unfortunately, accepted all his conclusions except
the last, and the missionary commerce continued.

What conclusion, therefore, can we come to? It would seem to this
commentator that the truth must be sought somewhere in the middle.
There does not seem to be any doubt that the Society of Jesus was a
truly powerful economic force in Brazil, although not as omnipotent as
Furtado and Nunes claimed. It would also seem clear that the professed high humanitarianism of Furtado and Pombal in freeing the
Indians was really somewhat of a ploy to break down the regular orders'
relative (in comparison to the secular clergy, which was more subservient) independence from heavy-handed despotism and absolutism.
The denouement of the religious orders in Brazil after the defeat of the
Jesuits was certainly at least partially due to the iron hand of despotism
which treated the religious like lower-echelon state employees. Once in
complete control of the salaries of the clergy, it was an easy matter to
begin the control of the entry of novices, which ended in the virtual
death of the religious orders in imperial Brazil.

In all of this, the source of all the wealth as well as of all the contention—the Indian—was all but forgotten. Certainly, the Indian lost most
in the suppression of the Jesuits and the heavy-handed shearing of the
religious' powers to protect them. The new system after 1759 of military
Indian agents did nothing but make a prophet of Duarte dos Santos,
the desembargador of 1734, who warned that the end of missionary
control would make the "aldeias soon but a memory." And, strangely

enough, the state did not become "richer" as Nunes and Furtado promised. Within three years after the Jesuits' expulsion, the money from the forced sales of their property was gone, and the governors complained of their utter inability to pay the *três folhas:* civil, ecclesiastical, and military. Could it be that the astronomical figures about the Jesuit riches had been exaggerated? More study is needed in the post-1759 period before this can be ascertained.

One thing is sure: today the Brazilian government relies heavily on religious missionaries to take care of the Indians. Perhaps missionaries are the only ones with enough altruism or virtue to carry on this thankless work. Certainly there is today more chance of success, since there is separation of Church and State now. But again in modern times, the Church has to have considerable economic resources for this expensive labor. This causes murmuring about the "wealthy Church" all over again, and the old vicious circle begins all over again.

In conclusion, I welcome Professor Alden into this fascinating field of research and assure him of any help I can give him. Bravery such as his should be rewarded.

NOTES

1 Arquivo Histórico Ultramarino, Pará, *Papeis Avulsos,* Caixa 3, and 1701–1750, maço 1.
2 João Lúcio de Azevedo, *Os Jesuitas no Grão Pará: Suas missões e a colonizção* ... (Lisbon, 1901) , p. 226.
3 *Ibid.,* p. 312.
4 Arquivo Nacional da Tôrre do Tombo, Ministério do Reino, *Papéis Diversos do Ultramar,* No. 601.

AZEREDO COUTINHO AND THE
INTELLECTUAL FERMENT OF HIS TIMES

Manoel Cardozo
The Catholic University of America, Washington, D.C.

IN his history of Portuguese America, published in Lisbon in 1730, Sebastião da Rocha Pita gives an incomplete list of persons, like himself born in Brazil, who were worthy of being remembered for the positions of responsibility they had held in the service of the Crown and of the Church in Portugal, Brazil, and elsewhere in the Old Empire. The list included a bishop; an abbot; cathedral canons; governors of Brazil and of Maranhão, of Rio de Janeiro and Pernambuco, of Angola, the Cape Verde Islands, and São Tomé; camp masters; members of the Overseas Council; justices of the high courts of Lisbon; justices of the district courts (*Relações*) of Bahia, Pôrto, and Gôa; secretaries of the State of Brazil; chancellors of the Royal Exchequer; a castellan of Mozambique; and a supervisor of the Exchequer of India.[1] Rocha Pita believed that "our Portuguese America . . . in the production of talented sons may compete with Italy and Greece. . . ." [2] When we realize how exiguous were Brazil's human resources during the period in question—an estimated free population of only 74,000 people in 1660[3]—we may readily understand why Rocha Pita was justified in memorializing his fellow Brazilians.

It is a pity that a man with Rocha Pita's pride in the land of his birth, "the best portion" of the New World, "a paradise on earth," [4] did not live to record the names of the far more numerous natives of Brazil who in the generations that followed his own were to contribute more abundantly and significantly to the civilization of Portugal. Suffering as he obviously did from a sense of inferiority, growing out of his status as the citizen of a colonial capital, he would doubtless have been pleased to know that in the eighteenth century no other colonial country, in proportion to its human and physical resources, may have exerted so great an influence upon the Mother Country. During the dark days of the Restoration, when Portugal's independence hung in the balance, Brazil had already become the "milch cow." During the brighter days of the Marquis of Pombal and Dona Maria I, Brazil was also indispensable, this time intellectually and economically, to the well-being of Portugal.

The influx of Brazilians into Portugal throughout the eighteenth century coincided with, and possibly contributed to, movements for economic modernization and religious *aggiornamento*. The movements themselves were part of the larger process that led to the overthrow of the *ancien régime*, but the conjunction of an overseas element in the Portuguese renewal was unusual. The Enlightenment in Portugal ought not, however, be looked upon as an imitation of what happened in France. Coeval Portugal was intellectually, culturally, and economically underdeveloped, as compared with France and England, and it would be foolish to expect that the Enlightenment among the Portuguese, and by extension, among the Brazilians, was on the same plane or meant the same thing. There was resistance everywhere against the established order, with its appalling rigidities, but there was no thought in Portugal of "throwing the baby out with the bath." Having spent the seventeenth century in a kind of Spanish straightjacket—the influence of Spanish philosophers and theologians continued beyond the Restoration of 1640—the Portuguese began the eighteenth century, and lived through it, with the feeling that there was something wrong with society: not certainly with the absolute monarchy, which remained above criticism, but with the baroque Church and its legalism, its prying into all areas of intellectual life, its censorship; with the Holy See and the Roman Curia; with the philosophy of the Schoolmen, which continued to be the official philosophy of Portugal long after trans-Pyrenean Europe had turned to other, more modern systems. During the eighteenth century it became clear that Portugal had isolated itself from the rest of Europe in an "Island of Purity" and that its adherence to narrow orthodoxies had contributed neither to the prestige of Portugal's intellectual reputation abroad, nor to the economic development of the country.

The Brazilians who flocked to Portugal during the eighteenth century must therefore have felt, when they did not feel themselves in harmony with the establishment, a mixture of frustration and excitement. At least 1,752 of them, including some of the most prestigious names in Luso-Brazilian society, studied at the University of Coimbra.[5] Another 215, among them José Bonifácio de Andrada e Silva, were certified by the Court Royal (Desembargo do Paço), as was customary for positions in the judiciary.[6] Most of these people inevitably found their way into the establishment and became a part of it. Others, remarkably few in number, attacked the regime under which they lived, as did the Coimbra alumni involved in the Minas Gerais conspiracy of 1789. A few defections were to be expected in an age that was both revolutionary and absolutist.

The Brazilians who made their presence felt in the administrative and intellectual life of the Portuguese monarchy were no different basically from the Portuguese of other provenances. They did not form a special corporation within society, nor did their ideas differ from those of their fellow Portuguese. Very few of them, indeed, were willing to run the risk of antagonizing the establishment, or trade the good life of Portugal for the less sophisticated life of Brazil. Not many Brazilian students at Coimbra were as careless as Francisco de Melo Franco of Pernambuco, accused by the Inquisition in 1781 of being a heretic, a naturalist, and a deist.[7] Not many of them were as rash as Miguel de Sousa Borges Leal of Maranhão, who on July 31, 1803, at the moment when the degree of Doctor of Laws was being conferred upon him, "with temerarious, and never before known daring," insulted "with words, and gestures of arrogance" the professors and doctors of the School of Law. Though he had not been disqualified for the degree, he had nonetheless been given a failing grade in an examination and had earned a *simpliciter*, the customary passing mark for students like himself who had not received general approval *nemine discrepante*.[8]

It was difficult, in a disciplined country like Portugal, to maintain a rigorously independent stance. One could criticize the establishment, including the Church, provided that one's intention was to support the authority of the Crown or improve public morality. Matias Aires Ramos da Silva de Eça, for example, was born in São Paulo in 1705 [9] and lived at a time when Portugal "burned with the fury of sacred lasciviousness."[10] It was a time when making love to a nun, as João V did, was looked upon as the height of amorous sensitivity.[11] Eça said sharp things about convent life:

... what a great difference there is between a woman, who professed through force, and one who professed through an act of will! The latter truly left the world; the former merely changed houses. Both entered the Temple, but one entered to profane it. One was called by God, the other was sent by men. One went to find a divine spouse; the other, because she did not find a man. Both entered Religion, yet only one became a

Religious. Both professed but in opposite ways, because what one professed, the other did not. Both said the same thing, but one only mouthed it, while the other also said it from the heart. One made a sacrifice, the other a ceremony. . . . Finally, both were on the path of virtue, but both were not necessarily virtuous. . . .[12]

He said equally sharp things against the nobility and the idea of nobility. "Men", he said with the conviction of a moralist, "were born equal. . . ." In a passage reminiscent of Francis I's famous retort (conveyed to the Emperor Charles V by the Cardinal of Toledo) ,[13] Eça declared further that "the sun rises for everybody; dawn awakens everybody for work; the silence of the night announces the period of rest for everybody. . . . The world was not made for the greater benefit of some than of others. . . ." [14] Men are not born "wise, just, prudent, virtuous, good; and in the same way they are not born noble; it is here that they find nobility. . . ." [15]

The censor, who was rector of the Jesuit College of St. Patrick, saw nothing offensive to the Crown in these and similar remarks. On the contrary, the book "seems to me to be very useful to awaken men engulfed in the pride of the world, from the lethargy, and forgetfulness of life eternal, and to make them deaf to the deceitful adulations of vanity, a vice as old as the world itself, and as universal as mankind, which follows them in life, and ordinarily does not abandon them in death." [16] Had Matias Aires wanted to do more than point up the pitfalls of vanity on man's way to perfection at a time when public morals were notoriously debased, he may have had to pay for his temerity with exile, as was the lot of the Chevalier de Oliveira, Hipólito José da Costa, and, to a certain extent, Antônio Nunes Ribeiro Sanches. The eighteenth century in Portugal had many strange facets and, we must repeat, it will not do to assume that what happened was a mere reflection of the larger European movement. It was, ultimately, a part of it, but in Portugal the right to criticize and to question was limited in special, exasperating, and paradoxical ways.

The eighteenth century in Portugal, despite its contradictions and limitations, was a period of accelerated change and was much less rigid in its baroque orthodoxies than the seventeenth.[17] The spirit of innovation was more marked during the second half of the century, particularly during the time of the Marquis of Pombal (1750–1777) , but it began to be felt much earlier: conceivably from about 1692, when Catherine of Bragança returned to Portugal; [18] possibly in 1703, with the Methuen Treaty with England; [19] or at least by 1727, when delegates from Paris established a Masonic lodge in Lisbon.[20] However tenuous or inconsequential, these were breaches in the armor of conformity.

The return of Catherine to Portugal after the death of her husband Charles II of Great Britain, was quite unexpected. Had the Glorious Revolution of 1688 not taken place, James II not been driven from the British throne, and William and Mary not succeeded the hapless Jacobite, it is unlikely that Catherine would have cut short her thirty-year residence in England. During the last years of her life she served Portugal well, displaying as regent, during her brother's absence from the country as during his illness, qualities of leadership which the British never suspected she possessed. For the Portuguese, it could not have passed unnoticed that the widowed queen of a Protestant country had been called upon to rule a Catholic commonwealth.

Dom Pedro II followed his sister to the grave within a year after her death, and in 1706 his son and her nephew ascended the throne, at age seventeen, as João V. Nineteenth-century liberal historians, notably Oliveira Martins, belittled the achievements of the magnanimous João. They pointed to the glitter of the society of his times and to the pomp of the civil and ecclesiastical establishments. They criticized him for having built Mafra, the Italianate palace and convent whose dimensions were such that in the Iberian Peninsula only the Escorial exceeded it in size. Perhaps he was not always wise in the use he made of the gold and diamonds that came to him from the mines of Brazil, but he was nonetheless a monarch of taste. He created the Portuguese Academy in Rome, erected the grand libraries of Coimbra and Mafra, established the Portuguese Academy of History, transcribed 200 volumes of documents from the Roman archives, raised the archdiocese of Lisbon to the dignity of a patriarchate, and persuaded the Vatican to bestow upon the sovereigns of Portugal the title of Most Faithful. Other writers dwelt upon unsavory facets of his private life, of his numerous sins of the flesh. Yet we should not forget, for our purposes, that the first unmistakable glimmer of the Enlightenment was observed during his opulent reign. It was João who made it possible for Father Luís Antônio Verney, from the sanctuary of Rome, to write his enormously effective critique of Portuguese education.[21] João also weakened the Jesuits' monopoly over Portuguese secondary education by permitting the Oratorians to establish schools of their own. It was during João's reign that students, such as Alexandre de Gusmão, went abroad to complete their education in the new science of Newton, Descartes, Galileo,

Locke, and Ramus, studies that were not permitted in post-Tridentine Portugal.

The second half of the eighteenth century is dominated by the Marquis of Pombal and by his attempts to modernize the country. He did not seek political modernization, because it was never his intention to weaken the prerogatives of the Crown. He sought, rather, to reform the baroque Church. To men of our own times, when the role of the Church is clearly circumscribed and the secularization of society has proceeded to the point where prayers are no longer tolerated in public schools, it is almost impossible to conceive a period in history when the Church was more powerful than the State, its income larger, its social functions greater. Indeed, it was because of these conditions that the Church inevitably became the chief target of the Enlightenment in Portugal. Against its baroque triumphalism and the Roman Curia that had made it possible, many Portuguese, both within and without the official Church, aided and abetted by the Crown, rose up against it, in a powerful movement for aggiornamento. It was to be, in the long run, a premature movement (and a fanciful one in some of its ideals), because it necessarily had no focus beyond the national frontiers. In an age of absolutism it was idle to suppose that a reforming ecumenical council, on the pattern of Trent and Vatican II, might be called into session; yet the Portuguese movement needed precisely the kind of direction that such a council would have given it. It floundered instead in the quagmire of entrenched interests and ecclesiastical authority, but it prepared the way nonetheless for the intellectual revolution that would in time overthrow the *ancien régime*.

The movement against the baroque Church was characterized on the one hand by regalism and on the other by laicism. Among the favorite authors were Tommaso Tamburini, Justinus Febronius, and, for the official position on the Church-State issue, Antônio Pereira de Figueiredo. Educational reform was the province of Verney, whose tirade against the schools appeared in 1746 and 1747, in time to affect the generation that was to bring about the radical reform of the University of Coimbra in 1772. Being a priest, Verney concerned himself in particular with the ecclesiastical disciplines, courageously, to be sure, but not with much originality. He opposed St. Thomas Aquinas and his commentators. He railed against the way theology was taught in Portugal. "The first thing," he said, "that the student learns from the scholastic method is to convince himself that the Bible is of no use to the theologian. The second is to convince himself that there is no other theology in the world except for the four questions of speculative theology, and that everything else is superfluous quarrels and the lazy ruminations of foreigners." [22]

The Jansenists of France and other countries naturally played into the hands of the Portuguese reformers, many of whom were Jansenists themselves—the papal condemnations of their tenets in 1642 and 1653 to the contrary notwithstanding. The Portuguese of this religious suasion could be expected to applaud the Congress of Ems, the bishop of Blois, the Emperor Joseph II, and the Civil Constitutions of the clergy of France. They would be sympathetic to the reforms proposed by the Synod (or Council, as they preferred to call it) of Pistoia of 1786, which legislated against processions in honor of Our Lady, the rosary, the Stations of the Cross, the veneration of images, the devotion to the Sacred Heart, and the like—innovations in Catholic piety which Pius VI in 1794 declared to be heretical. Since their ideas were proscribed by Rome, it is understandable why they became staunch supporters of civil control of the ecclesiastical establishment.

The reformers had a field day and took advantage of it, in a less becoming way, when the Jesuits were expelled from Portugal and from the overseas areas of the Portuguese *padroado* in 1759, and again when the Holy See in 1773, (partly as the result of the relentless campaign waged against the Society throughout Europe by the Marquis of Pombal) banished them from the entire Church. A hateful and slanderous literature calculated to arouse a brutal loathing of the Jesuits issued from the presses of Portugal with the approval of the ecclesiastical and lay authority. In 1771 an anonymous treatise was published that bore the extraordinary title of *Infected origins of the relaxation of moral teaching among the so-called Jesuits; the Manifest fraud, with which they deduced it from the Ethics, and Metaphysics of Aristotle: And the obstinacy, with which, on behalf of the sophisms of their Logic, they sustained it contrary to the general good: Achieving the prevalence of the impious ideas of that Philosopher, who lacks all knowledge of God, and of future, and eternal life, Against Scripture, against the Moral Teachings established by the De Officiis of St. Ambrose, by the thirty-five Books of the Moralia of St. Gregory the Great, that constituted the promptuaries of Christian Moral Theology, While it was not corrupted by those malign artifices with lamentable havoc wrought upon the consciences of the Faithful.*[23] In the following year another anonymous, equally scurrilous tract appeared, again with an inflated title: *The* doctrines of the Church sacrilegiously offended by the atrocities of Jesuit moral theology . . . To serve as correction for the abominable errors, and the hateful impieties of that so-called Moral Theology, invented by the Jesuitical Society for the conquest, and destruction of all Kingdoms, and Sovereign States.[24] Finally in 1778, José de Seabra da Silva, justice of the Court Royal and procurator of the Crown, published in two parts his famous *Deducção chronológica, e analytica*. The first part concerned itself with "the horrible havoc, that the Company known by the names of Jesus, wrought in Portugal, and in all of its Dominions by means of a plan, and system followed by the Company from the time that it entered this Kingdom, until it was proscribed, and expelled through the just, wise, and provident Law of September 3, 1759." The second part described what successively took place in the different epochs of the Church with reference to the censorship, prohibition, and printing of books, "showing the intolerable harm, that the abuse of the same has caused the same Church of God, all the monarchies, all the sovereign states, and the public peace of the entire universe." [25]

The movement for the reform of the Church, which these books attempted to further, took advantage, as we said, of the discomfiture of the Jesuits; yet the period that followed the expulsion of the Jesuits produced nothing that could compare, in terms of the impact upon the process of modernization and change that Portugal was then undergoing, with the reform of the University of Coimbra in 1772.[26] Suddenly, a felicitous conjunction of forces played into the hands of the reformers and they achieved an overwhelming victory. Thenceforth, students from Portugal and Brazil would be informed by the revitalized and restructured university. What they would learn at Coimbra, the only university in the Portuguese-speaking world, would affect their thinking upon religion and the world about them. Nothing more clearly prepared the educated classes of the two countries for the adventures in doctrinaire liberalism that were to face them in the nineteenth century than the events that stemmed from the promulgation of the new statutes of Coimbra in 1772.

The victory at Coimbra must seem strange to us today because the reform of the curriculum meant to do in Portugal toward the end of the eighteenth century what the more enlightened nations of northern Europe had already achieved a hundred years earlier. The time lag is significant, and it speaks well of the effectiveness of the vigilance that was maintained for so long against the spread of condemned ideas. It

may also help to explain some of the destructive nature of the energies
that now came to the fore, after having been kept in check for so many
years.

The concern of the reformers for the teaching of philosophy and theology again may seem excessive in terms of a more modern secular
society, but Coimbra was substantially an ecclesiastical university, run
by ecclesiastics, in a country where ecclesiastics were likewise found in all
levels of government. To the reformers, therefore, the great culprits were
Thomas Aquinas, John of St. Thomas, the Schoolmen of Salamanca,
Aristotle, and the Arabs. Correlatively, they attacked the traditional
teaching methods that involved the memorizing of formulas and the
repeating of time-honored arguments. They insisted upon a return to
the Bible, along the lines earlier advocated by the Protestants of the
North. They knew that in the obscurantist past, Scripture was thought
to be useful only to preachers and that the study of Holy Writ did not
attract the students of the Faculty of Theology. They were aware that it
had been the pratice at Coimbra, before the reform, to teach theology
without any relation to history. What they insisted upon now was a
theology that was illuminated by the study of the history of the papacy
and of the Church in general. Moreover, they believed that the new
breed of theologians should know Greek and Latin, beyond the regular
requirement of Church Latin. They felt that the study of law should not
be limited to Justinian's Code and its commentators, or taught, like the
catechism, by rote. They made good their demands that Portugese law
be given a place in the curriculum and that the Socratic method be employed in the classroom.

The reformers did not believe in traditional philosophy at all, and in
its place they substituted Natural Philosophy, which was not speculative but practical. Their assumption was that works of authors formerly
proscribed in Portugal, such as Galileo, Copernicus, Newton, and Descartes, would furnish the key to the secrets of the modern world. Since
logic, metaphysics, and the like were mere exercises in reason which, in
the opinion of the reformers, served only to befuddle mankind, the new
curriculum would be pragmatic and scientific: the study of nature instead of the classical texts.

The reforms meant simply, as we suggested elsewhere, that the European scientific revolution of the seventeenth century had finally come
into its own. The Portuguese were to return to the observing of nature,
as they had done before—pragmatically, but without a philosophical
structure—during their Age of Discovery. It would no longer be forbid-

den, as it was before the reform, to teach mathematics at Coimbra without reference to Newton, Galileo, and Copernicus. Thus it was that the spirit of reform that was imposed upon Coimbra served as a tonic for the intellectual life of Portugal during the declining years of the *ancien régime*. From 1772 onward, the Portuguese, now more nearly reconciled to their times, went about trying to catch up with the rest of Europe and to find their way back into what they considered to be the mainstream of European life. That it was not easy, or entirely successful, is exemplified by the life of José Joaquim da Cunha de Azeredo Coutinho.

II

A thirty-three-year-old Brazilian, bearing the distinguished name of José Joaquim da Cunha de Azeredo Coutinho, with an entailed estate and a delayed desire for the religious life, enrolled at the University of Coimbra in 1775.[27] He had been born in Campos dos Goitacazes (Captaincy of Rio de Janeiro) in 1742, into a prominent and wealthy landed family. Azeredo Coutinho was descended from old Brazilian stock, notably from Vasco Fernandes Coutinho, the first donatary of Espírito Santo, and Amador Bueno, the patriotic Paulista who cast his lot with the Restoration party and thus won for himself an otherwise undeserved niche in history.[28] He was also related to two Brazilians who occupied eminent positions in the service of Portugal—patrons, indeed, of the first order. One was the friend and associate of Pombal, Francisco de Lemos de Faria Pereira Coutinho, rector of the University of Coimbra from 1770 until 1779, and from the latter year until his death in 1822, bishop of Coimbra, count of Arganil, and lord of Coja.[29] The other was Pereira Coutinho's brother, Dr. João Pereira Ramos, a magistrate of the Court Royal, procurator of the Crown, and lord of Pereira, who died in Lisbon in 1799.[30]

Azeredo Coutinho was one among many Brazilian students at Coimbra. Contemporaries of his at the university would also make names for themselves: José Vieira Couto, the mathematician and professor of the university; José da Silva Lisbôa, the economist and future Viscount Cairú; Manuel Luís Alves de Carvalho, the future director of medical and surgical studies for the Court and State of Brazil; José de Sousa e Azevedo Pizarro, canon of the Cathedral of Rio de Janeiro, archpriest of the Chapel Royal, and president of the Brazilian Legislative Assembly; Antônio de Morais Silva, the magistrate and soldier who compiled the famous dictionary of the Portuguese language; José Arouche de Toledo, the first director of the School of Law of São Paulo; and Antônio Pereira de Sousa Caldas, the poet.[31]

Following his graduation in canon law on May 30, 1780, and his ordination, probably in the same year,[32] he was appointed archdeacon of the Cathedral Church of Rio de Janeiro in 1784.[33] He did not leave Portugal at this time, however, since, Dona Maria I in the same year offered him, probably through the influence of Dom Francisco, the post of deputy of the Holy Office in Lisbon.[34] Azeredo Coutinho did not take up the new job until September 15, 1785,[35] because of a final stay at Coimbra to qualify for the degree of licentiate in canon law.[36]

His career was now launched. His first published work was a strange subject for an ecclesiastic: a little piece on the price of sugar, which appeared in 1791. In the following year he was elected to membership in the Royal Academy of Sciences.[37] On November 21, 1794, he was named twelfth bishop of Pernambuco, and he was consecrated on January 25, 1795, by the titular bishop of Algarve.[38] Before his departure for Brazil, and indeed before his consecration, business involving the diocese was routinely referred to him, as occurred on December 11, 1794, when Martinho de Melo e Castro, the overseas secretary, asked for his opinion in the filling of a number of vacant ecclesiastical offices in Pernambuco.[39]

The new prelate also took advantage of the delay in getting to his diocese by making arrangements to carry out a plan that was dear to his heart, the establishment of two schools in the Bishopric: one, the episcopal seminary of Olinda for boys, whether they wished to study for the priesthood or not; [40] the other, the *Recolhimento* of Our Lady of Glory of Boavista, a boarding school for the "truly poor" girls, to prepare them for marriage and motherhood.[41] In a captaincy that had few schools the efforts of the Bishop to improve the school system could only be applauded.[42]

For the proposed seminary, Azeredo Coutinho received from the Queen, on March 22, 1796, title to "the building, which once served as College and residence of the extinct Jesuits, with the respective Church, the furnishings belonging to it, and the enclosed field, which adjoins the said building, and College. . . ." [43] At the same time, he drew up separate statutes, or rules and regulations, for the schools, which, in accordance with the law, he submitted to the Crown for approval.[44]

Azeredo Coutinho finally left Lisbon on November 20, 1798, and thirty-six days later, on Christmas Day, reached his destination.[45] He was welcomed characteristically with a *Carmen Bucolicum* by Manoel dos Reis Curado, a Latin elegy by Francisco Sales dos Reis Curado, and a salutory ode in the vernacular by Antônio Lourenço da Silva.[46] He was not destined to remain simply as the head of the Church of Pernambuco. The controversial governor of the captaincy, Dom Tomás José de Melo, was removed from office, by letter of the Prince Regent dated August 20, 1798.[47] On December 29, 1798, therefore, in accordance with the law, the government of the Captaincy was turned over to Azeredo Coutinho in his capacity as bishop of the diocese; to Pedro Sheverin, the intendant of the Navy, as the senior military officer; and to Antônio Luís Pereira, *ouvidor* of the local jurisdiction *(comarca)* as the principal officer of justice.[48] Finally, on January 1, 1799, in order that he might be able to provide more effectively for the needs of the new seminary, as was the Prince Regent's wish,[49] Azeredo Coutinho also took over the office of director general of studies (or superintendant of schools) of the Captaincy of Pernambuco.[50] Through an unusual conjunction of circumstances, Azeredo Coutinho thus became the most powerful man in Pernambuco, politically, religiously, and educationally. It was not, however, a fortuitous choice. Pernambuco was considered in Lisbon to be a sick province, and the Prince Regent hoped that the new Bishop would be able to work a cure.[51]

Azeredo Coutinho was rather suddenly transferred from the See of Olinda to that of Bragança and Miranda in metropolitan Portugal and was thus obliged to give up his various posts in Pernambuco. The reasons for this transfer have never been made clear. Tollenare, undoubtedly repeating the gossip that he had heard, suggested (some twelve years after Azeredo Coutinho's return to Lisbon) that he was removed because he was not liked at Court.[52] Oliveira Lima surmised that it had something to do with the Crown's negative attitude toward the intellectual development of Brazil,[53] but this is nonsense. It is true that shortly after his arrival the Bishop aroused local enmities, which had repercussions in Lisbon, when he endeavored to straighten out the tangled mess of public education in the Captaincy by dismissing two school teachers and reducing the salaries of their colleagues,[54] but again this does not seem to be the answer. He alienated the entire religious establishment by requiring the orders, congregations, brotherhoods, and the like to supply him with an accounting of their income-producing properties. The Crown had, of course, ordered him to do this. As a means of meeting the financial exigencies of the war with Spain, the Church bodies of Pernambuco were to be urged to sell whatever property they held in mortmain, turn the proceeds of the sales to the Royal Exchequer, and receive in return the income of 4 percent per year upon the total proceeds of these forced liquidations.[55] This quixotic plan was obviously bound to fail, and it did.

In his endeavor to improve the quality of the ministers of the altar, he did not hesitate to advocate reform measures that again aroused local jealousies and animosities. Perhaps the discovery of the mysterious conspiracy of 1801, which purportedly advocated the establishment of a republic in Pernambuco under the protection of Napoleon Bonaparte and which implicated the Suassuna brothers,[56] may have been responsible for his recall, even though Azeredo Coutinho handled himself well in what seems to have been a trumped-up emergency.[57] Was it because he was a Mason? Oliveira Lima says that he was.[58] In the light of his subsequent career, it hardly seems likely that Azeredo Coutinho belonged to the fraternity. Besides, many other important people in Portuguese society were Masons; and although the Masons were persecuted from time to time, it was not until 1818 that they were formally proscribed.[59]

As one of the provisional governors of the Captaincy of Pernambuco, the Bishop did in fact carry out his civic duties with dynamism and imagination, as may be gathered from the account of his administration which he published in 1808;[60] and inevitably, as we have pointed out above, his zeal for improvement was not shared by many of the people whose lives he meant to change.[61] Yet nothing that we have said thus far can hardly be sufficient reason to remove a man from so important a post as that of residential bishop of Pernambuco.

Actually, the Bishop never seems to have been happy in Pernambuco, and almost from the day of his arrival he despaired of achieving the well-being of his subjects and the security of their lives, honor, and property.[62] Corruption and venality, he said, were found everywhere; it was impossible to extinguish monopolies, oblige the vagrant to work, and put things in order. He felt, as time went on, that he was the victim of calumny and intrigue.[63] Moreover, he complained bitterly of the decisions and directives of the *Mesa da Consciência e Ordens,* the administrative body in Lisbon that supervised the work of the Church, as they affected him. He accused the *Mesa* of acts of despotism against him.[64]

In the Church of Pernambuco, powerful voices were raised against the Bishop, whose actions involving appointments to ecclesiastical livings were often questioned and at times tumultuously opposed. In a particularly bitter letter to Dom Rodrigo de Sousa Coutinho, the Overseas Secretary, dated Recife, April 8, 1800, Azeredo Coutinho lashed out against those who had undermined his authority by accepting a complaint against him from the vicar of Tijucupapo. In Lisbon the Prince Regent's advisors admitted that the Portuguese bishops generally, but especially the bishops of the overseas dominions, were opposed to the Right of Recourse to the Crown, which the faithful enjoyed. They were nonetheless appalled at the "invective of the present Bishop of Pernambuco, bearing in mind the School, in which he was educated." They believed that Azeredo Coutinho should be censured for his "innovating, and intolerant spirit" when it was clear that the preservation of the tradition Right of Recourse was proper and convenient to the Royal Service.[65]

In another instance, involving the naming of a pastor for the parish of Santo Antônio de Tracunhém, where the peoples' choice was preferred by the *Mesa da Consciência e Ordens* over the candidate proposed by the Bishop, the Prince Regent himself, at the instigation of the *Mesa,* formally censured Azeredo Coutinho on October 3, 1801, by charging him with the "abuse of the Sword" that had been entrusted to him.[66] The Bishop replied to the censure by saying that he had been condemned without being heard and that His Royal Highness had been deceived by his advisors. He criticized the *Mesa* for its high-handed tactics, demanded an impartial trial by any body other than the *Mesa,* and pointed out that unless this were done he could not in conscience carry out his duties as bishop and as one of the provisional governors of the Captaincy.[67] He went even further: he asked that the deputies of the *Mesa* who had in this way censured him be reprehended.[68]

This conflict with the *Mesa da Consciência e Ordens,* which touched upon ticklish prerogatives of ecclesiastical administration, must surely have been the reason, as Sérgio Buarque de Holanda says,[69] why the Bishop was rather preremptorily removed by Royal Letter of February 25, 1802, from the diocese of Pernambuco to that of Bragança and Miranda and ordered to return to Portugal at the first opportunity.[70] Two years later, the Bishop published his famous *Alegasaõ juridica,* not only to complain once more against the "violences, and oppressions" of the *Mesa* but also to seek the "Royal Protection" of the sovereign. His treatise was indeed much more than a petition; it was his way of saying to the world that the churches, dignities, and benefices of the overseas bishoprics of Portugal, south of Cape Bojador on the African coast, including the bishoprics of Brazil, fell under the immediate ecclesiastical patronage of the Crown, not under the *Mesa da Consciência e Ordens* through the Military Order of Christ.[71] He was ready and willing to work under the Crown, not under the *Mesa.* In Pernambuco, Azeredo

Coutinho did not "flaunt with impunity the authoritative opinion of the doctors of the Mesa," as Buarque de Holanda writes,[72] but since the Crown did not side with the embattled Bishop, it is easy to understand why he was ordered back to Portugal. His usefulness in Pernambuco had obviously come to an end.

On July 12, 1802, the Bishop-Elect of Bragança and Miranda, after hearing four poems composed for the occasion by Frei João Batista da Purificação, Father João Pereira Rodrigues de Alcântara, his secretary, and Manoel de Araújo Lemos,[73] sailed on board the "Marquês de Angeja" for Lisbon.[74] He never took possession of the northern Portuguese see. Since the duly consecrated bishop of Bragança and Miranda refused to resign, the Prince Regent had perforce to find another place for Coutinho. An opening occurred in Elvas in 1806, when the local ordinary was promoted to the primatial see of Braga.[75]

Azeredo Coutinho would spend the remainder of his life in Portugal, through the French invasion, the flight of the royal family to Brazil and its return to Lisbon, the opening of the ports of Brazil to the commerce of friendly nations, the Peninsular War, the British occupation, the Gomes Freire conspiracy, the wars of independence in Spanish America, the Pernambuco revolution of 1817, and the agitation of 1821 in Brazil. He asked in time to be relieved of Elvas, but on the very day that his request was granted (November 15, 1817) he was transferred to the see of Beja, which he did not accept.[76] In the following year, on May 13, 1818, he became the Grand Inquisitor of the Holy Office and President of the Junta de Melhoramento das Ordens Regulares.[77] He was subsequently chosen as one of the delegates of Rio de Janeiro to the constituent assembly of the Portuguese monarchy and died, at the age of seventy-nine, two days after its deliberations began,[78] and one year before the formal independence of Brazil was proclaimed.

III

Azeredo Coutinho is very much a product of the Portuguese eighteenth century, with all its contradictions, and in a special way of the reformed University of Coimbra. He was neither more enlightened nor more liberal than many other natives of Brazil who also climbed the ladder of success in the Mother Country. They all knew that their criticisms of their society had to be made within the accepted canons of political and social expediency. Actually, Azeredo Coutinho's writings are singularly free of new ideas. There is basically nothing in them that could have disturbed the status quo; and the fact that Dom José Joaquim, who often gave vent to his combative nature, was able to speak out without endangering his career is proof enough that he never overstepped the bounds of political or religious propriety. Even when called to question for his ideas on ecclesiastical patronage, it surely could not have been his ideas of royal supremacy which disturbed the authorities.

It is, therefore, temerarious to say, as has been done, that Azeredo Coutinho had something special to do with the Enlightenment in Brazil and that he contributed in some way, through his writings and activities, to the independence of Brazil.[79] The Seminary of Olinda did of course produce men, largely priests, who were to make Pernambuco a hotbed of revolution, but it is hard to believe that Azeredo Coutinho had this goal in mind. Despite the deserved reputation that it quickly achieved, the Seminary was after all no more than a good secondary school. It is foolish to look upon it as a "new Coimbra." Even the Bishop himself, in his statutes for the school, declared, and we believe honestly, that his purpose was not "to establish a College of universal sciences; but rather no more than a School of elementary principles, proper not only for a good, and true Minister of the Church; but also for a good Citizen, and investigator of Nature, which adores the Creator in its works, and makes them serve the welfare of mankind. . . ." [80] More specifically, as he says in another connection, the purpose of his seminary was to educate "the Boys of our Diocese," not, certainly, the men.[81] His purposes were clearly pastoral and not as intellectual as later times have imagined them to be. To say, moreover, as he said, that anything not covered by his statutes would be governed by the new statutes of the University of Coimbra, was to follow the established pattern for all such schools.

When one compares the tone of Azeredo Coutinho's statutes of 1798 with the statutes of 1776 embodying the curriculum reforms of the Franciscan Province of the Immaculate Conception of Rio de Janeiro, one senses that much of the fire had died down in the intervening years. The French Revolution with its pestiferous doctrines was too close upon the Portuguese, too dangerous for the security of Throne and Altar, to permit the grand attacks against the educational system that the statutes of Coimbra of 1772 made fashionable. The Franciscans, however, were still close enough to the reform movement to share its enthusiasms and its indignation. They too flayed Scholasticism, berated it, hounded it to death. Any book, they said, composed in accordance with the Scholastic Peripatetic Method would inevitably contain "a hundred useless

Questions, and a thousand sophistical entanglements, which serve rather to confound the intellect, than to advance it along the truth path of Letters." [82] They were proud of the fact that Dom José I had been chosen by Providence "to free us from the shameful captivity of ignorance, and of fanaticism. . . ." [83] Twenty-two years later the job description for the chair of practical theology at Olinda was, by comparison, rather pallid and matter-of-fact.

The Teacher . . . should avoid following the path of the Casuistic Moralists, not only the bad ones, but also the good: because, in addition to their not giving the formulas together in one body, and not treating them with the good deduction which is necessary for the pupils to be able to conceive a good idea, and form a just system of all the Evangelical Moral Theology; they make them lose their time in the study of particular cases, disjointed without rule, without method, and without system, for that reason making it impossible for them to resolve any case with assurance, which they had not studied, or which was not in every respect similar to some of those that they had studied. [84]

Actually, what the Franciscans of Rio de Janeiro proposed to do was, in many ways, on a plane higher than the one that Azeredo Coutinho had in mind. In Olinda, only Latin was to be taught; among the Franciscans, Latin, Greek, and Hebrew. Olinda provided for elementary education, "primeiras letras"; the Franciscans did not. Theology at Olinda was to be covered in two years; in the Province of Rio de Janeiro, in nine. At Olinda students were to take Latin for three years; among the Franciscans, it was assumed that they knew Latin. The course in philosophy at Olinda included experimental physics, natural history, and chemistry, and the material was to be covered in two years. In the Franciscan province, three years were to be devoted to philosophy, including one year for geometry, natural history, and experimental physics. Olinda provided a one-year course in mathematics, i.e., geometry, trigonometry, and elementary algebra; the Franciscans made no provisions to teach mathematics as a separate discipline. Ecclesiastical history was a part of both curricula; it was to be taught for one year at Olinda, more than one year under the Franciscan plan. The Franciscans specified no fixed period of time for the study of rhetoric, Greek, and Hebrew; at Olinda, rhetoric, which also covered secular history, was a one-year course. The statutes of Olinda provided for the study of music; those of the Franciscans did not. Both made no provision for modern foreign languages, though the students at Olinda were to be expressly warned against the use of certain Brazilian sounds that had crept into the vernacular.

In his letter to the Bishop, offering him the *Festschrift* that appeared in Lisbon in 1808, Father Manoel Jácome Bezerra de Meneses called the Seminary of Olinda "the only one in all Brazil, with the necessary Sciences, and Wise, and Learned Masters for the education of those who are destined for the service of Religion, and of the State. . . ." [85] During Azeredo Coutinho's stay in Brazil, the seminary taught Latin grammar, rhetoric, poetics, history, geography, chronology, geometry, rational and moral philosophy, physics (i.e., natural history), dogmatic, speculative, and practical theology, ecclesiastical history, liturgy, music, and art *("desenho")*.[86] Bezerra de Meneses was probably justified in his praise, which referred to a situation in 1808, at the latest. The quality of the education ministered at Olinda should not be exaggerated however, nor should we forget that the seminary was a secondary school, whose business it was to prepare students for higher studies at the University. In short, there was no indication, when Azeredo Coutinho created it, that the seminary was to become what it did become, the alma mater of liberals who took an active part in the subsequent political life of Pernambuco. Times changed, and so did the men involved in the school's operation. But the Bishop who became the Grand Inquisitor of Portugal, proud though he was of his sowing, could hardly have been pleased with the harvest.

His ideas on the education of young ladies were also the usual ones of the Portugal of his day, as we shall see from an examination of the statutes for the recolhimento or boarding school that he set up in Boavista for poor white orphaned girls of the diocese of Pernambuco. By this we do not mean to belittle his achievement in this area, which, from a practical point of view, was very great. Yet the formal rules and regulations for his charity school for girls reveal another side of his personality that leaves us unimpressed with his pastoral concerns and old-fashioned attitudes.

Boavista was to be run by women of recognized virtue and mature years, twelve white women who would reside on the premises, one of whom would be appointed by the Bishop as superior or regent. These estimable women were not to form a religious community, nor were they to be allowed, without the Bishop's permission, to take the vow of chastity.[87] Even so, they were to live a cloistered life within the school and never permit themselves to be seen by visitors whenever the door to the cloister was allowed to be opened.[88]

The Bishop exhorted the women to practice Christian charity. "All disorders, all crimes, and trouble, that take place in the world, either in families, or in Cities, Provinces, and Kingdoms, all without doubt stem from the lack of Charity. . . .[89] Humility, the Bishop said, was the virtue that God prized most, and he urged the regent, as a mark of this virtue, to sweep the floors from time to time, wait on tables, wash the dishes, and nurse the sick.[90] Modesty was the handmaiden of humility, and modesty was practiced with the eyes, tongue, gestures, and other actions.[91] Girls should not be brought up in idleness, because such young people become bored and will not know what is good for them. Idleness fearfully leads to laziness, and laziness weakens the body as it does the soul. "This softness together wtih ignorance, which proceeds from laziness, produces in Girls, a pernicious sensitivity for all amusements, and shows," and of course weakens the character.[92] For their religious instruction, Dom José Joaquim recommended the catechism of Charles-Joachim Colbert de Croissy, Bishop of Montpellier, which, as he probably knew, was condemned, along with his other works, by the Holy See in 1743.[93]

In addition to his other recommendations, the Bishop hoped that the school would correct defects which he considered to be characteristic of the female sex, namely, timidity, the tendency to cry, telling lies, talkativeness, and vanity.[94] There were, in the Bishop's opinion, two states of life for women. Those who were destined for the religious life and planned to profess as nuns and sisters had to learn how to mortify their will and be proficient in Latin and music. All other women were expected to embrace the married state. For this purpose the latter were required to learn the "particular science" of living with their husbands in peace, of raising their children in virtue, and of running their households with economy. The pupils of the school ought to be shown, therefore, "that cleanliness when it is moderate is an agreeable virtue; but it is criminal, when it is excessive, through the pleasure, and the badly employed time that one spends on it. . . ." [95] They should also be taught how to manage household servants and slaves, since this is a great responsibility for mothers of families.

In describing how this responsibility should be carried out, Azeredo Coutinho gives us precious insights into the society of his times and the attitudes that people of his position had toward the serving class and domestic slaves. "The Directress should tell them [the pupils], that even though they should treat their maids and female slaves with love, and charity, they should not withal treat them with such familiarity as to breed contempt for them [their mistresses]. . . ." [96] On the other hand, the girls were to be made to understand quite plainly that servants and slaves were not to be looked upon as people of another kind, as though they had been created for the convenience of their employers and their masters.

. . . God did not create mankind to be servants, or slaves; . . . it is a brutal error to believe, that some people are born to flatter the laziness, and the pride of others; . . . we are all brothers, and children of the same Father: but . . . the necessity of some, and the slavery of others, imposed by human laws, or as a penalty for their crimes, or to save them from a greater evil, to which their very barbarity had subjected them, or their victorious enemies, were what established this accidental inequality, which we observe throughout the world; . . . the service, that one furnishes another, is for the interest of both; and . . . it is thus necessary to sweeten it, as much as possible, so that both may be satisfied; . . . if employers, and masters, who are born in abundance, and had a good education, are even so filled with defects, and of errors, it should not be looked upon as strange, that servants, and slaves have them too, in the absence of means of education, and of the examples of virtue, and of honor.[97]

Azeredo Coutinho would have his school girls learn that they must run their future households in such a way as to keep themselves and their servants and slaves busy. They must indeed learn that every man has the obligation to work in this life, which stems from God's injunction to Adam, that thenceforth he will live by the sweat of his brow. Finally, the girls had to be taught to handle money so as to avoid, on the one hand, extravagance, and, on the other, avarice.

The future mother and homemaker from Boavista likewise ought to know reading, writing, and arithmetic. She would begin with the alphabet and proceed from there, in studied progression, to words and sentences. Particular attention should be paid to pronunciation. Pupils should not be allowed to invert letters *("breço"* for *"berço")* or suppress them *("fio"* for *"filho," "Portugá"* for *"Portugal").* They should avoid reading haltingly or in a sing-song manner or through the nose. There were two nonacademic subjects, sewing and embroidery. Some also were taught music.

The rules and regulations that he prepared for the two schools of the diocese are a measure, in more than symbolic terms, of the kind of man that he was. He was not interested in philosophy or theology, and indeed he never wrote upon these subjects,[98] though he was aware of philosophical and theological principles and ideas. His publications are concerned with matters that were legal, political, and economic. Even his studies on slavery and the slave trade, which we shall mention below, may be classified under these latter headings. He must have been, on the level of his intelligence, the typical product of the new University of Coimbra, the man of action who was interested in the concrete, not in the theoretical. He himself was aware of the nonecclesiastical nature of his intellectual bents.

. . . I have to satisfy those who perhaps accuse me of occupying myself with a study that is more proper to a Farmer, and a Business Man, than to a Bishop; it is necessary to remind them that before I was a Bishop, I already was, as I still am, a citizen linked to the interests of the State; and that the objects, that I treat do not offend Religion, nor my state of life: when I was a Student I did not know, nor did I think, that I would be a bishop . . . it is a duty to serve the State, that honors me, that supports me, and that defends me. . . .[99]

What he thought about slavery and the slave trade he expressed in appropriate places throughout his published pieces, as, for example, in the statutes for the boarding school for girls of Boavista, but especially in two tracts.[100] The first was the better known in wider European circles. It was placed before the Congress of Verona in 1822 as a refutation of the English view on the abolition of the slave trade.[101]

Insofar as slavery itself was concerned, Azeredo Coutinho's ideas were those of a right-minded planter. He believed that slaves should be cherished and protected, if only for the self-interest of the master. As he pointed out in the statutes for his *Recolhimento,* a slave that dies prematurely through wretched treatment is a great loss to his owner. Referring to Brazil, the Bishop wrote:

Some Masters more through ambition, and force of temper, than through justice, punish their slaves with rigor, and cruelty, much more than their crimes require; and for that reason they give them the occasion, either to get sick, or to escape to the backwoods: others to save the little food, and clothing, that they should give their slaves, let them die of hunger, and of wretchedness without realizing, that they lose more than they gain; either from the profits, that might have accrued to them from the services of those slaves, if they had not fallen sick, or had not escaped; or from the losses, that occur when they have to spend large amounts of money, to buy new slaves to serve them; amounts very much above the sum of all of their stingy economies.[102]

Masters who acted in this foolish fashion, the Bishop said, totally lacked common sense and showed "a brutal ignorance of their own interests. . . ." [103] He went so far, in his concern for the well-being of the slaves and their greater productivity as workers, to draw up the text of a law that he felt should be passed "to oblige the master not to abuse the condition of his slave." [104] Yet he had no qualms of conscience about the morality of slavery itself, and he urged his fellow Christians not to allow themselves to be misled by the libertarian propaganda of their times.

> If in accordance with the principles of the [doctrinaire] partisans of the Philosophical Sect anyone upon his own authority is permitted to raise his voice in the midst of a nation to defend the rights that are said to be those of liberty and of oppressed humanity, they ought not to accuse me of commiting a crime if I, upon the authority of religion, and of the state, for the purpose of calming the consciences of the people of my Diocese, and of working for the welfare of all my fellow citizens, should also raise my voice against a sect of hypocrites, who with the pretext of defending the chimerical rights of liberty, and of humanity, have shown themselves to be the enemies of thrones, and of religion, arming their very own fellow citizens one against the others, tearing apart the bosom of the same Fatherland, that gave them being.[105]

In his historical account of the development of slavery as it was practiced by Europeans, Azeredo Coutinho pointed out that Negro slavery in America, and especially in Brazil, "was born, who would have believed it? from humanity itself, from the sweet, and tender affection, that Las Casas had for his beloved Indians, whose Protector he was at the time that he was also their Apostle." [106] The use of slaves in the New World, he thought, grew out of a perfectly natural situation. In any society whatever, or in a well-regulated nation.

> it is absolutely necessary for the welfare, and existence of everybody, that some people sow bread, others knead it, others bake it, others keep it, others distribute it, etc. Of all these kinds of work, the one that is carried out in the sun, and in the rain is the hardest, and demands proportionate physical strength; but it is absolutely necessary, and indispensable under pain of everybody's death: labor that is performed in the sun, and in the rain is always constrained, and imposed, either through the force of hunger, or through the force of those who have the greater force in their hands; Philosophers call those who work in the sun, and in the rain the slaves of others; let them call them what they will; the truth is, that much of the labor, that the workers of Europe used to do, was substituted, and done by the slave workers of Africa; those of Europe began to join the class of those who work in the shade, the class of crafts-

men, businessmen, scholars, and finally the class of the rich, the free, and the civilized.[107]

In other words, Europe could not have become rich, free, and civilized without slaves from Africa.[108]

Las Casas, Azeredo Coutinho said, by advocating Negro slavery as a means of protecting the Indians of the New World, "produced, even though unwittingly, an immense result; he stabilized without a doubt the bases of the wealth of the two Worlds; he was a great Statesman without wishing to be, more than a sensible man: without the Negroes the Colonies would have been useless. . . ." [109] Yet this wealth was being attacked by philosophers whose ideas against the right of property had spread with the spread of the ideas of the French Revolution; ". . . it is necessary that such Philosophers now appear without a mask in the face of the World, as leaders of indigent bands, fighting rich Property Owners in order to rob them of their lands, of their wealth, and of their industry. . . ." [110]

What then was the essence of Azeredo Coutinho's ideas on slavery? He believed that masters should treat their slaves well, not because he shared the humanitarian ideas of the European Enlightenment,[111] but because it was to their own self-interest. He was almost Protestant and English in his insistence that the individual should help himself and that the fruit of his labor, however exorbitant, was just and reasonable. Slavery was an integral part of the life that he had known in Brazil during his youth, and he felt no qualms of conscience about the morality of the institution itself.

His ideas on the economy of Portugal and Brazil were again neither seminal nor revolutionary. Sérgio Buarque de Holanda puts it very well when he says that "the Bishop did not belong, certainly, to the family of utopians. He fought for liberal measures or half measures, whenever they were viable and, apparently, of immediate and certain benefits." [112] It is true that he was among those responsible for the removal of certain restrictions on the Brazilian economy, such as the salt monopoly. It is true that he encouraged the development of Brazil's agricultural economy, and that he contributed, by the dithyrambic praises of the wealth of his native Brazil, to the latter-day *ufanismo* of his fellow citizens. But he could operate only within the established system, which he understood and which always merited his support.

When the events in French Santo Domingo led to the destruction of its flourishing economy, he urged the authorities to take advantage of the discomfiture of the French by increasing the production of sugar in Brazil.

His ideas on mining were basically negative, and the first chapter of his thin book on the mines of Brazil attempts to show that "gold mines are prejudicial to Portugal," [113] merely repeating what the Crown had said as early as 1700 and what Antonil wrote a few years later, that "the true mines of Brazil and Portugal" were sugar and tobacco.[114] The son of a rich landed family of the captaincy of Rio de Janeiro and, before his departure for Coimbra, a planter himself, Azeredo Coutinho's interest evidently lay in agriculture. Throughout his career he never failed to support the class from which he sprang. He was assuredly not concerned with the Industrial Revolution that was rapidly changing the face of Europe even in his own days, and he placed his faith in Portugal's economic future upon the raw materials of its colonies, upon a powerful merchant marine, and upon fishing.[115] Francisco Adolfo de Varnhagen, in his classic history of colonial Brazil, praised Azeredo Coutinho as a "great advocate of the development of the industry and commerce of Brazil," [116] but João Francisco Lisbôa did not share the encomium:

> ... what we know and read was that he advised and justified the memorable destruction of all our manufactories decreed by the Portuguese government [by the *alvará* of January 5, 1785], and later he changed his tune, even though with visible embarrassment, when the respective decree was revoked [by alvará of April 1, 1808]. He seemed to be one of those complacent and ready publicists, who write to be pleasing to royal courts, and he probably was at most a great Portuguese patriot, certainly not a Brazilian one.[117]

Lisbôa's mordant opinion of Azeredo Coutinho suffers from an apparent unwillingness to admit that a Brazilian colonial of the Bishop's generation could comfortably be both a Brazilian and a Portuguese. There was nothing unusual in this, and even José Bonifácio de Andrada e Silva, before he joined the revolutionary movement for the independence of Brazil, found nothing incongruous in his Portuguese citizenship. He had no qualms about referring to himself as a Portuguese, though a Portuguese from the principality of Brazil. Of course Azeredo Coutinho was a "great patriot" of Portugal, but this did not mean that he was not also a dedicated Brazilian.

As a matter of fact, throughout his long life, the Bishop nurtured a love for his native Brazil, suffered, indeed, from the *saudade* that comes to those, like himself, who knew that they would never go back. In his

study on the mines of Brazil, he declared that "to speak about the objects of my Native Land, or that are related to it, is a sweet pastime of
nostalgia; of that nostalgia that cannot be separated from the Native
Land, that presents itself by itself to the imagination." [118] This same
love of Brazil, and concern for Brazil's prosperity, will also help us
understand the dedication in his study on the morality of the slave
trade: "To you, fortunate Brazilians, my friends, my worthy fellow-
citizens and countrymen. . . ." [119] In the preface to his essay on the
commerce of Portugal and its colonies, Azeredo Coutinho again refers
to "the desire to serve my Native Land, even from afar, and beyond the
grave." [120]

On the other hand, as Lisbôa assuredly regrets, Azeredo Coutinho's
perennial interest in Brazil did not lead him along the path of treason;
and although biographers have said that he contributed in some way to
the independence of Brazil, there is no evidence to show that he ever
wavered in his loyalty to the Crown of Portugal. Indeed, everything
points up to the fact that, in the years following the outbreak of the
French Revolution, when subversive ideas were everywhere current,
Azeredo Coutinho wanted the Portuguese on both sides of the Atlantic
to be alerted to the dangers of their times. He exhorted his countrymen
from Brazil to remain firm in their allegiance to their legitimate sovereign. Brazil, he told them, had "hidden enemies," and he himself had
been "insulted, and persecuted . . . by inhuman and cruel agents or
sectaries of the barbarous Brissot and Robespierre, of those monsters
with a human figure, who established as a rule: 'rather the death of
colonies, than one sole principle'. . . ." [121]

He declared to his fellow Brazilians that when he wrote his tract on
the African slave trade the "principal object" was to "unmask the in-
sidious principles of the philosophical sect," to remove "from your
paradise the apple of the infernal serpent," to persuade them "to obey
the laws of your Sovereign." [122] He warned them against believing in
the sovereignty of the people, against democracy and democratic ideals.
The only person who could tell a citizen whether or not the law was in
harmony with natural law was the Sovereign himself. "There is no
longer law for man, once he sets himself up as judge of the justice of the
same Law. . . ." [123] He condemned "the system of social compacts" which
he considered to be contrary to man's nature and destructive of the
social order.[124] "Man deduces his natural rights from the necessity of
his existence." [125] He thought that the evils that surround human nature
are more than enough to torment it; "there is no need to reduce revolu-

tions to a system for its total destruction." [126] He berated the idea of popular sovereignty, that is to say, of the people understood as the lower classes. To him "people" were "a multitude of men who came together for any reason, without ties or subordination among themselves. . . ." [127] It followed, therefore, that "the system that admits the sovereignty of a rational being still in embryo" is patently absurd.[128] He admitted that what he had to say about the sovereignty of the people would not "please the person who calls himself a philosopher, this miserable being who, satisfied with himself, full of pride and arrogance, unwilling to recognize a God above him, wants to step upon and give laws to the whole world. . . ." [129] So deep were his convictions in this regard that he refused to accept the invitation to preside at a meeting of the populace of Elvas, convoked upon the departure of enemy French troops, on the grounds that he could not take part in any formal gathering that was authorized by the people.[130]

Even earlier, during his years in Pernambuco, he never once indicated in any recorded public or private utterance that he believed that the governed had any constitutional say in the conduct of the government. The parishioners of Santo Antônio de Tracunhém, as we have seen, would not tolerate the Bishop's attempt to interfere with their choice of a pastor, alleging that the election of pastors had always been a prerogative of the people ever since the first centuries of the Church. When the *Mesa da Consciência e Ordens* appointed the candidate of the parishioners to the vacancy, the Bishop complained bitterly. Writing to the Visconde de Anadia on February 2, 1802, Azeredo Coutinho stated that the *Mesa,* by so acting, had approved "tumultuous elections by the people; usurped the Right of Presentation" of the sovereign "to give it to the People, and established a rule for me to follow, which was that I should propose for Pastors, not those who in my opinion I judged to be the most worthy, or had the decisions of the examining boards in their favor, but rather those who might have more Protectors, or might be better able to carry out their intrigues, and collect the riff-raff in their support. . . ." [131] To have given in to these demands, the Bishop, told the Prince Regent in another connection, would now put us "in the midst of the horrors of the French Revolution, governed by the Sovereignty of the People, which had its origin in the daggers of the assassins of the infamous Orléans. . . ." [132] It seemed extremely dangerous to the Bishop to permit, at that critical moment, the spread of the then fashionable doctrines of elections by the people.[133]

IV

The life of Dom José Joaquim da Cunha de Azeredo Coutinho must surely have some secrets that his biographers have not yet discovered, but his stance on the issues of the day are clear from the tracts that he wrote and published. Unlike his celebrated contemporary, the Abbé de Pradt,[134] who advocated independence for the Spanish colonies, Azeredo Coutinho was determined that Portugal should hold on to its own. In other ways, both men had much in common. Both achieved success in the ecclesiastical hierarchy, even though de Pradt never truly enjoyed the episcopal dignity since Rome did not confirm his appointment by Napoleon as Archbishop of Malines. Both were journalists of the kind that had flourished in Europe since the time of Paul Jovius. Both were hard-working and well-meaning but superficial in their attitudes and ideas. Politically, however, de Pradt was much more liberal in his writings, much more the product of an advanced and dynamic society. Azeredo Coutinho sought only to improve the *ancien régime,* not overthrow it. He was its last apologist.

A kind Providence undoubtedly spared him much tribulation and soul-searching by taking him from this world on the eve of the collapse of the Portuguese colonial system in Brazil. Coutinho was not the political chameleon that de Pradt was, able to adapt to any situation and thrive under any change of setting, and his death in 1821, on the eve of the independence of Brazil, very likely spared him the necessity of making an agonizing adjustment to a new way of life. Probably because the Bishop was singularly untheological in his thinking and devoted to the pragmatic and practical, liberals have generally looked upon him as a precursor of the secular state, "in many ways a progressive spirit and even a herald of new times." [135] It would be more to the point to say with Sérgio Buarque de Holanda that "as a whole his work remains singularly unfruitful. The opinions and institutions with which he more generally identified himself, belonged to the past or were already in the midst of their agony. At the end of his life, on May 13, 1818, Azeredo Coutinho still accepted the appointment to the Holy Office, and he was the last Inquisitor of the Realm." [136]

NOTES

1   Sebastião da Rocha Pita, *História da América portuguêza desde o anno de mil*

e quinhentos do seu descobrimento até o de mil e setecentos e vinte e quatro offerecida á magestade augusta del-rei D. João V, nosso senhor (2nd ed., Lisbon, 1880), pp. 334–36.

2 *Ibid.,* p. 329.

3 Hélio Vianna, *História do Brasil,* I (São Paulo, 1961), 260n.

4 Rocha Pita, *História da América portuguêza,* pp. 1–2.

5 Francisco de Morais, "Estudantes na Universidade de Coimbra nascidos no Brasil," *Brasília,* supplement to vol. IV (Coimbra, 1949), pp. 75 *et seq.*

6 Luiza da Fonsêca, "Bacharéis brasileiros. Elementos biográficos (1635–1830)," Instituto Histórico e Geográfico Brasileiro, IV Congresso de História Nacional 21–28–Abril de 1949, *Anais,* XI (Rio de Janeiro, 1951), 113 *et seq.*

7 Morais, "Estudantes na Universidade de Coimbra," p. 302.

8 *Ibid.,* pp. 367–68.

9 *Ibid.,* p. 96.

10 L. Cabral de Moncada, "Mística e racionalismo em Portugal no século XVIII," *Boletim da Faculdade de Direito* (Coimbra), XXVIII (1952), 32.

11 *Ibid.,* p. 29.

12 Matias Aires Ramos da Silva de Eça, *Reflexões sôbre a vaidade dos homens, ou discursos moraes sôbre os effeitos da vaidade* (Lisbon, 1752), pp. 233–34.

13 See H. P. Biggar, *A Collection of Documents Relating to Jacques Cartier and the Sieur de Roberval* ("Publications of the Public Archives of Canada," XIV [Ottawa, 1930]), p. 190.

14 Eça, *Reflexões,* pp. 117–18.

15 *Ibid.,* p. 400.

16 *Ibid.,* preliminary unnumbered pp. 23–24.

17 For a general view of the period, see Hernâni Cidade, *Ensaio sôbre a crise mental do século XVIII* (Coimbra, 1929).

18 See the inadequate study by Augusto Casimiro, *Dona Catarina de Bragança rainha de Inglaterra, filha de Portugal* (Lisbon, 1956).

19 See A. D. Francis, *The Methuens and Portugal 1691–1708* (Cambridge, Eng., 1966).

20 *Astréa almanak maçônico para 5847* (Rio de Janeiro, 1847), p. 64.

21 Luís Antônio Verney, *Verdadeiro método de estudar* ("Colecção de clássicos Sá da Costa" [5 vols.; Lisbon, 1949–1952]). The most recent and most complete work on Verney (or Vernei) is Antônio Alberto de Andrade, *Vernei e a cultura do seu tempo* (Coimbra, 1966).

22 Verney, *Verdadeiro método de estudar,* IV, 229.

23 The shortened title of the original is *Origem infecta da relaxação da moral dos denominados jesuítas* (Lisbon: Régia Officina Typográfica, 1771).

24 The shortened title of the original is *Doutrinas da Igreja sacrilegamente offendidas pelas atrocidades da moral jesuítica* (Lisbon: Régia Officina Typográfica, 1772).

25 The *Deducção chronológica, e analytica* appeared in five volumes in 1778 and was printed by Miguel Manescal da Costa, printer of the Holy Office. The first part is in two volumes and 785 pages; the second part, in one volume and 357 pages. There are in addition two volumes of *Provas,* one for each of the two parts.

26 There is a brief account of the reform in Mário Brandão and M. Lopes d'Almeida, *A Universidade de Coimbra esbôço da sua história* (Coimbra, 1937). See also M. Lopes d'Almeida, *Documentos da Reforma Pombalina,* I *(1771–1782)* (Coimbra, 1937). There is a crying need for a complete study of the University of Coimbra before and after 1772.

27 There are numerous (though incomplete) biographies of Azeredo Coutinho.

The most recent are by Sérgio Buarque de Holanda, *Obras econômicas de J.J. da Cunha de Azeredo Coutinho (1794–1804)* (São Paulo, 1966), pp. 13–53, and by E. Bradford Burns, "The Role of Azeredo Coutinho in the Enlightenment of Brazil," *The Hispanic American Historical Review*, XLIV (1964), 145–60.

28 See particularly Morais, "Estudantes na Universidade de Coimbra," pp. 194–95, and *A gratidão parnambucana ao seu bemfeitor o Ex.mo e R.mo Senhor D. José da Cunha de Azeredo Coutinho . . . O. D. e C. os socios da Academia Parnambucana, e os alumnos do seminario olindense* (Lisbon, 1808), pp. 31–32, notes. Hereinafter cited as *A gratidão parnambucana*.

29 Morais, "Estudantes na Universidade de Coimbra," pp. 194–95.

30 *Ibid.*, pp. 163–64.

31 This biographical information is taken from *ibid.*

32 Heliodoro Pires, "Azeredo Coutinho," *Revista do Instituto Histórico e Geográphico Brasileiro*, Tomo Especial Consagrado ao Primeiro Congresso de História Nacional (Sept. 7–16, 1914), Part I (Rio de Janeiro, 1915), 789.

33 José de Souza Azevedo Pizarro de Araújo, *Memórias históricas do Rio de Janeiro*, VI (Rio de Janeiro, 1946), 111.

34 Pires, "Azeredo Coutinho," p. 789.

35 Araújo, *Memórias históricas do Rio de Janeiro*, p. 111.

36 The examination took place on July 30, 1785. Morais, "Estuantes na Universidade de Coimbra," p. 297.

37 Pires, "Azeredo Coutinho," p. 790, says that he became a member of the academy in 1791. In the secretariat of the academy, Azeredo Coutinho is today (1968) variously listed: as a "sócio honorário," elected April 18, 1792; as a "sócio livre," named on the same date; as a "correspondente," elected on the same date; as a "sócio livre," elected on March 17, 1794; and finally as a "sócio honorário," elected on Nov. 26, 1818.

38 Araújo, *Memórias históricas do Rio de Janeiro*, p. 111.

39 Azeredo Coutinho to Martinho de Melo e Castro, Lisbon, Dec. 20, 1794, Arquivo Histórico Ultramarino (hereinafter cited as AHU), "Pernambuco, Caixa for 1795."

40 See *Estatutos do seminário episcopal de N. Senhora da Grasa da cidade de Olinda de Parnambuco ordenados por D. Jozé Joaquim da Cunha de Azeredo Coutinho, XII. bispo de Parnambuco do Conselho de S. Magestade Fidelíssima, fundador do mesmo seminário* (Lisbon, 1798). Hereinafter cited as *Estatutos do seminário*.

41 *Estatutos do recolhimento de N. Senhora da Gloria do lugar da Bôa-Vista de Parnambuco: ordenados por D. Jozé Joaquim da Cunha de Azeredo Coutinho, bispo de Parnambuco do Conselho de S. Magestade Fidelisima* (Lisbon, 1798). Hereinafter cited as *Estatutos do recolhimento*.

42 In 1796 the school maintained by Oratorians of Pernambuco had a faculty of seven and a student body of twelve. Dom Tomás de Melo, governor of Pernambuco, to Luís Pinto de Sousa, Recife, Feb. 26, 1796, AHU, "Pernambuco," Caixa 8, 1796.

43 *Estatutos do seminário*, p. 105.

44 The approval for the seminary was dated Jan. 29, 1798. Published in *ibid.*

45 *A gratidão parnambucana*, p. 1, says that he arrived on Dec. 25, 1799, but this must be a typographical error. Azeredo Coutinho gives the date of his arrival in his letter to Dom Rodrigo de Sousa Coutinho, the overseas secretary, Recife, Feb. 9, 1799, AHU, "Pernambuco," Caixa 17, 1799.

46 The poems are published in *A gratidão parnambucana*.

47 There is a copy of the letter in AHU, "Pernambuco," Caixa 17, 1799.

48 Azeredo Coutinho to Dom Rodrigo de Sousa Coutinho, Recife, Feb. 9, 1799, cited above, n. 45.

49 Royal Letter to Dom Tomás José de Melo, Queluz, April 13, 1798, AHU, "Pernambuco," Caixa 15, 1798.

50 Azeredo Coutinho to the Provisional Governors of Pernambuco, Recife, Sept. 9, 1801, AHU, "Pernambuco," Caixa 33, 1801–1802.

51 Azeredo Coutinho to Dom Rodrigo de Sousa Coutinho, Recife, April 8, 1800, AHU, "Pernambuco," Caixa 31, 1802.

52 L. F. Tollenare, "Notas Dominicaes Tomadas durante uma Viagem em Portugal e no Brasil em 1816, 1817, e 1818," trans. Alfredo de Carvalho, *Revista do Instituto Archeológico e Geográphico Pernambucano*, XI, 436.

53 Francisco Muniz Tavares, *História da Revolução de Pernambuco de 1817*, ed. Manoel de Oliveira Lima (Recife, 1917), p. 39.

54 There are many pertinent documents in AHU, "Pernambuco," Caixas 18 (1799), 23 (1800), and 33 (1801–1802).

55 There is abundant documentation in AHU, "Pernambuco," Caixa 21, 1799–1800.

56 Holanda, *Obras econômicas de Coutinho*, p. 17.

57 *Ibid.* I did not find anything on the so-called conspiracy in any of the Pernambuco caixas that I consulted in the AHU.

58 Tavares, *História da Revolução*, p. 35.

59 Luís Gonçalves dos Santos, *Memórias para servir á historia do reino do Brazil, dividido em três epocas da felicidade, honra, e glória; escriptas na côrte do Rio de Janeiro no anno de 1821 e offerecidas a S. Magestade Elrei nosso senhor o senhor D. João VI*, II (Lisbon, 1825), 273–76.

60 *Defeza de D. José Joaquim da Cunha de Azeredo Coutinho, Bispo de Elvas, em outro tempo de Pernambuco, Eleito de Bragança, e Miranda, Governador Interino da Capitania de Pernambuco, Presidente da Junta da Fazenda, Director Geral dos Estados, do Conselho de S. Magestade, &c. &c. &c.* (Lisbon, 1808).

61 *Ibid., passim.*

62 See especially Azeredo Coutinho to Dom Rodrigo de Sousa Coutinho, Recife, Feb. 9, 1799. He gives his first impressions of Pernambuco in this letter.

63 *Idem* to *idem*, Recife, June 19, 1799, AHU, "Pernambuco," Caixa 18, 1799, cited above, n. 45.

64 Azeredo Coutinho to the Visconde de Anadia, Olinda, Feb. 2, 1802, AHU, "Pernambuco," Caixa 33, 1802.

65 The letter cited is in AHU, "Pernambuco," Caixa 31, 1802. The comments of the advisors (not identified) are appended to the Bishop's letter.

66 The Regent's letter is appended to Azeredo Coutinho's letter to the Prince Regent himself, Jan. 12, 1802, AHU, "Pernambuco," Caixa 35, 1802.

67 *Ibid.*

68 Azeredo Coutinho to the Visconde de Anadia, Olinda, Feb. 2, 1802, AHU, "Pernambuco," Caixa 33, 1802.

69 Holanda, *Obras econômicas de Coutinho*, pp. 18 *et seq.*

70 Provisional Governors of Pernambuco to the Visconde de Anadia, AHU, "Pernambuco," Caixa 35, 1802.

71 *Alegasaõ juridica, Na qual se mostra, que saõ do Padroado da Coroa, e naõ da Ordem Militar de Cristo, as Igrejas, Dignidades, e Benefícios dos Bispados do Cabo de Bojador para o Sul, em que se compreendem os Bispados de Cabo Verde, S. Thomé, Angola, Brazil, India, até á China. Oferecida a sua alteza real o príncipe do Brazil regente de Portugal* (Lisbon, 1804).

72 Holanda, *Obras econômicas de Coutinho*, p. 18.

73 *A gratidão parnambucana*, p. 195.

74   Provisional Governors of Pernambuco to the Visconde de Anadia, Recife, July 27, 1802 cited above, n. 70. *A gratidão parnambucana*, p. 195, says that he left on July 13. The date is given as July 5 by Lino do Monte Carmelo Luna, *Memória, histórica e biográphica do clero pernambucano* (Pernambuco, 1857) , p. 91.

75   Araújo, *Memórias históricas do Rio de Janeiro*, pp. 111–12.

76   *Ibid.*, p. 112.

77   *Ibid.*

78   Burns, "The Role of Coutinho in the Enlightenment," p. 158.

79   Tavares, *História da Revolução*, pp. 84–85, believes that Azeredo Coutinho's ideas on free trade served as a mental preparation for the independence of Brazil, and that his seminary still more directly served the same cause. Burns, "The Role of Coutinho in the Enlightenment," p. 145, says that Azeredo Coutinho contributed to the introduction of the Enlightenment in Brazil and significantly, albeit unintentionally, to the independence of Brazil. Both of these authors must be read, in this connection, with a grain of salt. I shall have something more to say below on Azeredo Coutinho's loyalty to the Crown.

80   *Estatutos do seminário*, pp. 60–61.

81   *Estatutos do recolhimento*, p. 1.

82   *Estatutos para os estudos da província de N. S.ra da Conceição do Rio de Janeiro, ordenados segundo as disposições dos estatutos da nóva universidade* (Lisbon, 1776) , p. 5.

83   *Ibid.*, unnumbered p. 3.

84   *Estatutos do seminário*, p. 79.

85   *A gratidão parnambucana*, preliminary p. 3.

86   *Ibid.*, p. 199, n. 1.

87   *Estatutos do recolhimento*, p. 12.

88   *Ibid.*, p. 22.

89   *Ibid.*, p. 30.

90   *Ibid.*, p. 37.

91   *Ibid.*

92   *Ibid.*, p. 61.

93   *Ibid.*, p. 70; *Index librorum prohibitorum ss.mi D. N. Pii PP. XII* (Rome, 1940) , p. 98.

94   *Ibid.*, pp. 80 *et seq.*

95   *Ibid.*, p. 88.

96   *Ibid.*, p. 89.

97   *Ibid.*, p. 90.

98   *Respostas dadas por D. José Joaquim da Cunha de Azeredo Coutinho, bispo de Elvas, então bispo de Pernambuco, ás propostas feitas por alguns dos parochos d'aquelle diocese* (Lisbon: João Rodrigues Neves, 1808) is a thin little moral treatise that hardly nullifies what we have said about his lack of theological and philosophical concerns.

99   *Discurso sôbre o estado actual das minas do Brazil dividido em quatro capitulos* (Lisbon, 1804) , pp. 9–10.

100   The first edition of *Análise sôbre a justiça do comércio do resgate dos escravos da costa da África* appeared in London in French translation in 1798; the second edition, in Lisbon, in Portuguese, in 1808. The second edition is reprinted in Holanda, *Obras econômicas de Coutinho*, pp. 231 *et seq.* I shall cite the Holanda edition as *Análise*.

    Concordância das leis de Portugal, e das bullas pontíficas, das quaes humas permittem a escravidão dos pretos d'Africa, e outras prohibem a escrivadão dos índios do Brazil (Lisbon, 1808) . Hereinafter cited as *Concordância*.

101   J. H. Pereira da Silva, *Plutarco brasileiro*, II (Rio de Janeiro, 1847) , 104n.

102 *Estatutos do recolhimento,* p. 91.
103 *Ibid.*
104 *Análise,* pp. 304–307.
105 *Concordância,* p. 3.
106 *Ibid.,* p. 11.
107 *Ibid.,* pp. 15–16.
108 *Ibid.,* p. 16.
109 *Ibid.,* p. 17.
110 *Ibid.,* p. 7.
111 Holanda, *Obras econômicas de Coutinho,* p. 53.
112 *Ibid.,* p. 37.
113 *Discurso sôbre o estado actual das minas do Brazil dividido em quatro capítulos* (Lisbon, 1804) , p. 13.
114 See my study "The Brazilian Gold Rush," *The Americas,* III (1946) , 148–49.
115 See his *Ensaio econômico sôbre o commércio de Portugal e suas colónias publicado de ordem da Academia Real das Sciências* (63rd ed.; Lisbon, 1828) . The work also appears in Holanda, *Obras econômicas de Coutinho.*
116 Visconde de Pôrto Seguro, *História geral do Brasil antes da sua separação e independência de Portugal,* V (3rd ed.; São Paulo, n.d.) , 17.
117 *Ibid.,* p. 17, n. 38.
118 *Discurso sôbre o estado actual das minas do Brazil,* p. 11.
119 *Análise,* p. 233.
120 *Ensaio econômico,* p. xx.
121 *Análise,* p. 233.
122 *Ibid.,* p. 233.
123 *Ibid.,* p. 235.
124 *Ibid.,* p. 238.
125 *Ibid.,* p. 239.
126 *Ibid.,* p. 304, n. 2.
127 *Ibid.,* p. 296.
128 *Ibid.,* p. 297.
129 *Ibid.,* p. 298.
130 *Cópia Da Carta Que a Sua Magestade o Senhor Rey D. João VI. (sendo Príncipe Regente de Portugal) escreveo o Bispo D'Elvas em 1816* (London, 1817) , pp. 20 *et seq.,* in Holanda, *Obras econômicas de Coutinho,* p. 26.
131 AHU, "Pernambuco," Caixa 33, 1802. My translation of the original is not literal, but a literal translation would not have conveyed, in my opinion, the meaning.
132 Azeredo Coutinho to the Prince Regent, Olinda, Jan. 12, 1802, AHU, "Pernambuco," Caixa 35, 1802.
133 *Ibid.*
134 See Manuel Aguirre Elorriaga, *El Abate de Pradt en la emancipación hispanoamericana (1800–1830)* (2nd ed.; Buenos Aires, 1946) .
135 Holanda, *Obras econômicas de Coutinho,* p. 53.
136 *Ibid.*

COMMENTARY

E. Bradford Burns
Columbia University, New York City

The Portuguese language, rich as it is, has no specific word to designate the Enlightenment, that intense questioning and reasoning which characterized the eighteenth century. Variously and indiscriminately employed are the words *as luzes, as idéias francêsas, o esclarecimento, a ilustração,* and *o iluminismo.* A few years ago I informally presented the problem to the second Simpósio dos Professôres Universitários da História being held at the Universidade do Paraná. After an animated discussion, they failed to concur on any one word which might designate that culminant period of intellectual ferment. Perhaps that imprecise approach to the subject indicates a lack of interest and, to some degree, lack of awareness. It certainly does not indicate that the Enlightenment failed to impress itself upon and manifest itself within the Portuguese Empire. Quite the contrary occurred in both the metropolis and its principal colony. The Enlightenment, whatever be its name in Portuguese, bloomed in Brazil where the urban elite carefully nurtured it. Its presence is probably most easily identifiable by its contributions to the mental formation of Brazil, the Brazilians' pride in and knowledge of their own land, and independence. Those formidable contributions apparently were not enough to entice even one Brazilian scholar to write even one penetrating essay on the subject. Although North American scholars have produced some gems of scholarship on the Enlightenment in Spanish America, they have been reticent to duplicate those accomplishments for Portuguese America. The one exception, Alexander Marchant's pioneer essay "Aspects of the Enlightenment in Brazil," deserves our applause.[1] Usually, however, when and if the subject of Brazil's colonial intellectual history is mentioned, we tend to la-

104

ment the lack of a printing press and university and mumble something about retarded intellectual development. But that is hardly the true story and one day this appealing and significant subject will attract the scholars it merits and we will all discover in due course that Brazil did indeed have an Enlightenment, not as glorious as that of France of course, but fully comparable to that of Mexico and Peru.

There are a number of rather obvious starting points to initiate such a study of Brazil's Enlightenment. One certainly would be the various academies of the eighteenth century which appeared and disappeared sporadically in the two principal cities. We all know them by name: Academia Brasílica dos Esquecidos (Bahia, 1724–1725), Academia dos Felizes (Rio de Janeiro, 1736–1740), Academia dos Selectos (Rio de Janeiro, 1751–1752), Academia Brasílica dos Renacidos (Bahia, 1759–1760), Academia Scientífica (Rio de Janeiro, 1771–1772), and Sociedade Literária (Rio de Janeiro, 1786–1794). Beyond those attractive names, surprisingly little is known. True, one can compile a respectably long bibliography,[2] but bibliographic length does not necessarily denote strength, and this bibliography is flabby. A general conclusion easily deduced after reading the material is that original research has been kept to a minimum and that what has been done has not been digested. For example, the Visconde de São Leopoldo reprinted a number of informative documents but failed to incorporate the new facts or the significance of them into his text. Broad horizons of investigation are open before the student interested in the academies.

A second approach to a fuller study of the Brazilian Enlightenment would be through the libraries extant in the eighteenth and early nineteenth centuries. Apparently, many of the literate *élite* collected books and boasted of excellent libraries. Travelers to Brazil in the early nineteenth century remarked on this. Thomas Lindley, visiting Bahia in 1803, remembered a Father Francisco Augustinho Gomes whose library was, to use Lindley's expression, "very complete" in English and French works. He mentioned by name Buffon, Lavoisier, and d'Alembert.[3] In Pernambuco, the Frenchman L.F. de Tollenare commented on the literary preferences before the Revolution of 1817: "The French works are the most sought after and among those all the writers . . . of the philosophy of the eighteenth century." [4] John Luccock spoke of the brisk book trade in Rio de Janeiro in 1818 where "French books are in demand." [5] And in Minas Gerais in 1828, the visitor R. Walsh admired the large selection of foreign books in evidence, calling special attention to the works of Voltaire, Rousseau, Raynal, and Adam

Smith and mentioning "many which appeared in the early part of the French Revolution." [6] As late as the early 1840's one can still find references which indicate that books were one of the main bridges over which the ideas of the European Enlightenment migrated to the New World. I quote here at length from Daniel P. Kidder partly because of his quaintness and partly because it sums up this point:

Book auctions, indeed, are of very frequent occurrence. Europeans who are about to retire to their native country, and Brazilians who go abroad, generally dispose of their libraries by public sale. It is often painful to witness, on these occasions, the vast amount of infidel literature in circulation. The works of Voltaire, of Volney, and of Rousseau, are offered almost daily to the highest bidder, and bidders are always found.[7]

The studies of late colonial libraries have been few but their quality surpasses those devoted to the academies. Outstanding among them is Eduardo Frieiro's *O diabo na livraría do cônego* (Belo Horizonte, 1957), a witty analysis of the library of Canon Luís Vieira da Silva, a participant in the *Inconfidência*. He owned a magnificent collection of nearly 800 books and 270 titles representing all of Europe's foremost thinkers of the seventeenth and eighteenth centuries. The implication was—and the Portuguese government did not hesitate to draw it —that he was influenced enough by what he read to conspire for Brazil's independence. Clado Ribeiro de Lessa has given a suggestive summary history of libraries in his "As bibliotecas brasileiras dos tempos coloniais" (*RIHGB,* CXCI [1946], 329–35). His footnotes reveal further sources to investigate. Religious libraries received the careful attention of Serafim Leite in his monumental *História da Companhia de Jesús no Brasil* (10 vols.; Rio de Janeiro, 1938–1950). In Volume IV, he listed the inventory of the Jesuit library at the Casa da Vigia, Pará, and commented: "That library, shining like a spotlight in the colonial forests of Brazil, contained a little of everything" (p. 410). In Volume V, he discussed the library of the Jesuit College in Bahia (pp. 92–95). Indeed, throughout his multi-volume study, references appear to Jesuit libraries. Sílvio Gabriel Diniz, in his "Biblioteca Setecentista nas Minas Gerais" (*Revista do Instituto Histórico e Geográfico de Minas Gerais,* VI [1959], 333–44), spoke in general terms of libraries in that captaincy of gold-mining fame and then listed books which belonged to some churchmen during the eighteenth century. A more revealing inventory can be found in "Sequestro feito em 1794 nos bens que forão achados do

Bacharel Mariano José Pereira da Fonsêca extrahido do respectivo processo" (*RIHGB,* LXIII, Part 1 [1901], 14–18). Many of the works were in French. In my own article, "The Enlightenment in Two Colonial Brazilian Libraries" *The Journal of the History of Ideas,* XXV [July–Sept., 1964], 430–38), I examined the books which belonged to Resende da Costa, Senior and Junior, both participants in the *Inconfidência,* and to Batista Caetano de Almeida, a liberal reformer of the First Empire and Regency period. The list of authors represented in those rich libraries reads like a roll call of the European Enlightenment.

These studies simply hint at the amount of research yet to be done. Gabriel Diniz mentioned in his essay a manuscript in the Arquivo Público Mineiro, classified among the miscellaneous books of the Delegacia Fiscal, Seção Colonial, which "gives as the property of the deceased some lists of books which constituted their libraries" (p. 338). His footnotes further disclosed other documentary material on this subject to be found in the Arquivo Público Mineiro. In the catalog *A Coleção da Casa dos Contos de Ouro Preto* compiled by Herculano Gomes Mathias (Rio de Janeiro, 1966) there is information (p. 145) about the library that the physician Antônio Teixeira da Costa brought to Minas Gerais in 1791. The names of Voltaire, Montesquieu, Raynal, and Rousseau figure prominently in that document. Neither the hearings on the Inconfidência Mineira or on the *Inconfidência* Bahiana have been fully studied for bibliographic information, although the documents from both inquiries have been published for some years now: *A Inconfidência da Bahia. Devassas e sequestros* (2 vols.; Rio de Janeiro, 1931), reprinted from Volumes XLIII, XLIV, and XLV of the *Anaes da Biblioteca Nacional* and the *Autos de devassa da Inconfidência Mineira* (7 vols.; Rio de Janeiro, 1936–1937).

I would venture to suggest that probably the richest source of information on eighteenth-century libraries will be the *inventários* meticulously drawn up after the death of men of property. Everything from the smallest *objet d'art* to the largest building appeared in those inventários. If the deceased owned a library, the books will be enumerated by author and title. The director of the Arquivo Público da Bahia informed me that his archive contained many such inventários. I checked the one left by the statesman-physician José Lino Coutinho (1784–1836) and found a careful inventory of his extensive library. A few of the many European authors present were: Jean Duplan, Johann Spurzheim, Henry Thorton, Condorcet, d'Alembert, Jeremy Bentham, Montesquieu, Holbach, Mirabeau, Pradt, Racine, and Voltaire. Also there were two titles by the chief representatives of the Enlightenment in North America: Benjamin Franklin, *The Works of Dr. Benjamin Franklin* (2 vols.; London, 1793) and Thomas Jefferson, *A Manual of Parliamentary Practice* (Washington, 1801) .[8] If my understanding is correct, the state archives throughout Brazil hold numerous such inventários. Not everyone owned a library, it is true, but certainly an informative intellectual profile of the educated elite in the late colonial period, when the Enlightenment flowered in Brazil, will come from an analysis of the book lists in those inventários.

Practically nothing is known of the book trade in colonial Brazil. An occasional visitor mentioned *en passant* the presence of some book dealer in one or another of the ports. The *Almanaques* for Rio de Janeiro prepared by Antônio Duarte Nunes reveal that for the years 1792 and 1794 there was a bookseller in the capital. In 1799 there were two. What they sold and how they obtained their books are simply two of many fascinating and unanswered questions. From the few studies made of private libraries, one cannot help but be impressed with the catholicity of languages which the books represented. The Portuguese, French, English, Latin, Spanish, and Italian languages were well represented, with Portuguese and French predominating. As impressive as the number of languages is the great variety of cities in which those books were published. All the major and many of the minor European cities were represented. Paris seems to predominate. Such diversity speaks well for the book agents of the period, who were able to gather volumes from all over Europe and market them in Brazil.

A third approach to the Enlightenment in Brazil is through the study of the men who contributed to it. Serious studies of such men are minimal, to be more realistic, almost nonexistent. Who best represents the applied Enlightenment in Brazil? Probably Alexandre Rodrigues Ferreira. That naturalist perambulated through Amazônia for a decade, 1783–1793, collecting specimens, sketching, writing reports. He was following the first dictum of the physiocrats who exerted such a powerful influence on the Luso-Brazilian Enlightenment: to study the land and to know its potential. Professor José Antônio de Sá had advised in his classic of Portuguese physiocrat thought, *Compêndio de observaçoens que formão o plano da viagem politica e filosófica que se deve fazer dentro da pátria:*

The entire country, in which reforms are to be instituted, must be visited. The best reason dictates this, and the practice of other nations demonstrates it. Agriculture is in a state of decadence. The cause is either moral or physical. In order to find suitable measures to overcome the obstacles and to make reforms, it is necessary to find out as much as possible about the talent, habits, and quality of the farmers; about their land and customs of leasing land; about their methods of farming; the nature of the land, etc. There is little industry in the provinces and one ought to find out the cause of it. Is it because of the carelessness of the inhabitants, because of the lack of primary materials, or because of the lack of suitable locations for factories? All these and other things should be observed by the traveler.[9]

Rodrigues was engaged in doing just that and it is not for nothing that he entitled his unpublished master work "Viagem Filosófica." Despite the Herculean contributions of this remarkably skilled intellect, there is not a decent essay, much less a worthy book, about him. Several biographical studies are, quite frankly, travesties. Brazilians readily acknowledge him as a genius, yet no one is willing to edit and publish the countless manuscripts he left, now lying restlessly in the achives of Rio de Janeiro, Belém, and Lisbon. Frei José Mariano de Conceição Vellozo has fared only slightly better. At least his magnum opus, *Flora fluminensis,* has been published. José Bonifácio de Andrada e Silva also qualifies as one of the major figures of the Brazilian Enlightenment but since he is also the national hero, "the Patriarch of Independence," it is impossible to make an impartial and critical study of him. Consequently, eulogistic pap has reduced him to a caricature, the traditional fate which befalls the "untouchables."

A fourth candidate to represent the Brazilian Enlightenment would be the good Bishop José Joaquim da Cunha de Azeredo Coutinho to whom my colleague, Manoel Cardozo, devotes some attention, for which I thank him. This complex man must baffle all who consider him seriously. In his complexity and contradiction perhaps he faithfully represents the entire colony at that perplexing moment of change and fluctuation. On the one hand, an enthusiast of the Enlightenment, he advocated new ideas and desired to implement them; on the other, the old conservative spirit breathed deeply within him. After all, he served as the Grand Inquisitor of the Realm. Someone should put the dear old man to rest on a psychiatrist's couch with the hope of finding some unity in his diversity. But that master study remains to be done.

Despite his high posts and prolific writing, Azeredo Coutinho has never had a biographer. Studies about him until very recently have been thumbnail sketches, with each succeeding author copying—and frequently miscopying—the bombastic phrases of his predecessors. The work of several scholars will be necessary to rectify the errors of the past and to put Azeredo Coutinho in the proper perspective.

A few years ago, in an article entitled "The Role of Azeredo Coutinho in the Enlightenment of Brazil" (*Hispanic American Historical Review,* XLIV [May, 1964], 145–60), I attempted to portray him as a transplanter of ideas from Europe to Brazil. One obvious example was the direct connection between the Coimbra reformed by the Pombaline statutes of 1772 and the seminary Azeredo Coutinho established at Olinda in 1800. Azeredo Coutinho had enrolled in Coimbra in 1775, at the very time Pombal's innovations were propelling the university out of the past and headlong into the contemporary intellectual changes besetting Europe. To an extent unthought-of before, the university's instructors replaced theory with practice, speculation with experiment, dogma with questioning. A new observatory, medical amphitheater, botanical garden, and physics and chemistry laboratories contributed to that trend. Many of the faculty adopted the ideas of the French physiocrats. Much of what Azeredo Coutinho observed and learned there appeared later in his seminary. He repudiated the Jesuit pedagogic methods, strongly influenced by Aristotelian theory, which still predominated in the moribund colonial educational system, and introduced enough innovation based on Cartesian doctrines to initiate a change in the intellectual atmosphere of Pernambuco. Those new ideas, clearly seen at work in his seminary in Olinda, emphasized the sciences and arts in order to "illuminate the darkness" of the past centuries and to dispel ignorance and superstition.[10] Perhaps one measure of his success in introducing new techniques and ideas into the colony was that a high percentage of the leaders of the Revolution of 1817 had studied at his seminary. Their words and actions testified that they had imbibed heavily of enlightened ideology.

More recently the Brazilians have re-edited four of his major essays on Brazil in a handsome volume, *Obras econômicas de J. J. da Cunha de Azeredo Coutinho* (São Paulo, 1966), first in a series entitled "Roteiro do Brasil." In a forty-page, perceptive introduction, the eminent Brazilian historian Sérgio Buarque de Holanda offered one of the most mature studies yet made of this churchman. Of considerable importance is an appendix, "Relação das Obras Citadas por Azeredo Coutinho," which carefully tabulates all the authors and works he quoted or referred to. The obvious conclusion drawn from an examination of this list is that the Inquisitor General read widely, was conversant with the latest European literature, and had immersed himself deeply in the ideas of the Enlightenment.

I noted with special interest that Azeredo Coutinho cited two works of the foremost intellects of the Portuguese Enlightenment, Antônio Nunes Ribeiro Sanchez: *Tratado da conservação da saúde dos pôvos* and *Dissertation sur l'origine de la maladie vénérienne.* There was no mention of a third, *Cartas sôbre a educação da mocidade.* Yet, I could not help think that the Brazilian must have read those well known "letters" also. One can trace in the writings of the Bishop many of the ideas his predecessor discussed. Ribeiro Sanchez, for example, believed that gold was the curse of Brazil and that agriculture would be its salvation. As a matter of fact, he pointed to agriculture, commerce, and shipping as the "holy trinity" for Brazilian development.[11] It might be just a coincidence, but Azeredo Coutinho likewise put forth the same ideas, about a half-century later.

This newly edited collection is both worthwhile and valuable, but it does not exhaust the possibilities. Still resting in the Seção de Manuscritos of the Biblioteca Nacional in Rio de Janeiro are two intriguing manuscripts by the Bishop which should be published: "Medidas e providências administrativas do Governo Internio da Capitania de Pernambuco desde 7 de Janeiro de 1799 até 4 de Decembro de 1802 e sôbre todos os ramos da economía pública" and "Proposta da creação do Seminário Episcopal d'Olinda e sua abertura." Other works of this fledgling economist and reformer which deal with Brazil less directly also merit republication in order to make them more accessible.

Professor Cardozo stressed several times that the eighteenth century within the vast Portuguese empire was, at least intellectually speaking, a contradictory and paradoxical period. I agree. Therefore, I propose that Bishop José Joaquim da Cunha de Azeredo Coutinho, with all his own ambiguities, can stand first as a satisfactory symbol of that fascinating century and second as a caution of the complexities of the Luso-Brazilian Enlightenment.

NOTES

1 It can be found in Arthur P. Whitaker, ed., *Latin America and the Enlightenment* (2nd ed.; Ithaca, N. Y., 1961) , pp. 96–118.
2 See J. Lúcio de Azevedo, "A Academia dos Renascidos da Bahia e seu fundador," *Revista de Lingua Portuguêsa,* XIV (Nov., 1921) , 17–29; Moreira de Azevedo,

"Sociedades Fundadas no Brasil desde os tempos coloniaes até o começo do actual reinado," *Revista do Instituto Histórico e Georgráfico Brasileiro* (hereinafter abbreviated *RIHGB*), XLVIII, Part 2 (1885), 265–322; José Vieira Fazenda, "Academia dos Felizes," *RIHGB*, CXLIX (1943), 433–37; Max Fleiuss, "As principaes associações literárias e scientíficas do Brasil (1724–1838)," in *Páginas brasileiras* (Rio de Janeiro, 1919), pp. 381–456; Barão Homen de Melo, "O Brasil intelectual em 1801," *RIHGB*, LXIV (1901), i–xxxi; J. C. Fernandes Pinheiro, "A Academia brasílica dos esquecidos. Estudo histórico e literário," *RIHGB*, XXXI, Part 2 (1868), 5–32, and "A Academia Brasílica dos Renascidos. Estudo historico e literario," *RIHGB*, XXXII, Part 2 (1869), 53–70; Visconde de São Leopoldo, "O Instituto Histórico e Geográphico Brasileiro he o representante das ideas de illustração que em differentes épochas se manifestarão em o nosso continente," *RIHGB*, I (1856), 66–86; Lycurgo Santos Filho, "Sociedades literárias do século XVIII," *RIHGB*, CCLXVII (1965), 43–60; José Joaquim Norberto de Souza e Silva, "Litteratura brasileira: as academias litterárias e scientíficas no século décimo octavo. A Academia dos Selectos," *Revista Popular* (Rio do Janeiro), XV (1862), 363–76. There is only one book on the subject, Alberto Lamego de Campos' brief *A Academia dos Renacidos, sua fundação e trabalhos inéditos* (Paris, 1923). Fidelino de Figueiredo treats the academies at some length in his *Estudos de história americana* (São Paulo, 1927), and most literary historians discuss them, some in considerably more detail than others.

3   Thomas Lindley, *Narrative of a Voyage to Brazil* (London, 1805), pp. 66–67.

4   "Notas Dominicaes Tomadas durante uma Viagem em Portugal e no Brasil em 1816, 1817, e 1818," trans, Alfredo de Carvalho, *Revista do Instituto Archeológico e Geográphico Pernambucano*, XI (March, 1904), 436.

5   *Notes on Brazil* (London, 1820), p. 575.

6   *Notices of Brazil in 1828–1829* (Boston, 1831), p. 84.

7   *Sketches of Residence and Travels in Brazil* (Philadelphia, 1845), I, 116.

8   Arquivo Público da Bahia, "Inventário de José Lino Coutinho," Document No. 357.919.62/M157/d4.

9   (Lisbon, 1783), p. 4.

10 Miguel Joaquim de Almeida e Castro, "Orasam academica," *Revista do Instituto Archeológico e Geográphico Pernambucano*, XXXV (1937–1938), 180.

11 Antônio Nunes Ribeiro Sanchez, *Cartas sôbre a educação da mocidade* (Pôrto, n.d.), p. 121.

THE CHURCH IN THE
SECOND REIGN, 1840–1889

George C. A. Boehrer
University of Kansas, Lawrence

GENERALISTS in the field of Brazilian history would have us believe that the Roman Church in Brazil, unlike that in Hispanic America, co-existed with the State in relative harmony. Certainly there is a great deal of truth in this observation if we examine the history of Brazil's neighbors. Outright conflicts, suppression of religious orders, expulsion of hierarchies, restrictive legislation in education—all illustrate the tumultuous times for the Church in nineteenth-century Hispanic America. In contrast to that area, Brazil witnessed an early conflict over the investiture of a bishop-elect of Rio de Janeiro, minor difficulties over jurisdiction, and one serious conflict culminating with the jailing of two bishops in 1874. The two major problems were easily resolved: the investiture problem was solved after a number of tedious years of negotiation and obstinacy on both the part of Rio and of Rome; the two bishops were amnestied a year later after the ministry had changed hands. On the surface, therefore, the generalists are correct. Brazil was free from the horrendous Church-State problems which afflicted Spanish America. This freedom has been ascribed to the natural *doçura* of the Brazilian people or to the tolerance and the patience of the second emperor.

The co-existence theory is, however, an overly simplistic view. It does not take into consideration any change in the Church both in Brazil and in Rome in the nineteenth century. It assumes that the Brazilian Church was as static as the Brazilian Empire. It assumes that ultramontanism, for the most part absent in the early years of Brazil's independence, had not gained in strength in Brazil at the same time that it was triumphing in the Church elsewhere. What the theory of relatively peaceful co-existence does not take into consideration is that, while the Brazilian

113

government continued in an eighteenth-century tradition of regalism, the Brazilian Church, as represented by the hierarchy and the newer clergy, was embracing the ultramontane Church of Pius IX and the First Vatican Council.

Religiously and intellectually, nineteenth-century Brazil was a Pombaline country. Among all the Catholic countries, Portugal was the most affected by the reforms of the eighteenth century. Nowhere else did the proponents of the Enlightenment gain such control over the university and, more central to our concern, the seminaries. Nowhere else were the Jesuits so completely and significantly overcome. Nowhere else was the new thinking embraced by the political and ecclesiastical hierarchy to the extent that it was in Portugal. What was true in Portugal was even more true in Brazil.

Pombal's successful suppression of the Jesuits in 1759, his rupture with the Vatican for a period of ten years during which reforms were made without direct observation by Rome, and his reform of the University of Coimbra and suppression of the University of Évora had immediate and far-reaching consequences in Brazil.[1] If, despite assertions to the contrary, the Pombaline reforms did not introduce radical departures in methodology and "philosophy,"[2] there is no question that what was introduced was a Gallican-regalistic spirit in theology and ecclesiastical discipline. The Portuguese clergy, from which Brazil's hierarchy was drawn, became the obedient servitors and cooperators of the Portuguese state. As the eighteenth century drew to a close, if the Brazilian clergy was found in opposition to the state in the Inconfidência Mineira, in the Pernambucan Revolt of 1817, and in the Confederation of the Equator of 1824, it was not because of religious doctrine nor the heavy hand of regalism on the Church, but rather because the clergy was at one with fellow Brazilians in opposing the political and economic policies of the Portuguese Crown. The Brazilian priest in the period of independence and, indeed, for most of the monarchical period, was hardly distinguishable in attitudes from his fellow citizens. An identity, not to be found in the Spanish American countries, had been achieved in the late eighteenth century and was not to begin to disappear until the middle of the nineteenth century. Thus, we find the Brazilian clergy, as represented by Diogo Feijó and Francisco Muniz Tavares, taking its seats in the Côrtes Gerais Constituintes of Lisbon and, aside from the peculiarly Brazilian questions, voting along with the Portuguese liberal faction then dominant in the Côrtes. When independence was secured, the Brazilian hierarchy and clergy went along with the tide, and, indeed at times, went in front of it.[3]

This identification with liberal movements which were currently being opposed elsewhere in Latin America and in Catholic Europe by the papacy and the hierarchies is somewhat unique. It has its origins in the period preceeding independence. As stated before, the Portuguese Church had been captured by Gallicanism and regalism more successfully than the Church in other Catholic countries. Moreover, Portugal did not suffer from the Napoleonic invasions nor react to them as strongly as did Spain. The French presence did not cause the Portuguese the humiliation the Spaniards underwent: the Crown and the elite had fled to Brazil carrying their ideas with them. The occupation was relatively short and the Portuguese elite, exiled either in Brazil or in Great Britain, did not undergo that repugnance to French revolutionary, hence, liberal, ideas which affected the judgments of post-war Spaniards. Just as important, João VI was not Fernando VII: Portugal and Brazil were relatively free from the wave of reaction which swept over Europe after 1814. The Brazilian clergy, reinforced by the clerical courtiers who arrived in 1808, continued in the pattern which had been established for them in the previous century.

While the Brazilian clergy remained in comparative isolation, the Church in Europe was evolving into a different institution than that which had existed before the Revolution. Rome, shocked by the excesses of the Revolution, temporarily stripped of its temporal power, reacted vigorously against those philosophies which it thought had brought about its degradation. Ultramontanism, seemingly defeated by the universal suppression of the Jesuits in 1773, became an approved philosophy. The very revival of the Jesuits in 1814 over liberal opposition shows the growing ascendancy of the ultramontane doctrine. The extreme positions of Joseph de Maistre, and later of Jaime Balmes and Donoso Cortes, and their popularity in Roman circles are well-known signs of Rome's relieved acceptance of the ultramontane position. The Brazilian clergy, isolated from Europe, protected by the vigorous enforcement of the imperial patronage, remained separate from the increasingly rigorous position of Rome. The succession to the papacy of Pius IX in 1847 and his reaction to the Revolution of 1848 completed the triumph of the ultramontanists in Rome. During his long reign, ultramontanism would reach various heights with the publication of the *Syllabus of Errors,* the proclamation of the dogma of the Immaculate Conception, and the holding for the First Vatican Council and its acceptance of the dogma of Papal Infallibility. His pontificate would see the most serious struggle between the Church and the Brazilian state. But more basically, it would also see the alienation first of the Brazilian hierarchy and then gradually of the Brazilian clergy from Brazilian society.

In the year that Pius IX ascended the papal throne, João Dabney de Avelar Brotero, a young Brazilian who was half-American, visited his mother's homeland, sending home letters and keeping a diary. He was Brazilian enough to want to attend Mass only on his second Sunday in Boston, but, going to church, he found it crowded with part of the congregation kneeling out-of-doors on the sidewalk. Unable to enter the church, he went instead to the Unitarian church.[4] Later in Baltimore, he visited St. Mary's Seminary, directed by the Sulpicians. There he talked with a Mr. (Fr.?) Raymon, a Professor of Philosophy. He writes:

Mr. Raymon gave me detailed information on the system and plan of the college, which is conducted according to the statutes of the Catholic Congregation of Saint Sulpice, whose superior resides in Paris, and to whom the direction of this College as well as of other Catholic colleges, except for [those of] the Jesuits, is subordinated. This subordination of the Catholic colleges to a supreme direction resident in a foreign country does not cause the slightest hesitation or suspicion in this country where the majority is made up of Protestants, which seems to me very noteworthy since in Brazil, a Catholic and Monarchical country, this union with the Sulpicians was denied to the Fathers of the College [Seminary] of Caraca [sic] (in Minas Gerais) [5] whose basis of teaching is the same as in St. Mary's College, and the very proposal of that plan caused a violent outcry against the Jesuits, religious brotherhoods, etc. . . . .[6]

Continuing his conversation, Dabney found a striking difference between the Brazilian and the American churches.

Mr. Raymon in his religious opinions is what is called in Theology an ultramontane—and it seems that this is the dominant system in the Catholic clergy in this country. Since here the Civil Government does not have any supervision over religious matters, all the theories of Ecclesiastical Law concerning the protection and inspection by the civil power over the Church are not used, and the direction of Ecclesiastical affairs is entirely given over to the Roman Pontiff. And not only are the Papal bulls promulgated without interference from the civil power, but there are even great invasions of what are called the prerogatives of the Bishops in their Dioceses: Here the Pope is not considered to be the Bishop of Rome, equal to any other bishop in many respects and enjoying merely some rights of jurisdictions over the Universal Church in order to preserve its Unity, but, as Mr. Raymon told me, he is considered to be the Universal Bishop of the world, to whom the highest Government of the Church is entrusted. . . .[7]

The Brazilian mentality can immediately be seen in Dabney's words. The national Church's divergence from that of the United States, which for historical reasons was in the nineteenth and twentieth centuries perhaps the most Roman in orientation, is also evident. Dabney in turn was questioned by his informant concerning the state of the Brazilian Church. He wrote: "It seemed to me that he gave little credence when I told him that our clergy was perfectly orthodox, containing some elements of superior intelligence and much wisdom, and that, on the whole, they were honest and virtuous. My first two observations were very truthful; as for the last, a lie was involved, [but] indeed the reverend Jesuits teach that there are justifiable lies." [8] Although Dabney was writing twenty-five years after independence, his words may be applied to 1822, and, indeed, to the time of Dom João's arrival.

When Brazilian independence was achieved under a monarchical form of government, the royal, now the imperial, patronage was continued.[9] The Church's position was a source for keen debates in the Brazilian Constituent Assembly and in subsequent sessions of the Brazilian Parliament during the course of the First Reign. That the Church was not severely restricted in its activities is evidently true; however, there is no question that the interference of the patronage which was strengthened by the Brazilian politicians during the first decade of independence did "sap its strength." [10]

In the tumultuous era of the Regency, the conflict between the Roman Church and the regalists reached scandalous proportions over the problem of the appointment of Antônio Moura to the vacant bishopric of Rio de Janeiro. While Moura was suspect of Gallicanism, his sponsor, Diogo Antônio Feijó, was notorious as an ardent propagandist of clerical marriage, as a ferocious liberal, and as priest who had gone to the lengths of proposing that Catholic missionaries to the Indians be replaced by the Moravian Brethren. Rome's refusal to invest Moura after the government had nominated him led to prolonged and heated debates. The situation was eventually resolved with a Roman victory, but not before the Rio diocese had suffered the absence of an ordinary from 1833 until 1839.[11]

When the Second Reign began, the Church was not in a good condition. Administratively, it was made up of one province with the metropolitan see at Salvador. There were eight bishoprics, with sees at Belém, Mariana, Olinda, São Luis, São Paulo, Rio de Janeiro, Cuiabá, and Goiás. The first six were created at various times during the colonial period, the latter two in 1826. In 1848, a ninth bishopric was created in Pôrto Alegre, which was dismembered from the diocese of Rio de Janeiro. Finally in 1854, the bishoprics of Fortaleza and Diamantina were created. These were the last creations during the imperial period despite petitions for more. Only at the very end of the Empire in the last Speech from the Throne was there a proposal from the government for the creation of more.[12] The areas covered by the bishoprics were enormous. Rio de Janeiro, for example, covered not only the city of Rio and the province of the same name, but also the provinces of Espírito Santo and Santa Catarina and the eastern section of the province of Minas Gerais.[13] With such large dioceses, it is evident that effective ecclesiastical administration was impossible.

A handy index of the condition of the Church may be found in the reports of the presidents of the provinces to the provincial assemblies. As the representatives of the imperial patron over the Church, they reported on Church affairs. In August, 1840, the President of Ceará reported:

Presently there are 32 parishes of which 27 are filled by permanent[14] pastors, in the others there are temporary vicars except in the new parish of Nôssa Senhora do Carmo dos Inhamuns.

It would seem prudential to me that in the future no new parishes be created without hearing first from our Diocesan Prelate. . . .

The worship given to the All Powerful according to the holy religion which we profess seems to be in decay in this Province, as it is in the other Provinces of the Empire. Some of the Parish Churches are in a state of complete ruin; others need considerable repair so that the sacrosanct mysteries of our Religion may be celebrated in them. Many of them do not have the altar cloths nor the vestments necessary for the celebration of the sacraments and other rites. The Parish priests (with rare and honorable exceptions) are not greatly troubled with the religious instruction of their parishioners, and, if at times they preach to them with the Word, they do not edify them by example and the practice of the Christian virtues which doubtless would have more effect than contrived phrases in Sermons. The hope of a proximate creation of a Prelacy in the Province and the coming of an Apostolic Pastor who may burn with religious zeal and who may begin the reform of the manners of the clergy and of the people should console us.[15]

In the following year, another *Cearense* president reported:

> It is . . . deplorable, Sirs, that, when in an opulent dwelling any sort of a citizen may make a show of luxury and pomp, the temple of God should be so poor, that the place where creatures go to give God the reverence and the homage of their adoration should be so despised and in such a ruinous condition. Cast your eyes over all the corners of this Province and you will see Churches in ruin, such as those of Vila Viçosa and of Missão Velha, or Churches begun but not completed. . . .
>
> One of the more vital measures which you can take for the improvement of religion would be to create a greater number of parishes, restricting the territory of those which are too large, not only to make it easier for the faithful, but also to remove from the indifferent the pretext by which they escape their Christian duties, i.e., the distance from their parish churches. It would also be very convenient if you would augment the salary of the Parish priests . . . so that, in the eyes of their spiritual flocks, they will always appear as worthy shepherds and never with the oppressive character of extortionists, which is so contrary to the spirit of the Gospels. . . .[16]

From Minas Gerais in 1840, the President reported:

> Presently there are 189 parishes in the Province which for the most part are provided [with parish priests]. It is not possible for me to give you in all exactness the number of those which are vacant or which are entrusted to temporary vicars. . . . It seems to be that the principal causes for [the shortage of contestants in the *concursos*] can be indicated as the lack of clergymen in a number corresponding to the necessities of the Church and the facility with which [the priests] may obtain [other] means of honest subsistence without subjecting themselves to the burdensome duties of the Pastoral Office.
>
> Speaking of the Episcopal Seminary, I [already] gave you information on the only course which it holds for the special instruction of the Clergy; truly many are the needs which we still feel in this matter, but we should hope that they will be satisfied when the widowhood of the Church of Marianna is terminated.[17]

In a shorter report made three years later, the then president used one illustration to show the difficulties of religious life in the interior:

> I ought to inform you that the place called Sacramento, below the sandbank of Matepoó in Rio Doce, and some three leagues distant from that River belongs to the parish of Cuieté with which it cannot have either any dealings or even means of communication, since it is some 30 leagues distant by the river; and through the bush, if there were a road, some 20 [leagues]. . . . According to my information, it is 16 years since

the vicar has appeared in that out-of-the-way place; and there are farm laborers who are not yet baptized.[18]

From the far south, the President of the province of Santa Catarina reported to the provincial deputies that:

The personnel in this branch of [civil] service is in the same, if not in a worse, state than was reported to you on the opening of the last session. My predecessor and I have in vain made representations to the Imperial Government and to the Reverend Diocesan Bishop; no remedies were taken because there is a shortage of priests in the Bishopric. In the 19 parishes of the Province, three are without pastors, six are ministered by foreigners; each of the remaining ten has a priest, only three of them temporary in the parishes of the City [Destêrro], São José, and Tubarão.[19]

Things were worse four years later when the same president reported: "Of the 19 parishes in the Province, three have permanent pastors, of whom two are not functioning . . . being aged and sickly; twelve have temporary pastors, five of whom are foreigners, and four [parishes] are absolutely without Pastors." [20]

Salvador, the only archbishopric and the oldest see in Brazil, was not in much better shape. In 1843 the President reported:

Our parishes outside the capital are for the most part in deplorable shape, as much because of the lack of means to repair them as because of neglect by the pastors: there are some who under the pretext that the quota which came to them (which has always been distributed according to the just discretion of the Reverend Prelate) is insufficient and [therefore the quotas] have not been converted for the benefit of the churches.[21]

The President and his successors frequently complained that whereas before the province had enacted special legislation for the upkeep of the parish churches the expenses had been borne by the priests and the parishioners, but that after the passage of the decree both the priest and the parishioners believed that their obligations had been terminated. They sat back and complained about the inadequacy of the grant.[22]

The reports presented above have been chosen at random from various parts of the Empire for the first years of the Second Reign. They are typical of the reports from the whole country. Needless to say, reports from such areas as Piauí, Mato Grosso, and Goiás are even more dismal. Several themes run through all the reports: the shortage of clergy, the ruinous state of the churches, and the laxity of morals among the clergy. Whatever the cause, a shortage of clergy had been endemic in Brazil since the beginnings of colonial times and, indeed, persists to this day. The physical state of the churches can be attributed to neglect on the part of the government, but, as has just been seen, in Bahia at least some of the clergy seem to have pocketed funds allocated for the restoration of their churches.

More than anything else, the moral laxity of the clergy contributed to the low state of Catholicism in the nineteenth century.

It is true that few went as far as the Vicar of Inhambupe, who celebrated a sung Mass for the souls of both his mother and of the mother of his mistress. The mistress had an important role in the ceremony. She declared that she saw the soul of her mother in front of the tabernacle. Her clerical lover then ordered the congregation to sing the Divine Praises.[23] Less flagrant and more typical was that priest of whom his descendant, Afonso de Melo Franco, wrote that Vicar Melo of Paracatú "was a priest characteristic of the Brazil of his time—valiant, a politician, contentious, living with his woman and tenderly rearing his children. . . ." The other priests of Paracatú in the nineteenth century were also heads of families.[24] When, in 1868, Dom Pedro Maria de Lacerda, who was to be a reforming bishop, was elevated to the See of Rio de Janeiro, he chose as his vicar general Msgr. Félix, whose violations of the vow of chastity were well known. Years later when the Bishop was questioned about his choice, he remarked that he had chosen Msgr. Félix because the whole chapter was equally corrupt and there was no one else to whom he could turn.[25]

The one element in Brazilian clerical life concerning which the presidents of the provinces did not complain was clerical involvement in politics. Frequently, to improve his financial status, the parish priest became a supporter if not a local leader of one of the two political parties. The very method by which they were selected as parish priests and by which they obtained future promotions conditioned them to become politicians. Entering the open contest *(concurso)* for the benefice, the choice of the victor eventually fell to the political party in power.[26] Some political priests remained purely local figures—for example, a Father Santa Cruz of Santa Catarina became the president of the Republican Club of Tijucas[27]—but others went on to national prominence, Diogo Antônio Feijó was, of course, the most renowned; he achieved the highest position in the realm. Father João Manuel de Carvalho typifies the political priest in the later Empire. Twice elected a conservative deputy from Rio Grande do Norte, he gained momentary fame by his "Viva á República," shouted out in the last Imperial Parliament. Earlier he had supported the Visconde do Rio Branco, his party's leader and President of the Council of Ministers during the Religious Question. As editor of the Rio newspaper *A União* and as a deputy, he clearly showed his divergence from the bishops and from Rome.[28] For his pains, he had been removed from the lucrative post as the appointed pastor of the Church of Nôssa Senhora da Candelária in Rio, which was run by one of the wealthiest brotherhoods in the country.[29] A different type of the political priest was represented by Father Eutychio Pereira da Rocha of Belém do Pará. As editor of the newspaper *O Liberal,* he also supported the government in the Religious Question. He was excommunicated when he refused to abandon his political position and, at the same time, declined to give up his irregular life. His reaction was violent; he attacked his bishop, the powerful Dom Antônio de Macedo Costa, and voiced public suspicions of Rome's integrity. His position was simple: he had been a Catholic before the *Syllabus of Errors,* the Jesuitical, i.e., First Vatican, Council, and the bishop existed. In brief, he rejected innovations. He also thought that the excommunication of Masons was unjust. For himself, he wasn't worried about not being able to be buried in consecrated soil since neither Christ nor the Apostles had been buried in such cemeteries.[30]

Certainly not typical of the political priest but rather his *reductio ad absurdum* was Monsignor Joaquim Pinto de Campos. Twice deputy from Pernambuco, he aspired to the positions of both senator and bishop. As a regalist, he questioned the right of the Church to supervise seminary courses.[31] He also supported the government during the Religious Question and effectively earned the hostility of the hierarchy. When his book on a trip to the Holy Land was found to be largely plagiarized, the bishop of Rio de Janeiro sanctioned a lengthy *exposé.*[32] To advance his cause politically, he wrote a sycophantic biography of Dom Pedro II which sickened his subject and, it is hoped, kept the monsignor from further preferment.[33] While Feijó, João Manuel, Eutychio, and Campos were among the most celebrated of the political priests, there were hundreds of others who played more minor roles. Furthermore, the political priest usually was the one who also led an irregular life. As Oliveira Lima succinctly remarked: "such political fathers could not be priests of a canonically exemplary life." [34]

The picture of the clergy during the first years of Dom Pedro's reign was this: regalist, badly-educated, politicized, and lax in morals. On the whole, the clergy more-or-less represented Brazilian society. In his thought and his activity, the Brazilian priest was hardly distinguishable from the Brazilian layman. Indeed, a reforming bishop of Rio had to struggle to get his clergy out of civilian dress and into clerical garb.[35] The identity between the Brazilian clergy and the Brazilian people did not pass unnoticed in Rome, where both were regarded with distaste. Pius IX's remark, "Sicut populus, sic sacerdos," was not made as an expression of joy.[36]

The second Emperor, in the eyes of his most adulatory biographer, eventually became a religious liberal.[37] Whatever that may mean, it is certain that he was not an orthodox Roman Catholic as that position was being defined in Rome throughout his reign. Raised in the Gallican tradition of his family, he was also tolerant by nature. Outwardly, he conformed to the Church and went through the Catholic observances required by his position, although with some reluctance according to not unbiased observers.[38] In the most serious religious struggle during his period in office, he was clearly aligned against the position of Rome. Earlier when the novitiates of the religious orders were abolished in Brazil, he not only was in favor but also later expressed himself as wanting a continued suppression.[39] Without novitiates the orders would die, as they were doing in the closing years of the monarchy. In one sense, the decree of 1855 was a logical culmination of Pombal's first assault on the traditional defenders of religious orthodoxy when the Portuguese minister suppressed the Jesuits. Now in Brazil, it would be the turn of all the other orders. Dom Pedro's liberalism or indifference to the position of even the feeling of the Church was well shown when he insisted on decorating Ernest Renan, at that time Europe's most famous apostate from Catholicism. He rejected the counsel of two bishops in this matter and was blocked only by more prudent members of his government.[40]

Philosophically, then, Dom Pedro II should have been satisfied with the Church in Brazil as he found it in 1840. Paradoxically, it would be Dom Pedro who, unconsciously, would begin that reform of the Church which would bring it into open conflict with himself and with the regalistic ideology of the State. If Dom Pedro was one with the Brazilian clergy intellectually, morally he was not. Despite recent speculations,[41] Dom Pedro was outwardly a moral man. In the Victorian era, he was a model Victorian. Distressed by the public decline and disorders of the clergymen, he sought to reform them. He could do this only by using the hierarchy.

Dom Pedro's nomination of the members of the hierarchy would cause a dilemma. Uniformly, those priests who conformed to his own religious ideology were either leading hopelessly lax lives or would never receive the approbation of Rome. Since reform was his major concern, he perforce had to turn to priests who were capable of reform but who were also ultramontanists. There is no doubt that he wanted a moral clergy. In supporting the bishop of Pará's refusal to give preference to an unworthy but politically suitable priest, the Emperor remarked, "Without giving moral support to the bishops who deserve it, as does Pará, we shall not have a good clergy." [42] In the instructions which he left for his daughter during his first trip abroad, he hardly referred to the Church but did recommend that she select good ecclesiastics.[43]

The Emperor's first major appointment was that of Antônio Ferreira Viçoso as the bishop of Mariana. The new Bishop was a Portuguese and a member and a former superior of the Congregation of the Mission. When he arrived in his diocese, the Bishop found it in a shocking state. In Mariana itself, Dom Antônio discovered that the Cathedral chapter "was with few but honorable exceptions made up of priests who were publicly keeping women." [44] He immediately began to reform his clergy. More important than his reform of the diocese was his influence on the seminarians at Caraça and on the younger clergymen. Selecting the most promising, he sent them abroad to Paris and Rome for study. Among those he selected were Dom Pedro Maria de Lacerda, the future bishop of Rio de Janeiro, Dom João Antônio dos Santos, the future bishop of Diamantina, and Dom Luís Antônio dos Santos, who was to be first the bishop of Fortaleza and then the Archbishop of Bahia.[45] Those in this first contingent which he sent out were witnesses to the revolutions of 1848 and the reaction which followed them. They returned from Europe, trained in ultramontanism and dedicated to a strict morality. Clearly superior in education and morals to their fellow Brazilian clergymen, they received preference from both their mentor and the Emperor. Once appointed to their own sees, they began the Herculean task of "moralizing" their clergy. At the same time, other Brazilian prelates were nominated by Dom Pedro. Two of them were Dom Antônio de Macedo Costa, a Bahian priest of irreproachable orthodoxy and morals, who became the bishop of Belém do Pará in 1859, and Dom Vital Maria Gonçalves de Oliveira. The latter was a Capuchin who had gone abroad to join his order despite governmental regulations. Educated in Paris, he received his preferment because of his politically powerful family and was made bishop of Olinda-Recife at a young age in 1872. Returning from Europe, he immediately began the most serious of the Church-State quarrels, in which one of his leading opponents was the cousin who had furthered his career. In the struggle, he was enthusiastically joined by Macedo Costa while the other bishops gave their moral support.[46]

The nomination and approval of these bishops would cause the slow divorce of the Church both from the Brazilian government and the Brazilian people. The bishops would try to bring first the clergy and then the laity into a more perfect conformity with Roman beliefs and practices. They strove to strengthen the nominal union between the Brazilian Church and Rome. Their legitimate pastoral efforts would bring them into direct conflict with the state. Their attempts to reform the manners and the beliefs of their clergy would inevitably affront the regalistic sensibilities of the Crown and the people.

The government was more than sympathetic with the bishops' desire for reform, which seems to have been the intention of José Tomás Nabuco de Araújo when he issued the decree which closed the novitiates. His son relates that, when in 1853 he came to the Ministry of Justice, under whose supervision the Church was then placed, he found the following situation:

> Unfortunately, the state of the clergy did not allow society to reap all the benefits from the religious principle. The effort of the Government ought to be concentrated before anything else in the formation of a clergy capable of serving religion; and as the public scandal was greater when the rule was the more severe, it was principally towards the Orders, some of them fallen into the most complete relaxation, that the spirit of reform should be turned. It was this thought which inspired the act of Nabuco suspending the reception of novices into the convents. No act of his ecclesiastical administration, nevertheless, was so opposed by the Catholic side. The provisional measure became permanent. More than twenty governments followed, not one revoked it, and only with the separation of the Church and State, in the new regime, were the novitiates . . . opened.[47]

No one doubted the low state of the clergy. In 1851, Dom José Antônio dos Reis, Bishop of Cuiabá, had reported to the government that "I continue to have the supreme displeasure of informing your Excellency that the . . . clergy of this Bishopric, including the parish priests, do not have that instruction and morality which would make them perfect in their condition as Ministers of Religion." [48] Nor did anyone doubt the low state of the religious orders. As his son states, Nabuco had the initial support of the bishops when he closed the novitiates and set about seeking a concordat with the Vatican which would contain provisions for conventual reform. If many of the bishops later repudiated their support, some at least continued to believe that the novitiates should remain closed.[49] But, whatever Nabuco's intention, it is a fact that a concordat was never negotiated nor signed and the Emperor, as we have seen, had no intention of restoring the regular novitiates.[50]

The failure to negotiate a concordat, without which religious reform was difficult if not impossible, later brought on the Catholic attacks on the decree of May 10, 1855.[51] The orders continued to decline. Two documents from Bahia attest to this. In a confidential report to the internuncio in 1882, Dom Luis dos Santos remarks on the decadent state of the orders in the Empire. In a scribbled aside to his secretary, he writes: "Find out if there are three or two friars in the Convent of Carmo."[52] Three years later, Father Santos Pereira, eventually a bishop himself during the Republic but then administrator of the archdiocese, reported to the new internuncio, Msgr. Rocchio Cocchia, that the convent of São Francisco had eight religious living in the convent and that there were at most twelve Franciscans living in the whole province. The convent of Carmo had two in the cloister and four friars outside. The convent of Lapa had four resident friars and two living outside. Santos Pereira was interested in using one of the buildings for a seminary. He warned the prelate that the government had its eyes on the convents for a public library and a medical school.[53] The Benedictines were hardly in a better position. In 1868, there were eleven monasteries and forty-one members of the order in the entire country. Two abbeys had over half of the monks, Rio with fifteen and Bahia with eleven. Olinda had four monks and the other abbeys and priories only one or two.[54]

The secular clergy was not better off. One problem, already mentioned, was the scarcity of priests. In the Diocese of Fortaleza, for example, there were eighty-nine priests ordained between 1861 and 1878. However, in the same period, seventy-two priests died and twenty-two left the diocese, leaving a loss of five.[55] The attraction of the youth toward clerical life diminished as the morality of the existing priests declined. The situation was made worse when priests were imported. In Rio, the Bishop's secretary remarked: "The priests coming from the other diocese of Brazil are almost to a man, not better [than our own]. They come drawn by ambition and other passions." [56] And the problem was not resolved by securing clergymen from abroad. The same source relates:

Those coming from foreign lands generally are worse than the national clergy. They have all the vices of our own and those characteristic of their own [nation]. We do not speak of the Italians, the true outcasts of society, capable of all [sorts] of villainies. Many could scarcely read Latin; they did not know how to recite the Divine Office nor how to celebrate the Holy Mass; and they were ignorant of the most simple elements of dogma and morals.[57]

As has been made evident, the bishops, nominated by Dom Pedro in the hope that they would reform the clergy, were faced with an almost impossible task. They could take superficial means as did Dom Pedro Maria de Lacerda when he insisted that the clergy wear the cassock. If the priests did not, they were not allowed to say Mass. Until his arrival, the clergy dressed as the other Brazilians. Obligatory use of the cassock at least made the clergy more reticent about frequenting places of ill repute.[58] This and similar measures might restrain the clergy but did not strike at the heart of the matter. To cure their clergy, the bishops would have to use other measures, which, if they were not illegal, certainly curtailed the government's use of the patronage.

One noncontroversial method was the renovation of the seminaries. Dom Antônio Viçoso of Mariana had brought in the Congregation of the Mission, whose members are more popularly known as Lazarists or Vincentians, to reform the Seminary of Caraça. His example was followed by Dom Pedro Maria de Lacerda at Rio. In 1865 only these two seminaries were in a good financial state. The Catholic press reported that those of Pernambuco and Rio Grande do Sul were about to be closed because of a shortage of funds. The others were short of both professors and funds.[59]

The seminaries, financially supported by the government, were subject to the interference of the government. Thus, in 1865, in an effort to conserve money, the government suppressed the chairs of Greek, natural law, sacred eloquence, and geography. This forced the bishop of São Paulo, at least, to raise funds elsewhere.[60] Throughout the imperial regime, the seminaries were subject to the imperial government directly through decrees in the changing of the curriculum, or indirectly through failure to pay salaries or subsidies. The bishops resisted as much as possible the interference in the curriculum. In 1878–1879, when changes were authorized, the internuncio, Msgr. Caesar Roncetti, suggested that the bishops wait for six months before holding concursos to fill the chairs. At the end of that time, they then should protest that they were unable to fulfill the wishes of the regime.[61] The archbishop, at least, duly protested[62] and received a commendation from the Roman diplomat who states that he was going to recommend similar protests from the bishops.[63] Despite protests, the seminaries continued to fare badly. Whenever possible, the bishops followed the example of Dom Antônio Viçoso and sent their most promising seminarians abroad. Thus, Dom Antônio de Macedo Costa, who had received his own training in Brazil, sent forty-seven students abroad between 1861 and 1873.[64] The bishops could also see to it that regalism was no longer taught in the seminaries. This Dom Pedro II discovered to his chagrin when, on a visit to Caraça, a student and a professor defended the ultramontane point of view.[65]

Seminary reform, however, could only have its fruits in the future; the reforming bishops had the present to consider. One method of controlling their clergy was in the filling of pastorates. Normally when a parish was vacant, an open competition (concurso) was held. The winner (o collado) was then appointed for life. Needless to say, under the best of circumstances, bishops rapidly lose control over life-time appointees. When, as in nineteenth-century Brazil, politics entered the lists and the successful candidate owed as much, if not more, to his political party as he did to his knowledge and virtue, a reforming bishop would find himself severely handicapped. The bishops found their way around this obstacle by the simple and legal method of not holding the concurso. Relying on various pretexts, they filled the vacancies with temporary pastors (encomendados), who usually received half the salary of the collados and who, of course, could be removed by the bishop at any time. In his reform of the diocese of Rio de Janeiro, Dom Pedro Maria de Lacerda suspended the concursos and declined to subject himself to the interferences of the civil government in these matters.[66]

The hesitancy, delay, and downright refusal of the bishops to hold the concursos for the positions of pastors, of course, caused dissension. Patronage was being withheld from whatever political party was in power. In 1876, the Minister of the Empire, under whose jurisdiction the Church now existed, wrote a circular letter to the hierarchy in which he pointed out that the government could not be indifferent to the situation and that certainly irremovable pastors were by nature better for their parishioners than the encomendados. The minister then went on to remind the bishops that the Council of Trent had recommended beneficios collados and that both canon and civil law had provided for adequate emoluments. The bishops, he continued, were both violating canon and civil law and were failing to fulfill their obligations.[67] The bishops, however, continued their policy. What may be considered to be an indirect reply came from Bahia in the form of three articles in the official Catholic press. The editors thought that it was useless to attempt to demonstrate that the lack of action on the part of the bishops was contrary to the Church's discipline. What had to be considered were the special circumstances of the Brazilian Church which in effect made those provisions of canon law inoperative. Secondly, it was argued that the deplorable state of the Church in Brazil was due neither to the policy of the hierarchy nor to the failure to hold concursos. Rather, it was the responsibility of the government, which had neglected religion. Finally, the root of the matter was the attempt by the government to make the Church a mere division of the state. The government wanted the Church to be passively and blindly obedient to a succession of imperial ministers.[68] The matter would not be resolved during the imperial period.

By withholding the concurso, the bishops could effectively control the new pastors. However, the problem of the already collado pastor represented a grave difficulty. To curb the most abusive of the priests, the bishops had recourse to canon law. Through it, they could remove or suspend priests from their functions *ex informata conscientia*. Theoretically, the bishops, informed of irregularities, might suspend the offending parties without making the reasons for the suspension public and without a formal trial. In this way, public scandal could be avoided. This provision was not covered by Brazilian law. Hence, the prelate could move against unworthy clergy who thus could not have recourse to the civil courts. The use of this device spread alarm among the political clergy. As early as 1855, a group of Gallican priests in São Paulo, fearful of Bishop Joaquim de Melo, founded a short-lived journal, *O Amigo da Religião,* which defended their interests. They saw in the shift in hierarchical policy a plot against those who, among other matters, thought that the ex informata conscientia provision was an abuse of ecclesiastical authority. Priests in Brazil, the editors stated, were as much citizens as military officers, physicians, magistrates, or anybody else. As such, they could not be denied their rights. They thought that the Brazilian Church as it had previously existed was in perfect harmony with the laws of the Empire and that the bishops by their actions were destroying this harmony.[69]

The device was used to good effect. It was most frequently used against those priests whose theological ideas were not in accord with Rome and whose moral life was notorious. By inferring that they were concerned with the latter, the bishops moved against their enemies with relative impunity. Ostensibly disciplining the clergy for infractions of the sixth and ninth commandments but in reality striking at them for unorthodox views, the bishops took refuge in silence. There was little that their ideological opponents could do. There was only the possibility of appealing the decisions to the Crown. This the brotherhoods of Recife and Belém would do successfully in 1873 and 1874. However, in their case, it was possible, because the bishops had given their reasons publicly and had infracted the civil law. With the individual clergymen, it was another matter. In 1864, Dom João Antônio dos Santos had refused to include an unworthy cleric in the triple list of successful candidates in the concurso for the pastorate of São Pedro de Muritiba. The priest appealed to the Crown, and the Council of State found for the bishop. It stated that both the Church and the State required that the bishops be guided not only by the intellectual ability of the candidates but chiefly by their moral qualities: "This is left to the private judgment and to the conscience of the prelates." [70] Later politicians would attempt to make it easier for disciplined priests to have recourse to the Crown, but the Church was uniformly opposed and successfully fought the issue.[71]

Other matters were also of concern to the bishops. One, which was linked to clerical advancement, was the creation of new parishes. By law, the creation of new parishes and the division of existing ones were vested in the provincial assemblies, which could act in these matters without consultation with the ecclesiastical authorities. When consulted on the matter, the Council of State ruled that, although the presidents of the provinces would do well to consult the respective bishop, acts of the provincial councils were nonetheless valid.[72] The creation of new parishes was a constant problem for the bishops. Certainly new parishes were needed, but priests to fill them were wanting. Frequently the bishops simply refused to hold the concurso or even to appoint temporary pastors. Sometimes they refused to give canonical approval to the new parish. In 1873, Dom Antônio de Macedo Costa refused to appoint a pastor to a new parish in Amazonas. The Bishop argued that, although the assembly had the right to create a new parish in civil law, it did not have it in canon law. Hence, he was not going to oblige the assembly.[73]

Santos Pereira, administrator of the Archdiocese of Bahia, stated the position of the hierarchy in his remarks to the new internuncio.

The division and demarcation of the territory for a Parish are made by the Provincial Assemblies with a hearing from the Diocesan authority. After it is decreed by the Assembly, the demarcation of the new Parish is converted into law by the Civil Authority (the President of the Province) and is sent to the Diocesan authority for canonical sanction. In the event that the Ecclesiastical Authority is not heard, or being heard is not listened to, it denies canonical sanction to the . . . law: and the latter remains without effect. This has happened frequently and only in this fashion can a brake be put on the insatiable political interests. The division of a Parish, which can barely support a Pastor, results in two parishes without pastors. . . . It is this frequent occurence which led the Diocesan authority to accept only those divisions which are made in an orderly fashion and which do not ruin the parishes.[74]

By their refusal to take action, the bishops effectively blocked the wishes of the provincial assemblies, which frequently acted not out of concern for the religious needs of the people, but rather on behalf of the advancement of political coreligionists. More important, it was one more method of expressing the new hierarchy's opposition to the regalism of the Empire.

The greatest irritation to the hierarchy was, of course, the *placet*. Enshrined in Portuguese tradition and law only since Pombaline times, this restriction on the promulgation of papal documents seriously inhibited the freedom of the bishops in their attempt to bring Rome and Brazil into harmony. On minor issues, the bishops sometimes ignored the restriction and promulgated papal documents. Regalists complained;[75] the government was, moreover, jealous of the placet and usually insisted that the hierarchy comply with it.[76] Before the momentous events of 1872–1875, diverse organs of the Catholic press had expressed their belief that the placet was basically antireligious,[77] but the Religious Question brought the issue to the fore. Certainly the two bishops had violated civil law; but, in the eyes of their supporters, the law was unjust.[78] As late as 1880, the leading Catholic journal, *O Apóstolo,* was protesting the existence of the placet.[79]

It is clear that, in the Religious Question, which may be regarded as a culmination of the reforming spirit of the hierarchy, the two bishops were attempting to lead the Church in a direction other than that which the politicians—clerical and lay—had chosen at the beginning of the Empire. Also clear is that what they were doing was not popular with either the government or the articulate elements of the population. An examination of the Religious Question may give us ample evidence. As has been ably demonstrated, the Question was not a clerical-Masonic dispute, but rather a more fundamental one of regalism versus ultramontanism.[80] The government, the leading lights of both political parties, the chieftains of the newly formed Republican Party, and the intellectuals united to repel the pretensions of the bishops to govern the Church according to Roman direction. The intensity of the struggle and the bitterness which resulted can be seen from an examination of the secular press, but most especially from the illustrated satirical journals, such as *O Mosquito,* which lampooned, distorted, and mocked every action of the hierarchy.[81]

More indicative of the bitterness than the cartoons, the hostile editorials, and the commissioned articles in the *Seções Livres* of the newspapers was the use of force on the clergy. The attacks on the Catholic press and on the Jesuits in Recife during the height of the Religious Question are well known. But there was also violence elsewhere. The Holy Thursday procession of 1873 was stopped in Belém on the flimsiest of pretexts despite orders to the contrary by the provincial vice-president.[82] Later in the year, it was reported in Rio that, after Father Almeida Martins, the Portuguese Masonic priest who had touched off the controversy by his activity in Rio, had been excommunicated, priests who used clerical garb in the streets were not safe from abuse.[83] In August, 1876, after the passions should have died down, the bishop-elect of Mariana, Dom Antônio María Corrêa Sá e Benavides and two priests, one of whom was later to be the archbishop of Rio de Janeiro, were first insulted and then roughed up in the capital. Twelve days later, the pastor of the church in the Largo da Glória was insulted in broad daylight.[84] The most serious event came several months later. On October 21, Dom Pedro Maria de Lacerda was preaching at the Church of Santa Rita. He was interrupted and then, while he was still in the pulpit, he was stoned. The Bishop fled the church but, as he departed, his carriage was stoned. There had been a previous warning that something untoward would occur. The pastor of the church had gone to the chief of police, who had not bothered to advise the police station in the neighborhood.[85] The usually regalistic press expressed its concern over the event,[86] but the most ferocious of the Masonic press of the epoch, *O Ganganelli,* had other ideas. The editors first thought that the incident merely presaged tumultuous times to come over religious issues and that the clergy, by their audacity, were forcing the people to react. Upon reflection, the editors came to the conclusion that the whole incident had been staged by the clerics to incriminate Masonry.[87] The American minister, in reporting the incident to his government, thought that "either party is capable of either committing or getting up the affair:—which is another proof of the condition of this question and the temper and feeling on either side." [88] Other incidents followed. In 1877, in Patrocínio de Araras, São Paulo, two Jesuits who were conducting a mission were publicly threatened and forced to abandon their work.[89] Four years later, Dom Antônio Cândido de Alvarenga, the Bishop of São Luis do Maranhão, ordered a religious ceremony halted and the sacrament removed after he had observed irreverence by a part of the congregation. A riot followed, and the sanctuary and altar equipment were overturned. The Bishop's carriage was stoned as he left.[90]

As we have seen, the reform of the Church had been initiated by Dom Antônio Ferreira Viçoso when he became the bishop of Mariana in 1844. The bishops, therefore, had some forty-five years to attempt reform while the Church was still united with the State. The odds against their success were enormous. What, in the physical order, they did not achieve can briefly be seen by the reports of the presidents of the provinces at the close of the monarchical period. Of Ceará in 1877, the President, in reporting an *ofício* of the Bishop, said:

In the same dispatch, His Most Reverend Excellency requests the attention of the public authorities, especially yours, towards the state, which he classifies as terrible, in which the greater part of the parish churches are to be found—some [have] scarcely begun to be erected and [are] very far from being completed, others [are] threatened with complete ruin, and, generally, all [are] lacking the vestments necessary for worship. Very few, he adds, are completely furnished and decently preserved: he goes on to observe that the good condition of the latter few is not the result of aid from the Province, but [rather] of the zeal of the parish priests, of the funds and generosity of the parishioners, and of aid furnished by the Central Government during the calamitous drought.[91]

From Santa Catarina, the President was as gloomy when he reported to the Assembly in 1888:

In this Province, as in all of Brazil, there reigns the most complete indifference in religious matters. This statement, however sorrowful it may be, is proved by the abandon in which all the Catholic temples are to be found, by the insignificant attendance at religious ceremonies, and chiefly by the insufficient number of vicars and priests of whom there are few who show zeal for the true interests of the sacred ministry.

Without leaving this island, we may see two or more parishes served by one priest, and, since the former are greatly distant from one another, without doubt there results the lack of spiritual help: children remain without baptism; marriages become scarce and illicit unions become frequent; ignorance of doctrine and of holy matters and a tendency towards superstition and fanaticism [have resulted].[92]

From Bahia in 1877, the President reported:

This province is divided ecclesiastically into 190 parishes; that of Andarahy, created by the law of 1878, still does not have a canonical institution.

The other 189 are furnished with pastors, 65 being *collados* and 124 are served by interim or temporary pastors.

The reason for these vacancies is the now very appreciable lack of priests. The decline in numbers of the clergy in the whole country is attributed to religious indifferences. . . .

Besides this, some parishes are very small and have a congregation which is so poor that to name a priest for them is the equivalent of condemning him to live in poverty, since having only the paltry salary, it is not possible to maintain oneself with the decency necessary for his [i.e., clerical] state.

According to the information which I have gathered, there are many churches in the interior of the Province which need repairs or reconstruction, and, usually, they do not have vestments and altar cloths for the celebration of religious ceremonies. Since the respective populace is poverty stricken, nothing can be done to make the repairs of the church in those places.[93]

After forty-odd years, the physical condition of the Church had not changed; indeed, it may have worsened. What had changed, however, was the mentality of the hierarchy and, to some extent, of the clergy. The Brazilian clerics had officially abandoned regalism. The clergy had moved, but the laity had not. Thus, among the laymen of the empire, we can find very few who supported the actions of the clergy. Cândido Mendes de Almeida, Pedro Antônio Ferreira Viana, Zacarias de Góis, and the Felício dos Santos are among those who stand out. When, in reaction to the Religious Question, there was an attempt to found a Catholic party, it failed.[94] The hierarchy, in breaking with the regalism of the Empire, lost the support of the Brazilian intellectual elite. The loss was not one of a calculated risk. By their training and convictions, the bishops could no nothing else. Indeed, in their eyes, Brazilians had ceased to support the Universal Church a century before.[95] When regalism died unexpectedly with the advent of the Republic, the hierarchy would be able to pursue its work to rebuild Catholicism without suffering the interference of the State.

What the bishops had accomplished during the imperial period has been ably pointed out by Gilberto Freyre in his recent "semi-novel." Although for artistic purposes he writes only of Dom Vital, what he attributes to that prelate may be credited to most of the other members of the hierarchy in the Second Reign. He rightly regards Dom Vital as a revolutionary who radically transformed nineteenth-century Brazilian Catholicism.[96] If Dom Vital revolutionized Brazilian Catholicism in his brief tenure in office, his fellow bishops equally deserve credit. The Church continued throughout the Second Reign, but the changes within it and with its relationships to the Brazilian state and society were major.

NOTES

1 See Tarcísio Beal, "A reforma da Universidade de Coimbra e o clero brasileiro, 1772–1842" (unpublished Master's thesis, The Catholic University of America, 1965), *passim*. The best general account of the state of Catholicism in Brazil in the nineteenth century is Júlio Maria, *O catholicismo no Brasil (memória histórica)* (2nd ed.; Rio de Janeiro, 1950). The author wishes to express his appreciation for a grant from the Joint Committee on Latin American Studies of the Social Science Research Council which made research in Brazilian archives possible. This essay is part of a larger study of the Church in the nineteenth century.

2 See Antônio de Andrade, *Vernei e a filosofia portuguêsa* (Braga, 1946).

3 See Dom Duarte Leopoldo e Silva, *O clero e a independência, conferências patrióticas* (Rio de Janeiro, 1923) for the role of the clergy in colonial and early nineteenth-century nationalistic movements.

4 Francisco de Barros Brotero, ed., *A vida do Dr. João Dabney de Avelar Brotero. Excursão aos Estados Unidos da América do Nôrte em 1817. Discursos. Relatórios. Família e dados biográficos organizados por seu sobrinho* (São Paulo, 1945), p. 31.

5 Here the author confused his congregations. The priests who were brought in to take charge of the Seminary at Caraça were members of the Congregation of the Mission. See Silverio Gomes Pimenta, *Vida de D. Antônio Ferreira Viçoso, Bispo de Mariana, Conde da Conceição* (2nd ed.; Niterói, 1892), pp. 118ff.

6 Brotero, *A vida do Dr. João Dabney,* p. 106.

7 *Ibid.,* p. 107.

8 *Ibid.,* p. 108.

9 For a general treatment of the Patronage, see João Dornas Filho, *O padroado e a igreja brasileira* (São Paulo, 1938). The most exhaustive treatment, albeit from an ultramontane point of view, is found in Cândido Mendes de Almeida, *Direito civil ecclesiástico Brazileiro antigo e moderno em suas relações com o direito canônico* [short title] (Rio de Janeiro, 1866), I, viii–ccccxxiv. For difficulties during the period of Dom João's residence in Brazil, see Maurílio César de Lima, "Crise religiosa nos primeiros decênios do século XIX no Brasil," *Revista do Clero* (Rio de Janeiro), V (Feb., 1948) and the same author's "Metropoli-

136   GEORGE C. A. BOEHRER

tanismo e regalismo durante a nunciatura de Lourenço Capelli," *Revista de História* (São Paulo) , V (1952) , 387–416.

10   Bede A. Dauphinee, O.F.M., "Church and Parliament in Brazil During the First Empire, 1823–1831" (unpublished Ph.D. dissertation, Georgetown University, 1965; University Microfilm, Ann Arbor, Michigan, 1966) , p. 228.

11   Manoel S. Cardozo, "The Holy See and the Question of the Bishop-Elect of Rio, 1833–1839," *The Americas*, X (July, 1953) , 3–73.

12   "1889. Falla do throno por occasião da abertura da 4ª sessão da 20ª Legislatura, em 3 de maio," in Barão de Javary, ed., *Fallas do throno desde o anno de 1823 até o anno de 1889 acompanhadas dos respectivos votos de graças da câmara temporária* (Rio de Janeiro, 1889) , pp. 870–71.

13   "Map HA Igreja Cathólica," in Cândido Mendes de Almeida, *Atlas do Império do Brasil comprehendendo as respectivas divisões administrativas, ecclesiásticas e judiciárias* [short title] (Rio de Janeiro, 1868) . The atlas also shows parish divisions for each province.

14   As shall be explained later, there were two types of parish priests in Brazil. The permanent or *collado* was one who had undergone a public competition *(concurso)* for the post. The temporary pastor of *encommendado* was one appointed by the ordinary. The former had life-time tenure; the latter could be removed at any time by his bishop.

15   Arquivo Nacional (Rio de Janeiro) , Ministério do Império [hereinafter cited as ANRJ,MI], Relatórios das Províncias, Ceará, 1839–1843, "Relatório que appresentou o Exmo. Senhor Doutor Francisco de Sousa Martins, Presidente desta Província, na occasião da abertura da Assembléa Legislativa Provincial, no dia 1º de agôsto de 1840," pp. 4ff.

16   ANRJ,MI, Relatórios das Províncias, Ceará, 1839–1843, "Discurso recitado pelo Exmo. Senhor Brigadeiro José Joaquim Coelho, Presidente e Commandante das Armas da Província do Ceará, na abertura da Assembléa Legislativa Províncias, no dia 10 de setembro de 1841," pp. 5–7.

17   ANRJ,MI, Relatórios das Províncias, Minas Gerais, 1835–1842, "Falla dirigida á Assembléa Legislativa Provincial de Minas Gerais na Sessão Ordinário do anno de 1840, pelo Presidente Bernardo Jacintho da Veiga, 1º de fevereiro de 1840," pp. 62–63.
      The see of Mariana was in effect vacant from 1835 until 1844. Dom Carlos Pereira Freire de Moura, appointed in 1840, died before being consecrated. *Anuário Católico do Brasil 1960* (Petrópolis, 1960) , p. 183.

18   ANRJ,MI, Relatórios das Províncias, Minas Gerais, 1843–1847, "Falla dirigida á Assembléa Legislativa Provincial de Minas Gerais na abertura das Sessão Ordinária do anno 1844 pelo Presidente da Província, Francisco José de Souza Soares Andréa, 3 de fevereiro de 1844," p. 16.

19   ANRJ,MI, Relatórios das Províncias, Santa Catarina, 1835–1843, "Relatório do Presidente da Província de Santa Catharina [Anthero José Ferreira de Brito] á Assembléa Legislativa Provincial no dia e de novembro de 1840," pp. 3–4.

20   ANRJ,MI, Relatórios das Províncias, Santa Catarina, 1844–1849, "Falla que o Presidente da Província de Santa Catharina, O Marechal de Campo Anthero Jozé Ferreira de Brito, dirigio á Assembléa Legislativa da mesma Província na abertura de sua Sessão ordinária, em o 1º dia de março de 1844," pp. 10.

21   ANRJ,MI, Relatórios das Províncias, Bahia, 1842–1846, "Falla que recitou o Presidente da Província da Bahia o Conselheiro Joaquim José Pinheiro Vasconcellos, n'abertura da Assembléa Legislativa da mesma Província, em 2 de fevereiro de 1843," p. 14.

22   *Ibid.;* ANRJ,MI, Relatórios da Províncias, Bahia, 1842–1846, "Falla que recitou o Presidente da Província da Bahia o Conselheiro Joaquim José Pinheiro de

Vasconcellos n'abertura da Assembléa Legislativa da mesma Província, em 2 de fevereiro de 1844," p. 16; and "Falla dirigida á Assembléa Legislativa da Bahia na abertura da Sessão Ordinária do anno de 1845 pelo Presidente da Província, Francisco José de Sousa Soares d'Andréa," p. 13.

It should be noted that the four provinces from which reports have been cited were chosen at random. They represent more-or-less four sections of the country. The reports of these provincial presidents do not differ greatly from those of the other presidents. The author has transcripts of the sections on the Church from all the extant reports.

23 Arquidiocese de São Salvador da Bahia, Arquivo da Cúria Metropolitana [hereinafter ASSB,ACM], Officios Diversos, 1833, "Muitos Parochianos a Msgr. Manoel Santos Pereira, Inhambupe, 3 de junho de 1833."

24 Afonso Arinos de Melo Franco, *Um estadista da república (Afrânio de Melo Franco e seu tempo)* (Rio de Janeiro, 1955), I, 44–45.

25 Arquidiocese de São Sebastião de Rio de Janeiro, Arquivo da Cúria Metropolitana [hereinafter ASSRJ,ACM], "Bullário de arcebispado," II, 476.

26 In a report to the new internuncio, Msgr. Santos Pereira of Bahia gives a good description of how greatly politicized the appointment of pastors was:

"The priest who wanted to be placed in a parish directed himself to the political leader. Without the recognition of this chieftain, he could not enter the contest nor approach his prelate: Having obtained the approval for this or that [parish] according to the wishes and designation of the politician, the priest was rather certain [of being] the Emperor's choice even though he might be the most unworthy [of the candidates].

"And when this happened and the bishop . . . explained the truth about the unworthiness of the candidate to the Government, he was nevertheless selected and presented to the benefice. if this was convenient politically. Brazilian bishops more than once caused a serious conflict by refusing the installation of unworthy candidates; at one time, the caprice of the Government, not long ago, came to the point of ordering that the candidate be installed . . . by the civil authorities."

ASSB,ACM, Gabinete Archiepiscopal, Manoel dos Santos Pereira, "Relatório da Archidiocese da Bahia apresentado ao novo Internuncio Apostólico, D. Rocchio Cocchia, Arcebispo de Otranto, em 1885"; See also Romualdo Antônio de Seixas, *Memórias do Marquêz de Santa Cruz, Arcebispo da Bahia* (Rio de Janeiro, 1861), pp. 149ff., for an earlier analysis on the difficulties over the concurso and the appointment of pastors.

27 *A Gazêta Nacional* (Rio de Janeiro), Dec. 18, 1887.

28 *O Apóstolo* (Rio de Janeiro), July 8, 10, 12, 17, 22, 24 and 29; Aug. 5, 1874.

29 The Gallican official history of the Brotherhood of the Most Holy Sacrament of the Parish of Candelaria, which would have its own troubles with the ecclesiastical authorities in the first years of the Republic, briefly mentions João Manoel but with praise. F.B. Marques Pinheiro, *Irmandade do Santíssimo Sacramento da Freguezia de Nóssa Senhora da Candelaria e suas repartições, coro, caridade e hospital dos lázaros* (Rio de Janeiro, 1930), I, 25.

30 Biblioteca Nacional do Rio de Janeiro, Coleção Ramos Paz, I, 3, 4, 26, 27, 30, Eutychio Pereira da Rocha to F, Ramos Paz, Belém do Pará, Dec. 20, 1876, May 17, 1877, and March 10, 1878; *A Bôa Nóva* (Belém do Pará), May 31, 1876, Sept. 1, 1880, and Aug. 28, 1882.

31 Instituto Histórico e Geográfico Brasileiro, Coleção Nabuco, Lata 382, Ms. 3, Joaquim Pinto de Campos to José Thomás Nabuco de Araújo, Oct. 29, 1855.

32 *O Apóstolo*, July 19 and 31, Aug. 5 and 12, and Sept. 13 and 20, 1874. See also *A União* (Recife), Aug. 1, 1874, *et seq.*

138   GEORGE C. A. BOEHRER

33 Joaquim Pinto de Campos, *O Senhor D. Pedro II Imperador do Brasil; biographia* (Pôrto, 1871). While he was writing the biography, he seems to have plagued the Emperor. For Dom Pedro's reaction, see Dom Pedro II, "Diário de 1862. Introdução e notas do Prof. Hélio Viana," *Anuário do Museu Imperial,* XV (1956 [i.e., 1960]), 115–17, 158, 196, 225, 290.

34 Manoel de Oliveira Lima, "Annotações," in Francisco Muniz Tavares, *História da revolução de Pernambuco em 1817. Terceira edição commemorativa do 1° centenário revista e annotada por Oliveira Lima* (Recife, 1917), p. 42.

35 ASSRJ,ACM, "Bullário," II, 166–67.

36 Pimenta, *Vida de D. Antônio Ferreira Viçoso,* p. 86.

37 Mary W. Williams, *Dom Pedro the Magnanimous* (2nd ed.; New York, 1966), p. 167.

38 John Codman, *Ten Months in Brazil: With Notes on the Paraguayan War* (Edinburgh, 1870), pp. 164–65; also see C. M. Andrews, *Brazil, Its Condition and Prospects* (New York, 1887), pp. 85–86.

39 Dom Pedro, "Diário de 1862," p. 20.

40 ASSRJ,ACM, "Bullário," II, 274–76; F. de Macedo Costa, *Luctas e victórias* (Salvador, 1916), pp. 245–48.

41 See Raimundo Magalhães Júnior, *D. Pedro II e a Condessa de Barral através da correspondência íntima do imperador, anotada e comentada* (Rio de Janeiro, 1956); Henri Ballot, "A face oculta de D. Pedro II," *O Cruzeiro,* April 22, 1967, pp. 115–21.

42 Dom Pedro II, "Diário de 1862," p. 78.

43 Dom Pedro II, *Conselhos à regente introdução e notas de João Camillo de Oliveira Torres* (Rio de Janeiro, 1958), pp. 35–36.

44 Pimenta, *Vida de D. Antônio Ferreira Viçoso,* p. 86.

45. *Ibid.,* p. 30. Little has been written about Dom Pedro Maria de Lacerda; the best source is the Bullário do arcebispado located in the Metropolitan Archive. On Dom João Antônio dos Santos of Diamantina, see José Teixeira Neves, "Aspectos do século XIX na vida de um prelado mineiro atividades e influência de Dom João Antônio dos Santos, Bispo de Diamantina," *Revista do Livro,* XX (Dec., 1960), 49–59; Severiano de Campos Rocha has published "Vida e obras de D. João Antônio dos Santos Primeiro e Santo Bispo da Diamantina," in *A Estrêla Popular* (Diamantina) in 1939 and 1940. The work was never brought together in a book and the only complete copy seems to be in Diamantina. Nothing serious seems to have been written on Dom Luis Antônio dos Santos. However, an incomplete diary and some of his notebooks exist in the Metropolitan Archive in Salvador.

46 The accusation has been made that the other bishops in Brazil remained silent. This is hardly true. For some of the support offered, see ANRJ,MI, Coleção Ecclesiastica, Caixa 893, Pac. 1, Doc. 75, Protest of Dom Manoel Joaquim de Silveira, Conde de São Salvador, Bahia, Jan. 8, 1874; ASSRJ,ACM, Dom Pedro Maria de Lacerda to Dom Vital, Rio de Janeiro, Aug. 30, [1873] and Dom Pedro Maria de Lacerda to Dom Antônio de Macedo Costa, Reservada, Rio de Janeiro, Sept. 8, 1873; "Bullário," II, 187–91; for published episcopal letters of support, see *O Apóstolo,* May 11, 1873; *A Bôa Nôva,* May 11, 1873; and *A Chrônica Religiosa* (Salvador), July 6, 1873, among others.

47 Joaquim Nabuco, *Um estadista do império, Nabuco de Araújo, sua vida, suas opiniões sua epoca* (2nd ed.; São Paulo, 1936), I, 220.

48 ANRJ,MI, Coleção Ecclesiastica, Caixa 885, Pac. 6, Doc. 21. Dom José Antônio dos Reis, Bispo de Cuiabá, to Eusébio de Queirós Coutinho Mattoso Câmara, Cuiabá, April 23, 1851.

49 The future of the religious orders seems to have been discussed by the Brazilians attending the First Vatican Council. Dom Pedro Maria de Lacerda argued

against Pinto de Campos. According to his chronicler, he also "did not agree with D. Antônio de Macedo Costa and other colleagues who looked towards their extinction in order to apply their wealth to the maintenance of the seminaries, of the missions, and of other diocesan works." ASSRJ,ACM, "Bullário," II, 197.

50 Cf. p. 123 and n. 39.

51 See for example *A Nação* (São Luis do Maranhão), July 29, 1869.

52 ASSB,ACM, Gabinete Archiepiscopal, D. Luis, Correspondência do Arcebispado, XXIX, 1881–1883, Draft of Dom Luis to Msgr. Mário Mocenni, reservado [July, 1882].

53 ASSB,ACM, Gabinete Archiepiscopal, Manoel dos Santos Pereira, "Relatório da Archidiocese da Bahia apresentado ao Nôvo Internuncio, D. Rocchio Cocchia, Arcebispo de Otranto, em 1885."

54 Joaquim G. de Luna, *Os monges beneditinos no Brasil. Esboço histórico* (Rio de Janeiro, 1947), pp. 36–37.

55 ASSB,ACM, Gabinete Archiepiscopal, Dom Luis Antônio dos Santos, "Diário," 1871–1874.

56 ASSRJ,ACM, "Bullário," II, 476.

57 *Ibid.*, pp. 476–77.

58 *Ibid.*, pp. 166–67.

59 *O Cruzeiro do Sul,* March 26, 1865.

60 *O Missionário Cathólico,* Aug. 13, 1865.

61 ASSB,ACM, Gabinete Archiepiscopal, XVII, Correspondência da Nunciatura, 1874–1881, No. 15/682, Msgr. Caesar Roncetti to Dom Joaquim de Azevedo, Petrópolis, Feb. 3, 1878.

62 ASSB,ACM, Gabinete Archiepiscopal, Dom Joaquim, Correspondência do Arcebispado, XXV, 1877–1879, copy of Dom Joaquim Gonçalves de Azevedo to Dom Pedro II, Salvador, April 4, 1878.

63 ASSB,ACM, Gabinete Archiepiscopal, XVII, Correspondência da Nunciatura, 1874–1881, No. 21/851, Msgr. Caesar Roncetti to Dom Joaquim Gonçalves de Azevedo, Petrópolis, May 4, 1878.

64 *A Bôa Nôva,* Dec. 6, 1873.

65 Dom Pedro II, "Diário da viagem do Imperador a Minas Gerais," *Anuário do Museu Imperial,* XVIII (1957 [i.e., 1964]), 97; Um Padre da Congregação da Missão [Antônio da Cruz, C.M.], *O centenário do Caraça 1820–1920* (Rio de Janeiro, 1920), pp. 56–57; *O Apóstolo,* June 12, 1881.

66 ASSRJ,ACM, "Bullário," II, 167.

67 ASSB,ACM, Gabinete Archiepiscopal, Sé Vaga, Monsenhor d'Amour, Correspondência do Governo Imperial, IV, 1874–1877, José Bento da Cunha Figueiredo, Rio de Janeiro, Jan. 31, 1876, No. 267.

68 *O Monitor Cathólico,* July 10, 17, and 24, 1887.

69 *O Amigo da Religião* (São Paulo), Aug. 24, 1855.

70 *Consultas do Conselho do Estado sôbre negócios ecclesiásticos compilados por ordem de S. Ex. o Sr. Ministro do Império* (Rio de Janeiro, 1869–1870), II, 165–68.

71 *O Apóstolo,* June 17, 1866; May 5 and June 2, 1867; *A Bôa Nôva,* May 7, 1873.

72 *Consultas do Conselho do Estado,* I, 71ff.

73 *A Bôa Nôva,* July 9, 1873.

74 ASSB,ACM, Santos Pereira, to the new internuncio.

75 *O Amigo da Religião,* May 29, 1855.

76 *Consultas do Conselho do Estado,* II, 265–74.

77 See for example *A Nação,* Oct. 14, 1869.

78 See *O Apóstolo,* March 9; April 13; and May 4, 1873; *A Bôa Nôva,* July 19, 1873; *A Ordem* (São Paulo), Feb. 7, 1874.

79   *O Apóstolo,* July 18, 1880.
80   See Sr. Mary Crescentia Thornton, B.V.M., *The Church and Free Masonry in Brazil, 1872–1875: A Study in Regalism* (Washington, 1948).
81   *O Mosquito,* Jan. 17, 24 and 31; Feb. 14, 21 and 28; and March 7, 1874, among many others. The author has a collection of those numbers of *O Mosquito* from 1871 until 1874 which were concerned with ultramontanism and the Religious Question. A convenient reference to the caricatures on the Religious Question may be found in Herman Lima, *História da caricatura no Brasil* (Rio de Janeiro, 1963), I, 238–47.
82   *A Bôa Nôva,* April 16, 1873.
83   *O Apóstolo,* Sept. 21, 1873.
84   *Ibid.,* Oct. 25, 1876.
85   *Ibid.*
86   *O Jornal de Commércio,* Oct. 22, 1876; *O Globo,* Oct. 22, 1876; *A Gazeta de Notícias,* Oct. 22, 1876; *O Diário do Rio,* Oct. 24, 1876; and *A Reforma,* Oct. 24, 1876, reprinted in *O Apóstolo,* Oct. 25, 1876.
87   *O Ganganelli* (Rio de Janeiro), Oct. 22 and Nov. 2, 1876.
88   Washington, D.C., National Archives, Department of State, Dispatches from Brazil, XCIV, James R. Partridge to Hamilton Fish, No. 348, Oct. 31, 1876.
89   Arquiodiocese de São Paulo, Arquivo da Cúria Metropolitana, Registro da Correspondência Oficial, 1876–1880, copies of o Vigário Augusto Cavalheiro e Silva to Dom Lino Deodato, Patrocínio das Araras, April 10, 1877, Arm. 5, Prat. 2, Num. 8, ff. 9v–10r, and Dom Lino Deodato to Sebastião José Pereira, Presidente da Província de São Paulo, São Paulo, April 13, 1877, Arm. 5, Prat. 2, Num. 8, f. 10v. The Republican and Gallican journal, *A Província de São Paulo,* in reporting the incident, argued that the mission had been stopped not to prevent it but rather to prevent scenes of fanaticism. Between two evils, the lesser was chosen. *A Província de São Paulo,* April 1, 1877.
90   *O Apóstolo,* April 27, 1881.
91   ANRJ,MI, Relatórios das Províncias, Ceará, 1886–1887, "Falla dirigida a Assembléa Legislativa Provincial do Ceará na segunda sessão da 26ª Legislatura pelo Presidente da Província Dr. Eneas de Araújo Torreão, fala de 1 de julho de 1887," p. 61.
92   ANRJ,MI, Relatórios das Províncias, Santa Catharina, 1888–1889, "Relatório com que o Exm. Sr. Coronel Dr. Augusto Fausto de Souza abrio a 1ª Sessão da 27ª Legislatura da Assembléa Provincial em 1º de setembro de 1888," pp. 40–41.
93   ANRJ,MI, Relatórios das Províncias, Baía, 1887, "Falla com que o Illm. e Exm. Sr. Conselheiro Dr. João Capistrano Bandeira de Mello, Presidente da Província, abrio a 2ª sessão da 26ª Legislatura Provincial no dia 4 de outubro de 1887," pp. 53–54.
94   There was agitation after the Religious Question for the formation of a Catholic party. A program was drawn up. See "Um Cathólico Brazileiro," *Ensaio de programma para o partido cathólico no Brasil* (Pôrto and Braga, 1877). An attempt to field Catholic candidates in 1876 in Minas Gerais came to naught, *Bom Ladrão* (Diamantina), Sept. 20, 1876.
95   The failure of Catholicism in intellectual circles has been negatively shown by João Cruz Costa, *A History of Ideas in Brazil: The Development of Philosophy in Brazil and the Evolution of National History,* trans. Suzette Macedo (Berkeley and Los Angeles, 1964). Mr. Costa devotes slightly more than a page (55–57) to Catholicism during the Empire. For some reason, Cândido Mendes de Almeida is not mentioned.
96   Gilberto Freyre, *Mother and Son: A Brazilian Tale,* trans. Barbara Shelby (New York, 1967), pp. 119–21.

COMMENTARY

Donald Warren, Jr.
Long Island University, Brooklyn, New York

PROFESSOR Boehrer is too much the classic historian to use jargon like "cultural lag," but that is the nub of his explanation for Brazil's freedom from the "horrendous Church-State problems which afflicted Spanish America." The *Dictionary of Sociology* defines cultural lag as "retardation in the rate of change of some one part of an interrelated cultural complex," [1] the latter in this case being the Roman Catholic Church and the retarded part being the Brazilian clergy and ruling class. I find his idea original and well reasoned. It is more than plausible. Thanks to extensive documentation, it is persuasive. Here I should like to draw your attention to some emphases Professor Boehrer makes which seem to weaken the force of his sound thesis, for I feel at times he places the theologically absolute too close to the historically relative. I shall raise these points chronologically rather than topically.

There is grand sweep to his assertion that in no other Catholic country "was the new thinking embraced by the political and ecclesiastical hierarchy to the extent that it was in Portugal." If we limit new thinking to regalism—that is, the "assertion of royal rights in ecclesiastical affairs at the expense of the Pope" [2]—we can perhaps let it stand unchallenged. In fact, it was during the very reign of the last of the Spanish Hapsburgs, Carlos II, when the pope "had been able to extend his influence over the Spanish branch of his universal church," [3] that the Bragança monarchy began to feel its regalist oats. In 1674 the pope, in response to anguished petitions from the New Christians in Portugal (and probably from their allies, the Jesuits, as well), had suspended the Portuguese *Santo Oficio* from its functions. For seven years the pope held out against petitions from all three *Braços* of the *Côrtes*. They were

141

urging him to re-establish the Inquisition as a matter of national necessity. He yielded to the Portuguese Crown only in 1681.[4] Then, with the
opening of the long prosperous reign of Dom João V (1706–1750), the
Golden Age of Brazil, the Crown freed itself from any papal restraint
and let the grand inquisitor (Cardinal Nuno da Cunha e Ataíde) run a
popular-type *Santo Ofício*. Thus, at the very time of and in sharp contrast to the coming of *las luces* to Spain, Portugal undertook the imposi-
tion of orthodoxy along the religious-racial outlook of the people. In
Spain one finds Frenchmen in the train of Felipe V bringing the
eighteenth-century form of what Friedrich Heer calls "the 'upper' culture of Christianity, educated humanism and rationalism," whereas in
Portugal the Crown was giving way to what he calls the "underground"
or "the 'lower' culture of the masses."[5] By the time Carvalho e Melo
came to power (1750), the *Santo Ofício* had completed its job so that
the future Marquês, one of its familiars, rightly regarded the political
and social problem of the New Christians as practically solved. He
turned his ferocious gaze from what the people regarded as the ultra-
marine to what he saw as the ultramontane faction, the Jesuits. To heap
humiliation upon their suppression and confiscation of property, he
used the same blunt instrument the previous regime had used on the
New Christians, the *Santo Ofício*. With the traditional public pomp of
an *auto da fé* the Jesuit Malagrida was garrotted, his body burned
forthwith, and his ashes scattered to the winds.[6] I find it misleading to
call this Pombal's "first assault on the traditional defenders of religious orthodoxy," when in Portugal the orthodoxy of the Society had
not always measured up. Professor Boehrer's wording appears to imply
that the Marquês attacked the order because it defended orthodoxy,
which seems as unlikely as asserting that it was for theological reasons
that he outlawed legacies and forbade religious orders to receive novices. His citation from Dabney on "justifiable lies" is but a minor instance of Jesuit unorthodoxy. "Regalist" is the *mot juste* to define Pombal's acts. Because they deprived the king's subjects of freedom of
conscience, "new thinking" does not fit. Certainly they cannot be called
"enlightened," at least in the sense Richard Herr uses it for Spain at
the time: "religiously unorthodox outlook on life . . . deep faith in the
ability of the human mind to learn the truths of nature through observation and reason, . . . [so that] by the end of the eighteenth century
experimental science had largely replaced theology in the minds of
educated men as the queen of the sciences."[7] That definition scarcely
describes the minds of educated men either in Pombaline or in post-

Pombaline Portugal and barely applies to Brazil. (*Pace,* Prof. Burns!) Professor Boehrer admits as much when he concedes that the Pombaline university reforms may not have introduced "radical departures in methodology and 'philosophy.'" Let us say rather that Pombal employed the new thinking only in the sense of "capable monarchs making use of personal power to reform their countries . . . [who] adopted legislation that would further the commercial economy so that it would enrich their states." [8]

In sum, Professor Boehrer would have strengthened his thesis that nineteenth-century Brazil remained Pombaline had he more sharply isolated regalism from other aspects of the new thinking. These aspects are only peripheral, not central, to his sound argument that educated Brazilians and their Catholic clergy were of like mind thanks to their mutual remoteness from Europe during the quarter-century of the French Revolution and Napoleonic Empire. With barely a disturbing breeze to change their serene climate of opinion they passed from the Pombaline Colony, through the co-kingdom and the hectic First Reign and Regency into the cozy Second Reign of the Bragança monarchy.

It is only fitting and proper that Professor Boehrer faults Williams for calling Dom Pedro a "religious liberal" (with a small "l") without defining her term. Yet on the next page he saddles the Emperor with a regalist "ideology." Ideology succeeded theology in the past century when the "ideology of Progress" (with a capital "P") held sway in much of western Europe and this hemisphere. In H. Stuart Hughes' words, "Ideology lies somewhere between *abstract* political and social philosophy and the *practical* activities of parties and pressure groups. Indeed, it provides the link between the two" [9] (italics mine). Without action, then, there is no ideology, merely idealism or *Weltanschauung*. Here is perhaps the closest Dom Pedro came to formulating a philosophy: "I am religious because morality, which is the quality of intelligence, is the foundation of the religious idea." [10] Since Dom Pedro did not clarify this circular philosophy, the historian can arrive at any ideology he may have had only from his practical activity—that is, look upon him as the head of the regalist party or pressure group. His prime minister, Nabuco, proposed in 1853 that the government prohibit monastic orders from receiving novices and got the controversial measure decreed in 1855, about a decade after the young Emperor had made his "first major appointment . . . of Antônio Ferreira Viçoso as the Bishop of Mariana. The new Bishop was a Portuguese and a member and a former superior of the Congregation of the Mission" (an order of secular priests

known as Vincentians) . By bringing up this appointment several paragraphs *after* discussing the novitiate decree, when in fact Viçoso's appointment preceded it, Professor Boehrer runs the risk of misleading us
about Dom Pedro's "ideology." Rather, the Viçoso appointment made
in the forties during the first decade of the Second Reign would seem to
show the Emperor's youthful conviction that clerical reform must come
either through the agency of European clergy or (we can infer from his
nomination of prelates in later decades) through the agency of Brazilian priests trained in Paris and Rome, which after 1848 became centers
of ultramontanism. If we are going to ascribe an ideology to Dom Pedro
on the basis of his actions and diary entries, would it not go something
like this? "A country's morals and culture are to a great extent shaped
by its clergy. Brazilian culture is low and our clergy is corrupt. It needs
to be reformed and I can find the best men to carry reform out among
native Europeans or Brazilians trained in Europe, whether secular or
regular is not important. I concur with my ministers who find the monastic orders here beyond redemption." Gallican, yes; regalist, to be sure;
and Pombaline, if you will! Still, there is no theological issue. The state
confiscated no property (it was German Benedictines who eventually
fell heir to Benedictine holdings) . Hence, I do not think it follows that:
"In one sense, the decree of 1855 was a logical culmination of Pombal's
first assault on the traditional defenders of religious orthodoxy when the
Portuguese minister suppressed the Jesuits. Now in Brazil, it would be
the turn of all the other orders." Dom Pedro was less concerned with the
absolute, the religious orthodoxy that the monastic orders displayed to
the faithful, than with the relative, their sexual and financial morality.
Agreed that the consequence of the imperial decree of 1855 was woeful,
the bane is not to be found in a decline in the intellectual level of theology but in the material exhaustion of the monastic orders which "fell
into the hands of foreign friars, summoned to repopulate the convents
which were weakened by the prohibition against receiving novices." [11]
Here I must raise the question why Professor Boehrer passes over in
silence the State's permission to let teaching orders like the Vincentians
and, yes, the Jesuits, educate the youth of the Brazilian upper class. I
find the Empire's reliance on regular clergy to educate the future leaders
of the country more pertinent to discerning the nature of Church and
State relations than Dom Pedro's decoration of Renan in the seventies,
after the Religious Question. As loyal patron of the Instituto Histórico
e Geográfico Brasileiro, Dom Pedro would admire a scholar who studied
religion from an historical rather than a theological point of view.[12]

The decoration (to which I can find no reference) of the "ex-priest" shows merely that the Emperor shared the conventional *Weltanschauung* (not necessarily ideology) of the Brazilian elite or "society" (as Professor Boehrer calls it). This was the society from which the new clergy and the new hierarchy were becoming increasingly alienated, thanks to their new European orthodoxy (ultramontanism)—new for Brazil at any rate. Hence follows the Emperor's feeling of outrage, a truly Pombaline-Bragança outrage, when the bishops he had fostered to reform the Brazilian clergy attacked as unorthodox the comfortable Brazilian convention that Masonry was compatible with Catholicism. Brazil's cultural lag from Latin Europe was palpable. A brief *Kulturkampf* ensued, the Religious Question.

The first footnote of this stimulating original paper draws attention to Padre Júlio Maria's *O catolicismo no Brasil,* which Professor Boehrer calls "the best general account of the state of Catholicism in the nineteenth century." [13] I agree. Júlio Maria was neither a conventional Brazilian priest nor a professional historian. Writing in 1899, he judged the colonial period one of religious splendor, the imperial period one of regalist decadence, and the first decade of the Republic one of hopeful liberty. The Empire broke new ground by ensnarling the Brazilian clergy in the *"caatinga do regalismo."* The Second Reign was marked by the destruction of the regular clergy, by loss of clerical prestige, by the "energetic but ephemeral" reaction of the bishopric and Catholic elements during the Religious Question, and lastly by the rationalism and scepticism of the elite. He frequently cites a source Professor Boehrer calls reliable if ultramontanist, Cândido Mendes.[14] From his careful research, Cândido Mendes decided that the empire did not mean to reform the orders but to extinguish them, from which he drew the conclusion that under the Empire "Brazil never had even one truly Catholic government." Without entering the bog of what constitutes "a truly Catholic government," we historians cannot but agree with Cândido Mendes and Júlio Maria that in the period 1840–1889 the state did have the "right to police religious worship and to inspect doctrine and discipline." And it exercised that right. The outspoken priest said many a time that in the face of this regalist right and practice the clergy remained for sixty-seven years "mute, impassive, resigned to everything imposed upon it, [and] woke only for a moment, returning again to its lethargic slumber of indifference." Only by coming down so hard on clerical laxity does Professor Boehrer part company with Júlio Maria's trenchant conclusions. Much more enlightening than Júlio Maria is

Professor Boehrer's detailed analysis of the ecclesiastical hierarchy's all-too-light hand in the selection of and control over parish clergy. His analysis brings home to us, who are more-or-less accustomed to a free Church in a free State, why the Brazilian bishops could lend mere "moral support" to their imprisoned colleagues. Júlio Maria, though, had respect only for the teaching and the new orders (perforce mostly foreigners) to whom the rich, he thought, should be—but were not—most thankful. The Salesians arrived in 1883 and set a social Catholic example by erecting poor boys' orphanages. Such good works, he felt, lessened the poor's envious hatred for property and wealth. Ralph della Cava, looking through a different lense, has perceived that these new orders constituted a form of ecclesiastical neocolonialism which gave rise to nationalist resentment.[15] French and Italians, with the Emperor's approval naturally (and now Germans, Belgians, and Americans), simply replaced the Portuguese clergy of the colonial period. Della Cava cites some telling examples late in the Second Reign that show European clerical contempt for Brazilian Catholicism and culture, the culture that Dom Pedro wanted to raise.

In conclusion, I should like to bring up to date one of the issues Júlio Maria and George Boehrer have raised. The message of the *misionário do Brasil* (Maria's papal title) was, "Brazilian Catholics, rally to the Republic! Accept constituted authority and fight legislation. After all, the Republic has ended the suffocating regalism of the Second Reign. Now the Church has the glorious chance to 'christianize democracy' by bringing God to the People." Júlio Maria remained cheerful, pugnaciously so, even though a decade of liberty had persuaded him that the Brazilian clergy remained mute and impassive. He fervently desired what Professor Boehrer calls "the beginnings of a Catholic reformation in Brazil." But was there one and, if so, has it really continued "throughout the Republican period, gaining in vigor after the separation of Church and State?" I doubt if the "Catholic revival" has brought about any kind of what Júlio Maria called "a união da Igreja e do Pôvo." He wanted to "reconstruct the social edifice by infiltrating Catholic truth not only in souls but in politics, administration, and government." Have the books of Jackson de Figueiredo and Alceu Amoroso Lima and the ideas of Jacques Maritain passed beyond the seminaries and the middle class, and brought the Church any nearer to the people? The proliferation of cult and sect among the masses suggests an answer. More to the point of Professor Boehrer's well-researched paper is evidence that the Second Vatican Council has split the Brazilian Church, and that the present Government does not tolerate the idea of Churchmen free to preach the social gospel that Fr. Júlio Maria expounded in the nineties.[16]

NOTES

1 Ed. H. P. Fairchild (New York, 1944), p. 170.
2 Magnus Mörner, "The Expulsion of the Jesuits from Spain and Spanish America in the Light of Eighteenth Century Regalism," *The Americas,* XXIII (Oct., 1966), 157.
3 Richard Herr, *The Eighteenth-Century Revolution in Spain* (Princeton, 1958), p. 13.
4 J. Lúcio de Azevedo, *História dos christãos-nóvos Portuguêses* (Lisbon, 1921), pp. 311–23.
5 Friedrich Heer, *The Intellectual History of Europe,* trans. J. Steinberg (Cleveland and New York, 1966), p. 1.
6 "In 1751, Pombal curbed the Inquisition and ruled that henceforth no *auto da fé* should take place and that no religious executions should be carried out without government consent." Charles E. Nowell, *A History of Portugal* (Princeton, 1952), p. 166, cited from John Smith, *The Life of the Marquis of Pombal* (London, 1840), I, 65. Pombal regarded the Jews as a powerful commercial *república* with worldwide connections but, unlike the Jesuits, leaderless. J. Lúcio de Azevedo, *O Marquês de Pombal e a sua época* (2nd ed.; Rio de Janeiro, 1922), pp. 109–10. See also pp. 89–92, 96–97, 134–40, and 194–208.
7 *The Eighteenth-Century Revolution in Spain,* p. 85.
8 *Ibid.,* p. 8.
9 *Contemporary Europe: A History* (Englewood Cliffs, N. J., 1961), p. 11.
10 C. H. Haring, *Empire in Brazil* (Cambridge, Mass., 1958), cited in M. W. Williams, *Dom Pedro the Magnanimous* (Chapel Hill, N. C., 1937), pp. 166–73.
11 Fernando de Azevedo, *Brazilian Culture: An Introduction to the Study of Culture in Brazil,* trans. W. R. Crawford (New York, 1950), p. 161.
12 In point of fact, Renan was never a priest. In Oct., 1845, "shortly before the time arrived for him to be ordained a sub-deacon," he left the Seminary of St. Sulpice in Paris. Albert Schweitzer, *The Quest of the Historical Jesus,* trans. W. Montgomery (New York, 1961), p. 180.
13 Júlio Maria, *O catolicismo no Brasil (Memória histórica),* intro. Alceu Amoroso Lima (Rio de Janeiro, 1950), pp. 8–17 and 133–256.
14 See Boehrer's footnotes 9 and 92.
15 "Ecclesiastical Neo-Colonialism in Latin America," *Slant* (London), XVII (Oct.–Nov., 1967), 17–20.
16 Thomas G. Sanders, "Catholicism and Development: The Catholic Left in Brazil," in *Churches and States: The Religious Institution and Modernization,* ed. Kalman H. Silvert (New York, 1967), pp. 81–99.

THE TRANSFER OF THE PORTUGUESE COURT
TO RIO DE JANEIRO

Alan K. Manchester
Duke University, Durham, North Carolina

INTRODUCTION

THE transfer of the Portuguese Court from Lisbon to Rio de Janeiro in 1807–1808 precipitated developments of long-term consequence. It modified radically the relationship between the Mother Country and its most prosperous colony; it shaped the course of Brazilian independence; and it contributed materially to the preservation of the union. Like Spanish America, colonial Portuguese America suffered from accentuated regionalisms of geography, economic interests, clan loyalties, and cultural development; but unlike Spanish America it emerged from the independence movement as a single political unit. Considerable spade work has yet to be done before a reasonably satisfactory answer can be formulated as to why there is only one Brazil. But it is quite clear that one of the major reasons is the fact that on the eve of the independence movement Brazil possessed the attributes of an absolutist, centralized sovereign state. Why the founding fathers during the first two critical decades of the Empire elected to utilize the political machinery which they inherited is the subject of another study. This essay is concerned with the transfer of the government of the sovereign state of Portugal to Rio de Janeiro.

The discussion is divided into five sections. Section I focuses on developments which led to the decision on the night of November 24 to move the Court to Rio de Janeiro. Section II analyzes the embarkation with a view to determining whether the transfer was a precipitate flight or a planned and effective political maneuver. Section III identifies the elements of a sovereign state which were loaded aboard the fleet for shipment to Rio de Janeiro. Section IV concentrates on the way in which

148

the Court set up shop in the new location. And Section V brings the story to a climax with the Carta de Lei of December 16, 1815, which raised Brazil to the status of co-kingdom.

I. THE DECISION

As the summer and fall of 1807 wore on, Portugal came increasingly under a crossfire between France and England. After Tilsit (June 25, 1807), Napoleon was determined to close the remaining major leaks in his Continental System, namely, Denmark in the strategic Baltic-North Sea area and Portugal in the equally strategic southwest corner of Europe. The absorption of Denmark was a relatively simple operation, whereas the subjection of Portugal encountered troublesome political and military opposition and led to a totally different resolution.

Napoleon initiated action against Portugal on August 12, 1807.[1] On that date a joint note signed by France and Spain was delivered to Antônio de Araújo de Azevedo (later Conde da Barca), Minister of Foreign Affairs and War and Minister of State. The demands were precise and the time limit was specific. Portugal was to declare war on England by withdrawing its minister from London and requesting the recall of the English representative in Lisbon; the ports of Portugal were to be closed to British war vessels and merchantmen; and English residents in Portugal were to be imprisoned and their property was to be confiscated. A reply was to be made by September 1 and failure to comply with the demands would mean war.[2]

Between August 12 and November 24 the reaction of the Portuguese shifted by gradual and reluctant steps from the belief that an accommodation was possible to the comprehension that Napoleon did mean business. The transition is clearly evident in the recommendations of the councillors and the action of the Council of State.[3] On August 19 the Council voted to resist the demand to detain English residents and to confiscate their property. It hoped to adjust matters with reference to the other stipulations by arranging with England a "simulated" state of war.[4] By August 21 a new factor was under active consideration. In a *parecer* of that date João de Almeida de Mello de Castro (later Conde das Galvêas) presented his analysis of the situation and made a positive recommendation. It is obvious from his analysis that he was adequately informed as to the terms of the Treaty of Tilsit; that he was aware of the implications of the dissolution of the League of Armed Neutrals and the union of the Russian fleet with those of France and Spain; and that he foresaw clearly the reaction of England if Portugal acceded to Napoleon's demands. He realized that even if Britain should agree to the simulated state of war, Portugal would receive a grievous injury to her trade by virtue of the interdiction of communication with her colonies. In his mind there was only one solution, the immediate removal of the entire Court to Brazil.[5]

Five days later the council recommended to the Prince Regent (later João VI) that the Prince of Beira, the nine-year-old heir to the throne, should go to Brazil at the earliest possible moment and that the fleet be made ready not only to take the heir and his party but also to transport the Prince Regent and the entire Court.[6] Negotiations with the French and Spanish ambassadors postponed the September 1 deadline from day to day until the end of September.[7] In the course of negotiations the ambassadors agreed to modify the original demand for the confiscation of the property of British subjects to sequestration.[8] But this was as far as they would go: if Portugal refused, they would request their passports and France and Spain would consider themselves at war with Portugal.

The Council reacted at a session on September 30. On the proposal that Portugal should maintain its refusal to imprison English subjects and to sequester their property, opinion was divided. The Marquêz de Bellas and Fernando José de Portugal (later Conde de Aguiar) concurred. Araújo de Azevedo and the Visconde de Anadia favored compliance with all the demands. João de Almeida de Mello de Castro opposed the proposed reply. He was convinced that it would not satisfy Napoleon while it would inevitably lead to war with Great Britain and the immediate capture of Lisbon with results such as had just taken place in Copenhagen. Portugal would involve itself in two wars and would place its colonies at the disposition of England. This in turn would lead to the ultimate independence of the colonies in consequence of the necessity of initiating trade through channels other than Portuguese ports. He urgently recommended, therefore, that naval preparations be hastened for the transportation of the entire Court to Brazil, that the necessary paraphernalia of state, the archives, and the belongings of the personnel who would accompany the royal family be assembled, and that proper measures be taken to safeguard the property of Portuguese residents in England.[9] The Prince Regent, after listening to the divergent views of his councillors, refused to modify his position and the French and Spanish ambassadors departed.[10]

On October 12 and again on October 14 the Council, in spite of the strong opposition expressed by Madrid, reiterated its recommendation that the Prince of Beira be sent to Brazil.[11] The Prince Regent had approved the proposal and sanctioned a proclamation to this effect but he refused to give the order for the departure.[12] Until the middle of October the Court was tranquil, confident that Napoleon had objectives of greater importance than the invasion of Portugal.[13] Concern quickened soon thereafter, however. On October 20 at the recommendation of the Council—the *assento* was not signed by João de Almeida de Mello de Castro—the Prince Regent announced that Portugal, abandoning its policy of neutrality, now supported the Continental cause and in consequence he was ordering the ports closed to British naval and merchant vessels.[14] On November 1 Lourenço de Lima arrived from Paris with the alarming information that Napoleon was not satisfied and would not be unless English residents were seized and their property sequestered. This together with the news that Marshal Junot had left Bayonne with a French army and that Spanish troops were concentrating on the border tightened the screws appreciably.

The reaction of the council was expressed in three long pareceres presented by Fernando José de Portugal, the Visconde de Anadia, and the Marquêz de Pombal. With variants in their rationalization, they were in agreement that submission was the only alternative. Resort to force was futile: what the powers of Europe had been unable to do, Portugal obviously could not hope to accomplish. The final step of detention of the English and sequestration of their property was unfortunate but it could be alleviated by passing the word along that for those who wished to leave, flight would be facilitated not only with respect to the actual escape but also with reference to financial damage. War with England would result but this was preferable to war with France and Spain. Preparations for the transfer of the Court to Brazil should be accelerated in order to provide a means of escape in case Napoleon violated his promise to respect the integrity of the Portuguese boundaries and to maintain the Bragança dynasty.[15] On November 5 the order was issued to detain all English residents and to sequester their property and Strangford requested his passport.[16] The Marquêz de Marialva, his bags stuffed with a treasure of diamonds, was hurried off to Napoleon with the news of the final full compliance.[17] The Portuguese Court anticipated that these measures would induce Napoleon to halt the advance of the French and Spanish forces but should this not be the case, it was determined to retreat to Brazil. The decision to embark would be made the moment French and Spanish troops crossed the border.[18]

On November 16 Sir Sidney Smith arrived off the port of Lisbon with the British squadron and a force of 7,000 men. He had orders to blockade the port and, if necessary, to repeat the Copenhagen action—which was to say that rather than to let the Portuguese naval and merchant vessels concentrated in the Tagus fall into French hands he was to force his way into the harbor and capture or destroy them. On the other hand, if Portugal agreed to all of the terms of the Secret Convention of October 22 or if the Court moved to Brazil, he was to give every assistance.[19] After consultation with Strangford, Smith advised the Court that Lisbon was under strict blockade.[20] On November 23 [21] the news reached Lisbon that Junot had crossed the border and was then at Abrantes. Simultaneously there arrived a copy of *Le Moniteur*, the official gazette of France, which announced Napoleon's decision to dethrone the house of Bragança.[22] The cards were now all on the table and the moment of decision was at hand.

The decision was reached at a meeting of the Council of State on the night of November 24. The assento[23] of the session demonstrates that the members of the council were fully cognizant of the situation and that they responded with prompt and appropriate recommendations. At the outset of the meeting by explicit order of the Prince Regent three items of information were laid before the Council: *(a)* incontrovertible evidence was at hand that French troops had penetrated Portuguese territory as far as Abrantes (approximately four days by forced march from Lisbon) ; *(b)* Lord Strangford had requested through Secretary of State Araújo an audience with the Prince Regent in order to present proposals which would resolve absolutely and finally the relations between the two monarchies; and *(c)* Sir Sidney Smith had sent notice also to the Secretary of State that he was blockading the port and that he would take hostile action to secure the naval and mercantile fleet unless Portugal were to declare a friendly disposition. On the basis of this information and in the light of developments, particularly of the past four months, the Council recommended that since every avenue of negotiation had been exhausted without success in the effort to assure the independence and even the continued existence of the monarchy, the entire family should embark for Brazil without a moment's loss of time. Furthermore, the Prince Regent should grant the audience to Ambassador Strangford and inform him of the decision. Admiral Smith should be notified immediately that the port was open to British naval and merchant vessels, that the Prince Regent desired that the squadron should enter the harbor at the earliest possible moment, and that the commanders of the forts were being ordered to permit the entry of all types of English vessels. And finally, if the Prince Regent decided to go to Brazil, he should appoint a regency composed of prominent civil and military figures to act in a fashion similar to that of the past when the kingdom found itself without a legitimate sovereign. The Prince Regent approved the recommendations and immediate steps were taken to translate them into action.

II. THE EMBARKATION

It was close on midnight when a messenger awakened Joaquim José Azevedo (the future Visconde do Rio Sêcco) with orders for him to report to the Prince Regent. When he reached the Palace of Ajuda, he caught sight, through a half-open door, of the perukes of the Council members and heard excited voices all talking at once. Bypassing normal procedure, the Prince Regent gave him verbal orders to execute the plans for the embarkation of the royal family, which, he was told, was set for the afternoon of November 27. Rio Sêcco delayed long enough to obtain permission for himself and his family to accompany the Court and then hastened to fulfill his mission.[24] He alerted the Marquêz de Vagos, Gentleman of the Bedchamber, the Conde de Redondo, Comptroller of Provisions of the Royal Household *(ucharia)*, Admiral Manoel da Cunha, commander of the naval squadron, and key persons of the Church and Treasury. He obtained from Admiral da Cunha a previously prepared diagram of the number, size, and location of rooms available in the fleet as a basis for his allocations. He then set up shop in a shed *(barraca)* on the docks at Belém where he made cabin assignments and directed the disposition of volumes sent down by the Treasury. He kept at the job both day and night until the afternoon of the twenty-seventh. He not only superintended the embarkation of the fourteen members of the royal family but also, and this was beyond the call of duty, of the more than twenty courtiers and their families specifically designated to attend them and of other members of the Court and their families who were ordered or permitted to accompany the Prince Regent.[25]

The refusal of the Prince Regent to leave Portugal until he received incontrovertible evidence that all other measures had failed placed the embarkation under heavy pressure.[26] With Junot at Abrantes time was severely limited. In spite of the fact that most of them had to be brought in from Mafra,[27] the boarding of the members of the royal family was reasonably efficient. But this was certainly not true of the operation in general. Estimates vary widely but something in the neighborhood of 10,000 persons boarded the ships between the morning of November 25 and the evening of November 27.[28] The confusion was monumental. Baggage of all kinds was piled indiscriminately on the docks. In some instances the belongings of owners who were unable to get aboard were placed on the ships and in other instances the possessions of those who did embark were left on the docks. Families were separated, unaware, until a reunion in Rio de Janeiro, of whether relatives and friends managed to obtain passage. A cold rain, which had fallen for days, persisted until the morning of November 27. A sullen, resentful populace crowded the streets and port area, threatening violence and obstructing the operation. The departure resembled an ignominious flight, a *sauve-qui-peut*.[29]

All were aboard, at least with reference to the naval squadron, by the evening of November 27.[30] On the next day the Prince Regent ordered the naval vessels to report on their state of readiness. Certain deficiencies in food and water were indicated but the amounts were insignificant in comparison with the total requirements.[31] On the same day he made his peace with Strangford and through him with Admiral Smith.[32] On the previous day, immediately prior to embarking, he had signed the proclamation in which he announced the transfer of the Court to Rio de Janeiro, explained why he was going, appointed the Regency, and stated the instructions under which it was to operate.[33]

Preparations for the departure were thus completed but the order to sail could not be given until the strong south wind which had persisted for days should change. Reports which filtered in as to Junot's whereabouts placed him at Cartaxo on the evening of November 28. If this were true, and it was, he could be expected to reach Lisbon by November 29 or, at the latest, November 30. Fortunately, the morning of November 29 dawned bright and clear with the wind from the northeast. Anchors were weighed between seven and eight and the fleet, both naval and merchant, dropped down into the lower Tagus. Admiral Smith checked the fleet and provided supplies where necessary, relieved crucial spots of congestion by transferring passengers to English ships, discovered one vessel unfit for the south-Atlantic crossing and ordered it to England for refitting, and assigned four English warships to accompany the Portuguese to Rio.[34] By late afternoon of November 29 the sails were no longer visible from the hills of Lisbon.[35]

Was the departure a precipitate flight or the result of a sound policy decision? The events of November 24–29 unquestionably leave the impression that the former judgment is true. But contemporary observers such as Rio Sêcco were convinced that the removal of the Court from Napoleon's reach was the lamentable but inevitable solution to the developments of the latter half of 1807. The pareceres and assentos of the Council of State for the period give ample evidence in support of this viewpoint. Modern scholars such as Oliveira Lima, Ângelo Pereira, and Tarquínio de Sousa, in contrast to the traditional view, consider the removal of the Court sound policy. Oliveira Lima says that it is "far more judicious to consider the transfer of the Court an intelligent and fortunate political manoeuvre than a cowardly desertion." Ângelo Pereira, insists that "the retirement of the Royal Family to Rio de Janeiro was neither a desertion nor a disorderly flight but was instead an intelligent solution, long premeditated, which completely upended Napoleon's plans." Tarquínio de Sousa feels that the common people of the time lacked the subtlety with which to evaluate the political advantages which accrued from the transfer and questions whether even today the full extent of the act is realized.[36]

III. ELEMENTS OF A SOVEREIGN STATE

Life aboard the ships was deplorable. Baggage had been severely curtailed by the notice that household effects could not be accommodated and in many instances personal belongings had gone astray in the confusion of the embarkation. Some had boarded so hurriedly that there was not time to snatch up more than the most essential items—Chancellor Thomáz Antônio de Villa Nôva Portugal, for example, brought a few articles of clothing in a sack. Overloading resulted in shocking congestion. Men and children slept side-by-side on deck; women had a minimum of privacy. Cleanliness of person and linen was impossible under the circumstances.[37] To a contemporary observer the conclusion was inescapable that the departure lacked adequate planning. The conclusion is sound if its application is restricted to the actual embarkation, and even here an exception should be made with reference to Rio Sêcco's efforts in behalf of the members of the royal family, their immediate retainers, and selected members of the Court. But to extend[38] the application to the condition of the vessels and the adequacy of supplies is questionable. To do so ignores the readiness reports of November 28, Admiral Smith's review of the fleet on November 29, and the obvious fact that in spite of two bad storms the passage was eminently successful. One ship, the "D. João de Castro," was forced to land in Paraíba for emergency repairs and the "Medusa" put in at Pernambuco, but both were able to join the Prince Regent in Bahia. Although rationing obviously was necessary, there is no record of a critical shortage of food or water, nor is there a report of the death of anyone prominent enough to warrant notice.[39] This was a notable achievement, particularly in view of the excessive overloading.

There is other evidence of advance planning. Pedro Gomes, a wealthy merchant of Lisbon, writing to his father-in-law, the Conde da Cunha on November 2, 1807, reported that "we have not as yet been able to arrange firm passage for there are many who wish to leave and the ships are few. . . . We shall keep you acquainted with developments. We are determined to leave this Capital. . . . The ships continue under hurried preparation and all signs indicate some kind of embarkation." [40] One Christiano Muller, writing from Lisbon to Dom Domingos de Sousa Coutinho in London, reported that some months earlier he had been charged with the task of inventorying the papers, books, maps, and prints belonging to Antônio de Araújo de Azevedo, and that on the night of November 25 he had been awakened with instructions to pack up everything belonging to the Ministry of State. This he had done in thirty-seven large boxes which were sent aboard the "Medusa" during the day of November 26.[41]

These are two examples, in different areas, of the preparation which preceded the departure. They illustrate a crucial aspect of the transfer of the Court to Rio de Janeiro. On board the fleet were the essential elements of a sovereign state: the personnel of the civil, religious, and military hierarchies; members of high society, the professions, and business; and the paraphernalia of government. The whole machinery of state was being transported, lock, stock, and barrel, to a new location overseas where it would take root and continue its accustomed ways.

The members of the royal family were distributed among three of the ships-of-the-line. On the "Príncipe Real" were the demented Queen; the Prince Regent; the Prince of Beira, heir to the throne and future Emperor Pedro I; Miguel, his younger brother; and the young Spanish prince, Dom Pedro Carlos, a favorite of the Prince Regent and the future husband of his eldest daughter. On the "Afonso de Albuquerque" were the Princess Regent, Dona Carlota Joaquina, sister of Fernando VII of Spain; the eldest daughter, Dona Maria Teresa, the Princess of Beira; and three of her sisters, the *Infantas* Dona Maria Izabel, Dona Maria d'Asumpção, and Dona Anna de Jesus Maria. On the "Rainha de Portugal" were the Princess of Brazil. widow of the older brother of the Prince Regent; two more *Infantas,* Dona Maria Francisca and Dona Isabel Maria; and Dona Marianna, sister of the Queen. Accompanying the Prince Regent were the Marquêz de Vagas, Gentleman of the Bedchamber, Fernando José de Portugal, Councillor of State, and other retainers. The Condes de Caparicá and Cavalleiros attended the Princess Regent and her party while the Marquêz de Lavradio watched over the welfare of those on board the "Rainha." Scattered throughout the squadron were Anadia, Bellas, Araújo, Pombal, Almeida de Mello de Castro, and Rodrigo de Sousa Coutinho,[42] all councillors of state; the Conde de Redondo, Comptroller of Provisions of the Royal Household; Thomáz Antônio de Villa Nôva Portugal, Justice of the High Court of Appeals and Inspector in the Royal Treasury; the Duke of Cadaval, cousin of the Prince Regent and a prominent nobleman of the realm; General John Forbes Skellater, a militarist with a long record of distinguished service in Portugal; Monsenhor Joaquim da Nóbrega Cam e Aboim, and many more.[43] The papal nuncio and the bishop of Rio were invited to accompany the Court and they accepted, but they were unable to get aboard the ship assigned to them and were forced, therefore, to make their own way to Rio at a later date.[44]

There were others, less prominent but significant in the society of a sovereign state. There were José Egydio Alvares de Almeida (later Marquêz de Santo Amaro) , a Brazilian by birth who was in charge of the King's Cabinet and served as confidential advisor to the Prince Regent; the brothers Lobato, Keepers of the King's Wardrobe, who were much in the confidence of the Prince Regent (later in Brazil both were made viscounts) ; Manoel Vieira da Silva (later Barão de Alvaiazere) , also Brazilian-born, the personal physician and confidant of the Prince Regent;[45] Theodore Ferreira Aguiar, Surgeon of the Fleet;[46] José Correia Picanço (later Barão de Goiana) , First Surgeon of the Royal Chamber and Professor of Surgery at Coimbra;[47] Friar José Marianno da Conceição Velloso, noted botanist, member of the Academia Real das Sciências de Lisbôa and one of the literary directors of the Régia Officina Typográphica (precursor of the Imprensa Régia) ;[48] João Ignacio da Cunha (later Visconde de Alcântara) , judge of the affairs of orphans *(juiz dos orphões)* in Lisbon;[49] Felisberto Caldeira Brant Pontes (later Marquêz de Barbacena) , Brazilian-born graduate of the Colégio dos Nobres, Capitão de Mar e Guerra at nineteen, adjutant to the governor of Angola, holder of the badge of the Ordem de Christo, lieutenant-colonel of a regiment of the line, and owner of rich estates in Bahia and Minas Gerais;[50] and a countless number of business men, some more, some less affluent than Pedro Gomes. And to these more useful members of society were added what Tarquínio de Sousa termed an "immense retinue of nobility, and functionaries more or less poltroons, more or less parasites." [51]

Every minister appointed by Dom João VI in Brazil until the final two years of his residence there were on board. Members of the Council of State, justices of the Court of Appeals and the High Court, officials of the Treasury and the various juntas, the hierarchy of the Church, army and navy officers, courtiers, professional and businessmen, functionaries of the lower levels, servants, and a multitude of hangers-on were on their way to the New World, eager candidates for posts in the new, yet old bureaucracy.

The utilization of Portuguese vessels for the transfer of the Court to Rio assured possession of what in the overseas area was a sizable navy. Authorities differ as to the number of ships in the squadron, but even at the minimum estimate of fifteen there was a sufficient number to provide a respectable fighting unit. There were eight ships-of-the-line with batteries ranging from seventy-four to eighty guns, most of them 74's. The three (or five) frigates carried thirty-six to fifty guns with 44's predominating. The two (or four) brigs were armed with twenty-two guns; the storeship (charrua) with twenty-six; and the schooner with twelve. The schooner turned back to Lisbon but another brig got out before the port was closed. An additional brig lay at anchor in the harbor of Rio and a schooner in Pernambuco.[52]

The merchant marine, such as it was, likewise escaped Napoleon's grasp. The twenty to twenty-five commercial vessels which accompanied the squadron belonged to the Brazil fleet. Additional ships were saved through an order, issued on October 7, 1807, by the Visconde de Anadia, Secretary of State for the Navy and for Overseas Dominions, which prohibited the departure of all Portuguese vessels from Brazilian ports. The order reached the colony during the last part of December and the early days of January. The time factor cut down the effectiveness of the embargo but, even so, it produced results. When, for example, the Prince Regent landed in Bahia on January 22, he found the port crowded with ships although the embargo had been in force for only three weeks.[53] The resource of a merchant marine was still available.

The inability of the Peniche regiment to find accommodations on board the fleet was not of crucial importance. The essentially military nature of the Brazilian colonial administration necessitated an adequate armed force. This consisted of regular troops *(tropa da linha)*, militia *(milícias)*, and territorial units *(côrpos de ordenanças)*. The regular troops were composed initially of regiments sent out from Portugal but reinforcements were recruited in the colony. Every free male between eighteen and sixty, unless he were specifically exempted, was obligated to serve in some branch of the armed forces.[54] The colony, thus, was already in a position, both in military organization and in manpower, to maintain internal order, resist outside attack, and even undertake aggressive action.

Aboard the fleet were other essentials. The contents of the Royal Treasury and the immense store of diamonds from the Crown monopoly accompanied the Court. The royal family, nobility, businessmen, and clerics loaded silver plate, jewels, heirlooms, books, cash, and any other movable assets which were at hand.[55] The treasury and equipment of the Royal Chapel were taken along in order to assure appropriate facilities for religious ceremonies. A printing press[56] with type was shipped on the "Medusa"; Antônio de Araújo de Azevedo managed to salvage the collection of books, papers, maps, and prints which Christiano Muller had inventoried several months earlier; and somewhere in the fleet were the Royal Library of Ajuda and a mass of government files.[57]

The last two items merit special mention. The primary, although by no means the sole value of the Ajuda Library lay in the Barbosa Machado Collection. Diogo Barbosa Machado, a cleric who was in his ninety-first year when he died on August 9, 1772, spent his long life in assembling printed works, most of them original editions, manuscripts, maps, prints, portraits, pamphlets, and fugitive pieces. His eclectic interests ranged through sacred and profane history, biographies of illustrious men and women, poetry, letters, geography, grammar, orations, genealogy, coats-of-arms, dictionaries, politics, and current events. The quality of his collection is suggested by his Camões items, which included a 1572 first edition and a 1597 edition of the *Lusíadas,* half a dozen commentaries dating from 1639 to 1759, and translations in Spanish, Italian, English, and Latin. In a catalogue which he himself prepared he lists thirty-four classifications with 4,301 works in 5,764 volumes. A single volume might consist of scores of items, as, for example, in the case of the fugitive pieces which were bound in some eighty-five volumes.

The fact that the Royal Library had been partially destroyed and the remainder severely damaged by the earthquake of 1755 led Barbosa Machado to donate his collection to the Crown. The transfer to the Palace of Ajuda was made between 1770 and 1773. There it was incorporated with a reconstituted Royal Library and now the whole unit was on its way to Rio de Janeiro where it was to become the basis for the Bibliotheca Pública and later for the Bibliotheca Nacional do Rio de Janeiro.[58]

The second item, the mass of government files, is surprising in both its bulk and coverage.[59] Three sources provide information on the amount and content. The first is a document in the Orem Papers in the Arquivo do Instituto Histórico e Geográphico Brasileiro entitled "Relação dos Officios, Notas, Tratados, Livros, e mais papeis que existem no Archivo da Secretaría de Estado dos Negócios Extrangeiros e da Guerra no Rio de Janeiro, e que ora se Remettem para Lisboa em 10 Caixões." [60] The second is a catalogue, issued by the Ministério das Relações Exteriores, of items in the Arquivo Histórico which pre-date 1822.[61] Pre-1808 papers are identifiable both as to date and as to whether they are originals or copies. The third source is the impressive collection entitled "Negocios de Portugal" in the Arquivo Nacional.[62]

Boxes I through V of the Orem inventory contained dispatches to and from fourteen foreign capitals. In spite of wide variation in starting dates, the documents pretty well covered the period from the mid-eighteenth century to 1807. The Paris dispatches began in 1743; London dispatches in 1753; The Hague, Madrid, Naples, and Rome in 1756; Vienna in 1758; Turin in 1761; Copenhagen in 1768; St. Petersburg in 1780; Berlin and Hamburg in 1790; Philadelphia in 1791; and Stockholm in 1793. With the exception of Paris, which terminated in 1795, and London, which continued on to 1809, all ended in 1807. In quantity the dispatches ranged from the eighty-four bundles for Madrid, through thirty-seven for London, thirty-four for The Hague, twenty-six for Vienna, twenty-four for Paris, and twenty-one for Rome to three for Stockholm. There were 299 bundles in these five boxes.

Boxes VI and VII contained items which, with the exception of eight bundles for Paris dating from 1796 to 1807, were all post-1808. Box VIII consisted of a mixture of bundles and bound volumes of correspondence, Court functions, and miscellaneous dispatches. Box IX dipped into the more remote past with eighteen entries, each entry containing from one to twenty-two volumes, the latter being letters dating from 1697 to 1734. One volume related to the arrival, hospitality, and departure of princely guests from 1713 to 1753 and several to instructions for ministers in foreign courts. Box X was a composite of treaties, letters, material which "through forgetfulness was not included in its rightful place," and a final group of "letters of certain Cardinals and other papers all of great antiquity."

As voluminous as the material was, it by no means exhausted the files of the Foreign Office, which were brought over in 1808 or in subsequent years. The inventory lists only those items which were taken to Lisbon in 1821. Much remained in Rio de Janeiro, as the pre-1808 papers still in the *Arquivo Histórico do Itamaraty* demonstrate. The Orem document does suggest, however, the content and the volume of the paraphernalia of government which were transferred with the Court and it provides some insight into the criteria of selection. That the Ministry of Foreign Affairs was not alone in its foresight is evident from Christiano Muller's thirty-seven large boxes of material belonging to the Ministry of State which were loaded aboard the "Medusa."

The second source, the catalogue of pre-1822 documents in the Itamaraty archives, is, with some exceptions,[63] less specific as to which papers were brought over from Lisbon and which were already in the archives of colonial Rio de Janeiro. Some which are distinctly Brazilian in content might well have been in the viceroy's possession in Rio. In other instances where the material refers to the relations of Portugal with the courts of Europe, there would have been no reason to send copies to the colony. The notations *original, cópia manuscrita moderna*, or *cópia manuscrita antiga* throw some light on the problem, but in the final analysis the identification of documents which accompanied the Court in 1807 is a matter of judgment. It is safe to assume, however, *(a)* that a great deal of material found its way to the archives of Brazil which under normal circumstances would have been located in Lisbon and *(b)* that an imposing amount of documentation on the foreign affairs of Portugal both pre- and post-1808, was left in Rio when the Court returned to Portugal.

It is only in the last decade that the third source, the "Negócios de Portugal," has received attention.[64] The papers apparently remained intact when the Court left Rio de Janeiro and, as far as the record shows, none have been sent to Lisbon since the departure. The collection is impressive both for its massiveness and for its breadth of coverage. As summarized in a typed catalogue, it includes: *(a)* correspondence with the Regency in Portugal, 1808–1821; *(b)* correspondence and papers of the Secretary of State, the Secretary of the Navy and Overseas Dominions; the Secretary of War and Foreign Relations, and of the Royal Treasury; *(c)* papers of the Mesa do Desembargo do Paço and the Mesa da Consciência e Ordens as they relate to the overseas dominions (The Azores, the Madeiras, Cape Verdes, S. Tomé and Príncipe, and the colonies in Africa and Asia) ; *(d)* documents of the Companhía Geral de Agricultura e Vinhos do Alto Douro; *(e)* documents of institutions and schools—hospitals and the University of Coimbra; *(f)* documents concerning political and ecclesiastical matters; and *(g)* *generalidades*—documents so varied that classification is difficult. Almost all of these are addressed directly to the king. They comprise topics such as representations from municipal governments, petitions for and the awarding of honors, general correspondence, personal matters of the royal family, and miscellanea.

This summary, with the exception of the first item, does not date the material. Keeping the problem of the transfer of government files in mind, we can organize the documents into three groups: First, papers which pre-date the removal of the Court, such as Caixa 623: Ministério da Guerra e Estrangeiros — Legações Portuguesas na Europa 1800–1801 and Na Tunis, Argel e Morrocos 1793–1803; or Caixa 725; Correspondência de Pombal, 1741–1776; or Caixa 641: Assuntos Políticos, 1792–1807 (correspondence of Araújo, Anadia, and others). Second, papers which both pre-date and post-date 1808, such as Caixa 622: Ministerio da Guerra e Estrangeiros, 1790–1821; or Caixa 627: Assuntos Eclesiásticos, 1750–1820; or Caixa 723: Consultas de Vários Orgãos Administrativos, 1762–1810; or Caixa 726: Universidade de Coimbra — Diplomas, 1770–1819; or Caixa 644: Cia. Geral de Agricultura e Vinhos do Alto Douro, 1783–1819. Third, papers which post-date 1807, such as Caixa 616: *Generalidades,* 1808–1820; or Caixa 618: Desembargo do Paço, 1808–1822; or Caixa 633: Contas dos Governadores do Reino, 1813. The heaviest concentration lies between the early 1790's and 1820.

The major part of the material in the collection falls in the pre-1808 period and yet many of the runs extend into the time when the Court was resident in Brazil, and a not inconsiderable number of items is restricted to the latter years. Apparently, papers resulting from new business in Rio were classified according to the same system and in some instances were placed in continuing files.

Inadequate as this listing is, it nevertheless suggests the predominance of the "business of Portugal." A sampling of the documents themselves reinforces this impression, as the following examples demonstrate:

Caixa 640, Pacote 2, Real Erário, Contadorías de Províncias do Reino, Documents 2–8, presents a detailed accounting of receipts and expenditures of the Royal Treasury for the six-month period ending June 30, 1802. The file begins with a printed folio-size document which lists in tabular form the various sources of receipts and the items of expenditures of the Royal Treasury. The space for amounts is left blank. Succeeding documents are reports, using this form, sometimes with modifications, from the city of Lisbon, the provinces of Portugal, and all overseas dominions. The reports contain illuminating notes on the sources of income and the nature of expenditures. A final document gives a summation and strikes a balance for the Royal Treasury—in favor of receipts.

Caixa 685, Ministério da Guerra e Estrangeiros, Pacote 3, consists of reports on the military posture of Portugal in the late 1790's, plans to accelerate preparations for the defense of the country, the threatening movements of French and Spanish troops, and the equipment and manpower needed to bring the armed forces up to the required level. The reports are detailed and some are quite extensive. The report of the Marquêz de Alorna, Marechal do Campo, dated 1799, on the economics of the army, runs to two documents of 113 folio pages. The total number of folios in this bundle alone exceeds two hundred.

Other less extensive documents further illustrate the point. The abbess of Santa Clara in Évora petitioned the Crown for a cistern with which to supply much-needed water for the convent (Caixa 622, Pacote 4). In the same bundle there is a description of the postal service in Portugal with an excellently designed map of the route and the cities served from the Algarves to Pôrto, and a request for an investigation by the Crown into the unseemly conduct of a priest. Other bundles (Caixa 627, Pacote 2 and Caixa 652, Pacote 2) contain official correspondence with the rector of the University of Coimbra, appointments to the faculty, and information on the recipients of degrees from 1795–1796 to 1809–1810.

From the Orem document which lists files which were but are no longer in Brazil and from pre-1808 material in the Arquivo Histórico do Itamaraty and the Arquivo Nacional it is quite clear that an abundance of government files accompanied the Court when it sailed from the estuary of the Tagus on the morning of November 29. The shuffling of papers by the bureaucracy could be resumed as soon as both were housed in Rio de Janeiro.

IV. SETTING UP SHOP

From the foregoing discussion it should be obvious that the removal of the Court from Lisbon to Rio de Janeiro involved far more than the turbulent days of the embarkation, and it should also be evident that from the broader viewpoint the operation was notably successful. The personnel, the appurtenances, and the paraphernalia of the sovereign state of Portugal were safely aboard ship, well beyond the reach of Napoleon. The next step was to set up shop in the new location.

The second storm divided the fleet with the result that the "Príncipe Real" with the Prince Regent and male heirs, the "Afonso de Albuquerque" with Dona Carlotta and some of the Infantas, the frigate "Urânia," and one of the English ships put in at Bahia. The "Rainha de Portugal" with the Princes of Brazil and more infantas, the "Conde Dom Henrique," the "Martim de Freitas," the "Principe do Brazil," the frigates "Minerva" and "Golfinho," and three of the English ships sailed directly to Rio de Janeiro. They arrived on January 17. The "D. Joao de Castro" on February 10 and the "Medusa" on February 16, after emergency stops, joined the Bahia contingent prior to its departure. The Prince Regent and his party arrived in Bahia on January 22, 1808, sailed for Rio de Janeiro on February 26, and entered the harbor on March 7.[65]

Thus, during the first five weeks of his residence in Brazil, the Prince Regent was forced to operate without his usual mechanics of administration. There was no ministry through which he could channel business, no Council of State to which he could turn for advice. Instead, he used the governor of the captaincy, the Conde da Ponte, as the instrument for the dispatching of business, Dom Fernando José de Portugal as his Minister of State, and the two of them plus the Marquêz de Bellas as his principal advisers. The procedure developed, apparently, without a priori planning, as a means by which to carry on the affairs of state.[66]

The Prince Regent arrived in Bahia at a time of severe crisis. The embargo regulation of January 1 prevented the departure of the ships which had been attracted to the port by the harvest season. The holds were full, warehouses crammed, and sugar, tobacco, and cotton were flowing to market. But from the news which accompanied the Prince Regent it was clear that the raising of the embargo would not solve the problem. By laws of long standing ships could clear colonial ports only for Pôrto and Lisbon, both of which were now in the hands of the enemy and both of which were under blockade by England. Moreover, the utilization of foreign merchantmen to relieve the congestion was equally prohibited. In sum, Portuguese ports at home and overseas were sealed off from communication not only with each other but also with all foreign ports. And yet to permit Portuguese merchantmen to determine their own destination or to allow entry to vessels of a foreign flag would violate the fundamental tenet of colonial administration. The problem was crucial and the decision would be far-reaching in its consequences.[67]

In spite of the absence of his accustomed administrative machinery, the Prince Regent was not without advice. This he received with reference to the commercial issue from three major sources: a parecer by the Marquêz de Bellas, a *Representação* presented to him by the Conde da Ponte on behalf of the mercantile and agricultural elements of the city, and the views of José da Silva Lisbôa (later Visconde de Cairú) which were transmitted through Fernando José de Portugal.

The date of the Marquês de Bellas parecer[68] is uncertain, but that is was prepared prior to the carta régia of January 28 is obvious. In it he urged that since the Continental ports were closed from within by the French and from without by the English, the ports of Brazil should be opened to all friendly nations, not to any single one since the latter would result in a species of slavery. He was uncertain whether importation should be permitted in all ports or whether it should be restricted to the place where the Court would be established. But a measure of some sort was essential to the financing of the government in its new location and to the welfare of the people of Brazil.

The second source of advice came from the citizens of Bahia in the form of a *Representação* signed by the Conde da Ponte and dated January 27, 1808.[69] In it the people of Bahia petitioned in behalf of commerce and agriculture and for the benefit of the royal revenue: *(a)* that the embargo be lifted, public announcement be made that France and Spain were enemies and England an ally, and permission be granted for ships to seek whatever ports seemed to offer the best advantage; *(b)* that all merchandise without exception be cleared on payment of duties to be determined by the governor of the captaincy together with appropriate officials of the Customs Service and the Royal Treasury—these to be in effect until such time as the Prince Regent could issue a general order; and *(c)* that the ships, cargos, and persons of the two enemy nations be seized. The three requests, submitted in the perplexing confusion of the moment, were designed to prevent continuing serious damage to commerce, the imminent loss in agriculture, the misery of the inhabitants of the colony, and the stagnation of the royal income. And finally, immediate action was imperative.

The third source of advice was José da Silva Lisbôa, native of Bahia, distinguished graduate of the University of Coimbra, so able in Greek and Hebrew that he was appointed substitute professor in these subjects immediately on graduation. He soon returned to Bahia where he taught Greek and philosophy. In 1797 he again visited Lisbon, returning shortly thereafter with the lucrative post of inspector (deputado e secretário da mesa da inspecção). In the meantime he had been reading in the field of political economy. In 1801 he published the first edition of his Tratado do direito mercantil and in 1804, after digesting Adam Smith, his Princípios de economia política. By 1807 he was well known and highly respected as a specialist in the new "science" of political economy.[70]

The evidence of his participation in the events which led to the carta régia of January 28 is less tangible than that of the Marquêz de Bellas and the Conde da Ponte, but that he exerted influence is undeniable. Bellas in his parecer urged that "we listen to the great economist whom we shall encounter in Bahia." Fernando José de Portugal was persuaded[71] by Silva Lisbôa to make an unsolicited direct approach to the Prince Regent with the objective of obtaining a measure consonant with the new economic principles. Through his books and conferences with the persons of influence he provided the theory and rationalization for and in part shaped the action urged upon the Prince Regent by the practical men of business.

Six days after he sailed into the harbor of Bahia and four days after he went ashore, the Prince Regent issued the carta régia of January 28, 1808.[72] It was addressed to the Conde da Ponte. In it the Prince Regent assured the Count that having considered the Representação which informed him of the suspension of commerce resulting from the critical developments in Europe and consequent grave damage to his vassals and to the Royal Exchequer and wishing to take prompt and effective measures to remedy the situation, he now decreed, as an interim provision, valid until a general order could be formulated, that: first, all items of whatever genre be allowed to enter the customs houses of Brazil whether in ships of friendly nations or ships belonging to his vassals, on payment of 24 percent tax, payment to be in conformity with regulations then in force, with the proviso that molhados (such as wine, spirits, and olive oil) pay double the current amount; second, not only his vassals but natives of friendly nations be permitted to send commodities to any port which in their opinion offered the best advantage, the permission to hold for all colonial products except brazilwood or other well-known monopolies, on payment of taxes already established in the respective captaincies; and third, all laws, edicts, and other decrees which hitherto had prohibited in Brazil reciprocal commerce and navigation between his vassals and foreigners be suspended and without force. The Conde da Ponte was to execute the decree at once, registering it in proper form and issuing the necessary orders.

From the outset the carta régia was recognized as a landmark in the transition of Brazil from colony to sovereign state. Silva Lisbôa called it the Magna Carta of Brazil and supported his statement by emphasizing the absurdity of a policy which would have continued the colonial status of the land in which the sovereign resided.[73] Luís Gonçalves dos Santos, a contemporary, hailed the happy results of a liberal, enlightened policy which triumphed over deeply rooted practices and injurious monopolies.[74] Mello Moraes, writing from the perspective of the mid-nineteenth century, insisted that once the ports were opened Brazil could never have reverted to colonial status, regardless of whether the Court did or did not return to Portugal.[75] Pereira da Silva, a contemporary of Mello Moraes, argued that the carta régia had results which exceeded the anticipation or intention of its authors. As he saw it, the commercial emancipation produced a revolution which shook the entire social structure of the colony and led irrevocably to political independence.[76] Modern scholars agree. Wanderley Pinho, for instance, holds that the evacuation of the Portuguese troops from Bahia on July 2, 1823, was but the last link in a chain of events which was initiated on January 28, fifteen years earlier.[77] Tarquínio de Sousa, in more moderate but equally positive terms, considers that the abatement of colonial exploitation brought about by the opening of the ports and the transfer of the Court to Rio de Janeiro unquestionably effected a radical transformation in the life of Brazil.[78]

The decree was a provisional measure which was subject to revision when more extended consideration could be given to the matter, and changes did occur. By a decree of June 11, foreign trade was restricted to the ports of Pará, Maranhão, Pernambuco, Bahia, and Rio de Janeiro, a practical measure designed to facilitate the administration of customs, and coastwise shipping was restricted to Portuguese vessels. Rates were modified from time to time in response to local demand or to treaty negotiations, but the basic principle of reciprocal navigation with friendly countries remained intact.[79] The Prince Regent adhered to it as firmly as he would have done with reference to the ports of Portugal had he been ruling from the Ajuda Palace.

The period in Bahia was occupied largely in festivities with which the bemused and delirious populace welcomed the Prince Regent and his Court. Some business, much of it routine, was transacted, however, in addition to the carta régia. Utilizing the emergency administrative procedure, the Prince Regent reduced sentences and granted pardons; listened to pleas for promotions and the improvement of roads, imposts, and distilleries; determined reprisals with reference to a Dutch brig anchored in the port; ordered the sequestration of a contraband shipment of brazilwood; granted licenses for manufacturing and industry; and authorized the organization of a marine insurance company. He created a school of medicine and surgery to be located in Bahia and he granted honors and decorations with a lavish hand.[80] But to pleas that he settle the Court in Bahia, he turned a deaf ear.

When the Prince Regent entered the bay of Rio de Janeiro on the afternoon of March 7, he still faced the task of setting up shop in the new location. The elements of the mechanism of a state were now safely in harbor. All that remained to be done, it seemed was to provide space in which the bureaucracy could do business and to pull the trigger which would set in motion the transplanted organism. Both of these the Prince Regent did but with an additional step by which the structure of the sovereign state of Portugal was recreated in Brazil. Each major feature of the central government was specifically established by appropriate decree, with the same name (sometimes with "do Brazil" added), the same powers, the same function, the same procedures as its prototype in Portugal. Where applicable the same precedents were used to legitimize a department, a junta, or a procedure. The removal of the Court to Rio de Janeiro, thus, was not simply the transplantation of a government; it was, rather the transfer of the elements of a sovereign state which in the new location were formalized into a new, yet old and familiar system. In the process the Portuguese government in Brazil became a Brazilian government.

The Prince Regent set into motion the transplanted organization by the appointment of a ministry. On March 10 he nominated Fernando José de Portugal de Castro (later Marquêz de Aguiar) as Minister of the Interior (Ministro dos Negócios do Reino), Rodrigo de Sousa Coutinho (later Conde de Linhares) as Minister of Foreign Relations and War, and João Rodrigues de Sá e Menezes (then Visconde de Anadia, later Conde) as Minister of the Navy and Overseas Dominions. On the following day the Royal Exchequer was added to Fernando José de Portugal's responsibilities and he was made Minister of State.[81] This and succeeding ministries were composed of men who in experience, point of view, and loyalties were continental Portuguese.[82]

The reproduction of parallel units of government began soon after the appointment of a ministry. By an *alvará*[83] of April 1, 1808, the Prince Regent created in Brazil a Conselho Supremo Militar which duplicated precisely one which had long existed in Portugal. The decree stated (¶ 2) that the council would take cognizance of all matters which were within the competence of the corresponding body in Lisbon and (¶ 3) that it would act under the same regulations as those which governed the council in Portugal, namely, the regimento of December 22, 1643, as amplified by further royal decrees and ordinances. Paragraphs four through ten spelled out in detail the functions, precedents, personnel, time of meeting, extent of jurisdiction, and duration of the decree, with the repeated proviso that when clarification was needed, reference should be made to the Lisbon prototype.

During the following months similar decrees instituted other key features of the government. On April 22, the Tribunal of the High Court (Desembargo do Paço) and Conscience and Orders (Consciência e Ordens) with the Chancellor (Chancellor-Mór do Estado do Brasil) was authorized;[84] on May 9, a Register of Honor Awards (Registro de Mercês) ;[85] on May 10, the Intendancy of Police (Intendência Geral da Polícia) , and the Court of Appeals of Brazil (Casa de Supplicação do Brasil) ;[86] on June 28, the Royal Exchequer (Erário Real) and the Council of the Royal Exchequer (Conselho da Real Fazenda) ;[87] and on August 23, the complex, sprawling Junta do Commércio, Agricultura, Fábricas e Navegação do Brasil.[88] In the course of time, others were added. The formal institution of these branches of government did not mean necessarily that they began to function as of the date of the alvará. In some instances, as in the case of the Intendência da Polícia, this was true, but in others, such as the Royal Exchequer, the department had been in operation for some time. What it did mean was that "of Brazil" became deeply embedded in the governmental structure of Portugal.

Interspersed among these governmental decrees and a mushrooming amount of day-by-day business were items that were significant in the transition of Brazil from colony to autonomous state. On April 1, 1808, freedom of manufacturing and industry was granted to Brazil and the overseas dominions;[89] on May 13, the Imprensa Régia was founded;[90]

on June 13, following the death of the patriarch of Lisbon, the bishop of Rio de Janeiro was appointed Court chaplain (Capellão-Mór) with "all the ranks and benefits which have gone with that post";[91] on June 15 the Cathedral was declared to be the Royal Chapel (Capella Real);[92] on September 10, the official gazette began publication;[93] on October 12 the Bank of Brazil was founded;[94] and on November 25 ownership of land by foreigners was permitted.[95] None of these measures would have been approved had Brazil still been viewed as a colony to be administered in accordance with the principles of the old regime.

The determination of the Prince Regent and his advisors to make Brazil over in the image of the Mother Country involved more than changes in the governmental structure. It necessitated a sharp departure from traditional practice with reference to cultural development. The old policies which had resulted in the neglect of education[96] and public health, the suppression of literary, philosophical, and scientific academies, the disquietude inspired by libraries, the prohibition against newspapers, journals, and printing presses, and the exclusion of foreign influence were incompatible with the new status of the colony. The Prince Regent and his advisors, particularly Rodrigo de Sousa Coutinho and Antônio de Araújo de Azevedo, were aware of the fact and devoted considerable attention to it.

The Prince Regent began the reform early in his residence in Brazil. While he was still in Bahia he appointed a Physician-General (Physico-Mór) and a Surgeon-General (Cirurgião-Mór) and authorized the founding of a medical school in that city. Later in Rio de Janeiro, he founded (November 5, 1808) a School of Anatomy, Surgery and Medicine in connection with the Royal Military Hospital, appointed (July 28, 1809) a Commissioner of Public Health (Provedor-Mór da Saúde do Estado do Brasil), established (April 1, 1813) a course in surgery in connection with the Hospital de Misericórdia and (April 26, 1813) a chair of Hygiene, Pathology, and Therapeutics in the School of Surgery in Rio de Janeiro, and authorized (December 29, 1815) a full course in surgery in the city of Bahia. Still in the area of advanced education, he approved (April 23, 1811) a six-year course of mathematics, sciences, physics and natural science, and engineering in the Royal Military Academy and instituted (June 25, 1812) a course in agriculture in Bahia and a chemical laboratory in Rio.[97] On April 7, 1808, he set up a Military Archive (Arquivo Militar do Brazil) for the preparation, collection, and verification of maps of the coastline and interior of Brazil and the overseas dominions;[98] and on October 29, 1810, he made available to the public the Royal Library.[99] On October 12, 1813, he inaugurated the Teatro Real de São João[100] and in 1815 negotiated for a French mission of artists, sculptors, architects, and artisans and organized, in preparation for their coming, the Escola Real de Sciências, Artes e Offícios.[101] He welcomed and facilitated visits by distinguished foreign scientists, artists, musicians, engineers, and curious travelers.[102] These measures and others like them reinforced the effects of the new economic freedom. Together they exerted a profound influence on the cultural life of Brazil.

The influx of titled nobility raised the question of a comparable element in the society of the emerging state. Two factors were largely responsible for the answer. In the first place, it had long been the practice of the Portuguese Crown to utilize honors as a means by which to win the loyalty of the rural landowners. In the second place, an aristocracy of economic power and social privilege already existed in the colony. It consisted of the owners of sugar plantations, cattle ranches, and food- and commodity-producing farms, who, grouped into tightly knit clans, controlled the areas outside the major coastal towns. It was the result of an indigenous development with roots that extended far into the past, but it had not been formalized by official recognition. The answer was obvious: by utilizing his power to grant titles and to award honors the Prince Regent could establish an effective link between the Royal Person and this influential segment of Brazilian life and at the same time reinforce the nobility as an essential element in the monarchical system.[103]

Honors *(mercês)* were of various types. The most coveted were titles of nobility. They were granted in Brazil without regard to the traditional rules.[104] They were not hereditary and they carried no material advantage. There was always a reference to a town, a province, a river, a section of the country, a battle site, or even the name of a plantation but the relationship between the geographical terminology of the title on the one hand and reality on the other was purely honorary. To the recipient, if he accepted the award, a title meant prestige, personal satisfaction, the expense of living up to the new status in society, and a sense of obligation to the Crown. Of less prestige but nonetheless desirable was an assortment of decorations related to the five special orders, The Ordem de Christo, the Ordem de São Bento de Aviz, the Ordem de São Tiago, the Ordem da Tôrre e Espada, and the Ordem da Nôssa Senhora da Conceição, each of which had gradations of its own. One of the most highly prized honors was the Título de Conselho.[105] Both titles and decorations were awarded to Brazilian-born colonials, continental Portuguese, and foreigners. Recipients included politicians, magistrates, professors, men of letters, and the military. Even a businessman on occasion received recognition.[106] Awards to Brazilians were made largely but not exclusively to members of the landowning clans.

The Prince Regent was lavish in his distribution of titles and decorations. According to one estimate[107] he created in eight years twenty-eight marquises, eight counts, sixteen viscounts, and twenty-one barons. A partial list of decorations further emphasizes the point. During his residence in Brazil, according to another estimate,[108] João granted 4,084 knights, commanders, and grand-crosses of the Ordem de Christo, 1,422 awards of the Ordem de São Bento de Aviz, and 590 awards of the Ordem de São Tiago. The figures omit the Ordem da Tôrre e Espada, the Ordem da Nôssa Senhora da Conceição, and the Título de Conselho.

Somewhat different but closely related in its results was the practice of appointing Brazilians as officers of the militia. These appointments, also called mercês, involved more than military command. They granted certain administrative powers such as the right to convoke the people, recruit troops, collect revenue, and maintain order. The recipient, already a person of some importance in his community, became a member of the hierarchy with fidelity to the Crown.[109]

The prodigal use of titles and honors was politically shrewd. It broke the rigidity and weakened the privileged character of the select minority of nobility but by the inclusion of Brazilians it heightened the social prestige of the segment of the population which had long enjoyed a privileged position, extended the influence of the Court to the municipalities, and won support among the great landowners of the interior. Adapted to the social conditions of the country, it became an effective means by which to mobilize the Brazilian elite in support of the Crown.[110]

V. CONCLUSION

The transfer of the Court from Lisbon to Rio de Janeiro produced significant changes in the economic development, the social and cultural life, and the governmental structure of the colony. Some of these changes, particularly the economic and social aspects, penetrated to the grassroots of the interior, but politically the transformation was restricted to the central government. In setting up shop in Brazil, the Prince Regent left the administration of the captaincies intact.[111] As

Silvestre Pinheiro Ferreira reported on March 15, 1822, to a special committee of the Côrtes, nothing was done during the residence of the Court in Rio de Janeiro to modify the arbitrary, dictatorial character of the administration of the provinces.[112] The tax system, the administration of justice, and the military organization remained colonial in point of view and practice. Additional tribunals were instituted, more districts *(comarcas)* were established, heavier taxes were imposed, and countless jobs were created, but this was done at the local level without disturbing the pattern of colonial administration. The major concern of the Prince Regent and his advisors was to perpetuate in Brazil by the transfer of the superstructure of government the centralized, absolutist system of the Portuguese monarchy, and the monarchy itself.

The course of events which was precipitated by the action of the Conselho de Estado in the Palace of Ajuda on the night of November 24, 1807, culminated in the carta de lei[113] of December 16, 1815, which raised Brazil to the rank of kingdom, co-equal under the Crown with Portugal and the Algarves. The act[114] constituted an official confirmation of the fact that between early 1808 and late 1815 the colony had been transformed into an autonomous state with its own political, religious, and social hierarchies, its own mechanism of government, its own social and educational amenities, and the right of self-determination in economic policy. The Mother Country and the colony were joined, and in the process the colony in effect became the Mother Country.

NOTES

1   The following discussion is based primarily on documents in the Arquivo Nacional in Rio de Janeiro. They are included in a file classified as Negócios de Portugal, Caixa 714, Pareceres do Conselho de Estado, 1797–1807. Documents Nos. 88–102 of Pacote 2 date from Aug. 21 to Nov. 24, 1807. The papers classified as Negócios de Portugal were brought to Brazil with the Court in 1807–1808, or immediately thereafter, and were not taken back when the Court returned to Lisbon. The documents are not numbered in chronological sequence.

2   Pareceres do Conselho de Estado, No. 96, Session of Sept. 23. Also, Great Britain, Public Record Office, Foreign Office file 63 (Portugal), vol. 55 (hereinafter cited in the form F.O. 63/55), Strangford [Percy Clinton Sydney Smythe, Viscount Strangford, British Minister in Lisbon] to Foreign Secretary George Canning, Aug. 13, 1807, No. 46. Also 63/57, Letters and Papers from Chevalier de Souza, Portuguese Minister, and others, extract of a dispatch of Dom Lourenzo de Lima, Portuguese Minister at Paris, to Araújo, Aug. 7, 1807, and a certified copy of the note of Aug. 12, delivered at Lisbon. Souza was Portuguese Minister in London.

3   It was the practice of the Prince Regent to request of designated members of the

Council written analyses with recommendations (pareceres) on issues under consideration. With rare exceptions he attended sessions of the Council, but whether he was present or not the final decision was always his prerogative. And it was one which he invariably exercised.

4 F.O. 63/55. Strangford to Canning, Aug. 21, 1807, No. 48. Canning categorically rejected the proposal of a "simulated" state of war (Canning to Strangford, Nov. 7, No. 11) . The Portuguese proposed that the declaration of war be treated as a nominal statement only: the ships of the two belligerents would not fire on each other and Portugal would pledge itself not to issue letters of marque.

5 Council session of Aug. 21. Pareceres. Doc. No. 93. The idea was not new. It was proposed as early as 1580. It was considered seriously by José and Pombal after the Lisbon earthquake of 1755. It had been advocated by responsible persons at least twice since the outbreak of the French Revolution: in 1801 by the Marquêz de Alorna and in 1803 by Rodrigo de Sousa Coutinho. See Manoel de Oliveira Lima, *Dom João VI no Brasil, 1808–1821* (Rio de Janeiro, 1908) , I, 37–43. Oliveira Lima's work is the classic study of the Portuguese Court in Rio de Janeiro. It provides an essential background for this paper.

6 Council session of Aug. 26. Pareceres. Doc. No. 92. Strangford first noted unusual activity in the shipyards in a dispatch dated Aug. 2 (F.O. 63/55. Strangford to Canning, Aug. 2, 1807, No. 43) . In his dispatch of Aug. 29, Strangford reported that Araújo had explained this activity as preparation for the removal of the Court to America and had requested the aid of England if the transfer were to occur (No. 51) . On Sept. 8 Strangford passed on to Canning Araújo's statement that the removal of the Court to Brazil would result in the establishment of a "great and powerful Empire" which would be protected in its infancy by the naval power of England (No. 55) .

7 Strangford attributed the more moderate attitude of the French ambassador to the threat of the removal of the Court to Brazil (F.O. 63/55. Strangford to Canning, Sept. 25, 1807, No. 62) .

8 On Sept. 21, Strangford reported to Canning that he had secured a decree which would allow the English to withdraw all goods from customs houses and deposits free of duties and expense. This, however, would serve as only a partial safeguard against confiscation since most of the British property was in the form of sums due from Portuguese traders for woolens, salt fish, and other articles (F.O. 63/55. Strangford to Canning, Sept. 21, 1807, No. 60) .

9 Council session of Sept. 30, Pareceres, Doc. No. 97. The Marquêz de Pombal did not sign the acts (assento) of the meeting. He added his opinion later in his own hand at the bottom of the assento. The document becomes illegible at this point. When England learned that Napoleon planned to move on Denmark, it summoned the Danes to surrender their fleet for safekeeping. When they refused, the British navy bombarded Copenhagen for four days, Sept. 2–5. Denmark yielded the fleet and joined Napoleon.

10 F.O. 63/55. Strangford to Canning, Oct. 3, 1807, No. 68. He reported that Portugal still hoped to accommodate matters and that large sums of money and many diamonds had been sent to Paris.

11 Sessions of Oct. 12 and 14. Pareceres. Doc. Nos. 89 and 98.

12 F.O. 63/55. Strangford to Canning, Sept. 27, 1807, No. 66. The Prince Regent in a personal interview granted to Strangford stated that he could not abandon Portugal until the actual moment of danger to the monarchy. He was sure that England did not want him to lose his own country and he hoped that Britain would be magnanimous if he were forced in the end to close the ports against her (F.O. 63/55. Strangford to Canning, Sept. 26, 1807, No. 63) . As early as Sept. 8, Strangford was positive that the whole Court, not the Prince of Beira

alone, would move to Brazil if France continued to force its demands (F.O. 63/55. Strangford to Canning, Sept. 8, 1807, No. 55).

13 F.O. 63/55. Strangford to Canning, Oct. 14, 1807, No. 72. On Sept. 27 the Chevalier de Souza, Portuguese Minister in London, was instructed to negotiate a secret treaty whereby England was to be compensated for the closing of the Portuguese ports. By the agreement signed Oct. 22 England could occupy the Madeira Islands as soon as France made a hostile move or Portugal closed its ports to English vessels; Portugal guaranteed not to let any part of its naval or merchantile fleet fall into French hands; England promised an escort if the royal family fled to Brazil and assured Portugal that it would not recognize as king of Portugal any prince who was not the legitimate heir to the throne; and if and when the Court reached Brazil the two countries would negotiate a treaty of assistance and commerce. An additional article stipulated that if the ports of Portugal were closed, a port on the Brazilian coast would be opened to English ships. See José Ferreira Borges de Castro, *Collecção dos tratados, convenções, contratos e actos públicos celebrados entre a Coróa de Portugal e as mais potências desde 1840 até ao presente* (Lisbon, 1856–1863), IV, 236. The Prince Regent ratified the convention on Nov. 8 but with reservations which Canning rejected (F.O. 63/58, Domestic, Letters and Papers from Chev. de Souza, Despatch of Nov. 28, 1807, and Borges de Castro, *Collecção*, IV, 254–62).

14 Session of Oct. 20. Pareceres. Doc. No. 88.

15 Pareceres. Doc. No. 99, dated Nov. 2, 1807.

16 F.O. 63/56. Strangford to Canning, Nov. 9, 1807, No. 91. He had been warned by Araújo in advance of the issuance of the decree in order to allow the English residents to take necessary precautions.

17 Session of Nov. 8. Pareceres. Doc. No. 101. Also F.O. 63/56. Strangford to Canning, Nov. 17, 1807, No. 96. Marialva left Lisbon on Nov. 16. He never reached Napoleon.

18 F.O. 63/56. Strangford to Canning, Nov. 10, 1807, No. 93. Strangford had urged repeatedly that the entire Court move to Brazil and at the same time had assured the Prince Regent that England would cooperate in the most friendly manner. See F.O. 63/55. Strangford to Canning, Aug. 29, No. 50; Sept. 26, No. 63; and F.O. 63/56, No. 103.

19 F.O. 63/56. Strangford to Canning, Nov. 17, 1807, No. 96, and F.O. 63/56. Canning to Strangford, Nov. 7, 1807, No. 11 and Nov. 9, 1807, No. 13.

20 F.O. 63/56. Strangford to Canning, Nov. 20, 1807, No. 99. The dispatch was written on board the "Hibernia." Strangford left Lisbon on the morning of Nov. 18.

21 A. J. Mello Moraes, *História da trasladação da Córte Portuguêza para o Brazil em 1807–1808* (Rio de Janeiro, 1872), p. 84 and Ângelo Pereira, *Os Filhos de El-Rei D. João VI* (Lisbon, 1946), p. 111.

22 On Oct. 27 Napoleon concluded the secret Treaty of Fontainbleau with Spain by which Portugal was to be divided between Napoleon, Spain, and the Queen of Etruria. See M. A. Thiers, *Histoire du Consulat e de L'Empire* (Paris, 1849), VIII, 258 and 339–41.

23 Session of Nov. 24. Pareceres. Doc. No. 91. The assento is in the handwriting of João de Almeida de Mello de Castro. It was signed by him, the Marquêz de Pombal, the Marquêz de Bellas, the Visconde de Anadia, Fernando de Portugal, and Antônio de Araújo de Azevedo.

24 The following discussion of the embarkation is based primarily on three contemporary accounts: (a) A manuscript in the Arquivo do Museu Imperial in Petrópolis by the Visconde do Rio Sêcco [Joaquim José de Azevedo] entitled "Exposição Analytica, e justificativa da Conducta, e vida pública do Visconde

do Rio Sêcco, desde o dia 25 de Novembro de 1807 em que Sua Majestade Fidel-líssima o encumbio dos arranjos necessários para a sua retirada para o Rio de Janeiro, até o dia 15 de Setembro de 1821, em cujo anno dimittira todos os Lugares, e empregos de responsabilidade de Fazenda, com permissão de S.A.R. O Principe Regente do Brasil, Concedida por decreto de 27 de Agosto do mesmo ano. Publicada por elle mesmo. Anno de 1821." There is considerable doubt that the "Exposição" was ever actually published. (*b*) Camillo Luiz de Rossi. *Diário dos acontecimentos de Lisbôa, na entrada das tropas de Junot, escrito por um testimunho presenciar, Camillo Luiz de Rossi, Secretário da Nunciatura Apostólica, a caminho do Rio de Janeiro* (n.p., 1808), preface 1944 by Ângelo Pereira. The copy used was found in the Real Gabinete Português de Leitura do Rio de Janeiro. (*c*) An anonymous document entitled "Jornada do Sr. D. João 6° ao Brazil em 1807, o qual pertenceu a colecção do Conselheiro Francisco Gomes da Silva," written in 1812 and published by Pereira in his *Os filhos*, pp. 101–16. Rio Sêcco wrote his account fourteen years after the event and his memory slipped on occasion (he says that the last Council of State meeting occurred on Nov. 25 whereas the assento of the council is dated Nov. 24), but a citation accompanying the grant of a coat-of-arms on Sept. 8, 1808, substantiates the major features of his story ("Exposição," Doc. No. 2, folha 31). Rossi and the papal nuncio were unable to find room on the ship assigned them and were forced to remain in Lisbon until they could make their escape, cloak-and-dagger fashion, four and one-half months later. Rossi wrote his *Diário* on board ship between England and Rio de Janeiro prior to his arrival on Sept. 8, 1808. Rossi says that in addition to the long session of the council on the night of Nov. 24 there was another meeting on Nov. 25. The decisive meeting, however, obviously was on Nov. 24. The anonymous document merits confidence, says Ângelo Pereira, since it is in accord with "the secret documents which belonged to the Royal Cabinet of D. João VI."

25   "Exposição," Chap. I. In n. 6 Rio Sêcco states that the Prince Regent had already given orders to appropriate officials that they should honor his instructions. He gives the time of the embarkation of the royal family as three o'clock in the afternoon of Nov. 27, whereas according to Rocha Martins it occurred at eleven in the morning. See Francisco José de Rocha Martins, *A Côrte de Junot em Portugal, 1807–1808* (Lisbon, 1910) p. 18. Pereira, *Os filhos*, p. 119, cites a contemporary witness who confirms the morning hour. Rocha Martins' account merits attention by virtue of its careful, objective approach. It avoids the emotional interpretation characteristic of many of the versions of the story, such for instance as that by Raul Brandão, *El-Rei Junot* (Lisbon [1912]), pp. 100–12. Mello Moraes, *História da trasladação,* frequently cited in connection with the departure of the Court, repeats, sentence-by-sentence, without acknowledgment of the source, the anonymous account in Ângelo Pereira's *Os filhos*.

26   Brandão, *El-Rei Junot,* pp. 55–62, gives a detailed factual account of Junot's advance from the border to Lisbon.

27   Pereira, *Os filhos,* pp. 123–29, prints the text of an account by an unknown author of the events connected with the royal family from the departure from Mafra to the arrival in Rio de Janeiro. The family made the journey from Mafra by way of Queluz directly to the docks.

28   Pereira, *Os filhos,* p. 119, estimates 10,000, not including the marine brigade. The brigade numbered 1,600 men according to Mello Moraes, *História da trasladação,* p. 58. Thiers, *Histoire du Consulat,* VIII, 340, sets the figure at 8,000; Tobias Monteiro, *História do Império: a elaboração da independência* (Rio de Janeiro, 1927), p. 59, gives 15,000; and J. M. Pereira da Silva, *História da fundação do Império Brazileiro* (Rio de Janeiro, 1864), I, 121, agrees with Monteiro.

There is disagreement also on the number of ships. Lucas Alexandre Boiteux, *A Marinha de Guerra Brasileira nos Reinos de D. João VI e de D. Pedro I, 1807–1831* (Rio de Janeiro, 1913), pp. 9–13, lists twenty naval vessels ranging in size from eight ships-of-the-line to two small schooners. A manuscript in the Biblioteca Nacional entitled "Forças Navaes, que sahiram do Têjo em 29 de Novembro de 1807 . . ." (reproduced in *Annaes da Bibliotéca Nacional,* II, 13) names fifteen ships and identifies and locates the courtiers assigned to accompany the different members of the royal family. The "Memorias de Eusébio Gomes, 1800–1832," reproduced in part by Pereira, *Os filhos,* p. 119, places the number at fifteen and adds twenty-one merchantmen. Strangford reported that the fleet consisted of some thirty-six sail overall. F.O. 63/56. Strangford to Canning. On Board the "Hibernia", Nov. 29.

29 Rio Sêcco, "Exposição," Chap. I; Rossi, *Diário,* pp. vii, 11–14; "Jornada do Sr. D. João 6°," (above, n. 24), pp. 112–13; "Memórias de Eusébio Gomes, 1800–1832" (above, n. 28), pp. 119–20; Luiz Gonçalves dos Santos [1767–1844], *Memórias para servir á história do Reino do Brasil* (Rio de Janeiro, 1943), p. 209; Rocha Martins, *A Côrte de Junot,* pp. 15–23; and Octávio Tarquínio de Sousa, *História dos fundadores do Império do Brasil* (Rio de Janeiro, 1957–1958), II, 31–32. The infantry regiment ordered up from Peniche could not be accommodated and was returned to the shore (Rossi, *Diário,* p. 13). Thus, no troops of the line, only the marine brigade, accompanied the fleet.

30 Rio Sêcco got aboard about midnight. By good luck and quick thinking he outwitted the mob that attempted to obstruct his departure but he had to leave his hat, money, and papers in the shed. "Exposição," Chap. I.

31 "Jornada do Sr. D. João 6° . . ." (above, n. 24), p. 112. Mello Moraes, *História da trasladação,* footnote, pp. 58–59, gives an itemized list, by vessel, of the deficiencies reported. He agrees with the author of the "Jornada" that they were relatively insignificant.

32 Strangford conferred with the Prince Regent immediately following his return to Lisbon. He assured the Prince that by-gones were by-gones, that England would provide every assistance, and that he would notify Admiral Smith of the turn of events—provided the fleet sailed at once. F.O. 63/56. Strangford to Canning. On Board the "Hibernia," Nov. 24 and 29, 1807.

33 "Jornada do Sr. D. João 6°," p. 112; Mello Moraes, *História da trasladação,* pp. 55–56. Mello Moraes gives the text in a footnote.

34 "Jornada do Sr. D. João 6°," p. 112; Mello Moraes, *História da trasladação,* pp. 59–62; F.O. 63/56. Strangford to Canning. On Board the "Hibernia," No. 29.

35 Rocha Martins, *A Côrte de Junot,* p. 28, reports that the people of Lisbon "peeped out of their windows to watch the general enter the tower of Belém and stamp his feet in rage to see the last sail of the fleet disappear in the distance."

36 Rio Sêcco, "Exposição," Chap. I; Oliveira Lima, *Dom João VI,* I, 37; Rossi, *Diário,* pp. v–vi; Traquínio de Sousa, *História dos fundadores,* IX, 34–35. The Marquês de Funchal [Agostinho de Souza Coutinho], *O Conde de Linhares* (Lisbon, 1908), pp. 86–95, justifies the departure against detractors who call it a flight.

37 "Jornada do Sr. D. João 6°," pp. 112–15; Henrique Cancio, *D. João VI* (Bahia, 1909), p. 54; Mello Moraes, *História da trasladação,* pp. 62 and 65. In Cancio's words the passengers "gave the appearance of a tribe of Israelites being dragged off to slavery."

38 Brandão, *El-Rei Junot,* pp. 100–12 and Boiteux, *A Marinha de Guerra,* pp. 9–14, are but two examples of this point of view.

39 The "Medusa" proceeded on to Rio de Janeiro with the Prince Regent. The

"D. João de Castro" was held in port for repairs, and the personnel, with the exception of the Cadaval family, were distributed among the other ships (Conde da Ponta to Visconde de Anadia, March 8, 1808, in *Revista do Instituto Histórico e Geográphico Brasileiro*, XLV, Pt. II, pp. 8–10). The Duke of Cadaval, who became ill during the voyage, died on March 14, several weeks after he landed in Bahia.

40 The text of the letter is given in Ângelo Pereira, *D. João VI Príncipe e Rei: a retirada da família Real para o Brasil, 1807* (Lisbon, 1953), p. 171. That Gomes made it, then or later, is evidenced by a letter written in Bahia on Sept. 28, 1809. The text of this letter is given in Pereira, *Os filhos*, p. 150.

41 Oliveira Lima, *D. João VI*, I, 49. He located the letter among the *Papéis particulares do Conde de Funchal, 1806–1810* in the Collecção Linhares of the Biblioteca Nacional. The immense Linhares Collection in the Manuscript Section of the Biblioteca Nacional is being reclassified and it is impossible to identify the reference given by Oliveira Lima. A patient search failed to turn up the letter.

42 Rodrigo de Sousa Coutinho (later Conde de Linhares), brother of Domingos de Sousa Coutinho, Portuguese Ambassador in London, served as minister of the Navy and overseas dominions from Sept. 7, 1796, to June 14, 1801, and minister of finance from 1801 to 1803. During this period he was the leading figure in the ministry. His strong pro-English and anti-French position led to his withdrawal from politics until the middle of 1807 (Marquêz de Funchal, *O Conde de Linhares*, pp. 31–64). The Prince Regent recalled him to active duty in the early stages of the crisis of 1807. But Rodrigo in reporting to his brother the details of a council meeting charged Araújo with being a Francophile. The statement filtered back to the Prince Regent and Rodrigo was no longer summoned to sit in council. See Mello Moraes, *História da trasladação*, p. 41.

43 "Forças Navaes." The allocation is interesting. Had the "Principe Real" been lost during the passage, the entire male line would have been eliminated. There are two possible reasons for the arrangement; birthing was facilitated and a difficult problem of personal relations was resolved. The fondness of the Prince Regent for the three boys was matched by his distaste for his wife, Dona Carlota Joaquina. Gonçalves dos Santos, *Memórias*, pp. 229–31, lists one duke, seven *marquêzes*, two *marquêzas*, five *condes*, one *visconde*, five army officers, four *monsenhores*, and others of lesser rank. Most of them had wives and children with them.

44 Rossi, *Diário*, p. vii.

45 Mello Moraes, *História da trasladação*, pp. 30–31.

46 Carlos da Silva Araújo, *Figuras e factos na história da farmácia no Brasil Português* (Lisbon, 1954), p. 66.

47 *Ibid.*, pp. 64–68.

48 J. M. Pereira da Silva, *Os varões illustres do Brazil* (3rd ed.; Rio de Janeiro, 1868), II, 340–41.

49 Joaquim Manuel de Macedo, *Anno biográphico Brasileiro* (Rio de Janeiro, 1876), II, 229.

50 Alfredo Pretextato Maciel da Silva, *Os generais do exército Brasilerio de 1822 a 1889* (2nd ed.; Rio de Janeiro, 1940), I, 58–69; Sebastião Augusto Sisson, *Galeria dos Brasileiros illustres* (São Paulo [1948]), II, 57.

51 Tarquínio de Sousa, *História dos fundadores*, IX, 167. That there was an attempt to keep a record of the persons who came to Brazil is evidenced by a file entitled "Papéis Relativos a vinda da Família Real para o Brasil," Arquivo Nacional, Codex 730. The first folio presents a list of names headed by the "Duque de Cadaval com sua família." Almost all belong to the nobility. Folios 3 and 4 attempt a breakdown into the name of the head of the family, name of the wife,

number of children and servants, etc. In three instances a table of the crew of specific ships is given. And there is a report by the captain of a ship to the Conde dos Arcos on a voyage from Lisbon to Rio de Janeiro dated Jan. 27, 1808. The lists, although they are useful, are hopelessly incomplete.

52 Boiteux, *A Marinha de Guerra Brasileira*, p. 13; "Forças Navaes." The higher figures are from Boiteux.

53 Wanderley Pinho, "A abertura dos pôrtos — Cairú," *Revista do Instituto Histórico e Geográfico Brasileiro*, CCXLIII (April–June, 1959), 98–103. The embargo became effective in Bahia on Jan. 1.

54 Aliatar Loreto, *Capítulos de história militar do Brasil* (Rio de Janeiro, 1946), pp. 9–43, chapter entitled "A organização militar da colônia." A brief but excellent summary of both the military organization of the colony and the military nature of the colonial administration is given by Caio Prado, Jr., *The Colonial Background of Modern Brazil* (Berkeley, 1967), pp. 358–65. The translation is cited due to the apt English equivalents for the Portuguese terminology given by the translator, Suzette Macedo.

55 In the words of Tarquínio de Sousa, *História dos fundadores*, II, 31, to the bystanders the embarkation appeared to be a preview of the sack of the city by the approaching enemy.

56 The printing press was used for the founding of the Royal Press on May 13, 1808; See Oliveira Lima, *Dom João VI*, I, 48.

57 "Jornada do Sr. D. João 6°," p. 112; Rio Sêcco, "Exposição," Chap. 1; Rossi, *Diário*, p. 13; Rocha Martins, *A Côrte de Junot*, p. 14; Pedro Calmon, *O Rei do Brazil: Vida de D. João VI* (Rio de Janeiro, 1935), pp. 113–14; and Oliveira Lima, *Dom João VI*, I, 48.

Araújo de Azevedo had assembled a notable collection of books, papers, maps, and prints in the course of his travels in Europe but particularly during his residence as Portuguese minister in the courts of The Hague, Paris, and St. Petersburg. He had encountered serious difficulty in transferring the library from The Hague to Lisbon when he was called home in 1804 to serve as Minister of Foreign Affairs and War. He was determined that it should accompany him to Rio de Janeiro. By 1819 when it was purchased on orders of D. João VI for the Biblioteca pública, the Collection numbered more than 74,000 items (volumes). See J. Z. de Menezes Brum, "Do Conde da Barca, de seus escriptos e livraría," in *Anais da Bibliotheca Nacional do Rio de Janeiro*, II (1876–1877), 5–33, 359–403.

58 B. F. Ramiz Galvão, "Diogo Barbosa Machado," *Anais da Biblioteca Nacional do Rio de Janeiro*, I (1876–1877), 1–43; 248–65; II (1876–1877), 128–91; III (1877–1878), 162–81, 279–311; VIII (1880–1881), 221–431.

59 João Pandiá Calógeras in his *Formação histórica do Brasil* (Rio de Janeiro, [1930]), p. 95, says that "All of the administrative paraphernalia of government, archives, documents and papers, were aboard, arranged in such fashion that at the moment of desembarkation no difficulty would be felt in continuing the operation of the Monarchy on the New Continent in as normal a fashion as it had been administered in Lisbon." He does not, however, identify or describe the "paraphernalia." Due to recent discoveries in the Arquivo Nacional and the Arquivo do Instituto Histórico e Geográphico Brasileiro and to the publications of the Itamaraty it is now possible to identify them.

60 Carta de José da Silva Areas, Official Maior da Guerra, filho do Orem. Collecção Orem, Documento No. 18, Lata No. 164. The ministries of foreign affairs and war were under the same official. When the ministries were separated, the document, instead of being transferred to the files of the Ministry of Foreign Affairs, remained in the Orem papers.

61   Ministério das Relações Exteriores, Departamento de Administração, *Arquivo Histórico do Itamaraty:* Part III-30. *Documentação anterior a 1822.* Introducção do Embaixador José Carlos de Macedo Soares. Serviço de Publicações. The introduction is dated Rio de Janeiro, Feb. 28, 1956. In addition to the items of special interest to this discussion, the catalogue identifies the copies of documents which the Barão do Rio Branco and Joaquim Nabuco obtained from various foreign and national archives plus originals of the seventeenth to the nineteenth centuries acquired largely by Rio Branco.

62   Arquivo Nacional: Secção de Documentação Histórica: Relação de Documentos em Caixas: I. Negócios de Portugal 1555 a 1821, Caixas 612 a 732. A brief description in Sub-section I contains the statement that the documents for this collection came to Brazil with the royal family in 1808 or were sent for by the King during his residence there. It is filed in 120 *caixas.* The *caixas* are divided into *pacotes.* A *pacote* may contain scores of documents and a single document more than a hundred folios. Grouping by content and dates is a random affair. A typed catalogue, dated 1962, gives the number of the *caixa,* a general classification of the documents, and the dates covered in the bundles. A card file gives more detailed information. Helpful as the typed catalogue and the card file are— to work through the collection without them would be a hopeless undertaking —they are but the initial steps in the Herculean task of classification.

63   Some items left behind in 1821 have since been returned to Lisbon, e.g., The Conde de Lippe Collection, which in no way touched on Brazil (*Arquivo Histórico do Itamaraty:* Part III-30, p. 127) .

64   The Constitution of 1824 provided for a national archive but it was not until 1838 that it began to function and then in the Ministerio do Imperio. There the collection remained until it was moved to its current location when the Arquivo Nacional got its own building.

65   Mello Moraes, *Trasladação,* pp. 62–64; Pereira da Silva, *História da fundação,* II, 3–8; Tarquínio de Sousa, *A Vida de D. Pedro I* (Rio de Janeiro, 1952) , I, 37–52; Pinho, "A abertura dos pôrtos," 99–102. The Prince Regent did not go ashore until the afternoon of Jan. 24. He re-embarked on Feb. 24 but due to adverse winds could not set sail until two days later.

66   That this was an emergency arrangement is attested by the fact that the Prince Regent never referred to Fernando José de Portugal as Secretary of State but as his "Conselheiro." On the other hand, the Conde da Ponte addressed his communications to the Prince Regent through Fernando José de Portugal. Pinho, "A abertura dos pôrtos," pp. 102–103 and n. 26. This discussion of the opening of the ports leans heavily on Pinho's article since it is based on documents primarily in the Arquivo Público da Bahia.

67   Pereira da Silva, *História da fundação,* II, 9; Monteiro, *História do Império,* pp. 62–69; Calmon, *O Rei do Brazil,* pp. 129–30; Tarquínio de Sousa, *A vida,* I, 48–49; Pinho, "A abertura dos pôrtos," pp. 97–99, 102–103.

68   Pinho ("A abertura dos pôrtos," n. 31, pp. 126–28) , discusses the problem of timing and gives a resume of the parecer. He cites: Pereira, *D. João VI,* III, 38– 43, as a source for the text.

69   A copy of the Representação is in the Arquivo Publico da Bahia. The original is in the Arquivo Nacional in Rio de Janeiro. Pinho, "A abertura dos pôrtos," pp. 123–24, gives the text.

70   Macedo, *Anno biográphico,* II, 31; Sisson, *Galéria dos Brasileiros,* I, 105; Pereira da Silva, *Os varões,* II, 160–70. The two major sources for Silva Lisbôa's ideas on political economy are: *Estudos do bem-commun e economia política* (Rio de Janeiro, 1819–1820) and *Princípios do direito mercantil e leis da marinha,* (Rio de Janeiro, 1963) .

71 Mello Moraes, *História da trasladação*, pp. 70–72, gives a version of Silva Lisbôa's role which he obtained through personal conversation with Lisbôa's son. He states that Silva Lisbôa, after discussing the matter with Fernando José de Portugal and finding that they were in agreement, convinced Fernando to make a direct approach to the Prince Regent. This he did and the Carta Régia was issued with the desired terms.

72 The original is in the Arquivo Público da Bahia. A copy is in the Arquivo Nacional in Rio de Janeiro, Codex 952. Cartas Régias, Provisões, Alvarás e Avisos, 1662–1821. 50 vols. numbered 1 to 48. Vol. 48, 1807–1821. Happily, the original was in Rio de Janeiro when research for this essay was under way.

73 José da Silva Lisbôa, *Memória dos benefícios políticos do Governo de El-Rei Nosso Senhor D. João VI* (Rio de Janeiro, 1940), pp. 68–69.

74 Gonçalves dos Santos, *Memórias*, p. 203.

75 Mello Moraes, *História da trasladação*, p. 71.

76 Pereira da Silva, *História da fundação*, II, p. 12–13.

77 Pinho, "A abertura dos pôrtos," pp. 111–13.

78 Tarquínio de Sousa, *A vida*, I, 48.

79 Pereira da Silva, *História da fundação*, II, 49–50. According to Mello Moraes, *História da trasladação*, pp. 71–74, the Portuguese commercial element was shocked by the liberal terms of the carta régia. The decree, as it stood, would unquestionably abolish the jealously guarded monopoly which this element had long exercised over the commerce and business of Brazil. The opposition reached serious proportions in Rio de Janeiro. The propaganda of Silva Lisbôa, who accompanied the Prince Regent to Rio, and the support of Fernando José de Portugal, the Marquêz de Bellas, and Rodrigo de Sousa Coutinho reinforced the viewpoint of the Prince Regent and the basic principle of the carta régia survived the storm.

80 Pinho, "A abertura dos pôrtos," p. 101.

81 Max Fleiuss, *História administrativa do Brasil* (2nd ed.; São Paulo, 1925), pp. 71 and 97. Fernando José de Portugal had served as governor of Bahia, 1788–1792, and as viceroy in Rio de Janeiro, 1801–1806. Rodrigo de Sousa Coutinho had been Minister of the Navy and Overseas Dominions, 1796–1801, and Minister of Finance, 1801–1803. Anadia, the only carry-over, retained the same post. All three had been active members of the Council of State during the final four months in Lisbon. The organization of the ministry was in conformity with the alvará of July 28, 1736, which established the secretariats. See Mello Moraes, *História da trasladação*, pp. 395–400.

82 The thirteen years of João VI's residence in Brazil may be divided into three periods with respect to the ministries: 1808–1812, the period in which Sousa Coutinho was the dominant personality; 1814–1817, in which Antônio de Araújo de Azevedo (Conde da Barca) was pre-eminent; and 1817–1820, in which Thomáz Antônio Villa Nôva Portugal exercised major influence. Of the five ministers appointed prior to 1817 all had been active in Lisbon and all died in office—Anadia in 1810, Almeida de Mello de Castro (Galvêas) and Sousa Coutinho (Linhares) in 1812, Fernando José de Portugal (Aguiar) in 1814, and Antônio de Araújo de Azevedo (Barca) in 1817. Thomáz Antônio Villa Nôva Portugal, the personification of conservative absolutism, had exercised quiet but effective influence from the days when he was Justice and Chancellor of the High Court in Lisbon. Gonçalves dos Santos, *Memórias,* provides an indispensable contemporary account of the thirteen years of João VI's residence in Brazil.

83 Arquivo Nacional, Codex 528. Alvarás, I, April 1, 1808. Vol. I covers the period 1808–1813; Vol. II, 1813–1818; and Vol. III, 1818–1823. Vol. I begins with the alvará which created the Conselho Supremo Militar.

84   *Ibid.*, I, April 22, 1808.
85   *Ibid.*, I, May 9, 1808.
86   *Ibid.*, I, May 10, 1808. Both alvarás were issued on the same day.
87   *Ibid.*, I, June 28, 1808. The Erário and the Conselho were included in the same alvará.
88   *Ibid.*, I, Aug. 23, 1808.
89   *Ibid.*, I, April 1, 1808, and Pereira da Silva, *História da fundação*, II, 308–309, Doc. 3.
90   Oliveira Lima, *Dom João VI*, I, 48; Gonçalves dos Santos, *Memórias*, p. 256.
91   Arquivo Nacional, Codex 528. Alvarás, I, June 3, 1808.
92   *Ibid.*, I, June 15, 1808.
93   Fleiuss, *História administrativa*, pp. 79–80.
94   *Ibid.*, pp. 81 and 98.
95   *Ibid.*, p. 99, and Tarquínio de Sousa, *História dos fundadores*, IX, 35.
96   The concentration of higher education in Portugal was a conscious policy. When at the height of their prosperity the inhabitants of Minas Gerais offered to set up a medical school at their own cost, the Council of Overseas Dominions (Conselho Ultramarino) refused on the ground that "one of the strongest bonds that sustained the dependence of the colonials was the necessity of coming to Portugal to pursue advanced studies." Sérgio Buarque de Holanda, ed., *História geral da civilização brasileira* (São Paulo, 1960), I, Pt. 2, 72, with the result that "eighteenth century Portugal intellectually was half Brazilian." Oliveira Lima, *Dom João VI*, I, 243.
97   Fleiuss, *História administrativa*, pp. 83, 97, 99, 102, 103, 104, 106; Gonçalves dos Santos, *Memórias*, pp. 303, 305; Oliveira Lima, *Dom João VI*, I, 230–38.
98   Fleiuss, *História administrativa*, p. 98, and Gonçalves dos Santos, *Memórias*, p. 248.
99   The *Biblioteca Pública*, according to Maria Graham, *Journal of a Voyage to Brazil and Residence there During Part of the Years 1821, 1822, 1823* (London, 1824), pp. 300–302, was open six hours a day. She found from personal experience that the service was courteous and most helpful, and the resources excellent.
100 Gastão Cruls, *Aparência do Rio de Janeiro* (Rio de Janeiro, 1952), I, 255.
101 Fleiuss, *História administrativa*, pp. 88, 106; Oliveira Lima, *Dom João VI*, I, 243–47.
102 The number of foreigners who entered Brazil between 1808 and 1822 is startling. The official register of Rio de Janeiro alone lists 4,234, not counting, in many cases, wives, children, and servants. Some 1,500 were Spanish, primarily Spanish American, almost 1,000 were French, over 600 were English, and more than 200 were German. There were also Italians, Swiss, North Americans, Swedes, Dutch, Irish, Austrians, Danes, and Scotchmen. They came from China, Java, the Cape of Good Hope, India, Egypt, the Cape Verdes, the Canaries, Mozambique and Luanda, Malta, Greece, Russia, Martinique, and all parts of Spanish America. Among them were 23 physicians and surgeons, 17 painters, 15 professors, 14 musicians, 13 ballerinas, 10 actors, 4 chemists, 21 tailors, 17 shoemakers, 17 cooks, 10 bakers, 9 gardeners, 9 costumers, and a comparable spread of artisans. Many were in transit, some between foreign ports, but the great bulk remained in Rio de Janeiro. These added both numbers and new cultural elements to the capital and to the country. Arquivo Nacional, *Registro de estrangeiros 1808–1822*, Preface by José Honório Rodrigues (Rio de Janeiro, 1960), pp. 5–10.
103 Sérgio Buarque de Holanda, ed., *História geral*, II, Pt. 1, 31.
104 In the words of Pedro Calmon, *O Rei do Brasil*, p. 149, "to become a count in Portugal required five hundred years, in Brasil, five hundred *contos*."

105 This did not mean that the recipient sat on the Council of State. It was an honorary title which the Prince Regent referred to as "título do meu conselho." The alvará by which José Bonifácio was awarded the título de conselho illustrates the wording, the procedure, and the payment delivered to the treasury by the recipient (Arquivo Nacional, Codex 528, Alvarás, III, Aug. 18, 1820).

106 Pedro Calmon, *História social do Brasil* (São Paulo, 1940), II, 292–97.

107 Tobias Monteiro, *História do Império: O Primeiro Reinado* (Rio de Janeiro, 1946), II, 212. In contrast, says Monteiro, from the independence of Portugal in the twelfth century to the end of the third quarter of the nineteenth century there were created, in Portugal, 16 marquises, 26 counts, 8 viscounts, and 4 barons. Even with a liberal allowance for error, the difference is striking.

108 Buarque de Holanda, *História geral*, II, Pt. 1, 32–33.

109 Calmon, *História social,* II, 288.

110 *Ibid.,* p. 97, and Buarque de Holanda, *História geral,* II, Pt. 1, 31.

111 Buarque de Holanda, *História geral,* II, Pt. 1, 104ff., and Oliveira Lima, *Dom João VI,* II, 744ff.; *Correio Braziliense* (London, 1808–1822). The failure of the Court in Rio de Janeiro to modernize the administration of the captaincies was subject to continuing comment by Hipólito José da Costa. In the first issue, June, 1808 (I, 65), he could not understand how those who were then governing Brazil could have so little judgment as to continue the previous internal organization of the country. The criticism is repeated like a refrain throughout the life of the journal. Particularly apt examples occur in the issues of Nov., 1810 (V, 565–67), April, 1813 (X, 203), June, 1814 (XII, 917), Feb., 1816 (XVI, 184–87), and Jan., 1821 (XXVI, 167–76).

112 "Cartas sôbre a Revolução do Brazil pelo Conselheiro Silvestre Pinheiro Ferreira," *Revista do Instituto Histórico e Geográphico Brasileiro,* LI (1888), 371–72.

113 Arquivo Nacional, Codex 737. By the decree Portugal was to become the United Kingdom of Portugal, Brazil, and the Algarves.

114 Silva Lisbôa, *Memória,* p. 114; Gonçalves dos Santos, *Memórias,* p. 469; Tarquínio de Sousa, *História dos fundadores,* IX, 36; and Buarque de Holanda, *História geral,* II, Pt. 1, p. 149. Hipólito José da Costa, *Correio Braziliense,* Feb., 1816, (XVI, 187) felt that if the change in terminology meant that the colonial status was really ended and that internal reforms would follow, well and good. In the following number, March, 1816 (XVI, 296) he raised interesting questions, such as how two Juntas de Commércio, Agricultura, Fábricas e Navegação could operate within the same overall kingdom. Or what was it that was united under the "United Kingdom of Portugal, Brazil and the Algarves?"

COMMENTARY

Richard Graham
Cornell University, Ithaca, New York

PROFESSOR Manchester's paper throws light upon some very important events and suggests a burden of meaning in these events which has not heretofore been recognized. He also contributes to the revisionism launched almost sixty years ago by Oliveira Lima[1] and carried forward in Brazil by Tarquínio de Sousa[2] but still hardly noted in this country. It is my purpose here to highlight some of the points raised by Professor Manchester that appear to me to be most significant.

First of all, he points out that we must abandon the idea that the departure of the Portuguese Court from Lisbon was an unplanned action, undertaken on the spur of the moment. A leading textbook currently used in Latin American history courses across the country reports: "In November, 1807, a French army under General Junot moved into Portugal; *whereupon* the British Minister, Lord Strangford, and Admiral Sidney Smith . . . told Prince Regent John that the time had come to pack up his mad mother and get out." [3] Another textbook reportedly running a close second in sales to the one just cited puts it this way: "Late in 1807 a large French army led by Marshal Junot entered the peninsula and, with Spanish allies, overran Portugal. The mad queen, Maria I, her son, Prince Regent João, the rest of the royal court, and thousands of nobles gathered what they could and *clambered* on Portuguese ships just as Junot penetrated Lisbon." [4] If a student, bound by the English language as most of them still are, seeks a more complete account, he is likely to end up reading the fantastic cock-and-bull stories of Bertita Harding.[5]

It is against this backdrop that we can begin to appreciate the contribution of the paper now being discussed. Professor Manchester tells us of careful deliberations and precise contingency plans. Napoleon began to apply renewed and overt pressures against Portugal in mid-August, 1807. To this pressure the Portuguese reacted intelligently and with more success than could be reasonably expected from a small power faced with such a threat.

There were three alternative courses of action, all of which received support from some members of the Council of State. One was to surrender before the armed might of the French colossus. What several coalitions of major powers had failed to stop could not be realistically opposed by little Portugal. So the best thing to do, it was argued, would be to join the French side, declare war on Britain, and be done with it. But this would mean the end of Portuguese dominion in Brazil since Great Britain controlled the seas.

The opposite course of action available in August, 1807, was to throw Portugal completely into the hands of England. And the British urged the immediate removal of the Court to Brazil. The British were hard pressed by Napoleon's Continental System. Manufactured goods were piling up in London warehouses. Even in the months of peace after the Treaty of Amiens British businessmen had found that they were unable to restore pre-war commercial relations with the Continent. Now that war raged once again, the economic plight of Great Britain was intensified. The invasion of Buenos Aires and the aid and comfort extended Francisco de Miranda were part of the business community's interest in finding markets for their goods.[6] Now, Brazil had a population of some three million. Granted that not all of them were consumers; granted also that, with the century-old commercial ties between England and Portugal, British exporters to the Mother Country were in effect exporting to Brazil; yet the advantage of permanently breaking the Portuguese restrictions upon British penetration of that market were obvious in any British counting house. So they demanded the immediate transmigration of the Portuguese Court. But for the Portuguese to follow this advice was surely to abandon the Mother Country to the French and, as long as any chance remained that this result could be avoided, responsible statesmen would eschew that course of action.

The third possibility was delicately to play the French against the British, desperately trying to save through sophisticated diplomacy what Portugal's limited military capability could not hope to safeguard. On the one hand, negotiations were spun out so that Napoleon's ultimatum requiring compliance by September 1 was not carried out until late November. Anyone in Brazil who has tried to speed up delivery of a pair of shoes or the replacement of damaged merchandise will recognize this technique! On the other hand, an attempt was made to persuade Britain to agree to a false declaration of war *para francês ver*. The good Protestant nation found this duplicity distasteful and was too anxious to get its hands on Brazilian trade to play that game. The Portuguese then moved at the beginning of November to comply outwardly with French demands while keeping the British informed of every step, indeed warning them well in advance of every move.

Meanwhile, a course of action was laid out in case these steps failed to halt the French. This contingency plan was to move to Brazil. Every detail was foreseen. A "diagram of the number, size, and location of rooms available in the fleet" was prepared.[7] A line of command established. Papers selected. Treasury accounts put in order. Packing materials gathered. In short, every step was carefully planned. But no overt actions could be taken. Before the French armies crossed the border, the wisest course was to hold tight. Any sign that the Court was indeed planning to flee as the British desired would, in itself, provoke an invasion. It was a game of nerves and no one in Lisbon broke under the strain.

Only one problem could not be overcome: Portugal's small size meant that a Napoleonic invasion would be known in Lisbon only four days before French armies would arrive at the city. The Portuguese gambled that this would be long enough to carry out the massive task of removing not just the sovereign but the entire machinery of government. They won that gamble. If the actual pace of events during those four days produced frenetic activity, helter-skelter scurrying about, and an appearance of total confusion, it could have been no other way.

The second point which emerges from Professor Manchester's exposition is that the Prince Regent João (later João VI) was no fool. It has long been the practice among those who teach Latin American history in this country to enliven their discussion of Brazilian independence—so lacking in vibrant personalities or blood-and-gore—by eliciting laughter in describing João VI. He is characterized as "stodgy," [8] "a fat, sluggish fellow," [9] or a "vast hulk of inertia." [10] Even the generally balanced C. H. Haring refers to him as "well-meaning but temperamentally timorous." [11] Yet Professor Manchester notes that "with rare exceptions he attended sessions of the Council" and the final decisions were always his.[12] He resolved the opposing points of view of his counsellors and on several occasions overrode the bad advice of the majority. Nowhere does the strong-willed Dona Carlota—who at their wedding is alleged to have viciously bit her husband when they kissed—nowhere does Dona Carlotta appear as exerting any role of significance. The Prince Regent made the decisions in those crucial days and they were wise decisions. The rehabilitation in English of João VI is long overdue and Professor Manchester has contributed to it.

The third point raised here that seems to me to merit special attention is that the Portuguese Court in Brazil was not simply a government in exile. It was really to be a new empire. The large number of people who fled Lisbon at the end of 1807 is partly explained by this factor. It was not only the royal family that had to be evacuated, but also the civil, religious, and military administrative machinery including much more than the highest echelons, but also "functionaries of the lower levels." [13] In addition, "professional and businessmen," [14] as well as members of the social elite, went along to lend genuine luster to the new court. The accouterments of government also had to be transported. Obviously, the treasury and the royal jewels would be safeguarded from French seizure. But more striking is the transfer of a mass of government files chosen not so much regard to French cupidity as to Portuguese imperial purpose, for some papers dated as far back as 1555. The search for precedents so dear to lawyers could be carried out in Rio de Janeiro just as had been done in Lisbon.

It is notable how extensive was the Portuguese, now Brazilian, bureaucracy of that time. To the present day it is customary for foreigners and Brazilians alike to decry the multiplication of posts, the constant paperwork, the progressive multiplication of offices, agencies, departments, and superintendencies. Hélio Jaguaribe not so long ago spoke of the "notarial state." Forty years ago Oliveira Vianna pointed to the end of slavery as its cause, for "this aristocracy, stripped of its great landholding industry, then found in the State a new economic base to substitute for the one destroyed." [15] But Joaquim Nabuco, writing before the abolition of slavery, had insisted that "the class that thus live with their eyes turned toward government munificience is extremely numerous and the direct *result* of slavery." [16] Yet it is clear from Professor Manchester's paper that the bureaucracy was brought over by the Portuguese Crown as early as 1808, and anyone who has done research on the Iberian Peninsula knows that excessive paperwork antedates this event by several centuries.

Fourth, Professor Manchester has brought up the contradictory nature of these events. On the one hand, as he points out, "between early 1808 and late 1815 the colony has been transformed into an autonomous state with its own political, religious, and social hierarchy, its own mechanism of government, its own social and educational amenities, and the right of self-determination in economic policy." [17] With good reason many historians have argued that the date of Brazilian independence was not 1822 but 1808 or at least 1815. Certainly, the opening of the ports in 1808 broke the economic ties with the Mother Country; if the colonialism of that day was mercantile, then the end of the trading monopoly must be equivalent to independence. Furthermore, Brazilians now had a popular ruler among them—perhaps more popular there than in Portugal itself. It also had in Rio de Janeiro all the paraphernalia of government, it could trade with any country. Was not this independence?

Yet, in the paper now under review, we also find that "the tax system, the administration of justice, and the military organization remained colonial in point of view and practice." "The pattern of colonial administration" remained undisturbed.[18] We all know the later demonstrations of the truth of these assertions: the way in which Brazilian resources were used to pursue dynastic ambitions in the Rio de la Plata; the cruelty with which the Revolution of 1817 was put down; the supercilious way in which the Portuguese looked down upon the Brazilian-born thus creating, perhaps for the first time, a real sense of injustice similar to that felt by Creoles in Spanish America; and the perpetuation of many of these characteristics, not only until 1822, but until 1831. And what was the meaning of the opening of the ports? Had not British goods monopolized the market even before that date? Has Brazil yet become economically independent? Could the measure not have been reversed by João VI at any time? Was it not in fact only when an attempt in this direction was rebuffed by the Brazilians well over a decade later that we can begin to speak of "independence"? And if one maintains that it is not objective reality that must be considered, but rather what men thought of these events at the time, then we must ask with renewed scepticism whether 1808 can really be considered the date of Brazil's independence from Portugal. So Professor Manchester has raised issues which force us to define independence itself.

Finally, we have before us the interesting question of the comparability of these events with those in Spanish America. The superficial differences leap out at the observer. Yet, as Professor Manchester has pointed out, there are points of similarity. The regionalism which dominated the Spanish American struggles of independence was also important in Brazil. The clan loyalties that were to underlie Brazilian politics until the 1930's are also to be found in Spanish America. The economic interests of landowners clashed with those of Peninsular merchants in Brazil as in Argentina or Venezuela.

Yet, the experience and the results were different. The union was preserved, legitimacy assured, and political stability safeguarded. The marching feet of armies destroyed no crops, and no hordes were to wreck the mines or pillage the towns. The weakening of the social fabric which accompanied the political disruption in Spanish America was only dimly reflected in Brazil through the distribution of titles and, eventually, of power to Brazilian landowners. The rise of the Spanish-American *caudillo* from relatively humble origins—made possible by the collapse of ancient sanctions, the capture of the "Lord's Anointed," and the new demand for men of (military) talent—was avoided or postponed in Brazil. Indeed, if the caudillo be considered an inevitable concomitant of the breakup of the corporate society, then the transfer of the Portuguese Court to Brazil may be thought of as slowing down the course of Brazil's progress. In any case, in the complex interplay of men and events, the decisions taken by the Council of State and Prince Regent João between August and November, 1807, were to have far-reaching consequences in Brazil.

NOTES

1 Manoel de Oliveira Lima, *Dom João VI no Brasil, 1808–1821* (2nd ed.; 3 vols.; Rio de Janeiro, 1945).
2 Octávio Tarquínio de Sousa, *História dos fundadores do Império do Brasil* (Rio de Janeiro, 1957).
3 Hubert Herring, *A History of Latin America from the Beginnings to the Present* (2nd ed.; New York, 1961), p. 288, italics added.
4 John Edwin Fagg, *Latin America: A General History* (New York, 1963), p. 419, italics added.
5 *Amazon Throne: The Story of the Braganzas of Brazil* (Indianapolis, 1941).
6 William W. Kaufmann, *British Policy and the Independence of Latin America, 1804–1828* ("Yale Historical Publications Miscellany," 52 [New Haven, 1951]).
7 Above, p. 153.
8 Harding, *Amazon Throne*, p. 16.
9 Herring, *A History of Latin America*, p. 287.
10 Harding, *Amazon Throne*, p. 16.
11 *Empire in Brazil: A New World Experiment with Monarchy* (Cambridge, Mass., 1958), p. 12.

12   Above, pp. 173–74, n. 3.
13   Above, p. 156.
14   Above, p. 156.
15   Francisco José de Oliveira Vianna, "O idealismo da constituição," in A. Carneiro Leão, *et al.*, *A margem da história da república (ideaes, crenças e affirmações)* (Rio de Janeiro, 1924) , p. 143.
16   *O abolicionismo: conferências e discursos abolicionistas* (3rd ed.; São Paulo, 1949) , p. 160, italics added.
17   Above, p. 173.
18   Above, p. 173.

THE LISBON *JUIZ DO PÔVO* AND THE

INDEPENDENCE OF BRAZIL, 1750–1822:

AN ESSAY ON LUSO-BRAZILIAN POPULISM

Harry Bernstein
Brooklyn College of the City University of New York

THIS paper on the Lisbon *juiz do pôvo* and the independence of Brazil relates that important Luso-Brazilian official to the dynamic years of growth and change from Pombal to the Peninsular Wars. Portuguese history and Brazilian independence were both greatly affected by the domestic forces, international crises, and men of those times.

The origins, status, and roles of the Portuguese juiz do pôvo have received scattered mention in the administrative histories of Gama Barros, the guild histories of Franz-Paul Langhans, and the *senado da câmara* histories of Durval Pires de Lima and Eduardo Freire de Oliveira. Charles Boxer gives the office in Bahia some attention for the late seventeenth and early eighteenth centuries. The only Brazilian historian I know who gave attention to the juiz was João Ribeiro. His brief and isolated mention also deals with events of 1710, and his historical judgment was hostile: "This experience proved that the juiz do pôvo obstructed and often nullified the action of the government. It was characteristic of this revolutionary tribune to agitate the low passions of the masses and found his unique prestige among them. That is why it was abolished." But the office of the juiz do pôvo was not abolished, and we will hear the voice of the Bahia juiz later on. That picture of the Bahia juiz in 1710 is quite different from the much more attractive portrait of the role of the Lisbon juiz in Portuguese history. How it was in Brazil has yet to be carefully researched and studied.

The juiz do pôvo of Lisbon was a favored figure throughout most of the history of the Aviz and Bragança dynasties. The instances of abolition of the office by King Manoel in Lisbon, or by Minister Pombal in Pôrto, were temporary; the Lisbon official had a long life. There was

191

good reason for the Lisbon juiz to appear on the balcony of Government House in the revolt of 1820, alongside the other political and military supporters of the revolt. As we shall see, the views of the Lisbon juiz in 1820 affected the elections and reception of the Brazilian deputies to the *Côrtes* in 1821.

The Lisbon juiz do pôvo was the head of the Lisbon Guildhall, or Casa dos Vinte e Quatro. His political leadership was very important in the great political revolutions of 1375, 1580, 1640, and most important, 1808–1820. He was chairman or presiding officer of the Casa and was an elected (not appointed or hereditary) member of the senado da câmara. Although chosen by the twenty-four guilds of Lisbon (other cities entitled to a juiz had twelve guilds, like Pôrto), the juiz in Lisbon had direct access to the Crown on the same footing as royal ministers, and even on the same day set aside for such royal audiences.

In over 450 years of known existence, from 1375 to 1835, this unusual Luso-Brazilian tribune of the people acquired, held, lost, and then reassumed a great range of powers. Most of these were socioeconomic. Political leadership was always present, especially when Portugal's independence and nationality was in danger. He confronted the Crown, defied Spain, took a leading part in public ceremonies, festivities, and rituals. In 1788 the juiz do pôvo put together and printed an invaluable Mappa Geral of the Lisbon guilds, numbers of masters, apprentices, and journeymen, and the *bandeiras* where they worked and lived. Arrested by the *senado* for this, the Guildhall appealed at once to the Crown and had the juiz set free. And in 1820, the juiz do sat at the right hand of the liberal patriots and drew up bold political statements for both the deputies and the people.

Historians differ as to whether the juiz do pôvo, although a *mester* and member of the Guildhall, should be classified as a leader of the Third Estate or of the working class. Alexandre Herculano, the noted Portuguese historian and historical novelist, never mentioned the juiz in his histories. But, in his novel *O Monge de Cister,* Herculano is amiable toward João I, founder of the House of Aviz, stating that the people were still great and strong under João I and that Portuguese municipal life, the only possible guarantee of true liberty, had not yet been rendered farcical by absolute monarchy. Although King Manoel abolished and then quickly restored the juiz in 1502, Herculano, as is known, was most bitter toward João III, who declared that no master or officer of a guild who was New Christian could be elected master of a guild. He ordered the juiz do pôvo not to recognize or validate any such election. "The King went further than the Inquisition," writes Herculano in his *History of the Origins of the Inquisition in Portugal.*

This was the legacy of Brazil and the Brazilian guilds and senados during the early colonization, under the Aviz. By the time of the Bragança, however, things had changed. From 1640 to 1820, the juiz do pôvo stood close to the Crown, at least in Lisbon, and showed power and force both in Brazil and Portugal. Between 1750 and 1820 he stood publicly in the full light of his title of Muito Honrado (Right Honorable) and repeatedly asserted his rights before the Lisbon senado and the Crown. Although quite alive and alert in public during the two generations from Pombal's time to the Peninsular War, the juiz remained a forgotten man for intellectuals, or one whom people wanted to forget. The eighteenth-century learned work, *Prelecçõens de direito público de Portugal recitada no anno do 1788 para 1789* for example, deals with all sorts of magistrates and *juizes* but does not mention the juiz at all.

The Bragança, however, never forgot the juiz do pôvo. In the revolt of 1640 Dr. João Pinto Ribeiro, agent of João IV, went to the juiz do pôvo to get and secure his support and to share with him the political secret, according to the contemporary Pedro de Mariz. And because the juiz do pôvo did such a good job of announcing the uprising to selected *fidalgos,* the Bragança never forgot him. The great seventeenth-century Lisbon publishing house of Craesbeeck had several descendants who were both publishers and writers in their own right, prefacing their authors' books with literate and well-written essays of their own. One of the last of the publishing Craesbeecks, Antônio Craesbeeck de Mello, an historian and cultural figure of merit, wrote that "John IV loved the people with truly paternal affection and promulgated various decrees in their favor. Many times he gave ear to the juiz and charged him with the care of pointing out what was good for his subjects. He never permitted the powerful to prevail with force over them."

There must be an interesting document in the Bibliothêque National, Paris. Alfred P. V. Morel-Fatio refers to it in passing; he merely calls it "Ao Povo" and gives the first line as beginning "Vinte e quatro pôvo amado . . . ," placing it in the seventeenth century. Other fond and poetic allusions to the forgotten juiz do pôvo and his Casa survive down to the present. I take the liberty to cite a letter sent me last year by a major figure in Portuguese higher studies: "There is an old story on the juiz do pôvo, which I was told in the second grade at school. In Lisbon the city Council was called, as you know, the '*Casa dos 24*' [*sic*] with the

juiz do pôvo in the Chair. Once, the King was too impatient to receive
a delegation of the 24 and he himself decided to pay them a visit instead.
Then the juiz do pôvo told him not to proceed because that was the
'Casa dos 24' and not 'dos . . . 25.' " Even if it is not 100 percent true, it
is a good one! It is also a clue to the long memory of folklore in Portuguese history.

Even Pombal shared this benevolence and good will toward the juiz
do pôvo. What Boxer and Ribeiro pointed out about the hostility of
Crown officers and the Brazilian senados, especially Bahia, toward the
juiz overseas is not true for Lisbon. In fact, as we will see, after Pombal's
son, who was president of the Lisbon *senado* for years, fled to Brazilian
safety in 1808, the Lisbon juiz drew a new political strength from his
position of dignity and leadership. A letter drawn up by the powerful
minister of João VI, Thomáz Antônio Villa Nôva Portugal, and sent to
the Lisbon juiz in 1820 in the name of João VI shows (as in 1640) the
historic link forged by the Bragança with the juiz. If, as Herculano says,
the Aviz dynasty, or at least João III, imposed his absolutism over the
Portuguese cities and the juiz do povo, and the Spanish Felipes of the
"Babylonian Captivity" did as much and more, certainly the House of
Bragança changed the behavior of the Crown toward the Casa and its
juiz.

In Pombal's time, from 1750 to about 1790, the prestige of the juiz
do pôvo was strengthened. Lúcio de Azevedo, in his economic history of
the Pombal era, mentions a donation made by the Patriarch of Lisbon
at the request of the Casa. He also suggests that the juiz do pôvo and
the Casa backed Pombal's position against the Jesuits, in order to assure
national and Portuguese leadership under regalism *vis-à-vis* the Petrine
Doctrine and papal powers.

This instance of backing to the royal *padroado* over Jesuit ultramontanism is only one part of that picture. The Visconde de Carnaxide, in
his study of Brazil during the administration of Pombal, stresses the
economic side. He asserts that Pombal created a Fourth Estate, a bourgeoisie, while he reduced the organic basis of the old society in the old
nobility and the Church. To do this, he adds that Pombal tried to kill
off the arts and crafts of Lisbon, to back up his action repressing the juiz
do pôvo of Pôrto. I cannot agree with this: the Mappa Geral of 1788
shows the size and number of the growing guilds in Lisbon. One reason
for Carnaxide's position is that Pombal helped the growth of national
industry, and especially the rise of what can be called "industrial parks"

in the suburbs of Lisbon, about which the contemporary Jacome Ratton writes so pertinently.

The relationship of the guilds, their Guildhall of twenty-four and their juiz do pôvo with the coming of industry to Portugal between 1750 and 1825 is of the greatest importance in explaining the rise and fall of the juiz do pôvo during these same seventy-five years. The creation of the Real Junta de Commércio in Portugal, the ban on industry in Brazil, and the slow but steady industrial revolution which came to Portugal were all to provoke the attention of the juiz in due time. The earliest manuscript to which I found reference on these points is in *Miscelânea,* of the *Pombalina Coleção,* of the Biblioteca Nacional, Lisbon. Number 647, which is apparently from the eighteenth century, contains the "Representação do Juiz do Pôvo relativo a commércio e navegação para o Brasil." And, nearer to 1800, Langhans located a representation sent to the juiz, reporting the losses caused by the companies of America. He adds, "this is an important document showing the fight by the guilds against the new economic tendencies."

The juiz do pôvo is clearly an institution with native, grassroots Portuguese characteristics and interests. It is also clear that as the voice of the arts and crafts his office, at least in Lisbon, focused more upon European and domestic economics than upon overseas Portugal. Like half of Portugal's historians, the juiz do pôvo identified more closely with Portugal's European interests than with the concerns of her overseas Empire. Although the juiz, so far as I have found, never prophesied any dire consequences from discovery and empire, as did Camões' "Old Man of Belém," the juiz naturally had an interest in Portugal first and Brazil second. This traditional attitude of Mother Country and colony yielded only to the idea of "an overseas province" in Brazil, as opposed to the idea of independence, an idea which prevailed between 1816 and 1825. The juiz and the twenty-four guilds spoke only indirectly about Brazil. That is, they were more interested in protecting the prosperity and economic leadership of Portugal.

If this is so, then other queries arise. How did the juiz do pôvo protect his guild masters, artisans, and mechanics from the competition of the manufactures of the British industrial revolution coming into Portugal? What position did he take, after the Methuen Treaty, toward British factories and merchants in Lisbon? How badly were the guilds in Lisbon and Pôrto hit by the Strangford Treaty and its preference for British goods? Did the Strangford Treaty, and the already strong British *juiz conservador* of the British traders, make Brazil a *de facto* economic colony of Britain, while Portugal held on politically by a thread?

Since it is safer to ask than to answer questions on this vast and complex subject, a companion query also appears: what was the economic view and vested interest of the juiz do pôvo in the rise of the Portuguese factory system and the appearance of economic liberalism in Portugal? The guilds were a monopoly, a restraint on trade. They limited the supply of apprentices, and they controlled skilled labor. They had no freedom of contract. Last, but not least, how did the juiz treat the agency of the middleman-merchants, the Real Junta de Commércio, which had the full and ominous title of Real Junta de Commércio, Navegação, e Fábricas, and was the voice of big Portuguese capitalists and the newly emerging industrial class?

The independence of Brazil has been amply studied; the juiz do pôvo has never been studied. All we know, as Boxer has shown, is that the juiz as an institution was transferred to Brazilian cities, where guilds, artisans, mechanics, and masters had a life of their own in cities. Yet the guild bandeiras of Bahia and Recife are not nearly as well known as the *bandeirantes* of São Paulo. Those of Lisbon and of Pôrto (in its irregular existence) had wealth, importance, political voices, and an active ceremonial and fraternal life. Their treasuries also seem to have been rich.

Yet the institution of juiz do pôvo was not transatlantic. It was regional and Brazilian in Brazil, Portuguese in Portugal. There was no correspondence or contact or identity between the colonial juiz and the high counterpart officer in Lisbon. They went separate ways. The Bahia *senado* sent its *procuradores* to Lisbon but did not employ a juiz do pôvo there to sue, protest, or petition on their behalf.

In the process of the rise of industry, although there were several hundred gold and silversmith masters, journeymen, and apprentices in Lisbon, well protected in their crafts, it does not seem that the juiz do pôvo or the *Casa* was responsible for the Portuguese decrees which abolished these and other industries in Brazil after 1751, and again in 1785. The Lisbon juiz may have quietly approved the restraints on Brazilian industry, but I have so far seen nothing to show that he initiated the pressure to bring it about. He was mostly concerned about protecting the guild interest in Portugal from British and Portuguese machine-made products and techniques.

The earthquake of 1755 renewed the vitality and role of both the *Casa* and the juiz do pôvo. The matter of prices, supplies, as well as health and fuel, gave impulse to a modernization of the two guild agencies in the city. Pombal depended on them. The *Casa* had been located on the east side of the Rossio, at the foot of the hill. Earthquake and fire completely destroyed the Guildhall and its entire *cartório*. Documents were restored by copy by order of the juiz in 1786. The Crown undertook to restate in writing the ancient powers and rights of both Guildhall and the juiz do pôvo, which stood in timely stead in the quarrel with the municipal senado two years later over the Mappa Geral.

The increasing power of the guilds and of the juiz do pôvo is apparent in the economic sphere before 1808. But after 1808, from 1808 to 1821, the guilds and the juiz were to become more and more political. The build-up of guild power in the face of the coming of industry is evident in their outspoken demands. Two examples are enough, one in 1772, and another down toward 1820. Both show how deep was the protest of the juiz toward economic change (more in Portugal than Brazil), even though that voice seemed silent or to be directed only at political, educational, and constitutional matters. But silence by the juiz certainly did not mean consent.

The issues that arose over the coming of industry, and especially the introduction of the manufactures of foreign interests to compete with manufactures by home guilds, is excellently brought out in the following situation. The juiz do pôvo in an address to the Lisbon senado in 1772 (and not to the Junta do Commércio, be it noticed), showed how the juiz and his *Casa* ingeniously managed to accept the coming of the manufacturer and still keep the guild monopoly over production intact: they simply made the manufacturer take the test of admission to that guild as a master! That did not settle the differences between the old crafts-artisans and the new mechanics; but it did make the capitalist join the guild system. For a time, then, between 1772 and 1820, the new economics "married" the old and, except for an occasional economic writer on Portuguese manufactures of that day, most of those concerned seemed satisfied.

The statement of the juiz do pôvo for the year 1772 may also have been addressed to Pombal. It was printed by Freire de Oliveira in his *Elementos* . . . (Vol. XVII, 385), who added that he was never able to find the reply. João Chrysóstomo Rodrigues, juiz and chairman of the *Casa* for that year, filed an answer to the request of a Frenchman who had asked permission to set up a plant that would use the findings of mechanics, optics, and physics. It was the unanimous opinion of the *Casa,* based upon the survey of their guilds, that first, he should be naturalized, in due form, and then he should choose one of the guilds

suited to his work, be examined, and seek admission to that corporation, "as is done with other foreigners." In that way he could only
practice one occupation, since even nationals were only permitted to
practice one art (craft). Thus, naturalization by the *Casa,* or one of its
guilds, went economically together with the political naturalization of
the foreign businessmen in Portugal.

No wonder Freire de Oliveira can report, in another part, that the
juiz do pôvo Manuel José Gonçalves was a person "highly esteemed by
the Marquês de Pombal" and that the feeling was reciprocated, because
"the Marquês de Pombal had many friends and admirers among the
guilds." This same juiz was nominated by the Crown (i.e., Pombal)
for his election and also his re-elections by the *Casa.* As we will see below,
between 1808 and 1820 re-election for a second, third, and fourth term
began to suggest a continuity parallel to the Lisbon senado. In 1772 the
ministry and monarchy were still powerful, and the juiz openly led the
complaints (which we know Pombal and many others shared more dis-
creetly) against "the invasion of foreign plants and workmen to the
detriment of national concerns." And again in 1791 the juiz and the
Casa, seeing the handwriting on the wall, protested the introduction of
machines into the Rio Algebibe district.

Neither Pombal nor the juiz do pôvo could stem the tide of industrialization. On the very eve of the emancipation of Brazil from Portugal in 1821, the juiz do pôvo politically stronger after the Pôrto Revolt
than at any time in nearly five hundred years of Portuguese life, snapped
out a "complaint of the juiz in the name of the *Casa,* against the *Junta
do Commércio* for issuing licences to establish factories whose manufactures are related to or analagous [i.e., in competition with] the mechanics' guilds, or the *embandeirados,* and asking that the jurisdiction
of the Junta do Commércio be restricted."

But the Lisbon juiz do pôvo had outlived his usefulness. The abolition of his office was already being discussed in the Côrtes committees
of 1821–1822. Portuguese industry had come surprisingly far since
Pombal had befriended the juiz. The difficult and painful reconstruction
after the French invasions required new manufactures which needed
workmen the guild system did not make available. Brazil, in the economic sphere, was now moving toward England. The juiz still thought
of Brazil only in terms of its connection with Lisbon, though he may
have considered improving its condition from colony or Estado do Brasil to the new liberal one, that of "an overseas province" of Portugal,
equal to the traditional provinces in the home country. The juiz, how-

ever, broke away from the Bragança during the Peninsular Wars. The Strangford Treaty and the costs of rehabilitating striken Portugal led to rejection of the new Brazilian kingdom within the United Kingdom of Portugal and Brazil, the royal solution of 1816. The neat, compromise approach of an "overseas province," suggestive of the Spanish Constitution, reflected the indirect interest of the juiz do pôvo in Brazilian matters and in Brazilian independence. On a more extreme hand, however, the enemies of the juiz were the new capitalists of Portugal. They learned between 1821 and 1834 how to get along both without Brazil, whose separation was almost a fact in 1821, and without the *Casa* and the juiz, whose abolition was already suggested in the Côrtes Committee on Arts and Manufactures in 1822, but which did not finally become law until 1834.

Some aspects of the rise of industry in Portugal harmed the Brazilian economy; other economic developments were a help. The economic position taken by the juiz do pôvo or the *Casa* cannot always be found by research or investigation—at least not up to now. Their arguments may be extant (and I believe they are), but much remains in manuscript, or without index, and is being slowly looked up. Some phases of the economic process are well known, such as those of the Pombal era. We know how Pombal got the consent of Lisbon senado as well as the juiz do pôvo and the *Casa* to allow Christian Henry Smith to build the sugar refinery in Lisbon in 1750. This was intended to help the northeastern planters of Brazil and also to break the Dutch monopoly and bring sugar refining to Lisbon. It helped both Brazil and Portugal (and the Crown). It was also good for the tobacco producers in Bahia to know that they had a sure market under Portuguese mercantilism in Portugal for their products and sure profits under Portuguese imperialism in Africa for their tobacco. They contrast with the first repressive law against industry in Brazil of 1751, which was followed by the better-known measures of 1784 and 1785.

It was in between these dates, during the peak of Pombal's era, in 1761, that the local interest of the Lisbon juiz do pôvo and the guilds of the *Casa* first clashed with the national Portuguese aims for the encouragement of manufacturing and industry. José Accursio das Neves, a clear and intelligent Portuguese economic writer in the troubled years from 1808 to after 1825, was an enemy of the guilds and their juiz do pôvo. Unlike contemporary economic writers on the Brazilian side of the Atlantic, such as Azeredo Coutinho, Santos Vilhena, Rodrigues de Brito, and the two Silva Lisbôa (Baltasar and the later Visconde de

Cairú), who were friends of mines, plantation crops, and freer shipping arrangements, José Accursio was a vigorous spokesman for manufacturing. While Brazilian political economy was attracted to the laws of commercial capitalism, Accursio struck out frankly for industrial capitalism.

The late colonial Brazilian economic writers are strangely silent about urban economics. The guilds are not mentioned, and the juiz do pôvo are ignored as a vested interest in the city. Not so with Portuguese writers such as José Accursio. When he wrote that the guilds *(Casa)* deserve discredit, general disapproval, and the sentence of proscription, he foreshadowed in 1814 what the deputies in the *Côrtes* of 1822 would try to take up again. He wanted freedom of contract for labor (to work in industry). He preferred manufactures over agriculture and the doctrines of the new economic liberals to those of the physiocrats.

It is worth the extra detail to add that he studied the different national systems for their encouragement of technology and machine production in their patent and invention policies. In this matter, we can add that he explicitly disagreed with the Brazilian José da Silva Lisbôa, who was content to get state help by government encouragement of the importation of machines (from England). Instead, Accursio asked the Portuguese government to help Portuguese invention, production, and ownership of machines, rather than their import from outside the Empire. Accursio, by the way, was a member of the Real Junta de Commércio, composed of big merchants, capitalists, investors, and factory owners, which overshadowed the Mesa do Bem Comum of smaller merchants and was the target of juiz do pôvo attack.

For his part, he was glad that the decrees of February 9, 1761, and April 18 of the same year allowed foreign craftsmen to work in Portugal and be "exempt from the obstacles and vexations of the guilds." "More laws such as these," he wrote, "would be blows that would stop the guilds from being oppressive to Portuguese industry." He clearly believed that the Methuen Treaty (and even the Strangford) ruined Portuguese manufacturers (as many others did), but he blamed the *Casa,* the guilds, and the juiz do pôvo for Portuguese backwardness in manufacturing. But, as we have seen, the *Casa* and the juiz sidestepped outright competition by requiring the masters and artisans of such mills and factories to apply for admission to the closed society of the craft guilds.

The closed society of the guilds led to trouble also in one last detail. The need for workers, free from guild wages and protection, carried over into a struggle affecting education and vocational training. In the 1780's the Crown and especially Diego Pina Manique, the strong superintendent of police, health, and welfare, helped found the Casa Pia school for children of the lower classes. The school gave a vocational training, as well as reading and writing, parallel to the more "white-collar" and commercial school run by the *Junta do Commércio*. The efforts of Pina Manique, and later by José Accursio, to equate the vocational training of these schools with the apprenticeship training run by the guilds themselves failed to open the guilds to these graduates, but the discussion did bring forward the whole issue of public education. An important document of 1815 shows that the juiz do pôvo of that later day again forestalled attempts to open up the guilds' apprentice system by putting forward his own interesting proposal for public education of artisans and those apprenticed to artisans. A stubborn, proud, yet popular official, this Lisbon juiz. How much he took from the Spaniard Campomanes on the education of artisans I do not know.

In brief, there were, between 1750 and 1825, two manufacturing interests side-by-side in Portugal. The royal *Junta do Commércio* was the voice of the more modern eighteenth-century machine industry; the *Casa* and the juiz were the guardians of the ancient handcraft and guild manufactures. Of the two forces, it seems that the *Junta do Commércio,* more than the juiz, was the direct source of complaint against the ban on industry in Brazil. Even this is not clear. The original decree of 1785 blames the reason on contraband from the illicit and early inter-American trade with the United States. Yet the fact is that officers of the *Junta de Commércio,* such as José Accursio, preferred to look on Brazil as a market for Portuguese manufactures. Indeed, Accursio after 1808 was optimistic about that role for Brazil. Unlike the juiz he even favored the move of the Court to Rio. Accursio compared the transfer of the capital of the Luso-Brazilian Empire to Rio de Janeiro with the transfer of the Roman empire to Constantinople under Constantine.

During the next twenty-five years, from 1785 to 1810, a generation of revolution, continued economic crisis, and international wars brought into the open many issues of debate. Some of these were old and had been dormant. A few were new and evoked by the peril of war and invasion of Portugal. The juiz do pôvo, who seems to have been silent about the abolition of industry in Brazil in 1785, complained about the damage caused by companies' trading with America. The *Recordações* (or *Memoirs*) of Jácome Ratton, who prospered in Lisbon's business and political world from 1747 to 1810, supply data about companies, stockholders, and rich company owners who were trading with America. Being an officer of the *Junta do Commércio* he had more than one encounter with the Lisbon juiz do pôvo. They confronted each other before the French Marshal Junot for the last time in 1808. When Ratton opposed the "desgraçado" Strangford Treaty in 1810, the Regency of João VI sent him off to England. During his sixty-three years in Lisbon his political world had changed. In spite of the loss of Brazil and the opposition of the Lisbon juiz, his pro-industry ideas, which were like those of Accursio, were to win out in Portugal.

One other step in that direction had already come in 1802. Accursio, who applauded the French Revolution's action in abolishing the guilds, published a document for the first time, which is still little-known. The Portuguese Crown now openly viewed the corporations or guilds in the light of "well-understood principles." Although the Crown warned against any sudden abolition of guild privileges, it nevertheless allowed factory owners to sell their manufactures in their own shops, subject to the *Mesa do Bem Commum* of the local merchants and the review of the *Junta do Commércio*. The *Casa* and the juiz do pôvo were not in a position to resist or oppose. The *alvará* also allowed the Junta to extend long-term credits to merchants who would sell national products, and the dark days of the Lisbon juiz do pôvo were on the horizon. But, with the international war and invasion from 1808 on, as the economic role of the juiz and the guilds were in decline, larger and larger opportunities of political leadership and power came into sight, which the juiz seized as a sort of compensation for the economic twilight.

In Brazil, meantime, the colony was already being moved to her new economic and political place within the Luso-Brazilian Empire. As Portugal sagged under the first French war of 1795 and Spanish invasion of 1802, even before the three French occupations of 1808, 1809, and 1810, Brazil was safe and sound. The rivalry of old and new economic forces in Portugal was not repeated in Brazil. The three million people of the colony in 1800 were really not held back by the anti-industrial measure of 1785. Brazil was already entering her own period of growth. The balance between Brazil and Portugal was more and more in favor of the former, according to Caio Prado Júnior in his *Formação do Brasil contemporâneo*. If the few handcraft producers of textiles were suppressed, there was a considerable expansion of Brazilian cotton-growing and export, both to England and Portugal. Exports went under the navigation laws, direct to Lisbon and thence to London, to compete with the East Indian Company's finished yet cheap imports. Cotton exports almost doubled between 1786 and 1790.

If the planters of the Brazilian northeast prospered, there were other reasons there for echoing the restlessness of the age. The vigor of the juiz do pôvo of Recife and Bahia, so politically alive in 1710 as Boxer has shown, reappeared not only in 1798 but also in 1820. I pick these two years because they are times of the Bahia *Inconfidência* and the Portuguese Revolt. There may have been many other times in between when the Brazilian descendant of the Lisbon juiz do pôvo bestirred himself as the Portuguese juiz do pôvo was also doing.

Prosperity is no cure for short-sighted government. Moreover, the Brazilian Northeast and the merchants there were chronically irritated by the lack of specie and cash money for their needs. Anyone who holds that the cities of Brazil were of secondary importance is possibly too attached to the view that plantation-slavery, mining, ranching, and the *sertão bandeirante* activity were the only forces at work in the colony. The protest of a Brazilian juiz could be heard, when it wanted in 1798, clearly in Lisbon, the Ministry, and the Court. It may be that the after-effects of the Tiradentes Conspiracy and the Bahia *Inconfidência,* combined with the propaganda of the American and French revolutions, made Portuguese officials attentive to complaints in the colonies. But I think that the historic practice of hearing a Portuguese or Brazilian juiz, or the *procuradores* of a city senado, was older than any fear of current revolutionary influence. The established Portuguese *foral* and the force of the juiz may not have been as disorderly as João Ribeiro indicated. José Maria Bello in his *História da República* repeats Ribeiro's charge that the juiz was at the head of "rebellion against authority." I doubt that such an officer rooted in both tradition and establishment can fairly be called revolutionary in the same breath and age with Tiradentes, Robespierre, or Thomas Paine. Resistance is not revolution.

Recently the urban factor in Brazilian history has increasingly been recognized, although the juiz do pôvo of the city is still not well studied. The published minutes of the senado of Bahia show that as well as do Freire de Oliveira's and Pires de Lima's histories of the *município* of Lisbon. Although there is still a vast amount of the Bahia municipal material in the Arquivo Ultramarino in Lisbon, part of which Almeida e Castro undertook to reproduce, those documents which José Honório Rodrigues reprinted in the series "Documentos históricos" of the Biblioteca Nacional do Rio de Janeiro only go to 1726. (Rodrigues, a deep student, admirer, and biographer of Capistrano de Abreu, disagreed with that pioneer historian of the frontier, the *sertões,* and roads.) Unfortunately, those who have begun to see *senado da câmara* power and self-assertion as part of the tradition of Portuguese liberties still fail to note the presence and role of the procurador and the juiz do pôvo. At least Oliveira Torres has insisted that guilds, artisans, mechanics, and *mestres* are also found in colonial Brazil.

As Portugal swallowed up the Lisbon Casa and the juiz do pôvo, so did Brazil after its independence. The juiz do pôvo vanished from Bahia as he vanished from Lisbon. But he left his mark in both places, an unusual Luso-Brazilian figure, sometimes democratic, often liberal, and an influential popular leader. Both João Baptista Cortines Laxe, who studied the first Brazilian Municipal Law of 1828, and the more famous historian A. J. de Mello Moraes agreed more than a century ago that Brazilian civic liberties came from Portugal. Cortines Laxe noted that the Law of 1828 which abolished the *senado da câmara* and the office of juiz do pôvo was signed by Emperor Pedro I. It was countersigned by José Clemente Pereira, who was oddly enough called the juiz do pôvo of Rio by one Portuguese historian of the Pôrto Revolt of 1820. "Little by little," wrote Mello Moraes in 1872, "it will be necessary to restore to the *senados da câmara,* the unique people's corporations of Brazil, those rights which the Portuguese *câmaras* always enjoyed, and which formed the base of the *Côrtes;* an important institution whose disuse led the nation rapidly to its destruction." Cortines Laxe had thought the urban *senados da câmara* might have survived if the centralist nationalism of the first Brazilian Empire had given them some sort of tax powers. Pedro I when he got to Lisbon also abolished the Portuguese Guildhall and juiz do pôvo in 1834.

The Brazilian senado and juiz do pôvo, especially in Bahia, Recife, and Rio de Janeiro, gave a good account of their willingness to challenge matters between 1800 and 1822. The juiz do pôvo shows up well in Pernambuco, where the Recife juiz rose to a level of political importance in 1798 and again in 1820. It might be logical to expect this in Pernambuco Revolt of 1817. On the other hand, the Bahia juiz moved as quickly as the Lisbon juiz do pôvo to support the Pôrto Revolt of 1820. These two transatlantic halves became whole for a moment in Luso-Brazilian history.

Documents printed in the "Documentos históricos" series tell something of how the Recife juiz do pôvo in 1798, Jerónimo José Gomes, joined with a solicitor of Real Fazenda to directly ask the Crown to appoint a *residência* to investigate the conduct of the then governor and captain of Pernambuco, Tomás de Melo. This direct petition for impeachment and removal carried up to both Martinho Mello e Castro and Rodrigo de Souza Coutinho, ministers of high intelligence and integrity. I have not investigated for this paper the cause of the complaint, but only wish to show that the Recife juiz do pôvo was heard, in a direct action, and the governor was soon referred to in the papers as "ex-governor." What is ironic is a manuscript in the University of Coimbra Library dated ten years before, 1788, in which the Recife senado da câmara asked the Queen to not only appoint Tomás José de Melo as Pernambuco governor but to extend his appointment over a long time because of his services! They even asked Martinho e Mello to get the Queen to make the appointment. How fickle that senado, or how independent that juiz do pôvo!

The role of juiz do pôvo in Lisbon, Pôrto, Bahia, Recife, and its counterpart in Rio de Janeiro became increasingly assertive politically from 1800 to 1822. Perhaps this role was implicit in the office, or the imminent crises of those days evoked the precedents of 1640. Certainly it can be repeated that as the economic importance of the guilds declined, the juiz sought to hitch his office to the star of political action, as the voice of the people. This political action between 1808 and 1822, and especially in the Pôrto Revolt of 1820, was to affect Brazilian independence, and we should now turn to the second part of this paper: the political powers of the juiz do pôvo.

When the Braganças fled Lisbon in 1808, members of the senado also fled. Large amounts of capital left the country for England and Brazil or was hidden in the country. The juiz do pôvo rose up from the ashes. The only elected official in the nation, the juiz do pôvo emerged from the stage of the municipal senado da câmara on to a more political national scene. More and more attention was given to the juiz. His speeches and oratory becomes known; pamphlets appeared. Treatises of considerable length were published on the respectable history of the office and the Casa. Lord mayor to some people, people's tribune and civic magistrate to others, the Lisbon juiz really became eminent from 1808 to 1822. With King, Court, president of the senado, and the superintendent gone, the juiz came face-to-face with his old enemy the Junta do Commércio (especially Ratton), the new enemy (the French), and the Regency. The historic ally and protector, the Bragança dynasty, was safe in Rio de Janeiro. Bahia benefited from this. But Lisbon and

Pôrto faced the ordeal of standing up to the dreaded French veterans and conquering French generals. The guilds supplied teen-age apprentices or young journeymen to the Portuguese armed forces.

In 1808, in Lisbon, the juiz do pôvo of Lisbon met Marshal Junot for the first time. In that same year the office of juiz do pôvo of Pôrto was reconstituted, and the juiz there met Soult for the first time in 1809. As the fidalgos, nobility, and officials fled, the guilds and juiz stayed behind to fight Massena in 1810 and endure "the Calvary of the third French invasion of Portugal. Until help came for the Portuguese patriots from themselves and the supporting British, the juiz do pôvo moved with care and caution. The juiz of Lisbon, who had been taken into the secret of power in 1640 when the Braganças accepted the monarchy, was now left in ignorance of the Bragança plans to leave Portugal. He knew nothing about the messages of the French invasion. When it came, then, the juiz do pôvo stood rather lonely but courageous in his leading position.

That year, openly unwilling to recognize the Junta dos Três Estados, he made his first speech on the subject of the election of a new king or regent to govern Portugal. There are some six such *fallas* (speeches) in printed pamphlets in the Pombal Collection of the National Library, Lisbon, and many more in other libraries. Soon after, Hipólito da Costa, in his *Correio Braziliense* in London, was jubilant about the appearance of the juiz do pôvo in Pôrto. The term or title of juiz do pôvo even carried an image and may have been emotion-laden in that terrible decade. According to *Investigcão Econômica*, published in London, the head of the merchants of Liverpool was called the juiz; so was José Clemente Pereira in the later events of Brazilian independence. The proud and self-conscious civic figure in robes, batons, and ribbons who led the bandeiras and the twenty-four guilds to the Old See was symbolic as well as real. His reality fell across Portuguese patriotic politics in that decade; his symbolism (and I venture an opinion here) may have been readily borrowed by Portuguese Masonry. Hipólito da Costa, whose portrait in Masonic regalia and robes I have located, praised the juiz as both legal fact and populist symbol.

This helped his popularity and leadership. But these were not the only things. In 1808 the juiz do pôvo asserted as political doctrine (as the Spanish Jesuits did) that the people of Portugal elected their kings. If, then, the King chose to leave his people, then the people (or their juiz do pôvo) could choose another king, in fact another dynasty. It might have been the Cadaval who would replace the Bragança, if they dared or would. But letting the Bragança go was one thing; letting Brazil go was quite another. Now, in 1808, Brazil was praised not as a colony, nor as an *estado*, but as an "overseas province." The juiz do pôvo said nothing of a Brazilian kingdom in a united Luso-Brazilian Kingdom (as in 1816) and revealed understanding of Portuguese national interests, as well as those of the city of Lisbon and the peoples of the guilds.

Breathing the same sort of good riddance that some members of the *Côrtes Geral* of 1821 offered to the Brazilians leaving that assembly, the juiz do pôvo had now to face the French. The crisis was near. José Abreu Campos, another three-term man, was re-elected juiz in 1808. (I give the names of the juiz because I think the elected magistrate of the Casa deserve recognition by historians as much as *fidalgos*, clerics, some writers, and political leaders). This Abreu Campos, whom Raul Brandão calls tough and stubborn, stubbornly opposed the claim of Junta do Três Estados to recommend a candidate for regent or king to Napoleon. The juiz insisted that they be excluded and that a constitution shoud be given to Portugal.

The *Junta do Commércio* had been brought together to swear allegiance to the French, and Ratton tells the story. The French, to collect their heavy fines, indemnities, sequestrations, levies, and other benevolent or forced loans, turned to the juiz do povo to make up the list of contributions that the guilds would have to make. The Mesa do Bem Commum, under the scrutiny of the *Junta do Commércio*, would do the same for smaller merchants. The French bled Portugal as much as they could in Pôrto as well as Lisbon, and in any city or country district where property, jewelry, art, or valued materials could be found and "fined."

Then came the Pôrto Revolt of June 1808, and the bitter civil and anti-French war began. The Regency left behind by João VI had accommodated and yielded to the French almost as much as he had but was under much more immediate and daily pressure. They did not order a fight. But Junot abolished this Regency and governed Portugal directly, thus giving Brazil a *de facto* independence, since Napoleon had also declared the Bragança deposed.

The revival of the Pôrto juiz do pôvo and the growing resistance to the French by the Suprema Junta there led to kindlier views about the Bragança. The expectation of British aid also secured the hold of the Brazilian dynasty. But it is hard to say whether the support was genuine or opportunist and political, designed to hold on to British help and to help the cause. Certainly, however, the idea of less absolutism and a more constitutional, elected monarchy, even if the Bragança remained, began to appear. How much of concern there arose in Brazil over this is hard to say. It first came out in Lisbon.

On May 23, at the called meeting of the *Junta dos Três Estados*, the Lisbon juiz do pôvo boldly took the floor and spoke to Junot: he requested a constitution for Portugal and said he would be happy to have a constitution and a constitutional king, who would be prince of the blood of Napoleon's family. "We should consider ourselves happy to have a constitution wholly similar to that which your royal Imperial Majesty decided to grant to the Grand Duchy of Warsaw, with the only difference that the representatives of the nation be elected by the Municipal Chambers, so we can conform to our ancient usage." He wanted a concordat with the pope, as the French had, "in which all religions are free and enjoy civil tolerance and public worship," in which "our colonies, founded by our ancestors and watered by their blood, are considered as provinces or districts forming an integrated part of the Kingdom, so that their representatives can find in our social organization the places which belong to them as soon as they come, or are able to come to occupy them." He asked for public education, free press, ministerial responsibility, independent judicial power, and circulation of the properties of mortmain. But Abreu Campos failed. Ratton reported that the notables and estates accepted Junot's personal powers, in spite of the juiz do pôvo. (So the juiz do pôvo charged.) He turned now to populism, the people, and patriotism. The British landed late in 1809. The juiz do pôvo turned from the French dynasty. He now moved in the footsteps of João Salter de Mendonça, who called on people to rise *en masse* and join the Spanish Revolt.

The Pôrto juiz was reinforced by the backing he received from the Suprema Junta there and the Pôrto Casa. He came into office on a wave of patriotism. It was felt that the revival of this ancient institution, which once was the glory of Portugal, would restore the nation to its old-time energy. The Pôrto juiz was João de Almeida Ribeiro. He took office with an immediate call to the people to stay with the junta and oppose the French by being loyal to the Bragança. "I will not treat you as your Judge, filled with authority, but as your friend, and in your behalf. You will at once lay your complaints before me. If they are more than I can take care of, I will take them in person to the Supreme Government, for them to say what is for your benefit; let us not be despots."

In Lisbon, the call came for a Portuguese nation-at-arms and an armed militia. The *senado* and the guilds of the Casa were asked to set up *ministros de bairros* to report and select those men who were most capable of command. Thus, the Portuguese Legion has its beginning. No wonder the juiz do pôvo hailed the return of the wounded, sick, but victorious Portuguese partiots in 1814. Many of them came from the guilds, barros, and bandeiras which he knew well. The juiz do pôvo did not hesitate at all to assert leadership. When the British landed, he wrote to draw the attention of General Sir Hew Dalrymple to the office and role of the juiz do pôvo. Next year he did the same with the Portuguese leader, Bernardim Freire de Andrade, and with other British generals. He brought letters to the British personally, "Eu em nome do pôvo deste Reyno," specially striving to get the British (before Cintra) to get back some of French loot.

In his new role, the juiz do pôvo spoke as representative of a voiceless and stricken population, as well as the delegate of guilds and a political leader in the city. He presented claims on their behalf, "Eu reclamo por êlles." The idea of the public and the concept of public as well as national and guild interest arise for the first time. The public deserves more than any private person. "It is for the public of all the People that my office requires me to make claim." As a real voice of the people, now, the juiz entered a decade of popular support. Public demonstrations gave him a leading place in Lisbon and, in 1820, a leading place in the Pôrto Revolt.

A Goya would be needed to paint the reality of Portugal under the French. The juiz do pôvo changed his tune about wanting any French-derived royal family or constitution. Hatred of the French and desire for revenge pervade the fallas and pamphlets of the day. Ignored by the British, the juiz now turned to the people and the Portuguese nation even before the Bragança. That is, the allegiance to Bragança returned, but constitution, national independence, and protection of the people came first. That was how the war with the French and the great French despoiling of Portugal came to move the juiz do pôvo forward into the nineteenth century, at least politically. He was still unable to keep up with the changes that were industrial and economic. Unable to induce British, French, or even Portuguese authorities to call a real Côrtes, instead of the controlled Junta dos Três Estados, the juiz saw the liberty of his office with the reflected light of the Spanish Córtes of Cadiz.

The changing political position of the juiz do pôvo was affected by the changed prospect of the day. Already in possession of a written set of grants, *forais* (chartered privileges), and an assertive position over the people, the political eye of the juiz do pôvo found much in the Córtes of Cadiz to implement and give Portugal on a national scale more liberties and representation. As time went on, he abandoned his interest in a French constitution and openly admired and demanded the Spanish Constitution for his country.

Greater changes came after 1815. The Napoleonic War was ended; the French were gone. Sadly enough, the promising Spanish Constitution was on its way out. Brazil was about to be raised to a kingdom. Already well off, and the beneficiary of British trade as well as her own economic growth, Brazil was far better off than impoverished and embittered Portugal, and the contrast struck home. Why the Pernambucans should have been the ones to revolt against the Bragança when the Portuguese did not is a question which loosens even further my use of an economic interpretation of history. The Portuguese were really poor and deprived in 1815. After the French troops had raided and gone and the British troops had foraged and gone, Portugal faced ruin. Out of the ordeal within Portugal and the changing status for Brazil, the Lisbon juiz do pôvo grew in importance. The fact that he had stayed behind during the patriotic war gave him an added emotional appeal, so that in the political events after 1820 great popular demonstrations and fervent feelings on his behalf were stirred.

While the patriotic struggles were taking place, some of the hard feelings against the Braganças had waned. The elevation of Brazil to a kingdom in 1816, however, rekindled memories of the secret and swift departure of the Court and the resulting sense of anomie among the Portuguese left standing on the quay. The aristocracy of learning and letters renewed their contempt for the Crown and the new attractions of Brazil. Many of these, like the juiz do pôvo, had also favored the replacement of the Bragança and a new king. The elevation in 1816 of Brazil to a kingdom brought memoirs and memories out. Meantime, the changing middle class and industrial capitalism in Portugal made an amazing comeback during the period of reconstruction. In spite of the economic mist of that day, Accursio das Neves, like the present-day Victorino Magalhaes Godinho, reported considerable recovery. Paradoxically, it seems to have begun with the Bahia decree reopening Brazilian industry. The need for industrial products at home, the reappearance of industry in Brazil, and the Strangford Treaty's preference for British manufactures had the effect of stimulating the return of capital, technique, and machines to Portuguese industry. As before, however, Portuguese manufacturing could do without Brazil more easily than it could get along without a freer supply of workmen. The juiz was as much or more of a troublesome monopoly from past Portuguese history as was their Brazilian colony. Institution and colony were solid legacies.

Manoel Pinto de Aguiar, in his *A abertura dos pôrtos,* points out how much Bahia had gained from the Braganças in Brazil and their remedial legislation. Most of this accrued to commerce, because Brazilian industry, although now favored by the repeal of the law, remained still unprotected by any tariff. The King knew this. After he had signed the Strangford Treaty, he issued a manifesto to the three estates of Portugal (which Pinto de Aguiar reprints) in which he says: "Do not be concerned that the introduction of British manufactures must endanger your industry." To balance the lowering of tariffs on foreign goods which helped the import of foreign (British) manufactures, Portugal was urged to become agricultural, wine- and olive-producing. But no matter what the Crown was doing for Bahia between 1808 and 1816, there is no doubt that Lisbon manufacturing was growing, in spite of the new royal attitude, and the privileges of Brazil on one hand and the vested interest of the juiz do pôvo at home on the other.

By this time, also, a polemical literature for and against the juiz do pôvo came from left and right, from both liberals and conservatives. Some of the debate took place among Portuguese in London; words and pamphlets also flew among conservatives and liberals in Portugal. One opposing argument was a denial that the juiz was a magistrate or had ever entered into the body politic. Critics stated the Casa had only a guild function, and the juiz who took on a political activity only abused his position. Tribunes of the plebs might be necessary in an aristocracy; they would be advantageous in a republic; they can only be dangerous in a monarchy such as Portugal.

The best liberal argument for the juiz do pôvo was published in 1814 in London. A 56-page history and description of the juiz and Casa of the city of Pôrto gave the origin of these public men and "representatives of the third order of estate."* This historical, legal, social, and political support of the juiz as an established institution in both Pôrto and Lisbon ignores the juiz in Brazil. In spite of this intellectual juridical and political disquisition, the revolts a few years later in Pernambuco and Pôrto also indicated that the political lines in both Brazil and

* Palha Collection, Houghton Library, Harvard University.

Portugal had not been closed. The *sinédrio* stir in Portugal in 1817 and the Pernambuco Revolt in Brazil that same year show again that the juiz and his people may have shared the same institution on both sides of the Atlantic although they rarely acted together.

Between 1815 and 1820 the Lisbon juiz do pôvo enlarged his interests to include speeches to welcome home the great troops of Portugal to celebrate the European peace and the 1814 Treaty. He sometimes spoke in name of the people of the capital with great emotion and with allusions to the former greatness of other Portuguese efforts in Europe, Asia, Africa, and at home. The juiz did not care about political, historical, or juridical theories of his office. He was neither a philosopher or a doctrinaire. (Literate though each juiz had to be, I find no evidence of contribution to the philosophy or history of his office or function.)

He went straight to the people, with many kinds of sentiment and action. After 1815 he sought a separate school system for artisans, separate from those supported at the Court (Casa Pia). His request was supported by the Lisbon senado but turned down by the King's minister. The senado agreed that "primary letters were the key to the sciences and arts," and that the artisan-mechanic class should have access to a cultural introduction to their times and the past. Though highly skilled, the Portuguese workman had few educational and cultural attainments. But when the Crown officer handed down his opinion about the danger of knowledge in certain categories and areas, and how the program proposed ought to be controlled, the Lisbon senado changed its mind and agreed with the minister. Thus, the juiz' proposal for more lower-class education had to wait for Herculano and the reformers of the mid-century.

The revolt which began at Pôrto in 1820 spread to Lisbon and then to Brazil. It pushed the Lisbon juiz do pôvo forward again into the arena of national and colonial politics, after the previous lull and his five-year concern with educational, guild, and economic matters. The chain reaction begun in Pôrto led to the eventual independence of Brazil. Ideas of colonialism, economic progress, political and religious liberty once again created a climate for conservatism versus reform in both parts of the Luso-Brazilian empire.

Matters were different in 1820. By that time, within the United Kingdom of 1816, Brazil was clearly senior partner over Portugal in prosperity, geography, size, population, and even empire. Portugal had lost territory to Spain and was struggling against the effects of occupation by French and British troops and a British regent. Brazil had expanded across Uruguay and occupied Montevideo. A contemporary Brazilian historian adds the psychological factors of Portuguese inferiority to Brazil, and even Portuguese jealousy of this state of affairs. The analogy of father and son is appropriate: as the son grew larger, the parent grew smaller with age, stress, and distress. Even so, the parent had retained great intellectual powers, made repeated attempts at self-help, and exercised a capacity to survive and grow, based upon forces deep in Portuguese history and enlightenment. The parent was surely long-lived, with much muscle and mental fiber.

The period from the so-called *sinédrio* (1817) to the Pôrto Revolt (1820) covers only a slightly shorter time than that from the Pernambuco Revolt (1817) to the independence pronouncement in São Paulo (1822). There are connections between the two pairs, but they are individual and isolated and not enough to prove an historical case. Ideas which appear in the former do not appear in the latter. Many of the leaders have nothing to do with each other, and no contact. Brazilian thought, influenced by the presence of Brazilian leadership and prosperity, was independent. Portuguese thought was much influenced by the Spanish Constitution of 1812. This weakened the possibility of real union still further. (By 1820 Lisbon and Pôrto received less and less Brazilian gold, and no diamonds, in balance of payment, since Portugal was providing few if any manufactures or food for the Brazilian market.) The political position of those days came first from the Coimbra *sinédrio,* which had wanted Brazil in the united empire not as a kingdom but as an "overseas province," or better still, several provinces. In 1820 and later, the Lisbon juiz do pôvo took the same position and also added his call for the Spanish pattern of colonial deputies in a constituent *Côrtes.*

The August, 1820, revolt in Pôrto soon spread from the richer provinces of the Portuguese north, south to Lisbon, where it got support from the senado, army garrison, and juiz do pôvo. The popular demonstration in the Lisbon Rossio clamored for the appearance of the juiz. Populism elevated him to a primary public role which overthrew João VI's regent and *junta.* The new Suprema Junta at Lisbon included the original figures of the Pôrto Revolt and therefore was national, as well as liberal. The public drama and celebration of the event and the political role of the juiz do pôvo were very high. Was a new social contract and basis for Portuguese government in the offing? Was the historic tie between the Lisbon juiz and the Bragança broken by the King's flight from the French in 1807 and his long prosperous stay in Rio de Janeiro ever since?

It would have seemed so from the desperate economic situation. The promotion of national industry, in spite of writings which favored it, had not been helped much by the guild system and by the closed Anglo-Portuguese commerce. Each year had seen a new reduction in the Portuguese navigation and fleet and in imports of prime necessities and raw materials. More and more, wheat had to be imported. Factories, even shops, closed down. Not even the guilds did well. Beggary and poverty increased. "Production was beaten down by British competition overseas . . . and workers became beggars or robbers. In 1820 penury reached its extreme." This dismal picture of a desolate land is from Gomez de Carvalho, who adds that the Treasury did not return deposits or pay officeholders. Soldiers complained of not getting paid for eight months. Even the Montepio did not pay, and "misery was joined to humiliation."

On the very brink of this revolutionary economic and political situation in Portugal, João VI in Brázil held on to his Lisbon link with the juiz do pôvo, as we see from an exchange of letters between the Crown and juiz. The influential minister of João VI, Thomáz Antônio Villa Nôva Portugal (the same who thirty years before had started the business school for the *Junta do Commércio* in Lisbon) wrote for the King. Once before, in 1809, João VI had written directly to the people of Pôrto and the newly revived juiz do pôvo there, in praise of their loyalty to the Crown and his regard for popular institutions. Now, in 1820, the juiz still found time and state of mind to be urbane and ceremonial with the far-off King, and His Majesty also took time to write. It gave him pleasure to see how the "faithful people of Lisbon keep interested in the permanent prosperity and glory of the Throne and the Nation." The Conde de Aguiar (who was Tomáz de Portugal) sent it from Rio, December, 1819, and the juiz of Lisbon gave it to the *Gazêta de Lisbôa* to publish, (Tuesday, March 14, 1820) . The two institutions were very old Portuguese friends, and juiz politeness and royal sentiment rose to the surface of the gathering storm waters.

Revolt broke out six months later, first Pôrto, then Lisbon, then in Rio de Janeiro and São Paulo within the year. The deaths of the Conde da Barca in 1816 and the Conde de Aguiar (Villa Nôva de Portugal) in 1821 removed two alert and very intelligent advisors of the Crown. The Brazilian Vasconcellos de Drummond had been private secretary to Conde de Aguiar, holding his economic measures in high esteem and evaluating him, in simple black-and-white, as friendly to Brazil. On the other hand, Drummond looked very differently (in his *Memoirs*) upon the European-trained diplomat, Duke of Palmella, who came to Rio to meet with José Clemente Pereira between December, 1820, and February, 1821. A month after the *Côrtes* opened in Lisbon, Pereira, presidents of the Rio de Janeiro *senado* called a meeting of merchants and people, now famous, which Vasconcellos do Drummond called "anarchistic." A Portuguese historian of the events of 1820–1821 calls José Clemente Pereira the juiz de pôvo of Rio de Janeiro. He certainly is neither, but it is hard to be precise since this man still has no biography in spite of the fact that he lived a very long life (1787–1854) in Portugal and Brazil under three kings and was always close to the core of the power struggles.

The so-called Portuguese Party, with names associated with Palmella and Pereira, is really no such party. The term offers a certain clarity or identity of ideas and interests on one side, against those taking shape on the other. Pereira, who helped create Pedro I in 1821 and Pedro II in 1840, was a prosperous lawyer, merchant, and influential politician, who seemed, to have had the same momentum in Rio de Janeiro's *senado* that the juiz do pôvo in Lisbon possessed. Their ideas also ran parallel, which is a safe way to say again that I have found no correspondence between them. Pereira was president and voice of the Rio *senado;* the Lisbon juiz had practically taken the place of the *senado* and its president since 1808.

None of the contemporary political actions, whether by the juiz do pôvo of Bahia in 1820, by the Rio *senado* in 1821, or by the Lisbon juiz indicate any conspiracy of contact or of power. They were institutions that had inherited a tendency toward separate political action, especially in crises, and what we have is a series of municipal actions, more complicated than appears here, with different towns resisting their senados, other opposing provincial-intendancy juntas. In view of these arguments within arguments, the largest picture possible for now is one of rising city political leadership in both Lisbon and Brazil. The *Gazêta de Lisbôa* published these parallel actions of the Bahia juiz and his Lisbon counterpart. The juiz do pôvo of Lisbon was also a sort of leader in a chain reaction of letter-writing and correspondence with at least Bahia and Coimbra. The municipal officer has also a real place in the movement which gave rise to the *Côrtes*.

The army and people had poured into the Rossio in Lisbon when the Pôrto junta and juiz do pôvo sent information about the revolt which took place on behalf of the Braganças. They wanted a liberal constitution. The call soon went out for the muito honrado juiz do pôvo of Lisbon to both lead a peoples' demonstration and receive the acclaim of the demonstrators.

This is what the *Gazêta de Lisbôa* said on Saturday, September 16, 1820, three weeks after the August Revolt in Pôrto: "An urgent message was sent to tell the Right Honorable juiz do pôvo that the people wanted him. Soon, he and his scribe, set out in a curtained stage, down Rua Áurea to the Rossio. When he got there, and opened the curtains, the people saw him and he was hailed with the greatest expressions . . . until he entered Government House, where the Count of Rezende met him." It was a genuine demonstration on behalf of a traditional leader, although many in the crowd may have been the hundreds of apprentices, journeymen, clerks, and others who were members of or dependent on the twenty-four guilds. The great outpouring of people clamored for another interim government, the resignation or overthrow of the Regency of João VI, and a new *Suprema Junta*. A sea of handkerchiefs waved from the crowds waiting for an answer. Soon, the ministers of the new government appeared on the balcony of Government House. The Right Honorable juiz do pôvo, João Alves, also stood there right along-side army and political leaders.

The senado of the city followed suit, calling on the people of the *Grande Capital do Reino Unido* to join the general call of the nation, of rich and poor, of proprietor and peasant, of businessman and artisan, for the Constitution.*

The juiz do pôvo, who once protested that he never got a seat in the Constitutional *Côrtes* of 1821, wrote letters all over the nation to get support for the new provisional government. One also wonders why the new Suprema Junta did not include the Lisbon juiz considering the strong organizational support he had, together with the popular backing. Perhaps it was because the office of juiz do pôvo was only good for the year, although we have already seen in crisis several incumbents who held it for four years. The fact that the juiz was never a deputy to the *Côrtes* leads consequently to the point that he was not a member of the committee which was quietly about to favor national industry against guild monopoly.

Over and over, the "muito honrado juiz do pôvo" stood in the public

* These sentiments are from the *Editaes* of the *Câmara Municipal de Lisbôa, 1763–1765*, Palha Collection, Harvard University, and reappeared texually in the *Gazêta de Lisbôa*, Dec. 12, 1820.

eye at political ceremonies, demonstrations, and receptions—but not at constitutional or political functions. After the falling-out between Pôrto and Lisbon had been healed on October 3, 1820, the "muito honrado juiz do pôvo" waited to greet both juntas. He escorted them into the Rossio to the wild applause and waving of handkerchiefs by the crowds. Lisbon was brilliantly decorated. The city was alive with lights; the people's theaters were crowded. The guns of Castelo São Jorge saluted; river boats also echoed the juiz' welcome. No one can doubt the new leadership of the juiz when the army invited the "muito honrado juiz do pôvo da quelle fiel pôvo" to join their entrance into Lisbon and march with the officer at the head of the garrison.

Now in alliance with the Portuguese army, the Lisbon juiz do pôvo spoke out on several points that would be important to his status, power, and ideas. We will take up here only the point that affected not only him, but that also affected the election of deputies from Brazil and elsewhere to the forthcoming *Côrtes*. Politics has always made strange bedfellows, and the political alliance between the army generals and the juiz do pôvo may have appeared as strange as any, but it worked. It was put to the test on the issue, November, 1820, of how to base the elections of deputies for the coming constituent *Côrtes*. The juiz, backed by the army, challenged the arrangements of the new Suprema Junta and made them adopt the system used in electing the Spanish *Côrtes* for the Constitution of 1812. This is puzzling. The juiz do pôvo had been an historic enemy of Spanish monarchy and Spanish invasions of Portugal; with 1820, the juiz do pôvo was moving toward Peninsular popular liberalism. Portuguese guerrilla and liberal patriotism, since 1808, had learned to trust Spanish guerrilla and liberal patriotism.

This is what brought juiz do pôvo and army together in meetings and joint revolutionary politics, aptly described in d'Arriaga's *História da Revoluçao Portuguêsa em 1820*. While pressure was brought in 1820 to influence the basis of elections to the *Côrtes*, the effect two years later was to give rise in the *Côrtes* to the other Third Estate (national industry) and to push the juiz and the Casa toward their demise in 1834. But in 1820 the sun still shone on the popular and energetic juiz and the guild personnel who were close to the army. This was the greatest moment of the Lisbon juiz in the nineteenth century, almost as great as the national revolution against Spain in 1640. He put his demands squarely in the lap of the Suprema Junta, and they yielded.

His protest, as the *Gazêta da Lisbôa* then reported it, had its effect in November, 1820. João Alves, the "muito honrado juiz do pôvo" of

Lisbon, his scribe, Veríssimo da Veiga, and the generals and command-ers came to the meeting of the Suprema Junta in a deputation which expressed its chagrin that the preparatory commission of Côrtes had not adopted the election method used in the Spanish Constitution. "The Juiz do Pôvo in the name of the people, jointly with the Army, said it is absolutely essential to use that method." It was a just request, preventing a majority of the preparatory commission from going ahead, to the detriment of the nation. It reiterated that the deputies be elected by population rather than geography. It also provided for enlargement of the Suprema Junta by persons, whom d'Arriaga gives as popular, and whom the Gazêta de Lisbôa enumerates in detail. The juiz do pôvo and the army then dominated the junta. This I believe, is the higher point of the Lisbon juiz' political power in Portuguese history.

Effects in Brazil were varied. There was the "Representação ao Pôvo" made in Praça do Commércio in Rio de Janeiro by José Clemente Pereira. In other places preparations for election of provincial deputies to the Côrtes followed. The most interesting, and rather sympathetic, symptom of a once-vigorous institution stirred the juiz of Bahia, to en-thusiasm and support. Even there the poltics and prestige of the office seemed automatically to promote any guild or merchant leader into a juiz. Pereira was called juiz, but he at least was a member of the Rio de Janerio senado. Ten years before, the exiled Portuguese merchants in London referred to the Lord Mayor of Liverpool as the juiz do pôvo.

In Bahia, it is true, they were at least careful to say that the procu-rador do senado, acting in the manner of a juiz do pôvo, led the people and the merchants to a great meeting in the large square and to swear support to the same Suprema Junta which the juiz of Lisbon, Pôrto, Coimbra, and other cities were also upholding. The Bahia merchants, guildsmen, and other interests (including the archbishop) seemed bet-ter organized for continuation with Portugal and the Côrtes than they were for independence. Bahia, São Paulo, and Rio de Janeiro had their own separate interests to consider even while sending their deputies to the Côrtes Gerais, taking their stand on Pedro I and weighing the al-ternatives of independence as opposed to "overseas provinces." The merchant-lawyer of Bahia who "acted like a juiz do pôvo" wrote a letter to a friend in Lisbon (printed in the Lisbon newspaper) which showed the enthusiasm of the pro-Portuguese elements in Bahia. He even started to publish a newspaper to keep up with and explain those events.

When the juiz do pôvo backed by Bahia, Coimbra, Pôrto, and his own city, saw the prospect of the revival of the Côrtes, the return of the rights of the people, and the procedures of the Spanish Constitution brought into the Portuguese political scene, he grew proud and ecstatic. Of course, proportional representation meant more to Lisbon than to Pôrto or other Portuguese towns. It gave added emphasis to the distance of Brazil from the center of things. In fact, by the time the Brazilian deputies had arrived, the older slogan of "overseas provinces" meant less to the idea of representation than the election by population based upon key cities. And if the appropriate committee of the *Côrtes* followed the same principle, for which the juiz had asked, it meant that the priority of the Peninsula won out. Lisbon would have committee representation proportional to its population. But so also could Bahia. Distance also had a role to play and, as is known, the *Côrtes* met without waiting for the Brazilians to arrive. The archbishop of Bahia (born in Pôrto) was the first presiding officer. The Lisbon juiz now could praise the integrity of the Supreme Junta and the high promise of the Sovereign National Congress, just about to hold its meeting.

Perhaps so, but this very same *Côrtes* through this same *Suprema Junta* took up almost at once the inquiry into the usefulness of the Casa. The Brazilian deputies, on their way, were completely unaware of the deep-seated split and antagonism between *Côrtes* and juiz do pôvo, between the new economic liberalism and industrialism and the old, closed monopolies over labor and manufacturing. It brought the first hint of political clouds on the horizon of the great political fortunes of the juiz. The loss of Brazil in the *Côrtes* of 1821 and the Constitution of Portugal of 1822 was a threat to the Guildhall and juiz.

It started in the Committee on Crafts, with a guild matter originating in Pôrto. Then the committee acted on a report of the *Junta do Commércio*, asking the elevation of national industry to a better level. Senhor Miranda of the Committee opposed this, since he appeared before the committee on the behalf of the guilds. Discussions followed among the Committee members, and Miranda defended the corporations as doing much good. But one of the members, Borges Carneiro, wanted more study of the harm and benefit of those trades which enjoyed privileges, of the usefulness of the corporations established under laws and bandeiras and the privileges of sending men to the *Casa* and the senado. On the other hand, he pointed out the fiscal contribution to public expenses the corporations were making. He advised that the objectives of craft corporations be weighed with great maturity and that all the arguments in this matter be investigated carefully. Still, the juiz do pôvo and his ever-present scribe came almost daily to look in on the debates and discussions, to such an extent that the presiding officer complained about their taking up the time of the *Côrtes* in its national business.

The *Côrtes*, later on, voted that the *procuradores dos mesteres* and other members of the *Casa* in Lisbon, and other places in Portugal, should continue to be elected and hold office under the old statutes and laws; and their powers should continue so long as they were not "contrary to the constitutional system." No one could prove that they were contrary to the constitution until Pedro I of Brazil assumed the throne of Portugal. Then he closed the loophole provided by the charter of 1822 and, invoking his own charter of 1826, let fall on both Guildhall and juiz do pôvo the club first raised a dozen years before.

It is ironic that the *Côrtes*, which the juiz do pôvo sought to assemble on the model and pattern of Spanish constitutional populism, was the foe of Portuguese populism. The highly gifted and intelligent Portuguese liberals in the *Côrtes* also know that Spanish populism was in one of its forms influenced by Jesuits and in another inclined toward republicanism. In between was the commitment to peasants, land, and agrarian reforms. The Portuguese and Brazilian populist pattern was never so deeply based on doctrinaire juridical or legal and socioeconomic agrarian-peasant issues. It was, rather, urban and manufacturing, a civic populism which was easily replaced by new manufacturing and a new monarchy.

Although the more rural *sesmaria* of both Brazil and Portugal is an equally important aspect of Portuguese populism, especially agrarian populism, the urban juiz do pôvo as an historical legacy to Brazil is not linked to the country rich or fidalgo, but rather to the city's monied people. These two parallel institutions of a sociopolitical character provide a populist-secular-civilian character to the era of the early nineteenth century. The politics of populism and peoples' movements are very pragmatic and almost entirely lack intellectual and philosophical roots. No Age of Reason or Enlightenment in Portugal, or in Brazil, invented the concept of populism as in Spain. The Portuguese notion of pôvo goes as far back as the municipal *concelho*, which influenced both *sesmaria* and juiz, Portugal's real pillars of populism. Spaniards followed ideas; Portuguese proceeded on the basis of facts.

Basically, what were the relationship of the Portuguese populism, new ideas of economic industry, and the changing political conception of Brazil, Brazilian independence, and the Brazilian *senado*-juiz do pôvo tradition? What did the *Côrtes Gerais* intend to do—and what did it finally do—with Brazil? Did the juiz of Lisbon, an ancient ally of the Bragança, share the ideas of the new industry and the nationwide nationalism? How big was the Lisbon interest, the Lisbon *senado, Casa,* and juiz in the nonregional nationalism that was appearing in both Portugal and Brazil? The answers are even more complex than the questions, because we look in vain for counterpart matters in Brazil to throw added light. Bahia, certainly, and Pernambuco, most probably, were with Pará and Maranhão more bound to Lisbon than they were to Rio de Janeiro. African trade, sugar refining, tobacco exports, the Bragança favors to Bahia, also enter into the historical account. It seem to me that Recife, Bahia, and other parts of the northeast fitted better than central and southern Brazil into the juiz notion of Luso-Brazilian empire: overseas provinces sending deputies to a *Côrtes.*

The strongly nationalistic *Côrtes* wanted no Spanish ideas at first. Then, in opposition to the Guildhall and juiz do pôvo, it turned to Portuguese industrialism and constitutionalism. The *Côrtes* also threatened the end of Rio de Janeiro as the capital. While there might have been some few hopes and dreams in Bahia, that it could prove a better place for a restored capital with its Bragança favors and juiz do pôvo, the fact is that the ideas of the *Côrtes* were not those of the Crown or the juiz. Neither the current ideas of meetings attended by delegates from intendancy-provinces, or the rival one of representation based upon urban-senado units, found favor in Lisbon. The Lisbon *Côrtes* preferred to let Brazil "go it alone" rather than reduce the prestige or political powers of Lisbon and the new constitutional régime.

Only a few Brazilians echoed the juiz do pôvo's belief in a continuation of Portugal overseas, through provinces and representation. This idea was pulled apart, on one hand by patriotism and the independence movement in Brazil, and on the other by patriotism and nationalism in Portugal. Portuguese independence from Brazil also began at this time, because of these forces. The juiz, who was fearful of Peninsular unity and the invasion of Portugal, might also worry over the loss of independence from overseas. There was certainly enough precedent for the worry. The equality of Brazil with Portugal since 1816 was bad enough. The Revolt of Pernambuco in 1817 must have brought alarm over the possible loss of Brazil, even if Rio de Janeiro was far more active and repressive toward the Pernambuco Revolt than Lisbon. The best-known Portuguese historian of the *Côrtes Gerais* of 1821 also thinks that the idea of Portugal overseas and of overseas provinces provided *amour propre* and flattery than real power. Nor did it weaken the power and prestige of *Côrtes* or nation. At any rate, to the juiz do pôvo the idea of overseas provinces directly connected with Lisbon would control Brazilian centralism and political unity under a king or vice-king.

The politics of Lisbon and the juiz do pôvo and those of the new generation in the *Côrtes* were not the same as those of the Bragança King and his royal ministers. The position of the Duke of Palmella, which was a working compromise with José C. Pereira, favored a junta at Rio de Janeiro, made up of the towns and cities, so that the urban-municipal view could be kept intact and under Rio. The Conde de Aguiar (Thomáz de Villa Nôva Portugal) opposed this. The Palmella proposal was helped by the death of Aguiar, the determined nationalism of the *Côrtes*, and the competition for acquired power versus inherited powers between Rio de Janeiro and Lisbon. True, changes and revised ideas streaked through the atmosphere of those times like meteors, arousing people, but then extinguishing themselves. In the end the decision to send Prince Pedro to Lisbon "to hear the complaints of the people" was rescinded, and he became the leader that Palmella and Pereira, as well as Maria Leopoldina and José Bonifácio, wanted him to be—but with very complicated results on both sides of the Atlantic.

The economics of separation and independence adds further light to the political differences between the Brazil party and the Portuguese party. When João VI returned to Lisbon the *Côrtes* took control of the diamond industry and properties, a tremendous source of capital and revenue. The *Côrtes* created the Banco de Lisbôa to stand alongside the Banco do Brasil. The letters and writings of José Antônio Lisbôa, banker and Rio economist, implement the political stand of the *juiz de fora* and president of the Lisbon senado, José Clemente Pereira. Lisbôa's reaction to the Portuguese Constitution of 1822 was that it harmed and alarmed "the people of Rio de Janeiro," as it did others. He was strangely concerned with the lack of appreciation of that Constitution by the "least educated class," and wrote that the Portuguese position could also bring political sacrifice, even convulsions and other disorders inherent in any new and imperfect order of things. He seems to be, along with Palmella, Pereira, and the juiz do pôvo of Lisbon, on the list of those who preferred a Brazil which would enjoy greater liberty in Rio de Janeiro but which would still remain in the empire.

The Lisbon *Côrtes* crossed the Tagus (its political Rubicon) with the issues of Brazilian independence, the *Casa*, and the juiz do pôvo. In spite of dynastic and civil troubles at home, the political and economic principles of the *Côrtes* were strong enough to send Brazilians back to Brazil and to push them toward independence from the united kingdom. The same constitutional liberalism, after a short time, also nationalized the closed religious and guild congregations, although the reasons may be independent and unrelated. Only the Bragança dynasty connected both countries. Portuguese independence from Brazil made it possible for both branches of that house to rule for several more decades.

If we look for common explanations, I believe that notwithstanding all the complex questions—trade, diamonds, gold, public debt, Bragança, the *Côrtes*, Rio de Janeiro, Bahia, Lisbon, and the multitude of petty, local, and regional interests the one visible beacon of explanation is the rise of machine manufacturing and national industry in Portugal. The ideas of economic liberalism, the Third Estate, industrial capitalism, and bourgeois liberalism in Portugal made a real comeback after the costly Peninsular Wars and the flight of the Bragança and the nobility. Brazil needed Portugal less and less and turned more and more to British ships, capital, and supplies. Portugal relied on herself primarily and secondly on Africa. Portugal's wealth was now at home. The feudal monopoly over apprentices, mechanics, and even masters which the closed corporations of the *Casa* and juiz do pôvo represented had served its purpose. Monastic and hierarchic internally, and assertive and bold with urban populism externally, the juiz had to go. He had to be abolished by law, as Brazil had abolished itself *de facto* from Portugal.

In addition to the occasional and indirect factors which tie the juiz do pôvo in Lisbon, Rio de Janeiro, Recife, Bahia, and Pôrto to the restlessness of independence, the real connecting link is to be found in the rise of capitalism in Portugal. The guild merchant and the middleman merchant of those cities were dependent upon trade. Portuguese writers of that day said so, and modern economic historians restate it; I believe it to be the one fundamental reason why the Portuguese of the reconstruction period learned to do without Brazil on one hand and to bury their guild systems and its spokesmen on the other. Not that the juiz had a doctrinaire or colonial interest in Brazil, but that the two were part of an old order under the Braganças and helped ease the peaceful move of Brazil toward nationhood.

Perhaps the connecting factor is dynastic. It may be found in the outlook of Pedro I. Turning his back on his father's policy of support of *senado* and juiz do pôvo in both Brazil and Portugal, Pedro I abolished the Portuguese civic institutions in Brazil in 1828 and six years later abolished the urban guild organizations in Lisbon. Viewed as more of a liberal than his absolutist brother Miguel, it was Pedro I who finally terminated the feudal Guildhall and juiz in Portugal.

The meeting of the Brazilian deputies in Lisbon did more for their awareness of each other than it did for Portuguese concern about Brazil. As distinguished as many of these deputies were, and some were even members of the Academia Real das Sciências de Lisbôa, their company as intellectuals, scientists or even as political deputies was not welcome. On the other hand, Portuguese who wanted help in their own reconstruction and economic distress did not want to hear Brazilian demands; they did not relish what contemporaries called Brazilian arrogance. The *Côrtes* had, therefore, already arranged a great deal even before the different delegations had arrived. That made matters of tolerance of each other even harder than agreement with each other. Brazilians were badly regarded and rudely treated in hard political caricature, cartoons, and pamphlets—so satirical and insulting in Portugal.

The delegates from Rio de Janeiro were comparatively silent about Rio's loss of position as the capital of the Portuguese Empire and its return to Lisbon. They did nothing openly about the decision to replace courts and tribunals with new provincial governing juntas, appointed from Lisbon. Even though some Brazilians relished the idea of the reduction of Rio's status and the prospect of direct regional petition to Lisbon, the fact remained that it would still be petition and not equality. Brazil was let down, if not put down. Gomes de Carvalho thought the liberals in Portugal intended to go no further than equate Brazil with Africa and Asia in the general term "ultramar." That was why they were allowed to represent each other and even interchange with each other, as Brazil did with Angola. The success of the juiz do pôvo in getting the *Côrtes* to accept the Spanish constitution as a basis for electing deputies had the practical effect of reducing Brazil's representation, since they used an 1808 population count for Brazil, and not an 1821 count.

Putting the disappearance of Brazil from the Luso-Brazilian Empire and the disappearance of the Guildhall and juiz do pôvo from Luso-Brazilian civilization into the same historic movement and interpreting that process is both the argument and the conclusion of this paper. The idea is small but effective, the research vast, and the investigation as yet quite incomplete. It seems valid that as Portugal changed at home, she also changed with respect to the *fait accompli* of a vocal, capable, and independent Brazil. These are the two sides to that story. A new country and an old populist institution, by then almost half a millenium old, did less and less for the Portuguese and had reached a decisive stage in their respective histories. It is best to close as I started, repeating that Portuguese domestic history and Brazilian independence were both changed for good by the forces, crises, economics, and the men of the Peninsular Wars: a turning point in Luso-Brazilian and Spanish American history.

WORKS CONSULTED

Brazil

Aguiar, M. Pinto de. *A abertura dos pórtos: Cairú e os Inglêses* (Bahia, 1960) .

Arquivo Histórico Nacional, Madrid. Seccion: *América, Papeles que Interesan á Brasil.*

Annaes da Biblioteca Nacional.

Biblioteca Nacional (Lisbon) . Collecão Pombalina, Mss.

Biblioteca Nacional (Rio de Janeiro) . *Documentos históricos* (120 vols.; 1928– date) .

Boxer, Charles. *Portuguese Society in the Tropics: The Municipal Councils of Góa, Macao, Bahia, and Luanda, 1510–1800* (Madison, Wis., 1965) .

Carnaxide, Visconde de, Antônio de Sousa Pedroso Carnaxide. *O Brasil na administração Pombalina (Económica e política externa)* (São Paulo, 1940) .

Cortines Laxe, João B. *Regimento das câmaras municipaes ou Lei de 1º de Outubro de 1828* (2nd ed.; Rio de Janeiro, 1885) .

Costa, Hipólito da, ed. *Correio Braziliense* (London, 1808–1822) .

"Documentos officiaes inéditos relativos ao alvará de 5 de janeiro de 1785 que extinguiu no Brazil todas as fabricas e manufacturas de ouro, prata, seda, lã, etc." in *Revista Trimensal de História e Geographia* (Rio de Janeiro) , 2nd ser., Tomo III (Rio de Janeiro, 1848) .

Mello Moraes, A. J. de. *História da trasladação da Córte portuguêsa para o Brazil em 1807–1808* (Rio de Janeiro, 1872) .

Ribeiro, João. *História do Brasil* (Rio de Janeiro, 1954) .

Portugal

Accursio das Neves, José. *Variedades sôbre objectos relativos às artes, commércio e manufacturas, consideradas segundo os princípios da economia política* (2 vols.; Lisbon, 1814–1817).

Brandão, Raul, *El Rei Junot* (Lisbon, 1912).

Editaes da câmara municipal de Lisbôa: 1763–1835. 2 vols. In the Palha Collection, Harvard University.

Freire de Oliveira, E. *Elementos para a história do município de Lisbôa. Publicação mandada fazer a expensas da Câmara Municipal de Lisbôa para commemorar o centenário do Marquêz de Pombal em 8 de maio de 1882* (19 vols.; Lisbon, 1882–1943). Vols. 18 and 19 are indexes to the series.

Godinho, Vitorino Magalhaes. *Prix et monnaies au Portugal, 1750–1850* (Paris, 1955).

Gomes de Carvalho, M. *Os diputados brasileiros nas Côrtes Gerais de 1821 (Subsídios para a história de Brasil)* (Pôrto, 1912).

Langhans, Franz-Paul. *A Casa dos Vinte e Quartro de Lisbôa: subsídios para a sua história* (Lisbon, 1948).

Manuscript materials: British Museum, Biblioteca Municipal (Lisbon), Biblioteca Nacional (Lisbon).

Mariz, Pedro de. *Diálogos de varia história.* . . . (Lisbon, 1672).

Martins, Rocha e Lopes d'Oliveira. *Os direitos do pôvo. A Casa dos Vinte e Quatro* (pamphlet) (Lisbon: Cadernos históricos 194?).

Moral-Fatio, Alfred P.V. *Catalogue des manuscrits Espagnols et des manuscrits Portugais* (Paris, 1892).

Pires de Lima, Durval, ed. *Documentos do Arquivo Histórico da Câmara Municipal de Lisbôa* (Lisbon, 1957–1959).

Teixeira de Carvalho, J. M. ed. *Recordações de Jacome Ratton sôbre ocurrências do seu tempo de maio de 1747 a septembro de 1810* (2nd ed.; Coimbra, 1920).

COMMENTARY

George E. Carl
Georgia State College, Atlanta

M OST of those of us interested in Luso-Brazilian history are accustomed to following the Portuguese Court to Brazil when the Napoleonic forces approached Lisbon in the autumn of 1807. Between 1808 and 1820, Luso-Brazilian politics center in Brazil and we tend to overlook the developments in Portugal. In fact, general histories of Portugal in English devote a scant few pages to this period. Professor Bernstein has illustrated in his study of the *juiz do pôvo* that political leadership in Portugal was not altogether dormant despite the departure of the royal Court, a large portion of the nobility, and a great number of merchants and businessmen. According to Professor Bernstein, a public figure called the juiz do pôvo stepped forward to halt the total disintegration of Portuguese political life.

To understand better the role of the juiz do pôvo in Lisbon between 1807 and 1822, it is first necessary to describe his theoretic base of power, the Lisbon Casa dos Vinte e Quatro. The *Casa,* composed of twenty-four representatives of the craft guilds in Lisbon, was inaugurated by royal charter in 1384 to provide the Portuguese monarchy with the political support that would counterbalance the nobility, the merchants, and the Church. The twenty-four representatives were sent for one-year terms to the *Casa* from twelve *bandeiras* (religious fraternal organizations of artisans) . The delegates to the *Casa* were selected by the *juizes* or officers of the bandeiras to represent the artisan community as a whole, not the particular interest of one craft guild. The exact size of the artisan community in Lisbon is not known for each year during the period 1384–1834, but in 1788 there were approximately 14,000 masters,

227

journeymen, and apprentices engaged in more than sixty different crafts.

It should be emphasized that the delegates to the *Casa* represented the top echelons of the bandeiras; they should not be considered as spokesmen for the interests of all the members of the artisan community. A description of a delegate's qualifications for office will illustrate this point. Delegates had to be able to read and write well, they had to be sufficiently wealthy to devote proper time to meetings of the *Casa*, their wives could not be employed in public occupations *(ocupaçoens, públicas)*, and the delegates had to be experienced in the governing machinery of their respective craft guilds and bandeiras. As a further guarantee of their respectability, representatives were required to be Portuguese natives, married, at least forty years of age, humble, god-fearing, obedient to the laws of the realm, and free from scandal.

To assure that no special interest groups would form, the delegates to the *Casa* could not be re-elected to a second one-year term until four years had elapsed. Exceptions could be made during periods of extraordinary circumstances. Also, the new slate of delegates had to be approved by the incumbents. In this manner some continuity of the generally conservative nature of the body would be preserved.

Although the *Casa dos Vinte e Quatro* was designed to look out for the general welfare of the craft guild community, its most important function seems to have been the annual election of one of its members to the office of juiz do pôvo. This official served as a "watchdog" for the interests of the craft guilds. The juiz was not technically a judge nor a magistrate in the legal sense, but rather an advocate and protector. The juiz and his clerk, the *escrivão* (also a member of the *Casa*), attended meetings of the Lisbon *senado da câmara* and had the power of blocking legislation that might be contrary to the interests of the craft guilds. Furthermore, in their attending the *senado* meetings, the juiz do pôvo and the clerk were accompanied by four solicitors *(procuradores)* who were also members of the *Casa*. Thus, fully one-fourth of the members of the *Casa* could attend the *senado*, discuss legislation, vote on matters affecting the craft guilds, and, in the case of juiz, report directly to the king any infractions imposed on the crafts by the *senado*. How often the juiz exercised this function is not yet known.

As the chief representative of the corporation of artisans, the juiz do pôvo had significant ceremonial duties, both lay and religious. In the assembling of the royal court, the juiz stood close to the king, just above the benches of bishops and archbishops. Also, the juiz was expected to attend the king and queen on certain state occasions, as well as the baptism or funeral of any member of the royal family. He furthermore had the privilege of frequent audience with the king. In the religious sphere, the juiz accompanied the king at mass, especially on feast days. During the processions and functions of the Holy Office of the Inquisition, the juiz and his clerk were required to be present. In both lay and religious matters, therefore, the juiz symbolized the medieval ideal of corporate unity of king, Church, and people.

Because the juiz do pôvo was an important representative of the Third Estate, the monarch occasionally relied upon him for support. Although the Portuguese monarchy does not appear to have been as paranoiac as the Spanish Crown in maintaining a system of checks and balances, the *Casa* and its juiz do pôvo could act as a brake on the Lisbon *senado*, a body dominated by merchants and aristocrats. In exchange for this service, the Portuguese kings protected the interests of the craft guilds.

I have so far discussed the theoretical powers of the juiz do pôvo. His real powers are the subject of controversy among historians. Professor Bernstein has attempted to demonstrate that the juiz was a vibrant public official, representing the people, who stepped in to pick up the reigns of Portuguese political leadership when the royal Court and many officials departed in 1807. Furthermore, Professor Bernstein maintains that the juiz, as a "popular" leader, influenced the composition of the Côrtes of 1821–1822 and its subsequent attitude toward Brazil. This attitude of the Côrtes affected Brazil's status within the empire and thus precipitated the independence of that country. Therefore, the conclusion is inferred that the popularly supported juiz and Brazilian independence are related.

On the basis of present evidence it is difficult to establish that the juiz do pôvo represented the interests of the common people of Lisbon. The examples given in Professor Bernstein's paper do not prove this fact. The influence which the juiz do pôvo exercised with the Regency is unclear. Popular acclaim of the juiz's public appearances and utterances should not be construed to mean that he embodied the principle of common welfare. Whether or not the juiz do pôvo can be termed a "populist" leader is even more debatable. "Populism" refers to a strictly agrarian movement, whether in late-nineteenth-century United States or in Czarist Russian political phenomena. The juiz do pôvo by the nature of his constituency, was an urban leader. Since the juiz was elected annually, and during the period 1808–1822 there were at least

fifteen different men holding office, it would be difficult to ascribe continuity of popular policy to the juiz. Moreover, it is possible for an institution composed of one man selected annually by twenty-three colleagues—and who actually did change office—to become a popular arbiter
of Portuguese politics?

WORKS CONSULTED

Balbi, A. *Essai Politique,* Vol. I (Paris, 1822) .

Boxer, Charles. *Portuguese Society in the Tropics: The Municipal Councils of
     Gôa, Macao, Bahia, and Luanda, 1510–1800* (Madison, Wis. 1965) .

Dicionário histórico português (Lisbon, 1966) .

Grande enciclopédia Portuguêsa e Brasileira, Vols. VI and XIV (Lisbon, 1945) .

Langhans, Franz-Paul. *A Casa dos Vinte e Quatro de Lisbôa, subsídios para a sua
     história* (Lisbon, 1948) .

Livermore, H. V. *A History of Portugal* (Cambridge, Eng., 1947) .

THE NONVIOLENT TRADITION
IN BRAZILIAN HISTORY:
A MYTH IN NEED OF EXPLOSION?

Henry H. Keith
University of South Carolina, Columbia

THE nonviolent tradition in Brazilian history grew out of the tumultuous period of the Regency (1831–1840). Brazilians loyal to the centralized institution of the monarchy, such as the historian Varnhagen in his *História geral do Brazil*,[1] marshaled an impressive array of arguments against rebellious violence in defense of the conserving, orderly tradition of the monarchy. Oliveira Lima, writing in 1914, summed up his frank admiration for the achievements of imperial Brazil and gave expression to what was becoming a full-blown myth to be believed in and invoked by Republican governments as well:[2] "Imperial Brazil constituted a model of liberty and peace for Latin America and furnished at least a real image of civilization, reflected from the throne, at the time when Spanish American societies struggled in disorder and savagery." The nonviolent myth could thus be invoked for the purpose of extolling the Empire and also establishing Brazil's difference from and superiority to other nations of Latin America. What began as an apologia for the eventual victory by the monarchy over liberal and separatist—not always allied—violence during the period of the Regency and following it became official dogma in the period stretching from 1845 up to the dissolution of the Empire and the foundation of the Republic in 1889. Republican governments were not dilatory in "dusting off" the nonviolent tradition in defense of the status quo and in the interest of maintaining themselves in power.[3]

In our more psychologically oriented age, Prado and Buarque de Holanda indirectly reinforced the nonviolent myth. Prado argued that "the indolence and passivity of our people facilitated the preservation of social and political unity of our territory."[4] But Buarque de Holanda then reasoned that Brazil's future progress actually depended upon a national revolution! [5] "In this morass we shall need to make a *tabula rasa* before undertaking a total renovation." Nonviolence had served Brazil well in her early history but now apparently had no place in the pre-revolutionary atmosphere of 1928. Buarque de Holanda's perceptions of Brazilian character lent a more singular reinforcement to nonviolence; the *homen cordial* (cordial man) theory, explaining the Brazilian's inherent good nature, gave added weight to the belief that violence was somehow to be regarded as an aberration in Brazilian life. However, more contemporaneously, Vianna Moog has called for a revision of the classic nonviolent (bloodless) myth:

> The time has passed when, deluded by hasty interpretations of certain facts of their historical development—the abolition of slavery without bloodshed, for example—Brazilians piously believed in the vaunted basis of their emotional equilibrium. Today, after the general revision of values that modern historiography, aided by modern psychology, is carrying on in all sectors of the social sciences—say what they will of the bloodless way the abolition of slavery was effected in Brazil, or the proclamation of the Republic or the founding of the New State (episodes in which the symptoms of immaturity are confused with the symptoms and evidences of common sense and cordial spirit)—the same errors can no longer be nourished.[6]

It is interesting to observe that the nonviolent theory of history was not applied by Portuguese or native Brazilian historians writing in the period prior to the Regency, which had its inception in 1831 upon the abdication of Dom Pedro I; this lends credence to the view that the nonviolent myth was probably a creation of historians who were searching for a justification of the period of "enforced peace" brought to Brazil during the reign of the strong-man-in-the-frock-coat, Dom Pedro II.

It will be the contention of this study that the "nonviolent" period of Dom Pedro II's reign—1853–1889—actually stifled an often constructive process which was necessary to the development of viable political institutions, given the relatively violent pattern of Brazil's historical evolution prior to 1853 (the year of the beginning of the policy of *conciliação* during which the Liberal and Conservative parties blended for the sake of temporary peace; it lasted until 1858) and after 1889 (until at least 1930). Thirty-six years of "enforced peace" under the Second Empire do not constitute sufficient proof of the basic nonviolent tradition in Brazilian history. Quite to the contrary, the periods preceding and following Dom Pedro II's reign are replete with examples of violent conflict in Brazilian life; and the first ten years of his reign were wracked by revolts in Rio Grande do Sul (the *Farrapos* war, 1835–1845) and in Pernambuco (the *Praieria* revolt in 1848). Far from being always deleterious to the development of social and political institutions, the many revolts, uprisings, movements, and *coups d'état* have often had the result of keeping alive criticism of the governments in power, whose natural tendency was to condemn violence in wholesale fashion as detrimental to order, legitimacy, and constitutional processes. Violent means of protest often served as a nasty reminder that the legitimacy of governments could be seriously questioned. For example, both the Second Empire and the Republic rigged elections in such a fashion that local and national candidates enjoying official support almost invariably won "elective office." [7] True, oftentimes violent protests were staged by disgruntled members of the party out of power; nevertheless, it was beneficial—in the long run—that they be able to do so because the corrupt electoral system offered no alternative.

A leading sociologist has recently pointed out the positive social functions of conflict, stressing the need for social dynamics as opposed to social statics.[8] "Conflict consists in a test of power between antagonistic parties. Accommodation between them is possible only if each is aware of the relative strength of both parties. However, paradoxical as it may seem, such knowledge can most frequently be attained only through conflict, since other mechanisms for testing the respective strengths of antagonists seem to be unavailable." [9] This lesson would seem applicable to Brazil's evolution during the bulk of its history. One might ask with Sílvio Romero, "Which is better: a nation that is uniform, dead, frozen; or one that is vivacious and multiple in its expression?" [10]

It was not, of course, that there was any conscious mechanism of flexibility built into the colonial rule of Brazil by the Portuguese which allowed for the positive function of conflict and violence. It was, rather, the fact that Portugal's rule was for so long weak and ineffective that the end result was a necessary accommodation, as Prado has indicated: "Backwardness and the very same vices and weaknesses of the Portuguese central bureaucracy were the preponderant factors in the process of unification." [11]

The native-born Portuguese in Brazil, especially those more distant from the center of royal power in Bahia first and later Rio de Janerio, grew accustomed to a home-grown variety of government and social organization in the often tenuous exercise of royal authority. Violent, armed struggles in the seventeenth and eighteenth centuries served the

purpose of defending local, particular interests against the foreigner—
whether he be Portuguese or not. The precursor movements leading up
to the independence movement had their genesis in violent local reaction
to many of the Pombaline reforms, which were considered onerous regal
interventions in the political, social, and economic lives of native-born
Brazilians.[12] The independence movement was local in nature, and it
took on liberal overtones, since liberalism was the natural enemy of
regalism, especially as practiced by Pombal.[13]

The violence which characterized these local struggles should come
as no surprise to the observer who is familiar with the Portuguese of
the fifteenth century, and his descendants in succeeding centuries. Capistrano de Abreu described him in stringent terms: "The Portuguese of
the fifteenth century was coarse, abstemious, ardent in imagination, independent of character, with a propensity to mysticism. . . . His tem-
perament was rigid, his heart hard. . . . It was customary to think in
terms of violence and pain, either inflicted or received." [14]

In discussing the role of violence in Brazilian history, one must be
careful not to fall into the error of equating violence with bloodshed,
as Rodrigues has done in his recent *Conciliação e reforma;* violence may
or may not be accompanied by bloodshed. The fact of bloodshed should
not negate beneficial results which may flow from such action. The essential criterion in evaluating the place of violence is that of its social
and integrative function. It is all too true, as Rodrigues has pointed
out: "Bloody and non-bloody events alternate in the Brazilian historical
process, although it is correct and proper to state that the examples of
compromise [*conciliação*] predominate." [15]

He then restates part of the nonviolent myth by singling out men such
as Caramurú, José Bonifácio, Carneiro Leão, and Caxias as "examples
of moderating leadership and bloodless history; they avoided the bru-
tality and immaturity which occurred among other peoples of America
with greater frequency and atrocity, such as Mexico, Colombia, and the
United States." [16] A government that does not devise a system of political compromise or accommodation of violence cannot long survive.[17]
As we have indicated, except under the Second Empire and after 1930,
Brazilian history has been characterized by repeated compromise with
violence. The official government's leniency in the matter of amnesties
to rebels against its authority can be interpreted as an example of the
desire to accommodate, even if only partially, the demands of those
who had resorted to violence against it.[18]

As part of the nonviolent myth, there is the belief that Brazilian independence was handily won, almost a gift from the Mother Country.[19] Rodrigues refers to Latin American and North American historiography as unaware of the struggles and bloodshed required to achieve victory; he might have added much of Brazilian historiography to his list.

One cannot consider the place of violence in Brazilian history without singling out three types of social movements in conflict with governments which have occurred at different times: Negro revolts, messianic movements, and banditry. All three have fared badly at the hands of most writers until very recently, with the exception of Euclydes da Cunha's sympathetic treatment of the Canudos messianic movement.[20] The point of view of most writers was that these groups posed a threat to Brazil and had, consequently, to be annihilated (not merely brought under control).[21] More recent scholarship is engaged in exploring these movements as social phenomena which were misunderstood and in demonstrating that Brazilian governments dealt with them respectively out of an inhumanity and an inability to remedy social ills.[22]

These movements have served social functions in the history of Brazil. The Negro slave revolts were constant, sharp reminders of the destructive, inhuman effects of slavery; the severe repressions of these revolts, especially that of 1835 in Bahia, made their weight felt in the minds of Brazil's *élite,* which eventually freed the slaves in 1888.

Messianic movements have been less well understood by governments and the intelligentsia, but since da Cunha's *exposé* of the brutal annihilation of the followers of Antônio Conselheiro, more soul-searching has been in order. As Pereira de Queiroz points out,[23] messianic movements are attempts by marginal groups (or groups which feel themselves to be marginal) to establish a community; in many instances this occurred when an old community was disrupted or when a new community was coming into being—always under the leadership of a prophetic figure. Such messianic movements would not have been possible had not the integrative functions of Brazilian society failed to operate effectively, thus cutting off great groups of people in the interior from regular contact with the urban centers, especially on the littoral.

Banditry was likewise an index of the failure of governments—local and national—to come to grips effectively with the conditions which caused the institution to flourish in rural Brazil; far from attempting the solution of such problems, governments in Brazil often depended upon *cangaceiros* and *jagunços* (hired outlaws) to buttress their authority and control. *Coronéis* (colonels, who are rural political bosses) regularly contracted for the services of these types, at the behest of local or state governments.[24]

The establishment of the Republic was largely the work of the leaders of Brazil's armed forces, because civilian leaders were so politically fragmented, a chronic problem since independence which was probably worsened by the long period of the exercise of the powerful right of royal intervention in national (and local) politics by means of the *poder moderador.* The long period characterized by the "incubation" of political parties had prevented evolution of political institutions responsible to the electorate, as Nabuco de Araújo explained: "For the monarchy, the falsification of elections is an abyss upon which it is poised, because elections, instead of being what they are supposed to be, are a lie which forces the monarchy to err, which will be the provocation to lead the country inexorably to revolution. Undoubtedly, the errors of the *poder moderador,* in judging political situations in the country, would not be inevitable if elections were free." [25]

Violent passions which had been forcibly pent up under the Second Empire were now unleashed with unprecedented fury, ushered in by the *régime* of Floriano Peixoto (1891–1894), a figure reminiscent of "the *caudillo* characteristic of Hispanic America." [26] The naval rebellion in Rio de Janeiro and the federalist rebellion in Rio Grande do Sul, Santa Catarina, and Paraná merged into a civil war which was to last two years before being quelled by federal government forces. The power and authority of the states emerged strengthened since the central government had defended their loyalist regimes against the federalist rebels; the state governments had benefited by the very rebellion which had been aimed at their destruction! [27] A better example of the efficacy of violence in a politically and socially functional role would be difficult to find.

Scarcely two years after the end of the civil war, the Canudos messianic revolt erupted. Here political compromises were unnecessary, and politicians and national leaders could use the uprising as a safety-valve, or worse, as a scapegoat for the shortcomings of the Republic. Canudos served an unfortunate social function at the national level; it also demonstrated the fundamental need for community among the *sertanéjos* (backlanders), a need the Republic was unable to fulfill effectively. Other messianic manifestations attest to this state of affairs, such as the Contestado "war" (1910–1914), the Beato do Caldeirão (1935),[28] and others up to the present.[29]

Beginning with the Campos Sales administration (1898–1902), a method was devised which would result in the stifling of political evolution, both at the local and national levels. This political strategy, termed the *política dos governadores* (politics of the governors), actually meant that the president supported local candidates who were personally loyal to him.[30] Thus, in effect, the president named governors and held them responsible to him; when governors deviated from this standard, the president would order federal intervention to insure state support. The *política dos governadores* was followed by the successors to Campos Sales in the presidency up until the Revolution of 1930 and was a principal ill which rebels in 1922, 1924, and 1930 wished to set right.[31] In actual practice, the system meant that the strongest states, São Paulo and Minas Gerais, controlled the presidency and thus the state governments. One of the principal aims of the system was the containment of local violence; once again, an "enforced peace," this time under Republican auspices, was largely responsible for the vitiation of the federal representative system in the name of stability, order, and continuity.

Discontent spread in the 1920's, and a recrudescence of the violence during the federalist civil war occurred in Rio Grande do Sul in 1923; once again rebels took up arms against their governor, Borges de Medeiros, who had been (and was to continue to be) loyal to the central power.[32] The year before, dissident young officers, the *tenentes,* had revolted in Rio in protest against the repressive measures of President Epitácio Pessôa, who was pursuing the same kind of policy of repression of opposition and federal intervention in the states. The federal government was able to suppress both revolts but in doing so laid the groundwork for the future violence of 1924 by the tenentes once again, who this time unsuccessfully attempted violence on a national scale. The old system was perpetuated—rigged elections, intimidation of the opposition, censorship, and federal intervention in the states. The different ingredient this time was that the federal government was not successful in suppressing violence by the dedicated band of rebels who began their revolt in the cities, but took it to the interior, in defiance of federal and state troops.[33] The tenentes gained fame and legitimized violence as the means of reforming the Old Republic's corrupt ways: the Revolution of 1930 was the product of this process.[34] The *gaúchos* from Rio Grande do Sul had another score to settle with the federal government: exclusion from the presidency. Trained in violence in the 1893 and 1923 revolts, gaúchos were formidable opponents and, when joined by the

tenentes, undefeatable. The 1930 revolution was the triumph of violence in the name of legitimacy and reform.

Upon coming to power in 1930, Getúlio Vargas forged a system of
political power based upon the institutionalization of violence by effective manipulation of his followers, his opponents, and most important, the armed forces; it was he who effectively centralized power in the
hands of the president in a fashion his predecessors would have en-
vied.[35] The armed forces, especially the army, became directly participant in the political process as a result of the Revolution of 1930;
although Vargas "tamed" the radical tenentes, the armed forces have
played the role of final arbiter over Brazilian governments. Since April,
1964, the military has changed its role from arbiter to governor.

Vargas was also able to succeed in forestalling violence largely because he was effective in remedying some of Brazil's long-standing social
ills; this gave him a popular legitimacy never before enjoyed so widely
by any president. The social function of violence was largely displaced
by this effort.[36]

The single serious outbreak of violence which challenged Vargas occurred in São Paulo in 1932. Although it was subdued, it was a warning
to him that he must be responsive to the power in that state. In the
future, Vargas took care to protect São Paulo's economic interests, while
hedging on the issue of carrying out elections and other constitutional
promises.[37]

The more democratic governments which followed the overthrow of
Vargas in 1945 have often lacked stability and have not attended sufficiently to the social well-being of Brazilians; although more representative (up to the Revolution of 1964), they have often been ineffective
in dealing with the problems of a country in rapid transformation to a
modern society. If future governments do not realize significant improvements for the growing millions of Brazil, there may be the ultimate resort once again to violence to insure the likelihood of social and
economic improvement. Increased central control of Brazil has made
the phenomenon of violence in Brazilian public life infrequent in the
years since 1930, but one must remember that violence can originate
from within agencies of control such as the armed forces—the mainstay
of governments in Brazil since the *coup* of April, 1964—in alliance with
other groups, if grievances—political, social, and economic—mount in
magnitude. The best guarantees against the resort to violence from any
quarter are increased socioeconomic benefits to the Brazilian popula-

tion, as well as effective representative government to insure the fair implementation of those benefits.[38]

NOTES

1 Francisco Adolpho de Varnhagen, *História geral do Brasil* (7th ed.; São Paulo, 1962), V, 149–50.
2 Manoel de Oliveira Lima, *The Evolution of Brazil as Compared with that of Spanish and Anglo-Saxon America*, ed. Percy A. Martin (Stanford, Cal., 1914), pp. 91–92.
3 José Honório Rodrigues, *Conciliação e reforma no Brasil* (Rio de Janeiro, 1965), pp. 113–17. In spite of the rather over-simple dichotomy between the forces of reform and the forces of "conciliation" (compromise), Rodrigues' analysis sheds fresh light on the violent character of much of Brazil's history.
4 Paulo Prado, *Retrato do Brasil* (Rio de Janeiro, 1962), p. 165.
5 Sérgio Buarque de Holanda, *Raízes do Brasil* (Rio de Janeiro, 1936), pp. 101–102.
6 C. Vianna Moog, *Bandeirantes and Pioneers*, trans. L. L. Bartlett (New York, 1964), p. 224.
7 Victor Nunes Leal, *Coronelismo, enxada e vôto* (Rio de Janeiro, 1948), pp. 27–32; Rodrigues, *Conciliação*, p. 120.
8 Lewis A. Coser, *The Functions of Social Conflict* (Glencoe, Ill., 1956), pp. 20 and 31.
9 *Ibid.*, p. 107.
10 Sílvio Romero, *História da literatura Brasileira* (3rd ed.; Rio de Janeiro, 1943), p. 135.
11 *Retrato*, p. 165.
12 Sérgio Buarque de Holanda, *História geral da civilização Brasileira* (São Paulo, 1960), I.
13 Luiz Vianna Filho, "Homens e causas da revolução Baiana de 1798," Congresso de História Nacional, *Anais* (Rio de Janeiro, 1941), pp. 641–63.
14 João Capistrano de Abreu, *Capítulos de história colonial, 1500–1800* (Rio de Janeiro, 1934), pp. 19–20.
15 *Conciliação*, p. 59.
16 *Ibid.*
17 Coser, *Social Conflict*, p. 79.
18 Francisco José de Oliveira Vianna, *Populações meridionais do Brasil* (4th ed.; São Paulo, 1938), pp. 410–13. He singles out the population of the center-south of Brazil as that with peaceful and orderly virtues, blandness, moderation, and horror of blood and struggle and credits them with conserving the unity of the country. Since politicians from this part of Brasil controlled Brasil from the end of the eighteenth century on, there is a certain validity to this argument. His delineation of the "violent types" in Brasil—the northerner (the sertanêjo, the jagunço, and the cangaceiro) and the far southerner (the gaúcho)—is based upon the need to control these unruly groups (see pp. 382–83).
19 Manoel de Oliveira Lima, *O movimento da independência, 1821–1822* (São Paulo, 1922), p. 7.
20 *Rebellion in the Backlands*, trans. Samuel Putnam (Chicago, 1944), p. 161.

21 On Negro revolts, see Nina Rodrigues, *A Tróia negra* (Bahia, 1954) , p. 20; on major messianic movements such as Canudos and Contestado, see the conventional treatment by José Maria Bello, *A History of Modern Brazil,* trans. James L. Taylor (Stanford, Cal., 1966) , pp. 148–55, 224, 232; on a critical approach to banditry, see Oliveira Vianna, *Populações,* p. 385.

22 On the metamorphosis of the slave in Brazilian society, see Otavio Ianni, *As metamórfoses do escravo: apogéu e crise da escravatura no Brasil meridional* (São Paulo, 1962); on banditry see Ruy Facó, *Cangaceiros e fanáticos* (Rio de Janeiro, 1963) ; and on messianism see Maria Isaura Pereira de Queiroz, *O messianismo no Brasil e no mundo* (São Paulo, 1965) . A growing body of creative literature also draws upon these themes; see, for example, João Guimarães Rosa, *Grande sertão: verêdas* (2nd ed.; Rio de Janeiro, 1958) ; Rachel Queiroz, *Lampião* (Rio de Janeiro, 1953) ; Graciliano Ramos, *Vidas sêcas* (Rio de Janeiro, 1947) . The recent cinema has also turned to Negro revolts, messianic movements, and banditry for inspiration; such films as *Ganga Zumba* (based upon the leader of the famous Palmares Negro revolt in the late seventeenth century) , *Vidas sêcas* (based upon the Ramos novel) , *Deus e diabo na terra do sol* (based upon the life of Lampião, the famous bandit) , and *A vida e môrte de Severino* illustrate this trend. The young cinema director Glauber Rocha typifies this trend.

23 *O messianismo,* p. 68.

24 Facó, *Cangaceiros, passim.*

25 Joaquim Nabuco, *Um estadista do império, Nabuco de Araújo* (São Paulo, 1936), II, 97.

26 Bello, *Modern Brazil,* p. 91.

27 *Ibid.,* pp. 131–38; and June E. Hahner, "The Paulistas' Rise to Power: A Civilian Group Ends Military Rule," *Hispanic American Historical Review,* XLVII (May, 1967), 149–65.

28 The film entitled *A vida e môrte de Severino* is based upon this episode; also see the play by Jorge Andrade, *Verêda da salvação* (São Paulo, 1965) on a similar messianic movement in the late 1940's.

29 Pereira de Queiróz, *O messianismo,* pp. 260–83.

30 Bello, *Modern Brazil,* pp. 162–71; and Antônio Campos Sales, Jr., *O idealismo republicano de Campos Sales* (Rio de Janeiro, 1944) , *passim.*

31 João Alberto Lins de Barros, *Memórias de un revolucionário* (Rio de Janeiro, 1953) , *passim.*

32 João Neves da Fontoura, *Memórias; Borges de Medeiros e seu tempo* (Rio de Janeiro, 1955) , pp. 15–17; Hélio Silva, *1922—sangue na areia de Copacabana* (Rio de Janeiro, 1964), pp. 283–90.

33 Hélio Silva, *1926—a grande marcha* (Rio de Janeiro, 1965) , p. 106.

34 Lins de Barros, *Memórias,* p. 217.

35 Jordan M. Young, *The Brazilian Revolution of 1930* (New Brunswick, N. J. 1967) , pp. 81–97.

36 *Ibid.,* p. 96.

37 Thomas E. Skidmore, *Politics in Brazil, 1930–1964* (New York, 1967) , pp. 18–19.

38 *Ibid.,* pp. 320–21; Young, *Revolution,* p. 118.

COMMENTARY

Joseph L. Love
University of Illinois, Urbana-Champaign

HOW does violence relate to social progress? To Americans ineffectively coping with domestic upheavals as well as guerilla insurgency in Asia, this should be an arresting question. Professor Keith tries to answer this query for Brazil. As I understand them, his two principal contentions are: *(a)* Violence can be socially beneficial, and on a number of occasions in Brazilian history, it has been. Violence, he asserts, should not be condemned out of hand but should be evaluated by "its social and integrative function." *(b)* Brazil, in any case does not have the nonviolent tradition that Oliveira Lima and a host of other historians have claimed for it. This revision of "nonviolence," as Professor Keith acknowledges, was recently put forward by Dr. José Honório Rodrigues in his *Conciliação e reforma.*

The validity of these judgments, it seems to me, depends in great measure on our understanding of the terms of the propositions. "Social and integrative function" is a phrase difficult to attach a precise meaning to, and Professor Keith uses the word "function" in such a variety of ways that it seems to mean little more than "consequence." Clearly, not all the instances of violence are "integrative." Some are plainly divisive—such as the Federalist Rebellion of 1893–1895, which split Rio Grande do Sul into two hostile camps for thirty-five years.

A term that merits more extensive discussion is the key word "violence." He tells us what he means by "conflict" but he does not define "violence" beyond remarking that it is not equivalent to bloodshed. I will therefore hazard a definition of violence and elaborate briefly on its forms. "Violence," it might simply be said, is the deprivation of well-being, life, or security, We can agree with Max Weber that the state has a monopoly on "legitimate" violence, where "legitimacy" refers to the accepted views and customs of politically mobilized groups in a given society.[1]

With no claim to great profundity or originiality, I think forms of violence as thus defined can be instructively classified in the following ways: *(a)* Political *versus* apolitical. An example of the first would be the assassination of an elected official for political ends, and an instance of the second, a common murder. Political violence in turn could be classified as *(b)* Conservative (or reactionary) *versus* progressive (or revolutionary). As examples one could cite the repression of a jacquerie *versus* Marxist guerilla warfare. Other ways of classifying violence relevant to Brazilian history are *(c)* structured *versus* nonstructured (for example, military units in combat *versus* riots) ; and *(d)* secular *versus* religious (e.g., slave revolts[2] *versus* millenarian insurgency).

This scheme is perhaps a little too facile, and two qualifications are in order: first, each dichotomy really represents poles of a continuum along which a given instance of violence might be placed. Secondly, the four types are obviously mutually inclusive in a wide variety of patterns: among forms of political violence in modern Brazilian history, the Canudos rebellion of 1896–1897 might be seen as unstructured, religious, and conservative. The Caldeirão uprising of 1935 would be unstructured, religious—and if we are to believe Ruy Facó[3]—progressive in its primitive communism. The *Farroupilha* rebellion of 1835–1845 was structured (led by professional soldiers), secular, and, insofar as it helped destroy *gaúcho* slavery, socially progressive. The Federalist revolt in Rio Grande fifty years later was led by members of the (imperial) Liberal Party and might be classified as structured, secular, and conservative. Lampião's *cangaceiro* raids (1918–1938) I would classify as unstructured, secular, and conservative, since Lampião often served local *coronéis*. To disagree with these classifications—to object, for instance, that Lampião's followers may have been occasionally motivated by religious convictions as devotees of Padre Cícero—is to emphasize that violent acts and movements pass elusively along a continuum from secular to religious, from conservative to progressive, from structured to unstructured, and from political to apolitical.

With these categories we can delimit our comparative generalizations more cogently than those who state categorically that Brazil had a less violent history in the nineteenth and twentieth centuries than Argentina or Mexico. In secular structured violence, perhaps this assertion is true. In unstructured conservative violence (for example, violence associated with *coronelismo* or its Hispanic equivalent, *caciquismo*), this may not be true at all. In religiously motivated violence, Brazil would clearly seem to have a greater incidence (in its millenarian uprisings) than Argentina.

In the national period, most Spanish American countries were spared one form of unstructured secular violence—slave uprisings—which beset Brazil.[4] Although Brazilians usually view their history as less violent than our own, an American historian has argued that servile revolts in Brazil were more frequent and involved greater numbers than those in the United States.[5] In fact, the very existence of slavery to 1888 would make Brazil one of the most violent countries in the nineteenth century if we consider "legitimate" (publicly sanctioned) deprivation of life and well-being as violence.

With this preface on definitions and typology, we can now take up Professor Keith's propositions. One of his principal theses is that violence or the threat of violence in Brazilian history has usually accompanied social reforms. Vargas' violent seizure of power in 1930, for instance, paved the way for a spate of welfare measures. Primarily basing his case on Vargas, the sociologist Jacques Lambert has even gone a step further than Professor Keith, arguing that dictatorships in Latin America (establishing or maintaining themselves through violence) are more often socially progressive than formally democratic (but really oligarchic) regimes.[6] In any event, it is hard to quarrel with his notion that violence or the threat of violence plays an essential role even in apparently peaceful reforms.[7]

Yet, I cannot accept so easily his observations on the "functions" of violence. These functions (or consequences) are so manifold it seems profitless to try to generalize about them. One corollary, however, merits our attention. Professor Keith says a "function" of a certain type of violence is to reveal the failure of a social and political regime to integrate rebellious groups into its system of values, rewards, and perquisites. I would hesitate to infer (as he implicitly seems to do) that such violence necessarily jeopardizes the stability of a social regime. As the sociologist Mauricio Solaún has argued, in Colombia the division of all classes into two antagonistic parties after decades of *violencia* has paradoxically helped produce a resilient political system and a stable social regime. Guerrilla leaders cannot organize Liberal peasants without alienating their Conservative counterparts. Each social stratum is sharply divided against itself. Violence has not "integrated" dissatisfied groups, but it may have helped stabilize the social regime and has not destroyed the traditional two-party system.[8]

I would agree with Professor Keith that certain forms of violence may have such desirable consequences that violent acts become an acceptable social cost. As an example from United States history, consider Barrington Moore's judgment on the necessity of destroying plantation slavery through the Civil War:

One need only consider what would have happened had the Southern plantation system been able to establish itself in the West by the middle of the nineteenth century and surrounded the Northeast. Then the United States would have been in the position of some modernizing countries today, with a latifundia economy, a dominant antidemocratic aristocracy, and a weak and dependent commercial class, unable and unwilling to push forward toward political democracy. . . .
  Striking down slavery was a decisive step, . . . an essential preliminary for further advances.

He argues, for instance, that organized labor might have had a much longer road toward achieving legal and political acceptance if slavery had persisted and expanded.[9]

Each can draw his own conclusions on Brazilian slavery, and it is true that Brazilians did not face the same historical options; but the judgment should not remain undisputed that Brazil "solved" the slavery issue by studiously ignoring it while the United States blundered into unnecessary violence.

If the presence of violence is not necessarily always an evil, it is conversely true that its absence does not necessarily indicate that all groups are integrated or satisfied. One may hold down the rate of revolutionary violence by increasing the power of the state as well as by ameliorating social conditions. In this connection it is noteworthy that the Brazilian army has grown 1,000 percent in numbers since 1910, while the national population has increased less than 400 percent.[10] Furthermore, one could point out that potential political violence, in the absence of ideological preparation, may be deflected into personal apolitical violence, such as robbery and murder by the "marginal masses" of the *favelas* of Rio de Janeiro.

Violence has its uses at every point along the political spectrum. In Brazil the most common forms of political violence have been conservative, especially the abuses related to coronelismo. As is well known, coronelismo appeared as a means of political control over the rural masses through a graded series of inducements and threats ranging from political patronage to murder. Although coronéis had their *capangas* in the imperial era, the use of these political enforcers flowered with the Republic, for three reasons: *(a)* a rapid expansion of the registered electorate, from about 1.5 percent to 5 percent of the total population; *(b)* the redistribution of revenues toward the *municípios,* where local notables began to compete for spoils; and *(c)* the great increase in elective offices, especially the governorships (formerly controlled from Rio de Janeiro). The institution of formal democracy turned out to be a victory for the landed élite.

Professor Keith suggests that Pedro II and Campos Sales stifled the growth of democracy through what he calls an "enforced peace" (which I understand to mean violence and the threat of violence) and the manipulation of political machinery. But I submit that without the social and economic infrastructures associated with industrialization—as well as a gradual extension of effective suffrage—the political solutions of Pedro II and Campos Sales were virtually inevitable. Victor Nunes Leal in his famous study of coronelismo asserts that Campos Sales introduced the *política dos governadores* to avoid military intervention in the states[11]—a more violent form of burlesquing democracy.

Though I disagree with Professor Keith concerning the implications of certain uses of violence, I would not quarrel with his second general proposition, viz., that Brazilians have mythologized their allegedly nonviolent tradition. Here it is appropriate to summarize Professor Rodrigues' counterthesis of "compromise and reform." He asserts that Brazilian history is far from nonviolent. Yet, when violence threatens the social structure, he avers, warring factions of the *élite* compromise to their mutual satisfaction at the expense of the masses. The failure to introduce reforms that might prevent further bloodshed and destruction produces a new cycle of violence, compromise, and postponement of reform.

Could such a book be written about a "violent" Spanish-American nation? Broadly speaking, one has been—Alberto Edwards Vives' *La fronda aristocrática en Chile,* published in 1936. Like Rodrigues, Edwards argues that nineteenth-century Chilean history was dominated by an *élite* that successfully settled its internal cleavages at the expense of lower strata. In the manner of Rodrigues, he declares *la plus ça change, plus c'est la même chose*. One could make a tenable case that between 1830 and 1891 Chile had a less violent history than Brazil by almost any definition of violence.

Yet, when all is said and done, the myth has an element of truth: Brazil does seem to have a political culture that tends to eschew broad applications of violence. Even though this trait springs from a patriarchal system and primarily characterizes *élite* relationships, who can say that this political "style" will not survive the eventual collapse of an *élite* regime?

In the past, preservation of national unity has been closely related to the genius for compromise among sectors of the *élite*. Let us give Pedro II and his ministers their due for holding the country together in an era of centrifugal revolts. In the 1840's the young Emperor's cabinets reversed the policies of Pedro I and conciliated leaders of regional rebellions. In Rio Grande do Sul Caxias not only amnestied the rebellious Farrapos, he even reintegrated rebel officers into the imperial army. One would be hard-pressed to find a parallel in Spanish- or Anglo-America. In Pernambuco Pedro II's government dealt lightly with Antônio Borges da Fonsêca, the ex-seminarian and socialist agitator of the Praieira revolt. In 1849 Borges had declared, "Who is not for us is against us, wrote our Lord Jesus Christ. Liberty and Peace to those who support me; annihilation and death to those who oppose me and aid the imperial government." [12] Though confined to Fernando de Noronha for three years, Borges da Fonsêca was allowed to return to Pernambuco in 1852; he thenceforth continued to agitate till his death twenty years later. Granted, if he had not been a member of an ancient *Paraibano* family, he might not have received such lenient treatment; but among the *élite* the spirit of compromise in the 1840's and later is a fact worthy of appreciation in its proper perspective.

NOTES

1 The state can obviously abuse its responsibility and forfeit the legitimacy of its violent acts.
2 See Maria Isaura Pereira de Queiroz, "Messiahs in Brazil," *Past and Present*, XXXI (July, 1965) , 75.
3 *Cangaceiros e fanáticos: Génese e lutas* (Rio de Janeiro, 1963) , p. 207.
4 Cuba and Mexico were exceptions. Negro slavery persisted in the former until 1886; in Mexico illegal but *de facto* chattel slavery was imposed repeatedly on the Mayas and Yaquis until the Revolution of 1910.

5 "Compared with the countless uprisings of the Brazilian Negroes, the slave revolts in our own country appear rather desperate and futile." Stanley M. Elkins, *Slavery: A Problem in American Institutional and Intellectual Life* (2nd ed.; New York, 1963), p. 136, n. 112. Elkins argues, however, that this fact shows Negroes in Brazil could more easily conceive of themselves as free men than their dehumanized American brothers.

6 *Le Brésil: structure sociale et institutions politiques* (Paris, 1953), p. 136. Gilbert Merkx recently demonstrated that of the significant social changes that occurred between 1930 and 1965 in the Latin American republics, twice as many were implemented by governments coming to power through force than by those which achieved power through constitutionally specified means. See his "Force, Political Shift, and Social Impact in the Changes of Latin American Presidents, 1930–1965," unpublished paper delivered at the annual meeting of the American Sociological Association, Aug. 28–31, 1967, San Francisco, Cal.

7 Sidney Hook once wrote, "the history of 'peaceful' social reform demonstrates that the shadow or threat of more violent action has been the prime catalyst of 'sweet reasonableness' upon the part of groups which possess power." *Encyclopedia of the Social Sciences* (New York, 1935) XV, 265 (entry on "violence").

8 It is nonetheless true, of course, that if violence rises above a certain threshold, it can threaten the existence of a social or political system. Colombia's political system was temporarily disrupted in 1953, when a high incidence of violence contributed to the nation's only *coup d'état* of this century. (Solaún's dissertation is in progress at the University of Chicago).

9 Barrington Moore, Jr., *Social Origins of Dictatorship and Democracy: Lord and Peasant in the Making of the Modern World* (Boston, 1966), p. 153.

10 It need hardly be added that the revolution in armaments since 1910—especially the introduction of armored tanks and aircraft—has expanded military power even beyond what the rise in personnel would indicate.

11 *Coronelismo, enxada e vóto: o município e o régime representativo no Brasil* (Rio de Janeiro, 1948), p. 178.

12 Cited in Vamireh Chacon, *História das idéias socialistas no Brasil* (Rio de Janeiro, 1965), p. 192.

OCTOBER, 1930–CONFLICT
OR CONTINUITY?

Jordan M. Young
Pace College, New York City

BRAZILIAN history, though riddled with contradictions, has an essential unity which continues to baffle and puzzle observers, both national and foreign. From Capistrano de Abreu and Robert Southey to José Honório Rodrigues and Alexander Marchant, the nagging question of continuity or conflict is always present.[1] And always unresolved.

Twentieth-century Brazilian history, and especially the course of events of October, 1930, demonstrates a peculiar ability of the nation's leaders to propose compromise political solutions to crises and of the people to accept them, thus avoiding disastrous civil disturbances. The avoidance of conflict by compromise is a definite fact of historical life in Brazil and one that provides an effective pattern of continuity from the colonial period to the present.

European states, after Napoleon's defeat in 1814, began to chart a new political course. Most of the Latin American countries after 1822 started their experiments in republicanism. Brazil in contrast adopted an imperial system that had more in common with the Portuguese past than it did with Brazil's future. It was an exotic political system that was shaped, changed, and buffeted by the demands of Brazil's geography, economy, and social structure. Portugal was a small country with two vital and important cities, Lisbon and Pôrto. Brazil had many urban centers. Bahia, Recife, Belém, and São Paulo were all significant cities and could, to some degree, compete with the nation's capital, Rio de Janeiro, for the loyalty of the local citizens. The economic life of a vast nation could not be controlled by one city, and Belém, Recife, and Bahia traded almost as much with Europe as they did with other areas of Brazil. The social structure in each of the power centers of imperial Brazil represented and reflected local conditions.

Throughout the period of the Empire there was a slow expansion of the political influence of a tiny but growing middle class. Dom Pedro II certainly did nothing to encourage the Brazilian military and thus for nearly a century Brazil was spared the "man on horseback" as a successful model and image to be followed by power-minded politicians. When the monarchy fell in 1889, Brazilians had a line of continuity in national government that stretched as far back as 1822, a continuity that was not snapped in 1889 when the Empire collapsed.

A letter of Capistrano de Abreu, who was living in Rio de Janeiro, to the Barão de Rio Branco clearly captured the political mood of 1889:

I have just come from Campo de Santana, impressed, as you can well imagine, after having seen a revolution. And what a revolution! There is only one word which can reproduce what I saw: piling-up. A brigade rose up, and batallions arrived one by one, with no unity, attraction, or resolution; they lined up one by one, like dried fish. When there was no batallion that was missing or doubtful, they proclaimed the Republic, with no reacting, no one protesting. Given the state in which things were, it was the only reasonable solution. . . . All Brazil joined it. . . . The general impression today with regard to the government seems to me to be that of indifference.

With relatively few modifications the same could be written shortly after the revolutions of 1930, 1945, and 1964.

The Brazilian army precipitated the 1889 revolution but they shared their power almost immediately with the civilian political leaders of São Paulo and Minas Gerais. Marshal Deodôro da Fonsêca, unable to govern and faced with civil war, resigned and turned his administration over to another military man, Vice-President General Floriano Peixoto. A perplexing figure in Brazilian affairs, Floriano Peixoto surprised everyone by following the 1891 constitution to the letter. In 1894 he turned over the executive office to a São Paulo civilian political leader, Prudente de Morais. From 1894 until 1964 the army shared its power with the civilians. Both the Hermes da Fonsêca (1910–1914) and Eurico Dutra (1945–1950) administrations were basically civilian-dominated regimes. Brazilian presidents were primarily civilians and the military was apparently content to play its role behind the scenes. This situation of course changed abruptly in 1964 when the military installed an army man as a leader of the nation and the civilians were relegated to the former role of the military: as the behind-the-scenes arbiter of national affairs, but with nowhere near the same veto power as the army previously wielded.

The civilian power structure that operated from 1894 to 1930 was clear-cut, relatively simple, and demonstrated a high degree of continuity. Basically it was big-state poltics of coordinated action by the governors of the largest states. This meant that political leaders of the major states would caucus and come up with agreed-upon policies and programs. Though many states were represented, it invariably came down to what the power brokers of São Paulo and Minas Gerais wanted. The politicians of these two states were the political "establishment." This situation was, of course, not a new development but one that began during the Empire and was simply continued into the Republic.[2]

Politicians from the state of Rio Grande do Sul, however, always presented a special problem. Gaúchos had their own political and economic life yet were also determined to obtain a greater share and voice in governing the nation. They could not be ignored by the establishment due to the congressional role of Rio Grande do Sul Senator Pinheiro Machado. Up to his death in 1915 he forced the Paulistas and Mineiros to recognize Rio Grande do Sul and his power.[3] Skillful control of substantial groups of senators and congressmen by Pinheiro Machado often checked São Paulo and Minas Gerais in the exercise of economic and political power and sometimes resulted in policies which benefited the other Brazilian states. Minas Gerais and São Paulo always had to take Rio Grande do Sul into account even if they did not take the state's political leaders into the "club." If Rio Grande do Sul was forgotten Congress was truculent and often in conflict witih the president.

Thus, built into the first thirty years of Brazilian twentieth-century history was an unstated but operating network of compromises. The first was between the state of Minas Gerais and the state of São Paulo. The second was between these two states and Rio Grande do Sul. The third compromise determined the relationship of the three to the other states of Brazil. The final compromise was the role of the military behind the entire civilian façade, either giving its blessing to existing political arrangements or indicating mild disapproval. Strong disapproval by the military meant revolution and in the twentieth century the dates that point this up are 1930, 1945, 1964.

Revolution in the Brazilian frame of reference means an extra-legal change of government which does not follow any of the constitutional and prescribed forms for this change. Revolution in the Brazilian *milieu* does not mean abrupt, deep social, economic, or political modifications. Brazil has never had that kind of revolution.

The year 1930 is a perfect example of a potentially revolutionary situation that was handled, certainly not consciously, by the political establishment, the military hierarchy, and the economic élite with typical adroitness, compromise, and continuity. When the tumultuous events of October 3 to October 24, 1930, were over, no one was quite sure what had happened to Brazilian society, to the coffee economy, and to the political structure. Thirty-seven years after the October, 1930, revolution there is still an amazing variety of contradictory viewpoints and opinions about what *really* happened in 1930. There is certainly no consensus among Brazilians.

José Honório Rodrigues, one of Brazil's outstanding historians, writing in his *Concilação e reforma no Brasil,* feels that the Liberal Alliance platform on which Getúlio Vargas ran for office in 1930 proposed small, superficial transformations such as the secret ballot and electoral justice and spoke in vague terms about justice for the working class; the 1930 Revolution was revolutionary only in its form of action but had no real intent of satisfying the demands of the lower income groups.[4]

Economist Hélio Jaguaribe, in his *Desenvolvimento ecônomica e desenvolvimento político,* describes the 1930 Revolution as the second coming to power of the middle class.[5] The slogan of the secret ballot emotionally mobilized the petty bourgeoisie, but they were ideologically disorganized and they refused to deepen the revolution in the economic and social sphere.

Celso Furtado's *The Economic Growth of Brazil* states that the 1930 Revolution was the culmination of a series of abortive military uprisings beginning in 1922.[6] The 1930 Revolution was based on the city populations and especially civilian administrative circles and industrial groups and their allies in international finance.

Hélio Silva titles the third volume of his Vargas cycle *1930: A revolução traída.*[7] His thesis is a simple one, that the men from Rio Grande do Sul took advantage of the situation created by the economic crises, the social unrest, and the public disgust with the Old Republic and led a revolution which did nothing more than bring a new group of unscrupulous politicians into power. Affonso Henriques, another contemporary writer, stresses Vargas' ability for intrigue and deceit.[8] For Henriques the 1930 Revolution was nothing more than a fraud and a deception. Nelson Werneck Sodré a militant Brazilian Marxist, writes in his *História militar do Brasil* that the Revolution may have brought some new elements into the military establishment but very quickly the Vargas administration took an antilabor posture. This was especially true in São Paulo, according to Werneck Sodré.[9] Wanderly Guilherme, in a provocative study entitled *Introdução ao estudo das contradições sociais no Brasil,* declares tha the objectives of the 1930 Revolution were quite clear.[10] It was a capitalistic rebellion to free Brazil from the coffee-planting economy which was stifling industrial development.

The opinions on what occurred in 1930 are varied and diverse.[11] What is sharp and clear, however, is that when the fifteen years that Getúlio Vargas dominated Brazilian political affairs ended, a dramatic change in the nation had occurred. What cannot be denied is that the entire period is filled with improvisation, experimentation, and modest social planning. As a result, Brazil in 1945 seemed to be prepared to enter the ranks of the nations that had to some degree, however small, come to terms with modern twentieth-century capitalism. Adjustments had been made in the economic sector which if carried to a successful conclusion might provide the environment for a functioning representative government. Neither political democracy nor representative government *per se* provides food or decent living standards for the bulk of its citizens. A modified capitalistic structure responsive to public pressure, geared to mass production, and spinning off benefits to more and more citizens, could provide the *milieu* for a successful representative and democratic state. The Brazilian economic and political pyramid was too sharply structured in 1930. The pyramid was somewhat flattened by the events of 1930, with more people making gains in the middle economic sectors, and the trend appears to be continuing in 1967. This same rate of growth and progress, however, has not been carried out in the political area. Successful representative government needs encouragement, support, and historical roots which too often have been torn out and destroyed before they could grow to maturity in Brazil.

Thus, the real change or revolution in Brazil occurred slowly and quietly in the fifteen years that Vargas governed. It occurred when the infrastructure of the nation was shifted. It occurred when the urban working classes received some tiny assistance from the state. It occurred when the middle class began to acquire material wealth and, to a slight degree, political power. This was the revolution in Brazil, and it came about perhaps in spite of the 1930 Revolution, not necessarily because of it.

The essential unity and continuity in the specific events of 1930 is revealed by a closer investigation of the political establishment of Brazil in 1926. Political peace seemed to have returned in 1926 after four agitated years under the presidency of Artur Bernardes from Minas Gerais. From 1922 to 1926, "state of siege" laws had curtailed civil liberties and the chief executive effectively used the Brazilian army successfully to curb military and civilian opposition to the political establishment. In 1926 the situation changed when outgoing President Bernardes gave his support to the São Paulo candidacy of Washington Luis. There was a tacit understanding that in 1930 a Minas Gerais political leader would return to govern the nation for the next presidential term from 1930 to 1934.

As the period 1926–1928 was one of general prosperity, an era of good feeling spread across Brazil, and President Washington Luis was able to lift the state-of-siege laws. The peace and tranquility lasted until 1929, when the world economy, and Brazil's along with it, collapsed, and political opposition to the president developed within the establishment.

The actions of President Washington Luis were a perfect example of what could go wrong with the unwritten system of compromise and continuity that existed in Brazil if a strong-minded individual became president and refused to recognize the informal political power structure. Washington Luis was a tough, arrogant single-minded executive.[12] (One is reminded of the intransigence of Juan Manuel Balmaceda in Chile in 1891 when he too refused to recognize the informal power structure of his own country and precipitated a disastrous civil war.) The myopic São Paulo focus of President Washington Luis made him apparently lose track of the fact that there was a great deal more to Brazil than simply the "red earth" coffee plantations of his native state.

Early in his four-year term, he decided to break the unwritten agreement concerning the alternating of the presidency. Washington Luis selected another Paulista, Governor Júlio Prestes, as the official candidate for the presidency. This meant that the entire weight of the exccutive office would be thrown behind the candidacy. By doing this President Washington Luis was effectively blocking the political ambitions of the Minas Gerais leader, Antônio Carlos de Andrada e Silva, who though a traditional member of the establishment was considered by Washington Luis as simply not sufficiently competent to continue successfully the financial and economic programs put into operation by the Paulista president. The success of some of the economic and monetary reforms introduced by Washington Luis depended upon the close cooperation and support of the coffee planters and the business interests of São Paulo.

The decision by President Washington Luis not to alternate the Executive office was not too extravagant and did not run counter to much that had occurred previously in Brazilian affairs. The first three civilian presidents of Brazil had been Paulistas, yet no politician from the state of São Paulo had occupied the executive office since 1910. Two Paulista presidents, one following on the heels of the other, did not seem unreasonable or even apt to create conditions which would cause the Old Republic to fall.

Everything indicated that Washington Luis would have his way. Most of the smaller states in Brazil followed the suggestions of the executive office. This was true in the decade of the twenties and remains equally true in 1967. The situation seemed especially viable in 1928 as Rio Grande do Sul, the only state that could possibly have caused any trouble for the administration, had been neutralized by the appointment of Getúlio Vargas as Federal Secretary of Finance. He served only briefly as he was recalled to run successfully for the governorship of Rio Grande do Sul. As soon as Washington Luis indicated his choice of Júlio Prestes, Getúlio Vargas promptly and cheerfully gave his support to whatever candidate the President felt would best serve the nation.

Thus, the normally allied states of Minas Gerais and São Paulo split. Mineiro politicians, enraged at the duplicity of the President, were determined to block the plans of Washington Luis and sabotaged any possible political understanding by deciding that if their candidate, Antônio Carlos, was not selected they would do all in their power to prevent a Paulista from attaining the presidency. Minas Gerais politicians sought out the state of Rio Grande do Sul to block Washington Luis' candidate. A political impasse developed as the political bosses of Minas Gerais and Borges de Medeiros, political chief of Rio Grande do Sul, selected a reluctant Governor Getúlio Vargas as the opposition candidate to Paulista Governor Júlio Prestes. Vargas' running mate was Governor João Pessôa from the northeastern state of Paraíba. Minas Gerais, Rio Grande do Sul, and Paraíba formed a new party, the Liberal Alliance, and presented a relatively conservative platform to the nation.

Neither Vargas nor Pessôa were radicals, revolutionaries, or even innovators. They were both members of the Brazilian political establishment. Thus, the struggle for control of the government in 1930 was definitely not a break with any previous event in Brazilian history. The situation was reminiscent of the presidential contests in 1910, 1918, and 1922: there was simply a power struggle within the establishment. What the Minas Gerais politicians may have been aiming at was a political compromise which would have resulted in Washington Luis' dropping the candidacy of Júlio Prestes. Then the Liberal Alliance would substitute another politician for Getúlio Vargas. If events followed in their usual historical pattern, another political figure would be selected as a conciliatory presidential candidate and all sides would reunite to continue the Brazilian pattern of continuity and compromise. That this failed to develop can be easily traced to two important factors. First, the intransigence of President Washington Luis and, second, the incredibly skillful maneuvering of Getúlio Vargas, who seemed to have lulled Washington Luis into a false sense of assurance that the Rio Grande do Sul governor really was prepared, willing, and able to avoid a split in the political establishment. As long as Vargas was the opposition candidate to Júlio Prestes, President Washington Luis was sure there would be no sharp break with the traditional settlement of the political problems.

But Vargas is the clue to the revolution. His political style completely deceived everyone. Governor Vargas was aware that he could not win the presidential election of 1930. Executive office power over the smaller Brazilian states was enough to give any official candidate sufficient votes to win the office. Minas Gerais, Rio Grande do Sul, and Paraíba, simply did not have the voters to overcome the ballots that would be cast in the other seventeen Brazilian states. Elections were not complete frauds, but in the less developed states local political bosses could normally deliver the vote.[13]

Extremely clever and knowledgeable concerning the Brazilian political power structure, Vargas quietly came to terms with President Washington Luis. Vargas promised that when the election was over he would give complete and unconditional support to the winner. In turn, Washington Luis promised full political and economic cooperation from the federal government for the state of Rio Grande do Sul. This agreement did not, however, cover the other states allied with Vargas, Minas Gerais and Paraíba.

The Brazilian electorate were, of course, not informed of any of these arrangements. The middle class, the urban workers, and many intellectuals thought they had a real candidate who was honestly challenging the São Paulo coffee aristocracy as represented by Washington Luis and his candidate Júlio Prestes. The enthusiasm of the Vargas supporters also reflected the depressed economic conditions. The common people felt they had a champion. Vargas seemed to be the perfect opposition candidate. He was the type of Brazilian physically, emotionally, and intellectually with whom the middle and lower classes could identify. This was in sharp contrast with aristocratic attitudes of Washington Luis.

Elections were held in March, 1930, amid a great deal of tension and excitement. When the votes were finally tallied Vargas had lost, as he had anticipated. The votes of the three opposition states were not sufficient to counterbalance the other seventeen. It appeared at first that a reconciliation of the ópposing political powers was possible, especially when the federal government upheld its end of the bargain by cooperating closely with Getúlio Vargas.[14] Unexpected was the manner in which a few determined young *Gaúcho* politicians such as Oswaldo Aranha and João Neves da Fontoura began to inflame public opinion and maintain a revolutionary atmosphere from March, 1930, until military approval for a revolution was obtained. Contact was also made with a group of young army officers who had clashed in the years 1924–1927 with the military and political establishment. When their protest movement failed, they went into exile. They were popularly called the *tenentes* (lieutenants) and were associated in the mind of the general public as reformers. But only after the professional military had been sounded out by the younger establishment politicians did the armed rebellion break out in October, 1930, and topple the Old Republic. Once military approval had been obtained, then amid charges of fraud in the March presidential elections, corruption in government, and promises to clean up the federal bureaucracy, Gaúcho armies moved and the public overwhelmingly supported the action. October, 1930, was a popular revolution.

For many the success of the revolt was an end in itself; for others it was the beginning of a new era in Brazilian affairs. Like most extra-legal changes of government in Brazil, after the first few months of enthusiasm many in the new establishment (middle class and lower income groups) were dismayed at what had occurred. Again, it is necessary to emphasize that the events of October, 1930, were not truly revolutionary. Extra-legal changes of government were well within the Brazilian historical tradition.

How few basic changes took place in the first few years is sharply pointed up by surveying briefly the power relationship of the major states to the national government. São Paulo must be analyzed first. According to the charges of the "revolutionaries," the action of Paulista President Washington Luis had precipitated the revolution. In part the armed uprising appeared directed against the coffee planters, who controlled the economic life of the nation. But the revolutionary government, composed of so many divergent and contradictory factions, approached the state of São Paulo gingerly. The *tenentes* had one approach; civilian politicians from Minas Gerais and Rio Grande de Sul had another. Businessmen counseled caution while the unemployed São Paulo urban workers shouted for action—now. The young and inexperienced revolutionary government rode off in all directions at once. Everyone felt victorious and cheated of victory at the same time.

The years from 1930 to July, 1932, when the Paulista rebellion broke, clearly illustrate the failure and inability of the Vargas government to carry out any basic reforms in the São Paulo political and economic structure. It is somewhat analgous to the victorious North's inability after our Civil War to destroy or alter profoundly the social, political, and economic structure of the defeated southern states.

When João Alberto, a northeasterner and former *tenente* of the Prestes Column, was named by Vargas as interventor or provisional governor of São Paulo, the move was cheered by the radicals and unemployed, who expected great changes. In contrast, the middle class, including most members of the Partido Democrático, who had supported the Vargas movement, suddenly discovered that they were Paulistas first and revolutionaries second.[15] And worst of all they were being ignored by the new governor. From November, 1930, to July, 1931, when João Alberto resigned, Paulista politics were in a constant turmoil, with no important political or social reforms being carried out. From July, 1931, to July, 1932, there was a simple struggle for political power as Vargas sought a governor who could gain the loyalty of the Paulistas and at the same time remain friendly to the "revolutionary" national government.

In the economic sphere, coffee was stockpiled at the expense of the Vargas government.[16] Instead of destroying the coffee planters, the government spent precious federal funds on coffee stockpiling. World prices were so low that there was little emphasis on exports and few dollar earnings were recorded.

Brazilians, unable to purchase consumer items on the world market, turned to national industry. As a result, the industrial plants of São Paulo began to supply domestic needs. Very quickly São Paulo once again became the locomotive pulling the other states of Brazil. In the context of Brazilian history this development demonstrates more continuity than conflict.

The dramatic shift in the São Paulo capital structure away from coffee to domestic industrialization was certainly not planned. It was a reaction to the demands of a situation. It is reminiscent of New Englanders' opposition to the War of 1812 as a threat to their lucrative maritime trade. When the War of 1812 was over, New England had benefited most. They had developed consumer industry to meet the demands of the local market which could not be supplied by British industrialists. But the São Paulo transformation was neither planned nor anticipated by those who led the 1930 revolution. Though the Paulistas were excluded from participation in the political process on the national scene, they were unhampered in their internal economic development. This was fundamentally what the Paulista élite wanted. The revolutionaries basically left São Paulo alone after 1932. It had become apparent that as long as Paulista businessmen could make profits and were politically left alone in São Paulo they had no special quarrel with Vargas. A workable, pragmatic *quid pro quo* had been achieved. The similarity to the post-1964 period does not have to be stressed.

A somewhat similar pattern of events developed in the state of Minas Gerais. The revolutionary *tenentes* were unable to unseat the elected governor of the state; as a result, no basic political or economic changes occurred in the state in the early years of the Vargas administration.[17] When Minas Gerais needed economic aid from the national government its requests were granted. As long as mineiro politicians were free to dominate their own small political fiefdoms scattered throughout the state, they too had no quarrel with Vargas and received central government support. With the possible exception of Juscelino Kubitschek, Minas Gerais politicians seem to have a provincial small-town and parochial approach to Brazilian national politics. The events, intrigues, and power struggles with Minas Gerais seemed to attract them more than the problems of the nation as a whole.

In the affairs of Rio Grande do Sul the *tenentes* and innovators were relatively insignificant. The governor appointed after the revolution was Flôres da Cunha, a civilian political leader and a member of the reigning establishment. There were no radical changes in the economic structure of Rio Grande do Sul in the years 1930–1945. Many of the best political leaders and younger administrators were attracted to Rio de Janeiro where Gaúcho control of the national administration made access to important positions relatively easy. The Brazilianization of the leading Gaúcho politicians took place as Vargas, Neves, and Aranha found the political and social atmosphere of Rio de Janeiro much more attractive than that of Pôrto Alegre.

Thus, the three major states continued to have a political and economic life of their own. The national government brought no startling changes to these sections of Brazil. And the political life of Brazil in this period flowed from these major states. They set the tone, style, and method of political operation for the nation. A drastic or even revolutionary change set in motion by a *tenente*, acting as governor, in a northeastern state caused very little change in the national political style. Changes in São Paulo, Minas Gerais, and, to a lesser extent, Rio Grande do Sul were much more significant.

The 1930 revolution did, however, disrupt the continuity of Brazilian political evolution. Some of the uneasiness and unsettled problems that exist in contemporary Brazil are directly traceable to 1930.

First and foremost, political party life was torn apart and destroyed by the 1930 revolution. It is not necessary to praise unduly the contributions of the pre-1930 Republican Party to representative government in Brazil. Nor were the smaller opposition parties that existed in São Paulo, Minas Gerais, and Rio Grande do Sul anything more than another sector of the elite and middle class seeking expression or possibly simply political office. But they were political parties; they did have a following and party discipline did exist to some degree.

All the experience of the monarchy, during which political parties had existed for over half a century, was naturally carried over into the republican period. This development came to a halt, however, with the 1930 revolution. What gave the Brazilian political apparatus some rationale and structure in the closing decades of the nineteenth century was the fact that all the monarchists were not found in the Conservative Party, nor were all the liberals dedicated to the idea of a republic. The existing political parties were made up of politicians who knew how to compromise and reconcile their opposing views. There were wide differences of opinion, but they could find expression within a formal party framework: opposition was channeled and focused. Thus, the monarchists were accommodated in the new powerful Republican Party of 1889 with relative ease and without blood, sweat, or even much toil.

Shortly after the 1889 revolution succeeded, many monarchists claimed that they had always been ready to support a republic. It was easy for most politicians to turn in their monarchist robes for republican broadcloth. This easy accommodation appears to be part of a Brazilian historical pattern, but 1930 broke the pattern. Politicians were ready to accept the change in government. After the revolution, however, there was no political party to turn to. There were groups, cliques, clans, and clusters of politicians but there was no formal structure. The *tenentes* had their pressure groups, civilian political leaders from Rio Grande do Sul formed another group, and all competed for the attention of Getúlio Vargas and his military alter ego, General Góes Monteiro. Politics in Brazil, though always reflecting a high degree of personalism, became even more personalistic as a result of the 1930 Revolution. Political power in Brazil from 1930 to 1945 depended to a large extent on one's circle of friends, which was hardly conducive to the development of representative government. The charge can forcefully be made that the Vargas revolution broke the line of continuity of a functioning political party system.

The dismantling of the Republican Party of Brazil was carried out in every Brazilian state. By catering to groups that had not been in power before 1930 the Vargas government was able to command the loyalty of wider sectors of the population. Though only the Republican Party was under attack by the 1930 revolutionaries, by the time the fifteen-year Vargas period ended the average Brazilian was completely cynical concerning the role and function of all political parties. The cost of this destruction of political parties has slowly become apparent in the years following 1945. Though three major parties struggled for power from 1945 to 1964, success almost exclusively depended on political personalities. Political parties need periods of success in the form of government patronage and sharing of the spoils of political victory. This is the cement of a political society, and for fifteen years the mechanism of political parties disappeared.

Another equally serious charge that can be brought against the Vargas revolution focuses on the closing of the Brazilian Congress by Decree Law 19,398 of 1930. This broke another precious tradition in representative government that had been slowly building up from the earliest times of the monarchy to 1930. Unrepresentative as the federal legislature may have been, it did function and did provide a platform and forum for opposition elements. It did serve to inform the middle class that there were congressmen and senators who on rare occasions would raise voices against the establishment. One should not overemphasize this point. Congress was tightly controlled by the oligarchy but opposition speeches were covered by the entire spectrum of the Brazilian press.

Also, whenever the political establishment split, one faction would use the Congress to attack the administration in power. Political compromises were often arrived at and carried out simply because a legislative body existed. Even the victors of the 1930 revolution owe a great deal of their success to their use of the legislative forum to attack the Washington Luis administration. The speeches of João Neves were especially dramatic and whipped the citizens of Rio de Janeiro into an emotional frame of mind that made the revolution ever easier.

A surprising number of Brazilians were brought into the web of government by the existence of the federal legislature. Congressional politics were one method by which political life was brought closer to the people. Congressmen did work for appropriations for the voters in their districts. Obtaining a road, a port improvement, or a small reservoir in the northeast often depended on the skill of a congressman.

All this ended in 1930. The "captive" Congress of 1934–1937 was not an independent legislative body. It operated to a large degree only because Getúlio Vargas and the military considered it docile and in no way a threat. When representative government returned to Brazil in 1945 the legislative branch had to start from a *tabula rasa,* as most of the independent congressional politicians of the 1920's had disappeared and in their place there remained only the Vargas lackeys or a cynical younger generation of politicians who had come of age during the Vargas dictatorship. For fifteen years they had been subjected to Vargas' political style and most had learned the lesson very well. Brazil paid dearly in the years 1945–1964 for the damage done to the legislative branch by the Vargas revolution. The Brazilian Congress was the weakest of the three branches of government during the nineteen years following the overthrow of Vargas. It did not play a proper and vital role in the post-Vargas period. A broken, spiritless, cynical Congress was a direct legacy of the Vargas revolution. Two vital historical props of an open, representative society had been destroyed by the Vargas Revolution. This certainly was not continuity in the Brazilian historical sense.

One of the most severe charges that can be brought against the Vargas revolution in breaking the thread of continuity in Brazilian history involves the role of the military in the political life of the nation. Though the army had always been in the position of a power broker during the Old Republic, as a result of the 1930 revolution it began to influence the course of Brazilian events in a much more determined and positive fashion. In the years up to 1930 the army was behind the scenes. After 1930 every extra-legal change of government resulted in more political power's being openly concentrated in military hands.

The military made the October, 1930, Revolution possible. In 1932, the army saved the Vargas régime from being toppled by the Paulista counter-revolution. In 1935, an abortive Communist uprising was smashed violently by the armed forces. In 1937 the army was the major force guaranteeing the success of O Estado Nôvo, which stripped Brazil of even the faintest vestiges of democratic government. In 1945 the military establishment decided that Vargas was no longer to be trusted and removed him from office. In the post-dictatorship period, the tempo of army participation in the political decisions of the nation accelerated, with interventions in politics in 1954, 1955, 1961, and ultimately in 1964, when the army took almost complete control of the political affairs of the nation. The Vargas revolution of 1930 did not initiate military participation in the political affairs of the nation, but it certainly increased both the scope and frequency of the phenomenon. The availability and apparent willingness of the military to "right the wrongs" of the civilian political structure comes from deep within the Brazilian past. The army was, however, certainly welcomed and used more openly by Getúlio Vargas. Whether the military can bring better brains and sophistication to the political process remains to be seen.[18] Military solutions to political and social problems are often only temporarily effective. It is also becoming apparent that some of Brazil's most pressing problems are not necessarily subject to a military solution.

The historical verdict on October, 1930, is certainly not clear. The events of October 3 to 24 did not conflict with the Brazilian past; indeed, there was a great deal that was almost traditional in this extra-legal change of government. It was a practical and successful response to a potentially dangerous situation; it effectively blocked what could possibly have been a broader, more profound political movement which the establishment could not control. But, one might conclude that what took place during the fifteen Vargas years was in conflict with certain historical traditions. But as losses were recorded in some areas, gains were made in others. Whether the price paid for the gains was too high still remains to be seen.

NOTES

1 Alexander Marchant, "The Unity of Brazilian History," in *Brazil: Portrait of Half a Continent,* ed. T. Lynn Smith and Alexander Marchant (New York, 1951), pp. 37–51.

2 Sílvo Gabriel Diniz, "Grupos políticos em Minas Gerais," *Revista Brasileira de Estudos Políticos,* No. 22 (Jan., 1967) , 225.

3 Daniel de Carvalho, *Estudos e depoimentos* (Rio de Janeiro, 1953) , pp. 181–92.

4 José Honório Rodrigues, *Conciliação e reforma no Brasil* (Rio de Janeiro, 1965) , p. 91. Professor Rodrigues further comments: "Pelos seus objectivos reformista-liberais, quase limitados à 'Representação e Justica' porque nascia da cúpula dos partidos excluídos na participação do poder, da cisão da minoría dominante, o movimento de 1930 só foi revolucionário na forma do comportamento, na reação às proscrições acumuladas. Não visava a atender, senão em parte mínima, às reivindicações populares, nem antendia às apirações de mudanca estructural do país. Antes pretendia, pelas reformas secundárias, especialmente eleitorais que permitissem o acesso das minorías oposicionistas ao poder, evitar ou retardar a revolução. . . . A vitória da Aliança Liberal nascia tarde, como tantos movimentos no Brasil. Seu programa não era inócuo e vazio, mas era obsoleto, era socialmente atrasado, uma relíquia que insistia em sobreviver e só se afirmava diante da fossilidade ainda maior da plataforma conservadora. A revolução que deve ser sempre um salto no progresso histórico contra o atraso, não tinha esta intenção. Não era intencionalmente um instante de aceleração, era a sobrevivência do não contemporâneo. Foi a liderança ajudada pelo insistência dos fatores economicos e sociais contemporâneos, que transformou a pequena reforma em comê ço de revolução. O carácter conciliatório de Getúlio Vargas, a principio meramente formal, isto é, de transação entre facções da minoria dominadora e depois fundamental, isto é de transação com o pôvo, dá ao movimento de 1930 o caráter de começo da revolução brasileira."
On p. 105 he further comments: "O único movimento armado vitorioso no Brasil, o de 1930, não exprimia as nôvas fôrcas do país, nem pretendia fazer alterações profundas. Mas aos poucos estas fôrças obtiveram alguns triumfões e um ajustamento social construtivo harmonizou umas e outros, sem maior ruptura com o passado. Outros vêzes pequenas alterações foram fruto de idéias vencidas nos prélios armados, proque o processo histórico não pertence sòmente aos vencedores."

5 Rio de Janeiro, 1962, p. 173. Analyzing Getúlio Vargas, Jaguaribe writes: "Coube a Getúlio Vargas, como coubera a Floriano, em relação aos jacobinos da República, dirigir o 'tenentismo' de 1930. Revelou Vargas nessa tarefa, um senso político insuperável. Trouxe à revolução em 30 as conotações sociais próprias ao tempo. O conteúdo trabalhista, mitigado a partir de 1935 por um corporativismo parafascista, mais do agrado da classe média a que conduziria a revolução de 30 ao seu desenlace político, O Estado Nôvo."

6 Trans. Ricardo W. de Aguiar and Eric C. Drysdale (Berkeley, 1963) , p. 173.

7 Rio de Janeiro, 1966.

8 *Ascensão a queda de Getúlio Vargas, O Maquiavélico* (Rio de Janeiro, 1966) .

9 Nelson Werneck Sodré, *História militar do Brasil* (Rio de Janciro, 1965) , p. 247. In an interesting observation on the 1930 revolution Werneck Sodré writes on p. 250: "A revolução de 1930 permitiu à burguesía ascensional, num primeiro lance, e com apoio do Tenentismo, apoderar-se do Estado, utilizando-o em seguida para realizar as alterções que a interessavam, vigiliante para não aprofundá-las. Na medida em que o Tenentismo representava o sentido de aprofundamento, foi alijado da composição, voltando-se a burguesía para o latifúndio e apoiando-se nêle para deter as novas fôrças que emergiam no cenário nacional, as fôrças populares, com o proletariado à frente. [Werneck Sodré quotes Martins de Almeida, *Brasil errado,* p. 124, as follows: "O recalcamento do Tenentismo . . . o levará talvez a acompanhar a movimento extremista das massas, a seguir, pela fôrça dos acontecimentos, o comunismo em marcha, se pretende

violentar as situações dominantes. Aí é que em tempos vindouros, outras revoluções virão."] É claro que nessa altura do desenvolvimento histórico, o Tenentismo estava liquidado."

10 Rio de Janeiro, 1963, p. 21. The author has no doubt in his mind concerning the revolution and writes: "O movimento revolucionário de 30 abre etapa qualitativamente distinta na história nacional. Apesar dos testemunhos de personalidades coevas daqueles acontecimentos, no sentido ne que os líderes da revolução ignoravam os objetivos que deviam atingir, juízo frequntemente repetido mesmo entre historiadores, a verdade é que os objetivos da revolução de 30, como movimento social, eram perfeitamente claros. Tratava-se de criar as condições para a rápida expansão do capitalismo no Brasil, o qual vinha sendo entravado, agora de modo intolerável, pelo completo domínio do apelho estatal exercido pelas oligarquías, voltadas para o exterior. E êste objetivo foi alcançado de maneira exemplar, não cabendo portanto a admoestação de que o movimento de 30 em nada, ou quase nada, alterou das condições vigorantes anteriormente. O sentido histórico daqueles acontecimentos não se resumia na mera substituição de quadros obsoletos ou na inovação moral das práticas eleitorais viciadas, as quais serviram de pretexto imediato para o movimento revolucionário. Êsse foi o verniz superficial do fenômeno de 30, mas apenas indica a tendencia subterrânea do processo histórico. É certo que se substituíram em parte os quadros dirigentes, mas fundamentalmente porque se alteraram as relações entre as classes que forneciam êsses quadros."

11 Octavio Ianni, *Estado e capitalismo* (Rio de Janeiro, 1965), pp. 134–35, and Leoncio Basbaum, in his *História sincera da República da 1889–1930* (2nd ed.; São Paulo, 1962), II, 431, writes: "Que houve pois realmente em 1930? A substituição de um setor dos classes dominantes por outro, sem que nada mais se alterasse no país. . . . A revolução não foi na realidade uma revolução, como não foi egualmente um movimento puramente militar e menos ainda uma guerra civil: talvez se pudesse classificar la como uma insurreicão, política-militar com apoio parcial do pôvo, embora possa continuar chamando-se a Revolução de 30, nome que, com as devidos ressalvas, não prejudica a ninguém."

12 João Neves da Fontoura, *Memórias: Borges de Medeiros e seu tempo* (Rio de Janeiro, 1958), I, 362.

13 Victor Nunes Leal, *Coronelismo, enxada e vôto* (Rio de Janeiro, 1948).

14 John W.F. Dulles, *Vargas of Brazil* (Austin, Texas, 1967), pp. 56–57.

15 Paulo Nogueira Filho, *O Partido Democrático e a Revolução de 1930* (2nd ed.; Rio de Janeiro, 1965), II.

16 Jordan M. Young, *The Brazilian Revolution of 1930 and The Aftermath* (New Brunswick, N.J., 1967), p. 85.

17 Benedicto Valladares, *Tempos idos e vivídos-memórias* (Rio de Janeiro, 1966). A very close look at politics in Minas Gerais in the Vargas period by one of his trusted lieutenants.

18 *Revista Brasileira de Estudos Políticos*, No. 21 (July, 1966). The issue was dedicated to national security in Brazil as defined by the Brazilian military. An incredibly presumptuous collection of articles by military men on various aspects of Brazilian problems.

COMMENTARY

Neill Macaulay
University of Florida, Gainesville

PROFESSOR Young makes some interesting points when he compares the 1930 revolution with the *golpes* of 1889, 1945, and 1964. The mechanics of the change, the compromises, and the public apathy were strikingly similar in these four cases. And each golpe set Brazil on a new course—at least in regard to form of government. The events of 1945 and 1964, however, were less sudden, more anticipated, and, perhaps, less consequential than those of 1889 and 1930.

The 1889 revolution, after seven years, gave birth to the *politica dos governadores*; the 1930 revolution, after seven years, produced the Estado Nôvo. The pattern of one post- golpe period fits the other. First, there was the delayed reaction to the *coup* by partisans of the old regime—supported by a few disgruntled revolutionists and some elements of the Brazilian armed forces. This reaction centered in Rio Grande do Sul and Santa Catarina in 1893 and in São Paulo in 1932. Then there were the esoteric revolts from Left and Right: Canudos and the *jacobino* conspiracy of 1896–1897, and the Communist and the Integralista revolts of 1935 and 1938. In 1897 and 1938 extremists attempted to kill the president, in last-ditch efforts to destroy systems that had already taken root. The Estado Nôvo had been proclaimed five months before the Integralista assault on the presidential palace. And, President Prudente de Morais had given form—if not name—to the *politica dos governadores* prior to the *jacobino* attempt on his life in 1897.

It was the Revolution of 1889 and the resultant *politica dos governadores*—not Vargas, as Professor Young states—that "broke the line of continuity of a functioning political party system." Prudente de Morais and his successor, Campos Sales, killed the Federal Republican Party.

Pinheiro Machado later revived the idea of a national political party, but his success was only temporary. The política dos governadores had already overwhelmed the great *Gaúcho* before an assassin's knife ended his life in 1915. Professor Herman James, writing in 1923, remarks on the "absence of any political parties in Brazil since the triumph of the Republican Party in 1889." [1]

James also notes the "preponderance of executive power" [2] in the Brazilian constitutional system in the 1920's. "A broken and spiritless Congress" was a legacy of the Old Republic. Vargas' Estado Nôvo, with its suppression of Congress and abolition of political parties, was the culmination of the dominant trends of the Old Republic. Dictator Getúlio Vargas was a natural successor to strong presidents like Artur Bernardes and Washington Luis.

But the Vargas era did, in other respects, represent a break with the past. Vargas based his regime not on the regional power centers of the Old Republic, but on a national bureaucracy—which he created—and on the national armed forces. The Brazilian army had been the only truly national institution during the Old Republic—and, hence, the presidents of the Old Republic, the powerful delegates of the state oligarchies, strove to curtail the power of the military. Vargas, however, as Professor Young points out, depended on the army. He pampered the military; he even gave it a foreign war to fight. And, of course, the heroes of Italy turned against Vargas in much the same way as the heroes of Paraguay turned against Dom Pedro—and with less delay.

The Vargas *régime* signified a return to the centralism of the empire, but without the Empire's pseudo-parliamentary system and national political parties. Getúlio Vargas brought into full bloom the nationalism that Dom Pedro had dreamed of. Many of the seeds of the nationalism of the Vargas era, however, had been sown during the Old Republic. The diplomatic triumphs of Rio Branco and Brazil's participation in major international conferences were sources of national pride for many upper-class Brazilians before the advent of Vargas. And the great advancements in internal communications after 1889 made it possible for Vargas to "sell" Brazilianism to his middle- and lower-class countrymen. During the Old Republic railroads, telegraph lines, and even motor roads pushed deep into the interior of Brazil, cutting through the old regional barriers. In 1923 Oliveira Vianna could foresee a new era of centralism ushered in by these improvements in communication.[3] The new era arrived in October, 1930.

In summary, I would agree with Professor Young that the events of October, 1930, were "not in conflict with the Brazilian past." But as for the developments of the succeeding fifteen Vargas years conflicting with "certain historical traditions," I would insist that the conflict was more apparent than real.

NOTES

1 Herman G. James, *The Constitutional System of Brazil* (Washington, 1923), p. 90.
2 *Ibid.*, p. 92.
3 Francisco José de Oliveira Vianna, *Evolução do póvo brasileiro* (2nd ed.; São Paulo, 1933), pp. 317–18.

CONFLICT AND CONTINUITY
IN BRAZILIAN HISTORY

Eulália Maria Lahmeyer Lôbo
Federal University of Rio de Janeiro, Brazil

ALTHOUGH the title of this paper and of the seminar emphasizes conflict by placing it first, I shall stress the element of continuity since this, in my opinion, seems to be the dominant feature of Brazilian history. This paper is divided into three parts. The first is an examination of the evolution of the social and economic foundations of Brazilian society. The second part is an analysis of developments in Brazil from 1929 to the present. It focuses on the potential sources of conflict which have arisen since that year. The third part is an examination of different prescriptions for future developments in Brazil.

SOCIAL AND ECONOMIC FOUNDATIONS

As a first approach to this broad and complex theme, I would like to stress the overwhelming importance of the pattern of land ownership to the continuity of Brazilian history. Land ownership influenced the economic and social structure of both the colony and the independent nation. Manuel Diegues Júnior points out that "among the institutions brought by the Portuguese in the process of settling Brazil since the sixteenth century none persisted less subject to change than land ownership. *Latifundia* established through the system of grants called *sesmarias* present nowadays features not so different from those of that early century of Brazilian colonial history." [1]

Latifundia had not been characteristic of the Portuguese mainland since the law of *sesmarias* of May 26, 1375, required the effective cultivation of the soil by the proprietors. Despite Crown policy, *latifundia* were introduced in the Portuguese Atlantic islands, in Brazil, in the

Zambesi Valley, and elsewhere. Several factors combined to promote the development of *latifundia* in Brazil, among which the scarcity of the Portuguese population should be mentioned. Rebelo da Silva estimated the population of the kingdom at 1,010,000 inhabitants in 1422, based on a ratio between total population and the known number of *besteiros* (able-bodied males).[2] The first census ordered by Dom João III (1527–1532) estimated a total of 278,000 households, the number of inhabitants being 1,100,000 or 1,390,000, depending upon the average size of a family (four or five) adopted. Not only was the population of the kingdom small, but it also remained stable from 1495 until 1527–1532 due to constant warfare, the recurrent plague (four times in the reign of Dom Manoel: 1502, 1506, 1513, and 1521), earthquakes (1512, 1531, and 1551), and the loss of population represented by the outflow of immigrants to America, Africa, and Asia not compensated for by the inflow of slaves.

The scarcity of population was such that the Portuguese employed mestizoes, mulattoes, and half-castes in the military forces, in public administration, in the clergy, in crews for ships, and so on. The lack of immigrants also favored miscegenation throughout the Portuguese empire. It was difficult to attract Catholic immigrants, and plans such as that of Duarte Salter Mendonça, in 1723–1726, to encourage large-scale immigration of Roman Catholic Irish families to Mozambique and Angola failed.[3]

Furthermore, the native population of Brazil was also scarce. According to estimates based on the level-of-subsistence criteria, the population of eastern Brazil on the eve of discovery amounted to 387,400 inhabitants, with a density of 0.3 persons per square mile; the population of the tropical forest amounted to 2,188,970, or 0.6 per square mile, except for the banks of the Amazon River and two strips along the coast where the density was 2 inhabitants per square mile.[4]

The large amount of land available also contributed to the implantation of *latifundia*, despite the efforts of the Portuguese Crown to avoid it. The royal decree of November 20, 1530, gave power to the Governor-General of Brazil, Martim Affonso de Souza, to give sesmarias to the settlers for one life-time, with the obligation that the grantee cultivate the soil within six years of the date of the grant and that he pay the tithe. The Crown's need to attract private capital to Brazil, however, made it prone to grant concessions. The 1530 decree was soon amended to provide for the granting of land with the right of inheritance, although the grantee was required to cultivate the land within two years.

The requirement to cultivate or forfeit the sesmaria was constantly re-peated in many laws because of lack of compliance. Laws requiring measurements of land grants were also frequently abused; this, of course, left the door open to possibilities of encroachments and undue expansion of private property. The size of Brazil and the relative auton-omy of the proprietary colonies prevented effective enforcement of the law of sesmarias such as had been possible in the Mother Country.

The size of the sesmarias varied considerably, but their area was usually between 10,000 and 13,000 hectares and the same owner could possess several sesmarias.[5] Large estates were not confined exclusively to the capitalistic or export sector of the economy (sugar cane and to-bacco); they were also found in the subsistence or domestic sector (cattle-raising). The very nature of the operation of sugar and tobacco plantations, based as they were on slave labor and large-scale production, as well as the extensive holdings required for cattle-raising, favored the formation of large estates in both sectors of the economy.

Another important element of continuity has been the pattern of induced growth based on the exportation of a few primary commodities. This point has, of course, been frequently emphasized, but a less obvious characteristic of colonial trade has been neglected, namely, its contin-uity. If Spanish and Portuguese Atlantic trade patterns in the seven-teenth century are compared, a marked difference between them can be observed. Whereas the Atlantic trade of Spain suffered a severe crisis in 1609 with the collapse of the Vera Cruz market, followed by a century-long downward trend, Portuguese Atlantic trade expanded, despite the loss of independence of the metropolis, the Dutch attacks and conquests in Brazil and Africa, and the British conquests in the Far East.[6]

In the Portuguese Atlantic trade in the sixteenth century, when Madeira Islands sugar production began to fall, Brazilian production increased steadily, especially from 1560 onward until 1670.[7] Between 1668 and 1688 the price of sugar in the Lisbon market declined 41 per-cent, that of tobacco 65 percent, and that of clover 72 percent. The sugar price drop was due partly to Dutch competition in the Caribbean, and the expansion in demand for slaves in that area caused their price to increase approximately 100 percent between 1640 and 1680. Further-more, other prices of Portuguese exports, such as olive oil, showed a marked decline. Exports of salt from Setubal also declined, thus reduc-ing the inflow of silver which Dutch and Spanish merchants paid for that commodity.

Portugal, thus, had a late commercial crisis; it also managed to overcome the crisis rapidly through a number of successful measures designed to achieve a prompt recovery in the balance of trade. Such measures included the substitution of nationally produced manufactures for imports, exploitation of other products (such as precious metals and stones in Brazil and wine in Portugal), restrictions on the importation of luxury goods for conspicuous consumption, and currency debasement (20 percent in 1688 and 10 percent in 1694) both to remedy the scarcity of silver and to curtail imports. From 1690 onward, a rise in the prices of wine, salt, and olive oil enabled both the volume and value of exports to recover; this took place mainly because of expansion in the production of wine destined for the British market where Portuguese wines enjoyed tariff preference over French wines.[8]

During most of the seventeenth century in Brazil there was an expansion of trade, an increase in population, and an incorporation of new lands into the market economy. These developments contrast with a decline in the rate of population growth and of trade, the failure to discover new accumulations of Indian treasure, and an insignificant incorporation of new lands in Spanish America in the seventeenth century.

The impact of the gold rush and the consequent development of cities, internal markets, and communications tend to make historians overlook the fact that the sugar planter, despite the 1670–1690 crisis, remained important throughout the eighteenth century. It must be remembered that the first half of the eighteenth century was a period of fluctuation in sugar prices but that they frequently reached the high levels of the seventeenth century. It is true that between 1762 and 1772 there was a drop of one-third in sugar prices in the Amsterdam market, and that they remained stable until 1776; but from 1777 to 1799 there was an increase of 252 percent, despite the accidental drop in 1783–1784.

It must also be taken into consideration that the profits of the sugar planters were very high in the peak period of the trade (the last quarter of the sixteenth century) and that even with the price fluctuations in the seventeenth and eighteenth centuries sugar was still a profitable business. Celso Furtado attempts a rough estimate of profits in the sixteenth century. He estimates that labor represented 20 percent of the fixed capital; payment for services (transportation, storage, and so on) 5 percent of the value of the product on the wharf; salaries at less than 2 percent; and cattle, wood, and so on, 3 percent. He concludes that the net income from sugar was approximately 60 percent of the total value of sugar exports and that 90 percent of the income generated by sugar was concentrated in the hands of the planters and proprietors of the sugar mills.[9] The planters and mill owners had free land and there was always the possibility of cushioning a commercial crisis by switching from the market economy to the subsistence economy.

Another indication of the continued importance of the sugar trade is the fact that the Bahia fleet, from 1739 to 1763, remained the largest in the Brazil trade. The annual average of merchant ships entering Portuguese ports during that period was 615, with an average of 21.6 from Bahia, 14 from Rio de Janeiro, and 17 from both Pernambuco and Paraíba. The majority of vessels from Macao, Gôa, and Coromandel stopped in Bahia for two or three months where they found a good market for textiles and porcelain from the Orient and ivory and slaves from Africa, and where they loaded cargoes of sugar, tobacco, and hides for Portugal. In this period, of a total of 43 vessels coming to Portugal from the Orient (35 merchantmen and 8 warships), 28 stopped in Bahia.[10]

In 1610, the Brazil fleet had 76 ships and carried 2,000 chests of sugar. In 1618 Mathias de Albuquerque estimated the average yearly traffic at 300 ships and from 70,000 to 80,000 chests of sugar. According to Father Antônio Vieira, 235 ships were used each year in the Brazil trade. After 1644, the Crown required vessels in the trans-Atlantic trade to be more than 200 tons, with the result that from 1680 to 1690 the Brazilian merchant fleet averaged from 70 to 90 ships per year. The Bahia fleets of 1725 and 1726 carried cargoes of 12,000 and 13,000 chests of sugar, respectively, which was considered a profitable trade by the viceroy. In 1748, the Bahia fleet carried 17,000 chests of sugar, while in 1749 the Rio fleet carried 3,000 chests and the Pernambuco and Paraíba fleet carried 13,000.

Sugar, thus, remained an important and profitable export commodity throughout the eighteenth century, even before the agricultural recovery in the latter part of the century. (This recovery was due in part to technical improvements which contributed to a lowering of production costs.) [11] Gold production began to decline significantly around 1770, but from 1774 to 1778 tobacco prices rose by 109 percent resulting in an 81 percent expansion in the volume of exports. Port wine prices rose 200 percent between 1773 and 1780 and the quantum of exports increased 51 percent. Finally, sugar prices increased 252 percent between 1777 and 1799, as mentioned above.

The importance of the northeast is also revealed by demographic data: "The census of the 1770's and early eighties reveal that 38.8 percent of the population lived in the Captaincies-General of Bahia and

Pernambuco, compared with 20.5 percent residing in Minas Gerais. On the other hand, about 14 per cent lived within the confines of the captaincy of Rio de Janeiro, and less than 16 per cent dwelt in the Captaincy-general of which it was the principal port." [12]

Between 1785 and 1807, Portuguese trade with India recovered, and Brazilian production of cotton, coffee, cocoa, rice, and spices expanded, with cotton becoming the main export commodity to Britain and France. European wars and crises in the British and French West Indies favored Brazilian export trade. In 1791 the price of cotton rose from 240 réis to 380 réis per pound due to the rapid expansion of British cotton manufactures. (In the period 1771–1774, British consumption of cotton was 4.76 million pounds and in 1791–1795 it was 26 million pounds.) Around 1786, the Portuguese balance of trade became favorable, owing mainly to the growth of Brazilian exports; this was maintained until 1807, except for the war years of 1797, 1798, and 1799. Industrial activity in Brazil was forbidden by the decree of January 5, 1785, and it became the main market for Portuguese manufactures. In 1796 Brazil consumed 6,106,000 cruzados worth of Portuguese manufactures and in 1801, 10,030,000.[13]

At the close of the colonial period, the planter-exporter was not only prosperous but also enjoyed a privileged position in society. He influenced the monetary policy of the Crown, fought against foreign capitalists, obtained flexibility in the fleet system (including the clearance from several Brazilian ports and unloading in various Portuguese ports), and maintained the freedom of intercolonial trade. The agents of the Portuguese merchants *(commissários volantes)* were suppressed at the time of the Marquês de Lavradio, thus leaving Brazilian trade in the hands of the planter-exporter. He controlled land, labor, and finance and represented the main element of continuity. It is true that gold mining gave rise to new urban centers, stimulated the internal markets, promoted the first forces of integration, stimulated the granting of small plots of land (called *datas*) and the freeing of Negro slaves, but it did not last long enough to change the fundamental colonial economic and social structure.

The first half of the nineteenth century was a period of potential disruption of the traditional society of the landed aristocracy. In 1808, Portuguese exports to Brazil dropped to one-sixth of the volume of 1807 and Brazilian imports of Portuguese manufactured goods fell to one-twenty-seventh of the previous level. Thus, the French invasion of Portugal severed the commercial links between the metropolis and its colony. Besides, the independence of Brazil coincided with the beginning of a long depression. Between 1821 and 1860, there was a consistently unfavorable balance of trade which was temporarily compensated for by foreign investment and gold outflow from Brazil and later Spanish silver coins obtained in the trade with Spanish America. The government was even forced to resort to debased copper currency, and finally to paper money. In 1808 one milréis had the value of seventy dinheiros and in 1831 of twenty dinheiros.[14] Right after independence, in 1825, the Brazilian debt to Britain amounted to three million pounds sterling.

There was a marked decline in coffee prices from 1822 to 1830, and in 1826 a decline of all prices of Brazilian exports which also continued until 1830. Britain had her own economic crisis from 1826 to 1829, as did the United States. The cycles in Brazil tended to last longer than those in Britain and the United States, countries with which its economy was most closely linked in the nineteenth century. Therefore, despite the recovery of prices in 1831–1832 in these two countries, Brazil had its worst depression year during the first half of the century in 1831. A mild recovery occurred between 1832 and 1836, but depression set in again in Britain and the United States from 1837 to 1842, and from 1837 to 1845 in Brazil.[15] The year 1849 was again a very bad one for Brazilian trade; in the period 1850–1853, prosperity returned in Britain and the United States, but for Brazil there was only a slow recovery of prices and an exceptional stability of the exchange rate. Thus, the period of independence, the reign of Dom Pedro I, and the Regency (until the coming to power of Pedro II) were characterized by a trend toward the disintegration of the country's market economy based on the export of a few staples.

Federalist, republican, separatist, and anarchial movements were frequent during this economically unstable period. Such movements included the 1817 revolution in Pernambuco, the 1824 Confederação do Equador, the 1825 rebellion in the Cisplatina, the 1831 soldiers' rebellion in Rio de Janeiro and the riots in Pará, Maranhão, and Paraíba; they also included the 1831–1836 Cabanagem in Pará, the 1838–1841 Balaiada in Maranhão (in which Negro slaves participated) , the 1835–1845 Farrapos War, and the 1848–1849 Praieira revolt in Pernambuco.[16] Simultaneously, the planters were fighting against British pressure to abolish the slave trade. Clear signs of the disruption of the *latifundia* appeared, such as tolerance of squatters who increased considerably in numbers during the first half of the century. Dom Pedro II, addressing the legislature on January 1, 1850, called attention to the need to re-organize and strengthen the military forces, to assure a supply of labor for agriculture, and to stabilize the currency. These measures would insure the maintenance of the old order.

Around 1850 the emergence of new, broader markets for coffee, such as the United States, revived the economy which had been traditionally based on exports of tropical commodities. Coffee exports, which started to expand in 1851, reached a level of 27,339 bags (of 60 kilos each) in 1860 and the balance of trade turned favorable in that year. Law No. 601 of September 18, 1850, denied squatters the right of becoming proprietors. The Law of January 30, 1854, required the measurement of private properties to confirm titles of ownership, established conditions for the sale of unused land, set forth the categories of land which should be retained as public lands, and, finally, gave jurisdiction to the common judges in suits involving undue appropriation of land. Thus, the trend toward disintegration of the latifundia was reversed and the export economy reinstated.

During the same period more capital became available for investment. British capital inflow, which had declined after 1827 on account of the incapacity of Latin American countries to pay the interest on their early loans (more than twenty-one million pounds sterling between 1822 and 1825), returned following the renewed prosperity. The era of railroad and public-service investments began in 1849. There was a boom in Latin American government bonds which amounted to 130 million pounds sterling on the London Stock Exchange between 1851 and 1880. Brazilian bonds represented 18.41 percent of that total.[17]

At the same time (1850) the abolition of the slave trade took place under British pressure, liberating Brazilian capital involved in this trade. Abolition of the slave trade at that time did not seriously harm the interests of the landed aristocracy because, on the one hand, the government was willing to finance immigration and, on the other, British capital installed (between 1875 and 1885) fifty manpower-saving sugar mills. Furthermore, the competition of Cuban sugar in world markets was causing difficulty for Brazilian sugar, and northeastern planters began to sell slaves to the South. In 1865, coffee exports were already exceeding sugar exports, and coffee plantations from the Fluminense plain, the Paraíba Valley, and the Coastal Range of mountains in the state of Rio de Janeiro tended to absorb slave labor. Around 1870, São Paulo coffee plantations were already relying partly on free labor and machinery.

In 1840, in a population of less than 5 million inhabitants, there were 2 million registered slaves; in 1871 the number of slaves barely reached 1,133,200; in 1887, 735,500; and in 1888, 600,000 or only 4 percent of the total population.[18] Thus, the increased demand for coffee safeguarded the old structure of land ownership and export-oriented economy despite internal dislocations following the shift of the centers of power from the Northeast to the South. The abolition of slavery, which was a potential element of conflict, did not disrupt the plantation system: the uncompetitive northeastern sugar production managed to survive since it had sufficient power to retain a quota of the internal market, to the detriment of the consumer.

In the Northeast, where unemployment prevailed and there was no access to ownership of land because of the latifundia system, the freed slaves remained as wage earners with practically no improvement in their standard of living. Moreover, cattle-raisers in the northeastern backlands resisted, successfully to a large extent, the migration of labor to the South. For them it was useful to have a supply of labor for temporary seasonal work which could live at subsistence levels on their lands for the remainder of the year. Celso Furtado notes, in this case, that in the government of Campos Sales (1898–1902) there was a project to finance the transfer of un- and under-employed northeastern laborers from Ceará to the South but that the project met with such strong opposition in the national legislature, where most representatives were landowners, that it was doomed.[19]

The theoretical possibility of the coffee plantations' recruiting field hands in depressed areas of the country is shown by the movement of 200,000 persons from the Northeast to the Amazon basin between 1900 and 1910. They were encouraged to move by the rubber boom, despite the fact that they had to pay their own travel expenses. Hence, when the stimulus for internal migration was sufficiently strong, it broke the resistance of the local landowners.

The southern landowners, however, found a solution to their labor problem in immigration financed by the taxpayer. It was easy for the new coffee plantations in São Paulo to attract immigrants, since conditions in Europe, especially Italy, were favorable to emigration. Furthermore, the government was willing to pay the cost of transportation and industry was too weak to compete with the planters for labor.

For all of these reasons, as well as others, the standard of living of the freed Negroes did not improve substantially in the depressed areas of the Northeast and in the state of Rio de Janeiro, nor did they benefit from the coffee boom in São Paulo. Consequently, neither the abolition of slavery nor the downfall of the Empire brought any important redistribution of wealth or power and therefore no conflict.

The immigrants might have been another element of change and potential conflict. They belonged to two categories: colonists and field hands for the coffee plantations. The former were an important force for change. They contributed to the emergence and the diffusion of small and medium-sized landholdings in the South of Brazil, but most of the immigrants were attracted to the São coffee plantations. Between 1881 and 1890, 530,906 immigrants came to Brazil, of whom 221,657 (41.75 percent) went to São Paulo. From 1894 to 1903 Brazil received 862,110 immigrants; 463,177 (55.73 percent) remained in São Paulo. From 1903 to 1913 out of a total of 1,006,612 immigrants, 559,437 (55.58 precent) were destined for São Paulo.[20] (In 1949, for the first time, there was a larger recruitment of immigrant labor by industry, 2,703, than by agriculture, 2,490, in São Paulo.)

In 1940 there were 1,283,833 immigrants in Brazil, but almost 60 percent were living in São Paulo and practically all of the remaining 40 percent in Rio de Janeiro, Rio Grande do Sul, Paraná, Minas Gerais, Mato Grosso, and Santa Catarina. The influence of the immigrants was thus reduced by the fact that they were dispersed in rural areas. In Argentina, by way of contrast, immigrants tended to settle in urban areas, mostly in Buenos Aires; they rapidly became influential in the political life of the country and came into conflict with rural interest groups.

An additional element of change and a potential source of conflict was the modest industrial growth which took place during the Empire and to which the immigrants contributed both as workers and as consumers. Rejection of treaties with Britain which maintained a low import duty on British manfactured goods, the liberation of capital with the abolition of the slave trade, foreign investment, and a favorable balance of trade due to increased coffee exports undeniably helped to produce the first steps toward the industrialization of the country.

Between 1880 and 1884, 150 industries were established in Brazil, with a capital of 58,368,338,000 réis, and between 1885 and 1889, 248 industries with a capital of 203,404,521,000 réis. At the close of the Empire there were 636 industries with a capital of 401,630,600,000 réis (1920 value), corresponding to 25 million pounds sterling. These industries employed 54,169 workers and production was valued at 507,-092,547,800 réis. Almost all of this investment was in light consumer goods industries and 60 percent was in textile manufacturing alone.[21] This modest industrial growth gave rise to a more diversified society and to the development of new classes, which could have brought conflict.

This modest industrial growth also led to the formation of a number of workers' mutual benefit societies between 1856 and 1884, as noted by Maurício Vinhas de Queiróz.[22] The typographers were in the vanguard of the movement. Several workers' papers were established, such as *O Jornal dos Tipógrafos* in Rio de Janeiro (1858), *O Trabalho* in São Paulo, the *Gutenberg* in Alagôas (1881), and *O Operário* in Pernambuco (1879). According to Vinhas de Queiróz, the first workers' strike was promoted by the typographers of the three main daily newspapers in the capital on January 9, 1858. During the strike they asked for salary increases and improvement in working conditions. The *Jornal dos Tipógrafos* accused the capitalists of exploiting men and called for a fight utilizing all available means to end oppression and exploitation. Several strikes followed this first one. The workers also participated in the campaign to abolish slavery.

Despite the improved economic conditions of the second half of the century, the landed aristocracy still remained the mainstay of society during the Empire, and they retained this position in the Old Republic. The Republic began at a time of worldwide depression which lasted from 1890 to 1897 in the United States, from 1890 to 1895 in Britain, and from 1890 to 1908 in Brazil, with only slight recoveries taking place in 1892–1893 and 1904. Under prevailing international conditions attempts to promote industry by inflation *(encilhamento)* were a complete failure. The power of the coffee planters during this period is revealed by the Taubaté agreement in 1906 in which the policy of price supports for coffee was adopted and its costs imposed upon the nation. The tacit political agreement of the Old Republic by which the federal government was held in turn by São Paulo and Minas Gerais is well known.

World War I brought a period of prosperity to Brazil, which lasted from 1915 to 1919, and a new impetus to industry because of the decline in foreign competition. The 1929 depression revealed dramatically the shortcomings of the Brazilian economy founded as it was on the export of coffee; it also produced a disillusionment with the tenets of the physiocrats' theory—faith in the free market and in spontaneous progress. It gave rise to nationalistic sentiments which attempted to develop industry and diversify the economy the objectives being to free the country from an overdependence on price fluctuations in foreign markets and to achieve a minimum of economic self-sufficiency. Laws were promulgated prohibiting foreign exploitation of sub-surface resources and power.

In a speech in 1931 Getúlio Vargas argued for the integral rationalization of the entire economic system. He pleaded for a strong central government capable of planning the needed measures for the country's economic recovery. On October 29, 1932, he stated his desire to convert labor into "an organic force of cooperation" with the state. Vargas was paving the way for state economic planning in Brazil. Such planning was becoming the "order of the day" in most countries through the works of Keynes, Dusenberry, Leontieff, and others. The drastic decline of world trade promoted the development of national production to replace imported manufactured goods.

Accumulation of coffee stocks in 1929, rapid depletion of Brazilian gold reserves, and lack of financing accelerated the decline of coffee prices from 22.5 cents per pound in September of 1929 to 8 cents in 1931. The lowering of prices resulted in an expansion of coffee exports by 25 percent between 1929 and 1931; this proved insufficient, however, to maintain exports and the Vargas government decided to stockpile surplus coffee already collected, bagged, and transported to the ports. According to Celso Furtado, this measure, designed to benefit coffee planters, was also highly beneficial to industry since it sustained the purchasing power of the internal market.[23] Industrial production grew by 50 percent between 1929 and 1937, giving full employment to industrial equipment installed during the 1915–1919 boom and not fully utilized during the 1920's.

In the late 1920's the Confederação Geral dos Trabalhadores do Brasil (Marxist) and the rival Confederação Nacional dos Trabalhadores (non-Marxist) were organized. The Socialist Party, organized in the 1920's, failed to gain leadership of the workers' movement. A labor party was founded in Pôrto Alegre in 1928, its purpose being to unify the central organization of the unions. It declined, however, with the growing paternalistic power of Vargas over the workers. Thus, 1929 marks the beginning of the accelerated transformation of Brazil's traditional society into an industrial society. It is to this transformation, with its associated problems and possibilities for conflict, which we must now turn our attention.

BRAZIL SINCE 1929

According to Gino Germani, to achieve this transformation it is indispensable to promote elective types of behavior at the expense of the prescriptive or traditional types of social action, to institutionalize change, and to substitute differentiated and specialized social institutions for undifferentiated ones.[24] This change involves the secularization of society and it is, of course, much slower and more difficult to change attitudes toward the church, the family, and the state than to change the economic structure. Naturally, secularization started much earlier, but from 1929 onward there was an acceleration of the process, even though acceleration did not take place at the same rate in all sectors of society.

Recent sociological, economic, and historical studies tend, in general, to identify the emerging classes or sectors (labor and the middle class) with the forces that promote change, and the landed aristocracy with the forces that resist change.[25] What seems to underlie recent analyses of Brazilian society is the classical model of development based upon the experiences of the pioneer industrial countries. In this model there was a displacement of the landowning class by the industrial class because the interests of the two are mutually exclusive. The "revolutionary way" was viewed as that best able to liquidate the internal contradictions.

Fernando Henrique Cardoso and Luciano Martins, among others, have tried to test the validity of this model for the interpretation of Brazil's recent economic and social evolution.[26] They have pointed to a number of significant differences between the classical model and Latin American developments. One such difference lies in the fact that in Latin America evolution has been induced to a large extent by events and pressures from outside a given society. Another difference noted by these authors is that the process of industrialization has not necessarily implied a conflict between industrialists and landlords. On the contrary, in Brazil there has been an association of industrialists and landlords.

It has also been asserted that the traditional planter-exporter became an industrialist when industrialization was stimulated by the slackening of demand for primary commodities, and the resulting deterioration of the terms of trade.[27] Luciano Martins, in a recent study, made a survey of 135 major coffee planters in 1913 and showed that only 11 were shareholders in joint stock companies, seven of which were industrial enterprises.[28] Luis Carlos Bresser Pereira and Manuel Diegues Júnior also point out that the majority of the industrialists were immigrants and did not belong to the old coffee-planters' families.[29]

Although it seems that the majority of the industrialists were not coffee planters, it is true that a substantial part of the national capital invested in industry came from agriculture. This transfer, however, did not imply a conflict. In the 1850's, for example, the slave trade was abolished because the planters lost interest in the trade and because the British applied pressure; the capital liberated by this move became available for industry. Wartime conditions in 1919–1920 also encouraged investment in industry. In the 1930's it was impossible to maintain the level of exports, and the government's policy of purchasing coffee surpluses to avert the bankruptcy of the planters was beneficial for the industrialists since it sustained the purchasing power of the internal market.

Agricultural exports are necessary for industry, since it is agriculture which provides the foreign exchange earnings needed for purchases of foreign equipment. Agricultural interests see in industrialists allies for their protective policies. Both planters and industrialists operate, to a large extent, under state protection, on a noncompetitive basis, with high costs of production and a wastage of productive factors. They cooperate in transferring to society the onus of the protective policies regarding exchange controls, customs duties, price supports, quotas for the internal market, monopolies, inflation, and so on. A conflict between planters and industrialists has thus not materialized because the latter have been too weak to promote the changes that a strong national bourgeoisie had achieved in the classical model.

Luciano Martins made a survey of managers in São Paulo and Rio de Janerio in 1914, 1938, and 1962.[30] He included in his concept of "manager" individuals who directed enterprises as well as major shareholders. He divided the managers into three categories: industrialists; industrialists with other activities; and nonindustrialists (managers or shareholders of agrarian enterprises, banks, agencies, distribution, import and export firms, real estate, services, and finance). For lack of sufficient data Martins limited his research to joint stock companies.

Martins found that only 8 percent of the managers in 1914 were still managers in 1938 and only 22 percent of the managers in 1938 remained in 1962. The changes within the managerial group (from one of the above-mentioned categories to another) were very extensive. Between 1914 and 1938, 40 percent changed positions and between 1938 and 1962,

21 percent likewise changed. There was also a general increase in the number of industrialists with other activities. In the first place, the number of managers who were only industrialists and who became nonindustrialists was 44 percent as compared with 21 percent for the second period. The number of nonindustrialists who became industrialists is also larger in the period 1914–1938 (38 percent) than in the period 1938–1962 (27 percent). In both periods one sector of the economy (services) attracted more industrialists who abandoned industry; it also supplied more managers who became industrialists. In both periods finance was an important area for receiving former industrialists and for furnishing new ones; in the second period (1938–1962) real estate had much the same function.

This study reveals the instability and heterogeneity of the group of industrial managers, conditions which reduce the potential political role this group might play in promoting change and creating conflict. Martins points out that the marked shift from one industrial activity to another can be attributed to a trend toward monopolistic or oligarchic enterprises which eliminates small and medium-sized units as well as to foreign enterprises which replace national ones. Finally, this shift could also be ascribed to the fact that the replacement of imported goods by nationally produced ones gives permanent advantage to a few industries which, because of their strategic position, deserve more protection from the state; they therefore offer a higher margin of profit and attract more entrepreneurs. It is obvious that the part played by foreign investment in national industry (we shall avoid a discussion of the merits or demerits of foreign investments) hinders the formation of well-defined political attitudes on the part of the large industrialists. Thus, an alliance between the industrialists and the planters contributed to the growing concentration of wealth which accompanied the process of industrialization in Brazil. The industrial bourgeoisie is far from being an active force working for socioeconomic democratization in Brazil.

The expanding bureaucracy, the other important segment of the middle class or middle sectors,[31] seems very unfit to initiate changes which would produce conflict situations. The bureaucrats have not played the role ascribed to them in works such as that by John J. Johnson.[32] When Vargas developed a strong federal government he expanded the bureaucracy through liberal use of patronage. Octávio Ianni and David H. P. Maybury-Lewis, for instance, view the relationship between the personal rule of Vargas and the bureaucracy as a transferral of rural *coronelismo* to an urban setting. This assertion could be extended, in my opinion, to the relationship between the government and labor.

Urban labor is also to a large extent devoid of class-consciousness because it did not grow spontaneously or organize itself politically. On the contrary, liberal laws were enacted as favors to labor, labor unions were organized under government control, and the Brazilian Labor Party (Partido Trabalhista Brasileiro—PTB) was created by the government. Furthermore, the federal government, to retain control of the labor movement, has always prevented the emergence of a spontaneous labor leadership; it has also pursued a policy of favoring a multiplicity of unions, thus avoiding the formation of a central labor organization.

Industry's inability to absorb the growing labor force also places organized labor in a bad bargaining position. Between 1938 and 1948 the average annual rate of growth of gross industrial production was 5.8 percent, whereas that of industrial employment was only 3.6 percent. Between 1950 and 1960 these rates of growth were 6.2 percent and 1.6 percent respectively.[33] In the classical phase of capitalistic development the disorganization of the pre-capitalistic forms of production was gradual and industry absorbed the liberated labor. In Latin America, disorganization of the pre-capitalistic forms of production is taking place in a much shorter period of time and industry cannot absorb the labor released by this rapid change.

It must also be remembered that Brazil is still a massively agricultural country, since 45 percent of the active population was engaged in agriculture as late as 1960. Thus, urban labor, already a weak minority, is further weakened politically by the difficulty of adapting their original rural way of life to the requirements of an industrial society. Recent sociological studies reveal that a large segment of urban labor preserves the traditional prescriptive kind of social action. Moreover, the big gap between the minimum wage-earners and the salary level of skilled labor is an element dividing labor. (The gap is 72 percent between minimum and maximum wage-earners in Brazil.[34])

Finally, powerful pressure groups like the Church and the military have been, to a large extent, operating to maintain the economic and social structure. The most liberal military interventions in Brazil have been restricted, to a large extent, to a progressive political attitude in favor of the republican form of government, or, later on, of the secret ballot. The army leaders in the early republic were influenced by Auguste Comte, whose political ideas were very conservative; this influence is reflected in the constitution of the state of Rio Grande do Sul, where the legislature's powers were restricted to voting the budget. It is true that the *tenentes* in the 1930's had very progressive ideas regarding labor rights, unions, and cooperatives, but under the impact of the recent inflation and labor strikes, the army, as well as the middle class, has tended to consider defense of the nation against communism as the primary goal. The navy, of course, has always been conservative.

The Church has tended to change recently, but the hierarchy remains very conservative. The Latin American Episcopal Council (Conselho Episcopal Latino-Americano—CELAM) recognizes that, while lay political, economic, and social leadership on the Continent is in the hands of the people between thirty and forty years of age, the leadership of the Church is dominated by people unable to act efficiently on account of old age.[35] The International Federation of Catholic Institutes of Social Research and Social and Religious Research (Federação Internacional de Institutos Católicos de Pesquisas Sociais e de Pesquisas Sociais e Religiosas) in Brazil, Argentina, Colombia, Chile, and Paraguay has been an active agency in changing the traditional outlook of the Church and has developed a very militant political action program in recent years. In Brazil, the Church has influenced labor unions and peasant leagues, has defended land reforms and the Brazilian Institute for Democratic Action (Instituto Brasileiro de Ação Democrática), and played an active role in the organization of the rural unions during the government of João Goulart.

Father Antônio Melo, vicar of Cabo, Father Crespo, vicar of Jaboatão (Pernambuco), and Father Caricio in Quipapá (Pernambuco) are representative figures of the new young clergy involved in the organization of the peasants. Antônio Callado refers to the fact that Francisco Julião ordered an effigy of the famous northeastern priest, Father Cicero, to be carried in a truck throughout the northeast. The effigy was to be placed on a farm in Bomjardim, in the backlands, in hopes that it would inherit the aura of the folk saint's prestige.[36] On the whole, however, the Church still continues to operate as a very conservative pressure group.

Agricultural workers, sharecroppers, land renters, and small landowners (called, for the sake of convenience, "peasants" in this paper) are a segment of society especially unfit for political participation. As a result, their potential as agents of social change and conflict are limited. Under present conditions the rural population is dispersed and isolated due to a lack of efficient means of communications and deprived, to a large extent, of education and ownership of land. In 1950, 74.9 percent of the families economically active in agriculture had no land or were owners of farms of less than 5 hectares. Illiteracy among Brazilians age fifteen and over was 26.6 percent in urban areas and 66.9 percent in rural areas in 1950.[37] Social mobility is restricted by three conditions: low agricultural productivity, inability of industry to absorb labor displaced from agricultural areas, and the high rate of population growth.

Pompeu Accioly Borges summarizes the main features of the Brazilian agrarian *milieu* as follows: *(a)* predominance of vast landed properties (more than half with an area in excess of 500 hectares) ; *(b)* increasing concentration of ownership of rural properties (8 percent of the farmers own 75 percent of the total area under cultivation) ; *(c)* large proportion of agricultural workers without land (approximately ten million in a total population of twelve million agricultural workers) ; *(d)* small percentage of land under cultivation (an average of 10 percent) ; *(e)* primitive agricultural techniques (such as burning to clear forest lands for cultivation and rudimentary crop rotation) ; *(f)* incipient use of mechanization, fertilizers, or techniques to combat plagues; *(g)* semi-feudal labor relations (such as sharecropping and free labor) , and low per capita income (around 100 dollars per year) ; *(h)* lack of security for agriculturalists; and *(i)* lack of incentives for new investments by landowners, sharecroppers, or renters.[38]

According to the last census (1960) , 63 percent of the total population is dependent upon agriculture. Each person engaged in agriculture depends on a mere 0.5 hectares for support. Illiteracy in rural areas is 66 percent. Only 1 percent of the houses in rural areas have running water, and only 4 percent have electricity.[39]

It was only in 1943 that rural workers benefited from a minimum wage law and only in 1963 that special legislation for rural workers was enacted. This legislation excluded sharecroppers (who represented 14.8 percent of the agricultural labor force in 1950) , minifundia owners, agricultural workers without written contracts, and agricultural workers hired for specific tasks. The 1963 law required professional cards for agricultural workers, a maximum of eight hours' work per day, a minimum wage, and paid vacations. It also stipulated that employers build and maintain a school when employing fifty or more heads of families, that they grant tenure with ten years' work, and that they recognize the right of collective bargaining. The law further provided for arbitration of disputes prior to an appeal to Labor Justice, and for the formation of a social assistance fund for rural workers financed by a 1 percent sales tax on agricultural products.

The Inter-American Committee for Agricultural Development, with the cooperation of a number of international agencies, surveyed land tenure conditions and agricultural developments in Brazil.[40] The committee's report points out that agriculture's contribution to total national wealth fell from 29 percent in 1950 to about 25 percent in 1960, while industry's share rose from 24 percent to 31 percent during the same period. Total agricultural production during the period increased by 52 percent while industrial production grew by 139 percent.

Coffee yields per hectare, despite the credit facilities and other forms of protection which coffee production enjoyed, were only 40 percent of those in Costa Rica.[41] Increases in agricultural production between 1950 and 1960 were due more to an expansion of the area under cultivation than to a substantial increase in productivity. There have been repeated assertions that a spontaneous trend toward the breaking up of *latifundia* existed; the report concludes that there is no such trend. Moreover, the report stresses that agricultural employers frequently deny the right of sharecroppers, renters, and agricultural workers to cultivate cash crops, and when they allow cultivation, the product has to be sold to the owner of the farm. For agricultural investments the peasants have to rely on credit extended by the farm owner at high rates of interest. Farm owners, or their managers, tend to forbid field hands' making improvements in their houses so as to prevent such improvements from becoming the bases for possible claims of ownership of the land.

The 1963 law allows the employer to deduct up to 20 percent of the worker's salary for rent and up to 25 percent for food. The report points out that the rent for houses offered to peasants by landlords could not have a higher value than 5 percent to 10 percent of their daily wage, based upon the number of days actually worked. Frequently, however, the 20 percent is calculated on the basis of all the days in the month. Furthermore, the archaic *cambão* system still survives. The peasant, besides paying a yearly tax to enjoy the right of using land (which varied from 10,000 to 40,000 cruzeiros in 1961), has to give ninety-nine days of work to the landowner, ninety of which are paid for at a lower level of remuneration than regular work days, and nine of which are free (cambão). Another abuse involves the deduction of rent for the lot upon which the peasant's house is located. Finally, other means of bypassing the 1963 law used by landlords include such devices as oral contracts, or hiring workers for specific tasks at less than the minimum wage.

The recent trend toward absenteeism among landlords has had an unfortunate result for the peasants, since the traditional patronage of the landlord is lost and no other modern form of protection for agricultural workers has arisen to take its place. The managers who have replaced the farm owners do not have the patron-client relationship which previously existed with the workers. The criteria in selecting the managers is their loyalty to the landowner; they are the landowners' men and are familiar with the traditional methods of cultivation. The managers and owners administer the farms in an autocratic manner and frequently have a private police force.[42] Finally, minifundia owners suffer from encroachments by their neighbors because of the lack of appropriate registration of precise land boundaries. Under such circumstances it is obvious that the organizing of peasant leagues first and unions later was fraught with difficulties.

The first Peasant League (Liga Camponêsa) was founded in 1955 and was intended to serve as a cooperative for mutual assistance, mainly burial. Francisco Julião, a northeastern lawyer, was asked by the cooperative to give legal advice on its organization, since unions were forbidden at that time. Julião suggested that they call the cooperative a "league." The Leagues soon multiplied, but their aims were mainly the suppression of the cambão, elimination of the tax on land renting *(fôro),* and salary increases. In 1961 the military estimated the membership of the Pernambuco League at 30,000–35,000 people; the estimate for the Northeast as a whole was 80,000. [43] Julião preached distribution of land to the peasants as the indispensable first step in coping with Brazil's rural problems, but he never developed a general plan, nor did he manage to establish a central organization for the Leagues.[44] It appears that the Arraes government was interested in using Julião as its instrument, and when he could not be controlled it tried to undermine his popular prestige. Therefore, the communists, Julião, and Catholic forces all tried to influence the Leagues.

The federal government authorized the organization of rural unions in 1961, which reduced the appeal of the Peasant Leagues. Furthermore, by this time the government's wage policy was to grant increases higher than the rate of inflation; these increases were also larger for the lower income brackets than for the higher ones. This policy, of course, diminished the possibilities of a rural revolutionary movement in the northeast. In 1963 a schedule of payments for field tasks was promulgated by the government. Between February and December of that year the unions obtained an increase in the minimum wage from 6,000 cruzeiros to 30,000 cruzeiros per month. On March 2, 1963, the Statute of the Rural Worker (Estatuto do Trabalhador Rural) became law, and discussions of land reform were the order of the day. Because of the changes contained in these measures immediate possibilities of conflict emerged.

Turning to the relative position of all salary-earners, we note that between 1955 and 1960 their share in the national income increased. Salaries increased 624 percent during this period, while national income increased by only 560 percent. Despite this increase, in 1959 salary-earners' share of national income amounted to only 47.7 percent.[45] Economic stagnation and the 80 percent rate of inflation in 1963, followed by deflationary policies since 1964, brought about a deterioration in the wage-earner's standard of living.

The new government presented an economic plan which had as its goals both deflation and development. The Economic Action Program (Programa de Ação Econômica) of the Castelo Branco government established goals of a 10 percent increase in the "means of payment" at the end of the period 1964–1965 and a return to a 6 percent rate of annual economic growth.[46] Despite the assertion of the desire to attain the two goals simultaneously, government action was restricted to deflationary measures. Even with the priority given to deflation in the government's policy, in the first three months of 1965 prices in general rose 22 percent and the cost of living 19 percent; the official forecasts for the entire year had been approximately 25 percent. The renewal of development was not realized in 1964 or 1965.

The government tried to stimulate forced savings by increasing taxes and reducing government expenditures. The objective was to eliminate the deficit in the National Treasury. To curtail consumption, which had been diagnosed in the program as excessive, salary increases were reduced and credit to private enterprise was limited. The result of these policies, which aimed at increasing savings, was to deplete individual savings in the middle and lower classes and in private enterprises and to transfer these savings to the government.

Private initiative was weakened as a result of these policies. The combined effect of the increase of taxes, revaluation of assets for taxation purposes, curtailment of credits, and reduction of purchasing power in the domestic market has been the bankruptcy of industries and the expansion of un- and sub-employment with all its consequences.[47] The policy of limiting salary increases and reducing purchasing power has also promoted a "brain drain," a reduction of efficiency, and conditions of extreme poverty.

The government expected to achieve the above-mentioned objectives with less hardship because it counted on substantial foreign investment. The program stated that around 20 percent of total capital formation would come from foreign sources. This would amount to 4 percent of gross national product, since the capital formation was expected to be raised to 20 percent of the GNP. Therefore, the increase of capital formation from 16 percent to 20 percent was expected to be covered by foreign capital. This 4 percent was equivalent to $600 to $800 million, depending on the criterion adopted for the estimation of the GNP. In no period in the recent past, however, has the liquid inflow of autonomous capital into Brazil surpassed $190 million per year, and even if added to compensatory financing, it never exceeded $350 million per year. In the government programs for 1965 and 1966 the estimated amounts of foreign capital inflow were $365 and $387 million, respectively. It was thus unrealistic to have set goals of $600 million in the original plan. Many other criticisms could be leveled against overdependence on foreign investment. Since foreign capital inflow was much less than expected, the deflationary goals were not fulfilled and the major share of sacrifice fell upon the wage-earners.[48]

The National Monetary Council (Conselho Monetário Nacional) officially set the rate of so-called residual inflation at 10 percent in 1966 for purposes of wage adjustments. This measure assumed that inflation in 1965 had been 25 percent as predicted. Nevertheless, in 1963 the price rise was from 81 percent to 83 percent. In the first three months of 1964, until the takeover by the new government, prices rose by 25 percent. In the first three months of 1966 price increases amounted to 14 percent, and approximately 40 percent for the entire year. Price increases in 1967 are estimated at 30 percent.

The government program had foreseen an expansion in the "means of payment" by 70 percent in 1964 and 30 percent in 1965, but the real figures were 86 percent and 75 percent, respectively. There is no overall study of the impact of this policy on salaries, only a few results for Guanabara state. In this area, the minimum wage earners' loss from 1964 to 1965 was 8 percent in their real salaries. The loss by Bank of

Brazil employees was 15 percent; textile workers' loss, 7 percent; met-
alurgical workers', 4 percent; and federal employees' (level nine), 13
percent. Only commercial employees gained, by 3 percent.

If one admits a 3 percent growth in national production in 1965,
which means an approximately stable per capita income because of the
rate of population growth, it is obvious that the salary-earner's participation in the national product has declined.[49] The Costa e Silva government announced in October of 1967, through its minister of labor,
that the same salary policy would be continued. For this purpose the
residual inflation for the present year is estimated at 10 percent. Employers have been forbidden to grant salary increases above the level
established by the government, levels which are based on this theoretical
rate of inflation.

Another phase of the government's plan for economic recovery which
has not materialized is economic recovery based on an expansion of exports. The emphasis on exports rather than on industrialization has
proven disappointing. The trade balance was favorable, basically, because of a drastic decline in imports which reflect the depressed economic condition of the country.[50] Furthermore, exchange-rate stability could
not be maintained, and there is now a growing black market for dollars.

Government control of unions and the closing down of political parties broke the natural channels of communication with the masses. Of
course, the abolition of the traditional party system is not too much to
be regretted since the two major parties, both conservative, represented
51 percent of the vote, and the Labor Party was very unrepresentative.[51]
Conditions remain very unfavorable for a reorganization of the party
system, and the legislature has gradually lost its independence due to
the cancellation of the civil rights of many leading politicians. It is very
difficult to assess the part played by university students in today's political scene. They have been unable to establish a link with labor as
many thought they would,[52] and their influence has thus far been restricted protest demonstrations.

PRESCRIPTIONS FOR THE FUTURE

What lies ahead for Brazil? Three main currents of economic thinking prevail in the country. The so-called monetarist current is represented by Roberto Campos, who was responsible for the Economic Action Program of the Castelo Branco government; the program has already been briefly analyzed.

A second position, more pragmatic in nature, is that of Antônio Dias Leite. In his opinion increased exports, one of the means presented in the government's program for achieving economic recovery, could not play a very significant part in Brazilian development. He pointed out that in seventy countries of comparable size, income, and population the average value of foreign commerce is 35 percent of national production. This relationship increases to 50 percent for colonial or semicolonial countries of equivalent dimensions and income. In general terms, there is a significant relationship between foreign trade and the size and population of a nation. For all large countries (excluding China for lack of data), both developed and underdeveloped, the relationship between foreign trade and national production is low. For the United States it is 8 percent, for Russia 4 percent, for India 11 percent, and for Brazil 12 percent.

Two new factors tend to depress this relationship even further in the case of Brazil: the occupation of new lands and the rapid increase of population. Furthermore, the products that Brazil could export in the near future in increasing volume would be iron, cotton, sugar, wood, and meat. Each of these products is subject to great fluctuations in price and demand in international markets commanded, as they are, by the developed consumer countries. Almost all are exported by underdeveloped countries with the same component of cheap labor. Basically, it seems that Campos was thinking in terms of expanding iron ore exports. Even if such an expansion would have brought about temporary recovery of the rate of economic growth, the nature of the external bottlenecks for Brazilian development would remain the same; coffee would simply have been replaced by iron ore. Obviously, Brazil lacks the competitive conditions which would increase exports of manufactured goods; these contain a high percentage of technological ingredients which must be imported.

Dias Leite thus thinks that emphasis should again be placed on replacement of imports by national production and that priority should be given to industries that require less technology and for which available supplies of raw materials exist. Such industries are nonferrous metals, fertilizers, wood products, and paper. In general, the policy of import substitution should be adopted, but he insists that in each case a careful study should be made of the costs of national production as compared with the costs of importing the same product. Dias Leite believes that Brazil's large area and growing population afford opportunities for expansion of industry to supply the domestic market.

Massive importation of foreign capital, the other tenet of Campos' plan, is considered by Dias Leite not only to be unrealistic, as facts have proven it to be, but undesirable. In his opinion, power, petroleum, and steel constitute the "nucleus of expansion" and foreign investment in these areas would be undesirable. These industries, he believes, should be government enterprises; they should not be developed to produce profit but rather because they are so vital for the country's economy that they represent "centers of decision." He also points out that in the five years preceding 1965 increases of capital in all Brazilian privately owned and joint stock enterprises was on the order of 400 billion cruzeiros per year (1964 purchasing power), while increased capital needs per year of the industries constituting the "nucleus of expansion" was on the order of 1,000 billion cruzeiros.

Development should have priority over deflation, in the opinion of Dias Leite. The urgent need to increase productivity and efficiency implies, in his eyes, the maintenance of a certain level of inflation to insure needed investments, especially in government-owned transport enterprises. Although he recognizes the need for increased saving and investment, Dias Leite believes that the increased savings should be obtained from increases in production. The restriction of purchasing power in the Economic Action Program of the Castelo Branco government, as well as its curtailment of industrial credits, were used to obtain savings at a time of economic stagnation.[53]

A third position is the so-called structuralist school. Celso Furtado, for example, believes that around 1955 Brazil lost the possibility of reaching the stage of self-sustaining economic growth by an evolutionary process based on import substitution. This possibility was lost because of the rapid deterioration in the terms of trade as well as increasing difficulties in replacing current imports with national products. Furtado identifies the present-day Brazilian situation as "pre-revolutionary," and he thinks that the recovery of a satisfactory rate of economic growth will depend on structural changes within Brazil.[54]

Caio Prado Júnior also seems to envisage Brazilian development within the framework of structual changes. In his program for the Brazilian revolution he condemns the association of "progressive groups" with the national bourgeoisie and the emphasis given to land reform by the Brazilian Communist Party (Partido Communista Brasileiro—PCB). In his opinion, agricultural workers do not aspire to land ownership but rather to an improvement in their standard of living. The appeal to the agricultural workers should thus be based on union organization, labor rights, and so on. Prado also denies the progressive character of the Brazilian bourgeoisie and he advocates an alliance of agricultural and urban workers to carry out needed reforms.[55]

Raúl Prebisch's general thesis concerning Latin America holds that

the ills besetting the Latin American economy are not determined by circumstantial or transient factors. They are an expression of the critical state of affairs in our time and of the inability of the economic system— owing to structural defects that it has been beyond our ability or power to remedy—to achieve and maintain a rate of development consonant with the growth of population and with demands for a speedy improvement in the standard of living.[56]

He also stresses that the "rapid penetration of technique demands and carries with it radical changes—both in the pattern of production and in the structure of the economy—which can not be brought about without a basic reform of the social structure." Prebisch considers the elements representing obstacles to economic and social development as lack of social mobility and privileged positions in the distribution of income and wealth. Privilege in the distribution of wealth is reflected not in a rapid rate of capital formation, but rather in extravagant consumption patterns. These patterns of consumption in the upper strata of society contrast markedly with the unsatisfactory living conditions of the broad masses. Prebisch and the Economic Commission for Latin America had first envisioned solutions to Latin America's problems in a system of price stabilization for the area's major export commodities. Later they attached considerable importance to an area-wide free trade zone. They now appear to focus their attention on capital formation by means of income redistribution.

There is, then, an increasing trend in economic thinking, at least on the theoretical level, toward solutions to current problems that involve conflict, since these solutions call for structural changes in Brazilian society.

NOTES

1 *População e propriedade de terra no Brasil* (Washington, 1959) , p. 7.
2 In *História de Portugal,* ed. Damião Peres and Eleuterio Cerdeira (Barcelos, 1929) , II, 415.
3 Charles Ralph Boxer, *Race Relations in the Portuguese Colonial Empire, 1415– 1825* (Oxford, 1963) , pp. 50–51.

4 Julian Steward and Louis C. Faron, *Native Peoples of South America* (New York, 1959).

5 Diegues Júnior, *População e propriedade*, p. 16; Felisbelo Freire, *História territorial do Brasil* (Rio de Janeiro, 1906).

6 Pierre Chaunu, *Séville et l'Atlantique* (Paris, 1959), Tomo VI, I, p. 344 and Tomo VIII, 2, 1, pp. 50–52.

7 Frédéric Mauro, *Le Portugal et l'Atlantique au XVIIème siècle, 1570–1670* (Paris, 1960), pp. 236ff. From 1560 to 1570, the production of sugar reached 180,000 arrôbas; in 1580, 350,000; in 1582, 500,000; in 1627–1628, 900,000; in 1630, 1,300,-000 or 1,500,000; in 1641, 1,800,000; in 1643, 1,000,000 to 1,200,000; in 1650, 2,100,000; and in 1670, 2,000,000.

8 Victorino Magalhães Godinho, *Prix et monnaies au Portugal* (Paris, 1955), pp. 245ff.

9 Celso Furtado, *The Economic Growth of Brazil: A Survey from Colonial to Modern Times*, trans. Ricardo W. de Aguiar and Eric Charles Drysdale (Berkeley, 1963; first paper-bound edition, 1965), pp. 47–48.

10 Eulália Maria Lahmeyer Lôbo, "As frotas do Brasil," *Jahrbuch fur Geschichte von Staat, Wirtschaft und Gesellschaft Latin Americas* (Cologne), IV, (1967), 465–88.

11 Charles Ralph Boxer, *Salvador de Sá and the Struggle for Brazil and Angola, 1602–1686* (London, 1952) and *The Golden Age of Brazil, 1695–1750* (Los Angeles, 1962).

12 Dauril Alden, "The Population of Brazil in the Late Eighteenth Century; A Preliminary Survey," *Hispanic American Historical Review*, XLIII (1963), 192–93.

13 Portugal, Arquivo Nacional da Tôrre do Tombo, Codice 126, Carderneta 467 do Inventário do Livros de Junta de Comércio, No. 26. "Livros da Balança Geral do Comércio."

14 Caio Prado Júnior, *História econômica do Brasil* (4th ed.; São Paulo, 1956), p. 137.

15 Pompeu Accioly Borges, "A conjuntura no Brasil desde 1822," *Conjuntura Econômica*, II, No. 4 (April, 1948), 19–27, and "Os Ciclos na Economia Brasileira," *Conjuntura Econômica*, II, No. 5 (May, 1948), 22–31.

16 Caio Prado Júnior, *Evolução política do Brasil e outros estudos* (São Paulo, 1953).

17 United Nations, Economic Committee for Latin America, *External Financing in Latin America* (E/CN.12/369/Rev. 1) (1957).

18 Nelson Werneck Sodré, *Panorama do Segundo Império* (São Paulo, 1939), pp. 81ff.

19 *The Economic Growth of Brazil*, p. 133, n. 6.

20 Manuel Diegues Júnior, *Imigração, urbanização, industrialização* (Rio de Janeiro, 1964), p. 53.

21 Roberto C. Simonsen, *A Evolução industrial do Brasil* (São Paulo, 1939), p. 24.

22 "Modernização no Brasil," *Revista de Ciências Sociais* (Universidade Federal do Rio de Janeiro), III, No. 1 (1966); Vinhas de Queiroz, "As primeiras lutas operárias no Brasil," *Revista do Pôvo* (Rio de Janeiro), II, No. 2 (1946).

23 *The Economic Growth of Brazil*, pp. 203–213.

24 *Política y sociedad en una época de transición: de la sociedad tradicional a la sociedad de masas* (Buenos Aires, 1965).

25 It is impossible to present here a complete bibliography on the subject. A few outstanding examples are: Luis Aguiar da Costa Pinto, *Sociologia e desenvolvimento* (Rio de Janeiro, 1963); Hélio Jaguaribe, *Desenvolvimento econômico e desenvolvimento político* (Rio de Janeiro, 1962); Celso Furtado, *Dialéctica do*

desenvolvimento (Rio de Janeiro, 1964) ; Centro Latino Americano de Pesquisas em Ciências Sociais, *Resistência à mudança* (Rio de Janeiro, 1959) ; and John J. Johnson, *Political Change in Latin America: Emergence of the Middle Sectors* (Stanford, Cal., 1958) .

26   Henrique Cardoso, *Empresariado industrial e desenvolvimento econômico* (São Paulo, 1964) ; Henrique Cardoso, "El proceso de desarrollo en América Latina," (Santiago de Chile, 1965) , mimeographed) ; Luciano Martins, "Formação do empresariado industrial no Brasil," *Revista do Instituto de Ciências Sociais* (Universidade Federal do Rio de Janeiro) , III, No. 1 (1966) , 1–139.

27   Nelson Werneck Sodré, *História da Burguesia Brasileira* (Rio de Janeiro, 1964) , p. 271.

28   "Formação do empresariado industrial no Brasil," p. 130.

29   Luis Carlos Bresser Pereira, "Origens sociais e etnicas do paulista," *Revista de Administração de Emprêsas,* II (June, 1964) , 83.

30   "Formação do empresariado," pp. 104–18.

31   Lack of space makes it impossible to analyze the concepts of class and sectors. The two words are used here to refer basically to the small industrialists, merchants, and bureaucracy within certain brackets of income and salary level.

32   *Political Change in Latin America.*

33   Raul Prebisch, *Toward a Dynamic Development Policy for Latin America* (E/CN.12/680/Rev. 1) (New York, 1963) .

34   Centro Latino Americano de Pesquisas em Ciências Sociais, *Situação social da América Latina* (Rio de Janeiro, 1965) . Hereinafter cited as *Situação social.*

35   Address of Father José Marins, meeting of CEMLA in Mar del Plata, Argentina, Oct., 1966, *Jornal do Brasil,* Oct. 16, 1966.

36   Antônio Callado, *Tempo de Arrais, padres e communistas* (Rio de Janeiro, 1964) , p. 64.

37   Solón Barraclough, *Estructura agraria y educación en América Latina* (UNESCO/ED/CEDES/30, ST/ECLA/Conf. 10/L.30; PAU/SEC/30), p. 1.

38   Pompeu Accioly Borges, "Brasil," in *Reformas agrárias en América Latina: processo y perspectivas,* ed. Oscar Delgado (Mexico, 1965) , pp. 713–14.

39   United Nations, *Statistical Yearbook: 1961.*

40   Inter-American Committee for Agricultural Development, "Land Tenure Conditions and Agricultural Development in Brazil: A Report" (Rio de Janeiro, mimeographed) . Hereinafter cited as "Land Tenure Conditions."

41   *Ibid.,* pp. 26–29.

42   *Ibid.,* p. 257. In Mediga the rate of interest was between 120 and 160 percent.

43   "As sementes da subversão — Nordêste," *O Cruzeiro,* Nov. 11, 1961, p. 8.

44   "Nordêste, as soluções da estupidêz," *O Cruzeiro,* Nov. 25, 1961.

45   *Situação social.*

46   The best analysis of Castelo Branco's economic policy can be found in Antônio Dias Leite, *Caminhos do desenvolvimento econômico, contribuição para um projecto Brasileiro* (Rio de Janeiro, 1966) . All of the data used in the following pages concerning developments since 1964 are taken from this source.

47   The government's ordinary income is derived from sales and income taxes, stamps, import duties, and other minor taxes. The percentage of ordinary revenues to GNP was as follows: 1963, 7.7 percent; 1964, 10.1 percent; 1965, 10.8 percent. Dias Leite, *Caminhos do desenvolvimento,* p. 217. Income tax revenues in 1965 increased (in real terms) by 40 percent over 1964.

48   Liquid capital inflow (in millions of dollars) was as follows: 1963: 195; 1964: 173; 1965: 87. The margin between plan and reality was thus 300 percent. *Ibid.,* p. 222.

49   The estimated growth in national production for 1965 was 3 percent. This

estimate excluded coffee production, which is extremely variable but which was very high in 1965. Sales potential was limited, however. Considering the growth of population, the per capita income remained stable in 1963, 1964, and 1965. For further details, consult *ibid.*, pp. 205–207.

50   Exports in 1965 reached $1,560 million. The increase in comparison with 1964 was $130 million, $41 million more than foreseen in the government plan. Imports amounted to only $970 million in 1965, that is, $447 million less than foreseen in the government plan. *Ibid.*, p. 220.

51   The Partido Social Democrático in the federal elections of 1958 obtained 3,593,000 votes (31.7 percent of the total), the União Democrática Nacional, 2,259,000 votes (19.9 percent), and the Partido Trabalhista Brasileiro, 2,238,000 votes (19.6 percent).

52   Jacques Lambert, *Amérique Latine: structures sociales et institutions politiques* (Paris, 1963), pp. 263–66.

53   Dias Leite, *Caminhos de desenvolvimento*, pp. 178–80.

54   *Dialéctica do desenvolvimento*, pp. 120–36.

55   Caio Prado Júnior, *A revolução Brasileira* (2nd ed., São Paulo, 1966), *passim*.

56   *Toward a Dynamic Development Policy for Latin America*, pp. 3–4.

IN MEMORIAM

Artur Hehl Neiva (1909–1967)

ARTUR HEHL NEIVA, Executive Secretary of the United States Educational Commission in Brazil (Fulbright Commission) since 1963, died on October 9, 1967. Born in Rio de Janeiro on June 9, 1909, he received his primary and secondary education in Rio and São Paulo. Although he achieved scholarly eminence in the social sciences, his formal training in higher education, like the vast majority of his contemporaries, was received in other fields. He was educated in engineering at the Escola Politécnica in São Paulo and the Faculdade Nacional de Engenharía in Rio de Janeiro, and in law at the Faculdade de Direito in Niterói. In 1939 he was married to Dona Beatriz Vaccani, who survives him.

As a young man, he entered government service and held increasingly important positions from 1930 until his retirement from the service in 1963. Most of the government positions which he held were in the field of immigration, colonization, and naturalization; the practical experience and scientific knowledge which he acquired in this service led him quite naturally into the field of demography, in which he became a leading authority in the later years of his life. Among the positions which he held in government service were: member of the Commission for the Reform of Immigration Laws (as early as 1934) ; member of the Council on Immigration and Colonization (from 1939 to 1947, serving as first Vice President and President in 1946–1947) ; head of the Brazilian Delegation for the Selection of European Displaced Persons (also 1946–1947) ; and Special Advisor on Latin America to the Director on the Intergovernmental Committee for European Migration (from 1952 to 1956) . In the 1950's he became Professor of Demography and of the Social Sciences of the Pontifical Catholic University of Rio de Janeiro.

At the same institution he later (1959) became the Assistant Dean of the School of Sociology and Political Science.

Artur Hehl Neiva was a dedicated scholar and constantly carried on research and writing during his entire adult life; it was most characteristic of his intelligence and discrimination that he was largely self-taught in those diciplines such as sociology and demography in which he came to be one of the outstanding talents in the international community of scholars. In the course of his career he contributed some eighty articles to professional journals; he also wrote widely on a variety of subjects other than professional ones, and a complete bibliography of these and the professional writings could run to hundreds of items. Among the most important of his professional writings was a series of nineteen articles published under the title of "Evolução da política imigratória do Brasil," in *Cultura Política* (1941–1942) ; "Estudo sôbre a imigração semita no Brasil," *Revista de Imigração,* II (June, 1944) ; "O problema imigratório Brasileiro," *ibid.,* III (September, 1945) ; "Aspectos geográficos da imigração e colonização do Brasil," *Revista Brasileira de Geografía,* XI (April–June, 1947) ; "Povoamento do Brasil no século XVIII," *Revista de História,* III (April–June, 1952) ; "La importancia de la inmigración en el desarrollo del Brasil," *Migración,* I (June–March, 1961) ; "Política imigratória," V Reunião Brasileira de Antropología, *Anais* (Belo Horizonte, 1961) ; and "International Migrations Affecting Latin America," *The Milbank Memorial Fund Quarterly,* XLIII (October, 1965) , Part 2. In addition to his numerous scholarly publications, Artur Neiva was a frequent participant in Brazilian and international professional meetings in the fields of anthropology, sociology, history, and demography.

His unique experience in government service and professional pursuits made Artur Neiva the best possible choice for the position of Executive Secretary of the Fulbright Commission, and he served in that capacity from April, 1963, until his death. He was imbued with a genuine liking for the United States and a deep love for his native Brazil; moreover, he was committed to the furtherance of scholarship in all scholarly fields. Although his contacts with American scholars and students had been widespread before his appointment, they were prevasive after his arrival at the Fulbright Commission. One can truthfully say that few American scholars and students did not benefit from his wise and patient guidance; he took a personal interest in their research and opened otherwise difficult doors to them. One of the most important activities in which he was engaged personally during the past few years was his work in stimulating the study of archeology in Brazil through a close working relationship between Brazilian and American archeologists.

During the time which I served as the cultural affairs officer at the American Embassy in Rio de Janeiro (1962–1965), I came to respect and value Artur Neiva's qualities as a counsellor and friend. Our frequent meetings were always events during which my knowledge and awareness of contemporary Brazil were enhanced. It was his presence at the Fulbright Commission which made certain that its objective of interchange of ideas and scholars was made more effective and cordial.

The United States has lost a great friend, Brazil a faithful son. It is fitting that this volume, written by a large number of participant scholars who knew him as a friend and aide, should be dedicated in his loving memory.

GEORGE C. A. BOEHRER
University of Kansas
Lawrence, Kansas
December 18, 1967

George C. A. Boehrer (1921–1967)

G EORGE C. A. BOEHRER, Professor of History at the University of Kansas (Lawrence), died on December 18, 1967. He was widely known as an authority on Portuguese and Brazilian history in international professional circles.

George Boehrer was born in New York City on June 20, 1921, and was descended from a family which had been established in the greater New York City area for several generations. He was a devout, practicing Roman Catholic all his life. He prepared himself early for the office of professional historian: he attended the Brooklyn Preparatory School (1934–1938) and took his undergraduate liberal arts degree at Boston College (1942); he then entered the Graduate School of The Catholic University of America in Washington, D. C., where he completed his Master of Arts and Doctor of Philosophy degrees (1943 and 1951, respectively) under the able direction of his mentor and friend Professor Manoel Cardozo. During the period of his graduate study, he was the recipient of fellowships and grants for travel and research in Portugal, Brazil, and the United States; he held the following grants and fellowships: National Knights of Columbus Fellow (1942–1945); U. S. Department of State/Office of Education, research grant (1947); Penfield Travelling Fellow, Portugal (1948); Instituto para a Alta Cultura (Portuguese government) Fellow (1948); Georgetown University Alumni Grantee, Portugal (summer, 1957); and Grantee, Joint Committee of the Social Science Research Council and the American Council of Learned Societies, Brazil (1960–1961).

George Boehrer married Joanne Fenzel on May 31, 1958, and a daughter, Anne, was born on September 3, 1960. Both survive him.

He began his professional teaching career in the fields of Brazilian,

300

Portuguese, and Latin American history as an instructor, first at Dunbarton College (1944–1946), and later at Marquette University (Milwaukee, Wisconsin) (1949–1951); at the latter he was appointed Assistant Professor in 1951 and remained there until 1955. In that year he was appointed Associate Professor of History at Georgetown University (Washington, D. C.), where he remained until 1962, when he accepted the invitation from the United States Information Agency to serve as Cultural Affairs Officer at the Embassy in Rio de Janeiro, Brazil. He served in that capacity until 1965, when he resumed his teaching career as Professor of History at the University of Kansas (Lawrence), at which he remained until the time of his death.

Many American scholars who visited Rio de Janeiro during the period when George Boehrer was Cultural Affairs Officer found in him an invaluable *amicus curiae* in obtaining reliable guidance on the best Brazilian scholarly sources, as well as making contact with outstanding Brazilian scholars. He was at all times the scholars' friend and put not only his office at their disposal, but also helped them in making many personal adjustments. George Boehrer thus served his profession and his country well.

He was not only the American scholar's friend: he was also accepted as a fellow professional historian and intellectual by Brazilian scholars, and he counted among his personal friends some of the most eminent intellectuals in Brazil, such as Sérgio Buarque de Holanda, José Honório Rodrigues, Américo Jacobina Lacombe, Luís Martins, and Luíz Viana Filho, to name only a few.

George Boehrer's contributions to scholarship in the fields of Brazilian and Portuguese history were significant for their originality and depth. His more lengthy publications include: *Da monarquia à república* (Rio de Janeiro, 1954); *Fátima na luz da história* (as translator and editor of Costa Brochado's *Fátima na luz da história*) (Milwaukee, Wis., 1955); and *Edição crítica dos Apontamentos para a Civilização dos Índios Bravos do Brasil* (Lisbon, 1963). He was also the author of a number of important scholarly articles, among them the following: "The Franciscans and Portuguese Expansion in the Mediterranean and Africa, 1415–1499," *The Americas* (January, 1955); "The Flight of the Brazilian Deputies from the Côrtes Gerais of Lisbon, 1822," *The Hispanic American Historical Review* (November, 1960); "The Brazilian Republican Revolution: Old and New Views," *Luso-Brazilian Review* (Winter, 1966); "José Carlos Rodrigues and *O Nôvo Mundo*, 1870–1879," *Journal of Inter-American Studies* (January, 1967); and "José

Corrêa da Serra e os índios brasileiros," *Revista de História* (October–December, 1966). At the time of his death, George Boehrer was awaiting publication of three studies, which should be forthcoming in the near future: "The Church and the Overthrow of the Brazilian Monarchy," published in the *Hispanic American Historical Review* sometime in 1968; "The Church in the Second Reign, 1840–1889," his contribution to this volume; and "Antônio Conselheiro e a Igreja durante o Império: documentos inéditos," *Revista de História* (future publication date unknown); in addition to the above, George Boehrer served as section editor for Latin American history for the *American Historical Review* (October, 1958, to October, 1960), and prepared the Brazilian history section for the *Handbook of Latin American Studies*, Vols. XIX–XXVI and Vol. XXVIII. His book reviews appeared in *The Americas*, the *Hispanic American Historical Review*, the *Catholic Historical Review* and the *American Historical Review*.

In recognition of his original contributions to Brazilian history, the members of the Brazilian Academy of Letters awarded him its Machado de Assis Medal in 1964.

George Boehrer's membership in professional associations included the following: American Historical Association (1949–1967); Catholic Historical Association (1949–1967); Conference on Latin American History (1951–1967); American Association of University Professors (as local and regional officer, 1950–1967); Council on Latin American Studies (Secretary, Regional Conference, 1957–1959); and Sociedade de História (São Paulo, Brazil) (1962–1967).

With the death of George Boehrer the historical profession has lost a luminary, Luso-Brazilianists a colleague, and intimates a devoted friend. It is an honor—and indeed a duty—to dedicate this volume jointly to his memory as well as that of his trusted friend and counsellor, Artur Neiva.

Henry H. Keith
Newcomb College, Tulane University
New Orleans, Louisiana
January 19, 1968

INDEX

Abreu, João Capistrano de, impression of Revolution of 1889, 249

Absentee landlords, influence of on rural labor, 297

Academies in Brazil, as source for study of Enlightenment, 105

Accursio das Neves, José, supports Portuguese industrialization, 199–201, 202; supports move of Court to Brazil, 201

Afonso Henriques, king of Portugal (1112–85), concessions to English, 3

Afonso V (1438–81), concessions to Flemings, 7

Agrarian conditions in Brazil (1963), 285, 286–87

Agriculture in Brazil, productivity of (1965), 286

Aguiar, Conde de. *See* Portugal de Castro, Fernando José de

Ajuda, Royal Library of, moved to Brazil, 158–60

Almeida de Mello de Castro, João de. *See* Mello de Castro, João de Almeida de

Anadia, Visconde and Conde de. *See* Sá e Meneses, João Rodrigues de

Andrada e Silva, Antônio Carlos, 253

Andrada e Silva, José Bonifácio, 73–74, 95, 109

Aranha, Oswaldo, 256

Araújo, José Thomás Nabuco de. *See* Nabuco de Araújo, José Thomás

Araújo de Azevedo, Antônio, supports French demands on Portugal (1807), 149–50

Atlantic exploration, international character of, 15 n. 9

Avelar Brotero, João Dabney de, compares Catholic Church in U.S. and Brazil, 116–17

Azeredo Coutinho, José Joaquim da

Cunha de, family background, 81; named Bishop of Pernambuco, 82–83; interim Captain-General of Pernambuco, 83; removed as Bishop of Pernambuco, 83–86; later career of, 86; and the Enlightenment, 86–87, 110; his views on his intellectual interests, 92; on Negro slavery, 92–94; on economics, 94–95; on mining, 95; on industry, 95; loyalty to Portugal, 95–96; views on popular sovereignty and absolute monarchy, 96–97; political views of compared with de Pradt's, 98

Azevedo, Antônio de Araújo de, supports French demands on Portugal (1807), 149–50

Azevedo, Joaquim José, Visconde de Rio Sêcco, alerts key people of planned departure of Court to Brazil, 153; prepares for removal of Court, 153–54;

Azores (islands), foreigners in, 6

Bahia, actions of Prince Regent João in (1808), 164–68

Ballester, Fr. Manoel, S.J., attacks Maranhão trading company (1755), 51

Banditry, as index of government failure to solve social problems, 235–36

Barbosa Machado Collection in Royal Library of Ajuda, moved to Brazil, 159–60

Barca, Conde de. *See* Araújo de Azevedo, Antônio de

Bardi family of Florence, privileges from Portuguese Crown, 4

Barreto, Francisco, criticizes Jesuits for refusal to pay tithe, 32–33

303

186–87; significance of, 187–89; impact on role of *juiz do pôvo* in Portugal, 205–06

Ultramontanism, revival of in Europe after 1814, 115; Pius IX and, 115–16

Vargas, Getúlio, policy toward São Paulo, 238, 257–58; political system devised by, 238; reactions of in election of 1930, 254–56; policy of toward Minas Gerais, 258; policy of toward Rio Grande do Sul, 258–59; political changes resulting from rule of, 252, 259–61, 266; enhances role of military in politics, 261–62; removal by military (1945), 262; his reliance on military, 266

Vargas Revolution. *See* Revolution of 1930

Verney, Fr. Luis Antônio, supported by João V, 76; on education in Portugal, 77–78

Vianna Moog, Clodomir, criticizes non-violent traditions, 232

Viçosa, Antônio Ferreira, Bishop of Mariana, sends students to Europe, 124; reforms seminaries, 127; appointment as bishop discussed, 143–44

Villa Nôva Portugal, Thomáz Antônio de, departure from Lisbon (1807), 155, as major influence in royal government (1817–20), 181 n. 82; mentioned, 214

Vicentians, 127

Violence, in Brazilian history, 232–33; purposes of (17th and 18th cents.), 233–34; and bloodshed, 234; view of José Honório Rodrigues on predominance of over compromise, 234; definition and typology, 241–42; in Brazil and Spanish America, 242–43; consequences of, 244; significance of absence of, 244; and social change, 247 n. 7; in Chilean history, 245–46

Washington Luis. *See* Pereira de Sousa, Washington Luis

Welsers of Augsburg, in Portuguese trade, 10–11

Wernecke Sodré, Nelson, on significance of Revolution of 1930, 251–52